Map of Girton Village, *c*1940.

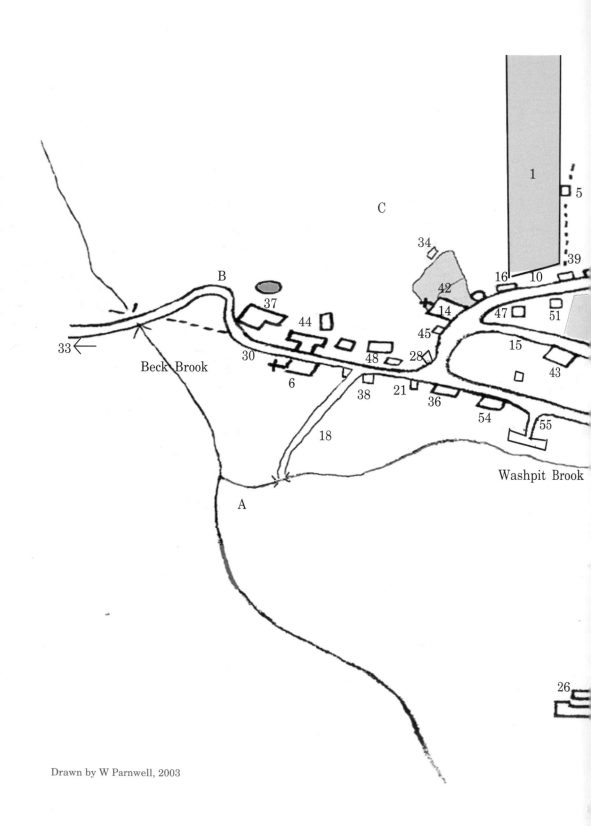

Drawn by W Parnwell, 2003

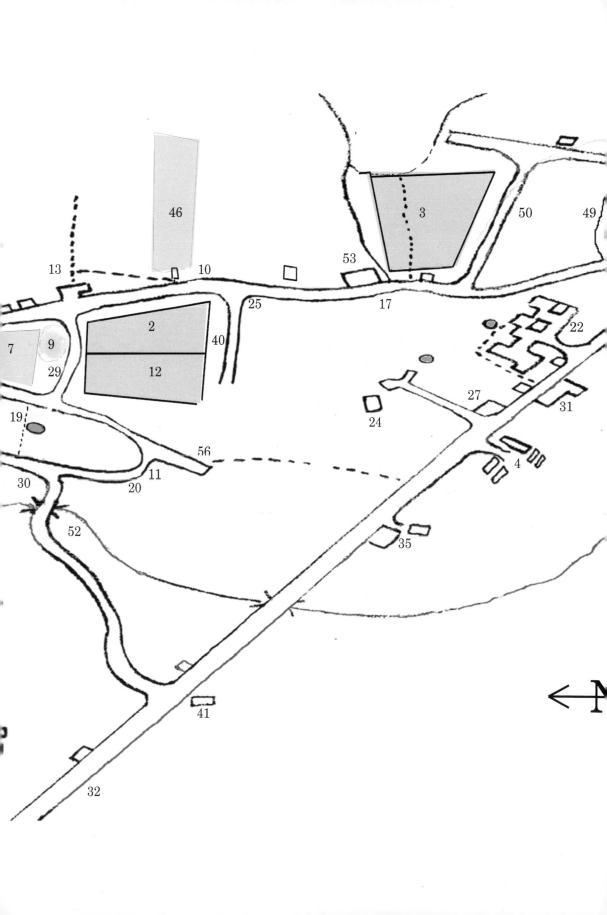

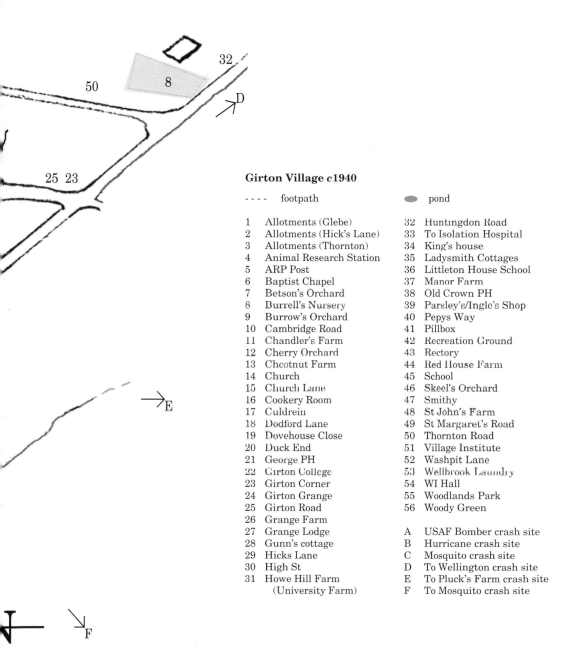

Girton Village *c*1940

- - - - footpath   ● pond

1	Allotments (Glebe)	32	Huntingdon Road
2	Allotments (Hick's Lane)	33	To Isolation Hospital
3	Allotments (Thornton)	34	King's house
4	Animal Research Station	35	Ladysmith Cottages
5	ARP Post	36	Littleton House School
6	Baptist Chapel	37	Manor Farm
7	Betson's Orchard	38	Old Crown PH
8	Burrell's Nursery	39	Parsley's/Ingle's Shop
9	Burrow's Orchard	40	Pepys Way
10	Cambridge Road	41	Pillbox
11	Chandler's Farm	42	Recreation Ground
12	Cherry Orchard	43	Rectory
13	Chestnut Farm	44	Red House Farm
14	Church	45	School
15	Church Lane	46	Skeel's Orchard
16	Cookery Room	47	Smithy
17	Culdrein	48	St John's Farm
18	Dodford Lane	49	St Margaret's Road
19	Dovehouse Close	50	Thornton Road
20	Duck End	51	Village Institute
21	George PH	52	Washpit Lane
22	Girton College	53	Wellbrook Laundry
23	Girton Corner	54	WI Hall
24	Girton Grange	55	Woodlands Park
25	Girton Road	56	Woody Green
26	Grange Farm		
27	Grange Lodge	A	USAF Bomber crash site
28	Gunn's cottage	B	Hurricane crash site
29	Hicks Lane	C	Mosquito crash site
30	High St	D	To Wellington crash site
31	Howe Hill Farm	E	To Pluck's Farm crash site
	(University Farm)	F	To Mosquito crash site

GIRTON'S WAR

GIRTON'S WAR

The Village 1939–1945

D R de Lacey

Illustrations prepared by
M Parnwell

With members of the Girton History Group

ISBN 0 9539007 1 1

Typeset in Great Britain by
Aslan Ltd, Girton, Cambridge CB3 0QB
in 11/13 New Century Schoolbook
and printed by
University Printing Services, University Press, Cambridge

First published 2003

This publication was enabled by a grant from the
Millennium Festival 'Awards for All' scheme

Contents

	Illustrations	vi
	Foreword	ix
	Acknowledgments	xi
	Abbreviations	xii
1	The War Years	1
2	ARP and the Invasion Committee	140
3	Replies to Freddie Barrett	174
4	Service Records	206
5	Adult Reminiscences	227
6	Children's Recollections	238
7	Evacuees	250
8	The Women's Institute	262
9	Girton College	280
	Index	305

Illustrations

Sketch map of Girton Village ⟨W Parnwell⟩   Frontispiece

An ID Card ⟨W Parnwell⟩   3
Girton AFS Squad ⟨V Smith⟩   5
Girton Endowed School, now the Cotton Hall ⟨Cambs
    Collection⟩   7
The Baptist Chapel, Girton ⟨Cambs Collection⟩   9
Girton Red Cross Unit ⟨D Tyrell⟩   9
A Searchlight Unit ⟨HMSO, from a war-time pamphlet⟩   13
Girton Cricket Team ⟨V Smith⟩   15
S Dixon ⟨S Dixon⟩   17
TG Impey ⟨His family⟩   19
ARP Officers with a cycle messenger ⟨HMSO, from a war-time
    pamphlet⟩   21
The Old Rectory (Littleton House School) ⟨W Parnwell⟩   23
Supermarine Spitfire ⟨W Parnwell⟩   31
Girton Home Guard Unit ⟨R Parr⟩   31
The Village Institute, Girton ⟨Cambs Collection⟩   35
Girton Church Magazine no 1 ⟨DR de Lacey⟩   37
Wedding Photograph of Eric Rowney & L Jean Evans. ⟨J
    Evans, now Mrs Wayman⟩   39
Stan Reader ⟨S Reader⟩   41
Girton Endowed School Cookery Room ⟨W Parnwell⟩   43
Iris Mayes ATS ⟨I Mayes⟩   45
Sgt Josef Kominek ⟨Czech Embassy⟩   49
The WI Hall's shuttered windows ⟨M & S Hornsey⟩   57
Ration book ⟨W Parnwell⟩   61
Archive photographs of Girton Church ⟨Girton College/PCC⟩   69
T Nightingale RAF Transport Command ⟨T Nightingale⟩   73
Frida Averne (Mrs HW Leakey) as an undergraduate
    ⟨Newnham College, Cambridge⟩   77
British Armed Forces currency note for 3d, in R Ellis'
    collection ⟨DR de Lacey⟩   80
M Ellis, injured at Marshall's early in the War ⟨M Ellis⟩   83
FC Barrett ⟨David Brown, The Portrait Studio, Histon⟩   85
Girton AFS Squad, Christmas 1944 ⟨V Smith⟩   87
V Pauley in India, July 1943 ⟨V Pauley⟩   93
Irvine King ⟨H Baggaley⟩   95

Alice Hibbert-Ware 1869–1944 〈photograph reproduced by
 kind permission of Cambridge Newspapers〉 100
TA Pauley 〈His family〉 107
The Rev G Hibbert-Ware 〈St Stephen's College, Delhi〉 111
The Hibbert-Ware Memorial Garden 〈W Parnwell〉 113
A Christmas card sent to FC Barrett 〈S Robey〉 117
F Evans RA 〈F Evans〉 121
Chestnut Farm 〈W Parnwell〉 123
German soldiers surrendering at Lüneburg 〈R Ellis〉 127
Girton Glebe School 〈J Harradine〉 129
MS Pease 〈His family〉 131
Ken Blunt RN 〈K Blunt〉 133
Post-war housing in Girton 〈W Parnwell〉 135
N Lewis RE 〈N Lewis〉 137
Pte Walter Dixon 〈R Lipscombe〉 137
Gordon Pluck 〈J Harradine〉 139
The Wellbrook Laundry, proposed HQ of the Invasion
 Committee 〈W Parnwell〉 142
The Rev PNH Palmer 〈V Smith〉 179
Roy Naylor 〈R Naylor〉 184
1944 Christmas card from the MEF 〈S Robey〉 192
Claude Kidman 〈C Kidman〉 197
Cyril Wilson 〈His family〉 199
TC Impey 〈TC Impey〉 205
WJ Claydon 〈WJ Claydon〉 206
R Coe 〈R Coe〉 207
L Collings 〈L Collings〉 208
CB Cundell 〈CB Cundell〉 212
R Ellis 〈R Ellis〉 214
T Evans 〈T Evans〉 215
MW Fordham 〈MW Fordham〉 215
Histon Despatch Riders 〈MW Fordham〉 216
L Hales 〈L Hales〉 217
RD Lipscombe 〈RD Lipscombe〉 220
K Matthews 〈K Matthews〉 222
K Mayes 〈K Mayes〉 222
D Mills 〈D Mills〉 223
R Nightingale 〈R Nightingale〉 223
Dick Watson 〈D Watson〉 224
R Wilson 〈R Wilson〉 224
Girton's Roll of Service 〈GPC〉 226
Girton Home Guard 〈R Parr〉 228

The brothers Will, Tom and Dick Evans ⟨Their family⟩   229
MS Pease ⟨D Pease⟩   234
Pillbox by the Huntingdon Road, Girton ⟨W Parnwell⟩   237
Marion, Alison and Isabel Bonny ⟨Their family⟩   238
Fins from an incendiary bomb of 1940 ⟨DR de Lacey⟩.   241
The George Inn, Girton ⟨W Parnwell⟩   244
The Pease family making hay ⟨D Pease⟩   246
Girton Follies, 1944 ⟨L Collings⟩   249
Jennifer Trusted (née Turner) ⟨J Trusted⟩   261
J Collings ⟨J Collings⟩   283
The Wisbech Fruiting Campaign ⟨J Storrs Fox⟩   285
A group of Girton tennis players, ⟨D Larrissy⟩   287
Two 'Infants' at Girton College. ⟨E Eadie⟩   292
Hermione Grammatike, the Girton mummy ⟨Girton College,
    Cambridge⟩   294
Treading silage at Girton College ⟨J Storrs Fox⟩   296
A student group at Girton College ⟨D Larrissy⟩   298
Students at the Wisbech Fruiting Campaign ⟨J Storrs Fox⟩   300
A group of Girton students ⟨D Larrissy⟩   302
Students at Girton, as portrayed in The Sketch ⟨E Eadie⟩   304

Foreword

The Village of Girton lies some 3 miles North of Cambridge on a gravel ridge which runs from Grantchester to Landbeach. The name means 'Gravel-Settlement'. It merited an entry in the Domesday Book, and parts of the church date from the eleventh century. In the Churchyard stands a War Memorial. 11 names commemorate those who fought and fell to preserve their Village and their Nation between 1939 and 1945. This is the story of that Village during those turbulent years, based on the memories of those who survived and on contemporary documents.

Our sources are of two kinds. There are the memories of those who can look back over 60 years to their youth or childhood. Members of the Girton History Group, including some whose own memories are part of this archive, interviewed and invited written records from as wide a range as possible of those who spent the war years in Girton or of Girton residents serving in HM Forces. As far as possible we have tried to tell their story in their own words. For recorded interviews the editing process has inevitably had to be greater since such recordings include broken sentences, interruptions and repetitions which become tedious on the printed page. Where possible the contributor has approved our work and we offer sincere apologies to any who may feel misrepresented.

There are also written sources from the time. We have used contemporary newspapers; the Minutes of the Parish Council, the Invasion Committee, the Reconstruction Committee and the Women's Institute; the College *Girton Review*; the Church newsletters; and letters written at the time, in particular those sent in reply to Mr Barrett's circulars. We are enormously grateful to those who allowed us access to these documents. We have tried to present this material in a clear and readable form which nevertheless preserves the integrity and historical value of the originals. While quotations from written sources have in general been abbreviated we have not changed the wording except in very rare cases, though we felt it too cumbersome to indicate every cut with an ellipsis. We have also standardised spelling and punctuation, and used abbreviations (as listed on page xii) where possible.

The various sections of this book were initially collected and collated by various members of the Girton History Group. To the

General Editor then fell the task of editing these into a coherent whole. The chapter on the Women's Institute, however, is the sole work of Maurice & Sheila Hornsey, by their own request.

FC Barrett and his News Letters

One set of documents has already been published by the Girton History Group. In the latter part of the War, the leader of the local Youth Group wrote a monthly circular, initially to members of his Group serving abroad, eventually to all Villagers in the Forces. *Keeping in Touch* (ISBN 0-9539007-0-3, privately published by GHG, Girton, 2001) collected these letters and illustrated them with contemporary photographs. They hinted at the richness and diversity of life in the Village.

Where appropriate we have used some of those photographs again here, and repeat our thanks to those who supplied them. We wish also to correct a few errors in *KiT* which have been brought to our attention: the M Rudd of the photograph on p41 is not the same as the M Rudd in the text; some of the names of the Red Cross contingent were given incorrectly and are corrected here; and K Deane should be K Dean. Our apologies go to all those concerned. Also, those involved would like it clarified that the reference on p1 is in fact to a double-bunk, not a double bed.

Sources

The various written sources used in this book are as follows:

Minutes of the Girton Parish Council, lodged in the CRO
Minutes of the Girton Invasion Committee, lodged in the CRO
Minutes of the Girton Women's Institute, now in the Cambs Collection
The *Girton Review*, from the Library of Girton College
North Stowe Deanery Magazine (ceased publication, Dec 1940), in the keeping of GHG
Girton Church Magazine (began publication Jan 1941), in the keeping of GHG
Memoirs of members of Girton College, now lodged in the College Archives
Diary of Mr CG Pluck, property of Mrs J Harradine
Diary of Mr R Lipscombe, in his own keeping
Letters and cards addressed to FC Barrett, property of S Robey, now in the Cambs Collection
The Memoir of Mrs HW Leakey, now in the keeping of GHG
Interview tapes and transcripts are all in the keeping of GHG.

Acknowledgments

This book could never have been contemplated without the input and help of a large number of people. It is a pleasure to acknowledge our debt.

For contributing their memories and photographs we are grateful to all of the following: Miss A Baker, Mr J Balaam, Mrs H Baxter, Mrs J Beavington, Mr G Betson, Mrs P Bickel, Mr K Blunt, Miss M Bonny, Mrs M Braddock, Mr J Brooks, Mr J Chapman, Mr W Claydon, Mr R Coe, Mr J Collings, Mr L Collings, Mr F Cracknell, Mrs J Cracknell, Mrs M Cundall, Mr C Cundell, Mr K Dean, Mr S Dixon, Mrs M Doggett, Miss A Duke, Mrs E Eadie, Mr M Ellis, Mr R Ellis, Mr F Evans, Mr R Evans, Mr T Evans, Mr M Fordham, Mr S Gawthrop, Mrs V Goddard, Mr P Graves, Mr L Hales, Mrs B Hancock, Mr K Hancock, Mrs J Harradine, Mrs P Hawker, Lady R Huxley, Mr T Impey, Mrs B Impey, Mrs D Larrissy, Mr K Lawrence, Mrs E Leakey, Mr N Lewis, Mr R Lipscombe, Mrs M Littlewood, Mrs E Matthews, Mr K Matthews, Mr M Matthews, Mr K Mayes, Mrs I Mayes, Mr D Mills, Mrs H Mills, Mr H Naylor, Mr R Nightingale, Mr T Nightingale, Mr & Mrs R Parr, Mr V Pauley, Miss D Pease, Prof F Pease, Mrs B Pepper, Mrs M Phillips, Mrs A Piper, Mrs J Pringle, Mrs J Rawlence, Mr S Reader, Mrs S Robey, Mrs M Rowlinson, Mrs V Sankaran, Mrs M Sharpe, Mrs V Smith, Mrs J Storrs Fox, Mr S Thulbourne, Mrs A Tole, Mrs J Trusted, Mrs M von Proschwitz, Mr D Watson, Mrs A Williams, Mr E Wilson, Mr R Wilson, and Mrs I Wilson. We apologise to any other contributors we have inadvertently omitted.

We received significant help and support from the Archivist of Girton College, the staff of CRO, the staff of the Cambs Collection, and Mrs P Knight, Clerk of GPC.

For editorial assistance the Editor is indebted to Miss J Blakeman, and for proofreading, programming and typesetting help and general support to Simon Buck and Dr D Galletly.

We have tried to contact all who have a copyright interest in materials published here. Our sincere apologies to any who feel we have infringed their rights.

The Millennium Festival 'Awards for All' scheme gave a generous grant to prepare and publish the text.

Abbreviations

AC(2)	Aircraftman(2)	CIPC	Cambridge Independent Press & Chronicle
AA	Anti-Aircraft [ack-ack]; Automobile Association	CM	*Girton Church Magazine*
AEF	Allied Expeditionary Force	CMF	Central Mediterranean Force; Commonwealth Military Forces
AFS	Auxiliary Fire Service		
AGM	Annual General Meeting	CO	Commanding Officer
APM	Annual Parish Meeting	Co, Coy	Company
ARP	Air-Raid Precautions	CPCC	County Parish Councils' Conference
ARW	Air-Raid Warden		
ATA	Air Transport Auxiliary	CPO	Chief Petty Officer
		CRE	Command Royal Engineers
ATS	Auxiliary Territorial Service	CRO	Cambs County Record Office
AW	Anti-tank Weapon		
BAD	Base Ammunition Depôt	CWN	Cambridge Weekly News
Battn	Battalion	DC	District Council
BEF	British Expeditionary Force	DE	Daily Express
		DEMS	Defensively-Equipped Merchant Ships
BLA	British Liberation Army	DFO	Divisional Fire Office(r)
BNAF	British North Africa Force	DM	*North Stowe Deanery Magazine*
BRCS	British Red Cross Society	DR	Despatch Rider
BSHF	Battle School Home Forces	DS	Daily Sketch
		EAA	East African Army
Bty	Battery	ENSA	Entertainments National Service Association
CC	County Council; [Police] Cambs County		
CD	Civil Defence	FA	First Aid
CDN	Cambridge Daily News	FAP	First Aid Party
		FE	Far East

GDNA	Girton & District Nursing Association		Women's Institutes
		NHS	National Health Service
GHG	Girton History Group		
GPC	Girton Parish Council	NIAB	National Institute of Agricultural Botany
GSM	Great St Mary's Church, Cambridge		
		NL	News Letter, see page x
HG	Home Guard		
HK	Hong Kong	OC	Officer Commanding
HMI	HM Inspector(ate)	PC	Parish Council
HyAA	Heavy Anti-Aircraft	PCM	Girton Parish Council Minutes
IC	Invasion Committee		
ITMA	Radio show *It's That Man Again*	PD	Diary of Mr CG Pluck
		PRC	Planning & Reconstruction Committee
IVC	Impington Village College		
IWC	Girton & Oakington Infant Welfare Centre	PT	Physical Training
		RA	Royal Artillery
KD	Khaki Drill [summer uniform]	RAMC	Royal Army Medical Corps
KiT	*Keeping in Touch*, see page x	RAOC	Royal Army Ordnance Corps
LA	Land Agent	RASC	Royal Army Service Corps
LDV	Local Defence Volunteer		
		RC	Red Cross (Society)
LEA	Local Education Authority	RCC	Rural County Council
		RCM	Reconstruction Committee Minutes
LHS	Littleton House School, Girton		
		RDC	Rural District Council
LtAA	Light Anti-Aircraft	Rec	Girton Recreation Ground
ME	Middle East(ern)		
MEF	Middle East Force	ROC	Royal Ordnance Corps
MI	Military Intelligence	RFA	Royal Fleet Auxiliary
MO	Medical Officer	SC	South Cambridgeshire
MSL	Missionary Service League	SEAC	South East Asia Command
MTB	Motor Torpedo Boat	SHAEF	Supreme Headquarters AEF
MU	Mothers' Union		
NAMCO	National Milk Cocoa drink	SOE	Special Operations Executive
NC	News Chronicle	Sqn	Squadron
NFS	National Fire Service	SS	Sunday School
NFWI	National Federation of	SSAFA	Soldiers', Sailors' and

	Airmen's Families	VI	Girton Village
	Association		Institute ['The Men's
TA	Territorial Army		Institute']
UL	Cambridge University	VJ	Victory in Japan
	Library	WAEC	War Agriculture
V1, V2	*Vergeltungswaffe*,		Executive Council
	'flying bomb'	WD	War Department
VAD	Voluntary Aid	WI	Women's Institute
	Detachment	WLA	Women's Land Army
VE	Victory in Europe	YMG	Young Men's Group

Mensuration

Original measures have been preserved throughout, but for those who are unfamiliar with them we offer rough equivalents.

Money

There were several ways of expressing sums of money; we have standardised them in the forms xd for pence; x/y or £$x/y/z$ for larger sums. 0 of any unit is represented by a dash (-).

  12 pence (12d) = 1 shilling (1/-)
  20 shillings = 1 pound (£1)
  1 guinea (1gn) = £1/1/- (1 pound, 1 shilling, 0 pence)
  1 half-crown (or half-a-crown) = 2/6
  Sums greater than £1 were often expressed in shillings.

Weight

  16 ounces (16oz) = 1 pound (1lb) = 0.454 kg approximately
  14 pounds = 1 stone (1st)
  112 pounds = 1 hundredweight (1cwt)
  20 hundredweights = 1 ton = 1 tonne approximately

Length

  12 inches (12") = 1 foot (1')
  3 feet = 1 yard (1yd)
  1,760 yards = 1 mile = 1.6 km approximately

Area

  1 acre = 4,000 m^2 (0.4 ha) approximately

Liquid Measure

  2 pints (2pt) = 1 quart (1qt)
  4 quarts = 1 gallon (1gal) = 5 l approximately

1: The War Years
M Parnwell

This section draws mainly on Council Minutes, the Press, and Church magazines (*North Stowe Deanery Magazine* until the end of 1940, then Girton's own *Church Magazine*). In parallel we have added, on the facing page, other war-time events particularly as these affected the Village or its servicemen abroad, to place this information in a wider framework. From Jan 1941 Girton's weather is given, as recorded in the diary of Gordon Pluck.

A number of significant issues raised here continued to concern the Village long after the end of 1945.

Victory celebrations were organised by the Council, which agonised over details and cost: £15 was allocated for fireworks and other suggestions included a cinema show and a band.

The PCM of Jan 1946 reported 'the hole at Girton Corner and the barbed wire had been filled in and removed'. In Feb the need to fill in a slit trench was noted. Sums of £7/5/- (sale of ARP blankets), 12/- (sale of lamps) and 15/- (salvage) were noted. In June the WD LA offered £36/15/6 compensation for the use of the Rec but the PC considered this inadequate.

In May 1946 the PC discussed a resolution of the PCC that the names of those who gave their lives in the recent war should be added on the Memorial, but not until July 1947 were tenders invited, and although a dedication service was planned for Armistice Day 1947, the names were still being discussed in 1948.

Two issues actively pursued by the PC and the Reconstruction Committee were new housing and education. Despite dissatisfaction with the original RDC plans, a new estate was named St Vincent's Close: 'Mr Ibbitt gave a report on the housing position and promised to produce a list of Council House applicants' [PCM, Feb 1948].

In October 1946 the PC wrote to the LEA 'requesting them to proceed with the new school building at once'. The Managers of the Endowed School had to agree to its closure [PCM, July 1947] but in Dec negotiations began with the Glebe allotment holders, and the new school was opened on 7 July 1951

In Feb 1946 'It was resolved to ask the Bus Co for a better service' and a year later 'resolved to make a strong complaint to the Traffic Commissioner respecting the very bad bus service 106' [PCM].

September 1939

3 'A special meeting of the Council was held on Sunday Sep 3, to consider the serious international situation. There were present Mr Pease (in the chair), Messrs Adams, Gawthrop, Gordon, Elwood, Lilley, Nightingale, Skinner, Searle, Miss Hibbert-Ware, Mrs JG Stewart.

A letter was received from Mr Garner, asking permission to dig trenches on the Recreation Ground for the use of the schoolchildren during school hours. After some discussion on the general question of trenches, it was agreed that permission be given. It was also decided to pass on to Mr Garner two suggestions, namely that the trenches be dug only 12" to 15" deep & that bales of straw be placed at each side, giving a total depth of about 3': also that they be dug near the N hedge so that they could be drained into Mr Searle's pit if necessary. It was also resolved to recommend the School Managers to provide a proper covered shelter.

It was also reported that all Wardens' houses would be clearly indicated, & it was agreed that the Constable be asked to provide some similar indication of his whereabouts, for the guidance of the public'. [PCM]

12 'Dr Arthur Walton, Head ARW, outlined the work of the ARP. Children's respirators were not yet available but would be distributed as soon as they came to hand. The whistle system of warning did not seem to be adequate, the Laundry hooter would be an excellent warning signal but it could only be used during working hours. The Directors of the Laundry had offered to install an electric hooter.

It was resolved to ask for a statement from the RDC on the present position of the fire service. It was suggested that one or two FA talks should be arranged. A letter was received asking for shelters to be erected for the use of Special Constable on duty and also for roads & kerb edges to be marked. It was resolved to pass this on to the authorities.

Miss Hibbert-Ware & Mr Skinner were appointed to attend the CPCC on 30 Sep'. [PCM]

21 & 24 Harvest Festival & Service. [DM]

22 Wedding of Thomas Charles Impey & Jennie Hancock. [CWN]

October 1939

1 Thursday prayer-meeting begun. Evensong moves to 3pm. [DM]

6 '**The Baptist Church** was filled to capacity for the harvest service. It was announced that the evening service would take

Elsewhere

Radio programme ITMA starring comedian Tommy Handley.

Italy remains neutral & calls for international conference.

First evacuation of children ('Operation Pied Piper').

Blackout introduced.

Ministry of Information established.

WAAF consists of 234 officers & 1,500 airwomen.

1–3 German troops invade Poland; start of WW2. Chamberlain forms war cabinet, Churchill is First Lord of the Admiralty.

4 *Athenia* sunk by U-boat with loss of 112 lives.

4 RAF attacks German Navy; 8 out of 29 bombers shot down.

5 US & Eire proclaim their neutrality.

7 National Service Act allows call-up of men aged 18–41.

18 Carrier *Courageous* sunk by U-boat: 515 lost.

24 Petrol rationed.

27 Income tax raised from 5/6 to 7/6.

30 National Registration Act introduces ID Cards.

NOTICE FA 523497

1. **Always carry your Identity Card. You must** produce it on demand by a Police Officer in uniform or member of H.M. Armed Forces in uniform on duty.

2. **You are responsible for this Card, and must not part with it to any other person.** You must report at once to the local National Registration Office if it is lost, destroyed, damaged or defaced.

3. If you find a lost Identity Card or have in your possession a Card not belonging to yourself or anyone in your charge you must hand it in at once at a Police Station or National Registration Office.

4. Any breach of these requirements is an offence punishable by a fine or imprisonment or both.

FOR AUTHORISED ENDORSEMENTS ONLY

T 51/2878 i

NATIONAL REGISTRATION IDENTITY CARD

An ID card, back and front

Elsewhere

1 Men aged 20–22 liable for conscription.

4 'Dig for Victory' campaign launched.

5 Fighting ends in Poland.

place from 3 to 4pm.

Conservative Association. At a committee meeting held at Mr & Mrs Searle's house it was decided to allow the FA detachment to use the Conservative Room as a centre for the duration of the war.

YMG. In the autumn session a number of interesting topics have been discussed, including "Experience" opened by Mr FG Evans, & "The Scout Movement' opened by the Secretary, Stanley Dixon. At a meeting last Sunday a report of the recent broadcast "The Church in War-Time" was read. This was followed by spirited discussion. Mr FM Dupont is speaking next Sunday on "The Art of Getting Along Together"'. [CWN]

10 'Miss Hibbert-Ware reported from the LEA that trenches should not be dug for the schoolchildren.

It was resolved to inform the RDC that the PC was not satisfied that the fire service could be relied upon, and to call on them to provide separate equipment and to train a fire squad in the Parish immediately.

It was resolved to call a Parish Meeting on Wed 18 Oct at 7.30pm in the VI to give residents an opportunity of discussing Air-Raid warnings.

Miss Hibbert-Ware reported on the CPCC'. [PCM]

13 'IVC. Evening Sessions will commence with a Social Evening on Mon 16 Oct at 7.30pm. Admission free. The bus will leave Girton Church at 7.13pm. Fare 3d return.

WI. At the monthly meeting Mrs Leakey occupied the Chair. Mrs Green gave hints on how members could help the evacuated women. Tea was served by Mrs Betson & helpers, after which the meeting concluded with singing. Owing to blackout, meetings will be held at 2.30pm until further notice'. [CWN]

November 1939

10 'YMG. "Why Pain & Suffering" was opened by Mr Tom Chapman. It was announced that the usual meeting would not take place next Sunday as members were attending the united service at the Parish Church. On Sun 19 Nov, Mr AR Thurlow will speak on "The discipline of one's self".

WI. At the monthly meeting, Mrs Leakey presiding, the question of holding an auxiliary meeting for members who could not attend the usual evening meetings owing to the blackout was discussed and an afternoon meeting will be held on the Wednesday prior to the usual meeting. Mrs Oxley then gave an interesting talk on "The Use of Fats in War Time" which set the majority of members'

6 Hitler peace proposals rejected by French & British.
9 Chamberlain announces committee of ministers to co-ordinate economy.
14 HMS *Royal Oak* sunk by U-boat in Scapa Flow.

Fire Service. The local AFS Squad, established after much wrangling with the central Cambridge Fire Service

Elsewhere
4 'Cash & Carry' clause introduced in US Neutrality Act permitting British & French to purchase arms.
8 Hitler escapes assassination attempt.
9 Venlo Incident: MI6 agents Stevens & Best kidnapped.
11 50,000 tons of merchant ships sunk off E coast by magnetic mines in one week.
16 'Received Degree 54 Years Late. Death of Woman Who Saw Girton Rise. There died today at the age of 87 a woman, one of the first students at Girton who saw the dawn of a new age for women. She was Mrs Amy Brooke of Bushey, Herts, who entered Girton College in 1870, a year after it was founded at Hitchin

minds at rest and was much appreciated.

Baptist Church. The combined service for young people & adults was conducted by Mr FM Dupont. Several of the SS also took part. The usual united service would be held at 3pm next Sunday. Owing to the confused & disturbing events of the present time this service has been viewed with mixed feelings. It is felt, however, that a simple service of remembrance and a re-affirming of one's personal ideals cannot be unfitting.

GDNA. A successful whist drive & entertainments were held in the VI on Saturday evening. 10 tables were in place. Mr Pease acted as MC and Mr Bowyer gave away the prizes to Mrs Wilderspin & Mrs B Gawthrop, Mr Foster & Mrs Kidman. It was agreed to send a message of sympathy and good wishes for a speedy recovery to Mrs Sadler. A musical entertainment followed led by Mr Williams of IVC.

Labour Party. Mr Albert Adams presided at the monthly meeting on Tuesday when Mr Jackson of Elsworth spoke on the war. He very much deplored that the leaders of the Labour Party had arranged a political truce. An animated discussion followed in which Miss Smelly, Mr Tingey, Mrs Pease, Mr Cobb, Mr Skinner & others took part'. [CDN]

14 'After further discussion on the RDC's proposals regarding fire-fighting the PC concluded that the matter was still unsatisfactory and it was decided to ask the DC for a copy of the actual schemes entered into with the Boro' of Cambridge and to make informal contacts with neighbouring Councils with a view to joint action being taken.

Mr Searle undertook to sink barrels into Washpit Brook at the bottom of Woodlands Park & Dodford Lane to provide adequate depth for suction should the main be damaged.

Dr Walton thanked the PC for calling the Parish meeting.

Miss Hibbert-Ware reported that children who would be left in school in the event of an air-raid would be very closely packed together. It was agreed that this was undesirable. Dr Walton was asked to form an opinion.

In response to a request from the RDC the Clerk had sent out 8 letters asking for the number of stack-sheets or tarpaulins available for use as temporary coverings for buildings which might be damaged in air-raids. Mr Hall [has] one, Mr Searle 2, University Research Station 2; it was decided to repeat letters to those who had not replied'. [PCM]

17 'A Special Service of Remembrance at the Baptist Church was

and the progress & development of which were synonymous with women's emancipation. Although she passed her examinations for the BA & MA she did not receive the degrees until 1928, 54 years afterwards. From Girton she joined the teaching staff of Manchester High School. She was a pioneer of the Labour movement and frequently spoke on its platform'. [CDN]

17 Supreme War Council agrees on co-ordination of British & French war production.

21 Chamberlain imposes embargo on all German trade in retaliation for sinking neutral ships.

28 'Rationing starts on 8 Jan. 4oz Butter & Bacon per person per week'. [CDN]

'Children ... would be very closely packed together'. Girton Endowed School, already too small for the Village in 1939.

well attended although it was noted with regret that there were
very few ex-servicemen amongst the congregation. The address
was given by Mr GW Hayed and selected passages of scripture
were read by Mr Roy Nightingale, Mr GE Canham of Swavesey
was the organist. Representations were present from the Parish
Church, the Village Scout Troop & YMG. A collection was taken
for the Earl Haig fund.

Poppy Day realised £24/16/2. The following were collectors: Mrs
Austin, Miss Bailey, Mrs Chaplin, Miss Garner, Mrs Gow, Mrs
Hancock, Miss Hunt, Priscilla & Colin Leakey, Miss Porter, Mrs
Teff, Mrs Thompson & Miss Tucker. Mr Bonsor again rendered
valuable assistance'. [CIPC]

December 1939

Organ Recital by Miss Frost for Christmas gifts to serving men
raised £2/5/-. [DM]

1 '**First Aid**. The first of a series of 3 talks about FA, organised
by FAP & ARW, was given by Mrs Hallam on 23 Nov and the
second by Dr Dwyer-Joyce of Histon on Wednesday. Both gave
interesting & instructive talks and appreciative audiences gained
valuable information. The last talk will take the form of a
demonstration by the RC in the VI on Thursday next at 8pm'.
[CIPC]

2 Funeral of David Childerley (93). [DM]

12 'The Chairman read a report on the school air-raid rehearsal and
it was resolved that protection for the school should be left to the
School Managers & the LEA.

Arising out of a further letter from the RDC regarding fire-
fighting the PC considered the matter still far from satisfactory
and resolved to press for a copy of both the peace & war-time
schemes arranged with the Boro' of Cambridge.

It was agreed that the sinking of the barrels into Washpit Brook
should be done by the RDC ditching staff'. [PCM]

15 'A Whist Drive in the WI Hall in aid of Girton RC detachment
raised £5'. [CIPC]

16 Funeral of Caroline Annie Martin (66). [DM]

18 Funeral of Maria Elizabeth Smith (55). [DM]

19 Wedding of George William Hall & Elizabeth Jean Herrow. [DM]

23 Wedding of Frederick Thomas Griffin & Frances Evelyn Bennett.
[DM]

23 Wedding of Leslie George Impey & Betty King. [DM]

25 Wedding of Cyril Leslie Moore & Hilda May Andrews. [DM]

29 '**YMG** spent a very pleasant evening at the VI last Friday with

Girton Baptist Chapel

Elsewhere
    4,500 girls working in WLA.
13 Battle of R Plate.
14 USSR expelled from League of Nations.
17 *Graf Spee* scuttled off Montevideo.
18 Canadian troops arrive in UK. Empire air training agreement
    signed.
25 Admiralty announce completion of E Coast minefield.
26 First squadron of Australian airmen arrive.

The Village Red Cross Unit, c 1939
Back: Alice Hall, Gert Lyons, Ginny Naylor, Doris Naylor, Margaret Hancock,
Heather Huddlestone, Honor Huddlestone, Alice Lee, Edna Johnson
Middle: Irene Nightingale, ?, Beatrice Turner, Joyce Bonsor, Mrs Marshall
Front: Mrs Burgh, Rose Evans

chess & other games. Mr Cecil Wilson, as usual, saw everyone was supplied with tea & biscuits. Mr FG Evans will give a talk on 31 Dec'. [CIPC]

29 Wedding of Geoffrey Cecil Edmunds & Evelyn Joyce Shead. [DM]

January 1940

3 Funeral of Jane Coe (68). [DM]

5 'Labour Party: Mr Percy Suttle presided at the monthly meeting when Dr EM Tillgard spoke on the Federal Union'. [CIPC]

9 'The Chairman explained the circumstances under which the Rec came to be occupied by the Military Authority and he was asked to negotiate terms for rent & compensation with them. He undertook to stress that the sanitary arrangements must be adequate and that lorries must keep off the turf and that the public must not be excluded. Mr Searle undertook to see the Sergeant in charge and ask him to assist by keeping lorries to the track. It was decided to suggest to the Cricket Club that they re-erect the fencing round the cricket table'. [PCM]

13 Baptism of Alison Margaret Bonny. [DM]

18 Funeral of William Kidman (87). [DM]

18 SS Prize-Giving Treat (with tea & games) for 50 children. [DM]

19 '**Baptist Church**: Sunday service was conducted by Mr PC Easter. The service for young people on Tuesday evenings will recommence this week.

Labour Party's Benefit Whist Drive for the benefit of Mr W Evans was a great success. $15\frac{1}{2}$ tables in play and thanks to numerous gifts over £6 was cleared and sent to Mr Evans. A letter of thanks was read from Mr Evans, who has been ill for over a year and Mr Cobb, the Secretary, expressed warm appreciation of the help given by non-members'. [CIPC]

21 Funeral of James Percy Vinall (63). [DM]

27 Funeral of Mary Alice Cooke (70). [DM]

27 Funeral of William Francis Watson (73). [DM]

February 1940

9 '**YMG**. An interesting talk on "Memory" by Mr Frank Twinn.

Labour Party. Mr Suttle presided. Dr Joseph Lock spoke of a scientist's view of politics. Dr Needham thought there were some problems on nutrition & public health. [CIPC]

13 'The WD had agreed to pay rent for the use of the Rec and compensation for any damage.

It was agreed to charge the Dept for water taken from the standpipe in excess of 5,000gal per quarter.

A further letter from the RDC regarding fire-fighting, stating that

Elsewhere

Council for the Encouragement of Music and the Arts founded as
an alternative to ENSA.

Free milk provided for mothers & babies.

George Cross instituted for acts of civilian bravery.

5 '1) Top Fruit. No further planting without sanction of WAEC.
2) Soft Fruit. The present acreage must not be increased.
3) Vegetables. a) Asparagus. No further planting will be allowed.
b) Rhubarb. The acreage must be reduced by 30%.
c) Seakale. The acreage must be reduced by 25% each spring.
d) Herbs. The acreage must be reduced by 30%.
4) Flowers. a) Perennial. No increase in the present acreage will
be allowed. b) Bulbs. No restriction has been made. c) Flower
Crops. 50% of the land must be made available for food crops.
5) Glasshouse Flower Crops. 25% of the area must be made
available for food crops.
6) Nursery Stock. a) No increase in acreage will be allowed.
b) Roses. Not more than 10% of the land cleared in any one
season must be replanted to rose or other stocks'. [Condensed
from *WAEC Emergency Regulations in Horticulture*]

9 German bombers sink 3 merchant ships in North Sea.

10 Allies obtain invasion plans after Luftwaffe officer crash-lands.

12 Conscription extended to ages 20–27.

15 Nearly twice as many Britons killed on roads since blackout
started than by enemy action.

31 Food subsidies running at £1M per week.

Elsewhere

16 HMS *Cossack* rescues 299 prisoners from *Altmark* off Norway.
Crews of HMS *Exeter* & HMS *Ajax* cheered through London on
return from S America & Battle of R Plate.

24 Germany revises attack plan to include Panzer assault through
Ardennes.

the Boro' Fire Brigade would answer all calls and that hose was to be provided and 3 men trained & equipped to deal immediately with fires arising from air attack.

It was agreed to remind the RDC about sinking the tubs in Washpit Brook and to ask Mr Amps to pipe the entranceway to his land adjacent to the Woody Green Path.

Some discussion took place over the apparent conditions under which the RE's occupying the Rec appeared to be living and Mr Searle undertook to make some enquiries'. [PCM]

16 '**LHS** Whist Drive raised £4/8/5$\frac{1}{2}$ for the Scouts' BEF Comforts Fund. This effort was a spontaneous one on the part of the school troop.

WI. Quite a number of members attended in spite of the black night to hand in their nominations for the new committee. The following social events had been arranged: 15 Feb Whist Drive in aid of the troops, 22 Whist Drive in aid of St Dunstan's, 24 Dance in aid of local troops' fund. Mr Hibbert-Ware gave an interesting lecture on Whipsnade Zoo'. [CIPC]

22 Bishop Price confirmed Betty Hullyer, Muriel Edna Pentelow, Hazel Daphne Blanch King, Walter Clifford Hankin & Kenneth George Naylor at Girton. [DM]

24 Baptism of Andrew David John Suttle, Jennifer Marion Lipscombe. [DM]

March 1940

 1 'AT Chenery fined 15/- for failing to obscure a light.

WI. Whist Drive raised £3/10/- for St Dunstan's.

YMG. "How we can help Girton" by Mr FM Dupont'. [CIPC]

 8 Organ Recital by Miss Frost for serving men (25/- raised). [DM]

10 Evensong reverts to 6pm. [DM]

11 Funeral of James John Crane (53). [DM]

12 'Mr Amps had piped the ditch under his entrance way and the tubs had been sunk into the Brook.

The WD had undertaken to reorganise the feeding arrangements for the men of the Searchlight Detachment and on Mr Nightingale suggesting that the men would appreciate an old wireless set & cooking stove, it was agreed that this might be discussed at the APM.

The WD had agreed to contribute half the cost of making up the Rec entrance roadway and had paid the sum of £1/13/4 for the use of the Pavilion for billeting. The Clerk has written to the CC pointing out that the gate and part of the fence had been damaged by the generator lorry and asked for the necessary repairs to be

The RE established a Searchlight Unit on Girton Rec

Elsewhere

Meat rationed to 1/10 worth per week.

12 Finns hand over Karelian Isthmus & part of E Karelia.

12 Treaty of Moscow ends 'Winter War'.

18 Hitler & Mussolini meet at Brenner Pass.

21 Reynaud replaces Daladier as French Prime Minister.

28 Allied War Council lays mines in Norwegian waters.

29 Molotov announces Soviet neutrality.

carried out. He was instructed to ascertain the attitude of the WD towards cricket on the ground. It was agreed that the ground should be cut and not grazed this year.

Mr Searle was asked to put in a new water tap. It was decided to ask Mr I King to pay the sum of 1/- *pa* for using the tap.

The Chairman made a statement on the taking over of Thornton Rd by the CC and said that the sewer which was the matter most likely to affect the DC & PC would not become public property until adopted by the DC.

It was agreed that for the summer months meetings should be held at 8pm'. [PCM]

12 Funeral of Allen Richard Stonebridge (79). [DM]

15 Funeral of Leslie John Wilderspin (74). [DM]

27 YWCA play 'The Happy Man' for Church funds (Feb). [DM]

April 1940

10 American Tea & Sale of Work at the VI. [DM]

14 Children's Service at 3pm with address by Mr Burgess, Master of Cambridge Central School. [DM]

16 'APM. Mr Pease was elected Chairman & Mr Lilley Vice-Chairman for the ensuing year. Mr Searle & Mr Elwood were appointed Assessors to assist the Rating Authority.

Mr Nightingale had made preliminary enquiries for running a Whist Drive to raise funds to provide the Searchlight Detachment with a cooking stove & wireless set, but that these had now been provided by the WD.

It was decided to ask Mr North to put in 4 oak posts to mark the roadway across the Rec and the Clerk was instructed to inform Messrs Isons that if their lorries continued to cross the Rec on the turf the PC would prosecute them for damage.

A tender was received from Messrs Skinner for providing a new gate post in place of that damaged by the Army generator lorry and it was agreed that this be passed on to the WD.

Permission had been given for cricket subject to the following conditions: 1) That the striking crease should not be less than 62yd from the Searchlight apparatus. 2) That the apparatus must be adequately protected by nets &c by the Club. It was agreed to inform the Club and ask for an assurance that they will be conscientiously carried out.

It was resolved to suggest to the PCC that the Churchyard wall near the children's playground should be rebuilt and also to ask for the old wire &c to be cleared away.

Girton Cricket Team, shortly after the War:
?, K Naylor, W Kidman, T Impey, J Balaam
R Dadswell, C Matthews, G West, P Alton, S Gawthrop

Elsewhere

Woolton appointed Minister for Food

8 Destroyer *Glowworm* sinks off Norway after ramming German cruiser *Hipper*.

German troops invade Denmark and land in 5 places in Norway: Oslo, Kristiansand, Bergen, Trondheim & Narvik.

15 Anglo-French troops land in Norway; British troops occupy Faroes.

25 Ministry of Health Survey shows that only 8% of children eligible for evacuation have been registered; 19% of parents refuse, no reply from 73%.

27 Himmler orders construction of concentration camp at Auschwitz.

30 German aircraft crashes at Clacton killing 2, the first British civilian casualties.

31 Oswald Mosley interned.

Mr Searle was asked to put up a notice board on the land used by the PC as a refuse dump, worded as follows: "Persons trespassing on this land will be prosecuted".

A circular was received from the RDC asking the PC to start a scheme of collection of waste paper &c. LHS Scout Group were undertaking a partial collection and it was decided to ask if LHS could provide a dump for any further paper.

Permission was given to the Cambridge Gas Co to erect a kiosk in High St near the Parish Pump, and Mr Searle was asked to carry out any necessary repair to the pump.

Miss Hibbert-Ware & Mr Frank Skinner were appointed representatives to CPCC.

In reply to a circular from the RCC regarding the Dig for Victory campaign, the Clerk was instructed to say that the Charity Trustees had ploughed up 2 acres of grassland for use as allotments and plots were available for immediate cultivation. The Clerk was appointed as Citizens' Adviser in the Parish'. [PCM]

26 Wedding of Mr E Melbert of Catherine St, Cambridge & Miss V Dixon of Cambridge Rd, Girton, and of Mr AE Chandler of Trafalgar Rd, Cambridge & Miss M Nightingale of Church Lane, Girton. [CIPC]

26 **GDNA**. At the AGM at the VI, Mrs Cyril Matthews, WE Bowyer, Mrs Cecil Turner & Mr Pease were elected to the committee for 3 years'. [CIPC]

May 1940

3 '**Baptist Church**. Arrangements have been made to celebrate Young Life Day as usual next Saturday.

YMG. Mr Tom Chapman gave a talk on "Cheerfulness" which led to general discussion. Members gave a hearty welcome to their former Secretary Sgt Stanley Dixon RAF on leave from active service.

For the Blind. A Whist Drive was held in the WI Hall on 25 Apr. 9 tables were in play and £9/1/- collected for the Association.

IWC. The 4th AGM took place on Wednesday week with Mrs Vellacott in the Chair. The Centre had had a very successful year. Members remained fairly constant at 128, average attendance at each session being 30 to 40. 76 children in all had now been inoculated against diphtheria. Mothers & babies evacuated to the district had been made welcome'. [CIPC]

10 '**YMG**. Mr WH Wosencroft gave a much enjoyed talk on "Religious Music". A welcome visitor was AC Maurice Songer on leave from

Flt-Lt Stan Dixon, who was in Girton on leave in May 1940

Elsewhere

50,000 car radios to be removed. A new Emergency Powers (Defence) Regulation stated "No person shall use or have in his possession or under his control any radio receiving apparatus installed in any road vehicle. The carrying of portable radio sets in cars also forbidden".

Concentrated tablets of synthetic vitamins, similar to those issued to German troops, are being manufactured in UK.

Less sugar for forces on leave. Maximum amount of sugar obtainable by members of the Forces (including women) on leave with the RB8 duty ration card reduced from 21oz to 16oz and with the RB8A duty card from 10oz to 8oz, with the domestic sugar ration reduced to 8oz. Seamen not affected. Reduction of butter ration allowance to catering establishments comes into force.

Anderson Shelters must be properly installed by 11 June or local authority to receive in writing a good explanation why'. [DE] the RAF.

WI. At the monthly meeting on 1 May members & others enjoyed a concert arranged by Mr Alan Williams, Music Director of IVC'. [CIPC]

12 Pilot Officer Norman Smith killed in Netherlands [DM]

14 'Dr Walton presented a statement setting out the functions & personnel of the various ARP services and general advice as to procedures to be adopted in an air-raid. It was agreed that the statement be duplicated & distributed to every house. Mr Radford of 11 Pepys Way had offered to organise a Utility Squad. It was agreed that Mr Radford's offer be accepted and that the CC be asked to supply steel helmets. If the CC were unable to do so they should be purchased by the PC.

Mr Fletcher had offered to lend & drive his lorry as a member of the Squad if the petrol could be made up. Agreed that the CC be asked to provide this.

Mr Impey reported on the FAP with special reference to the quantity of equipment. After discussion it was unanimously resolved that the PC augment the equipment by the provision of extra splints, 12 tubes tannic jelly, calico for bandages & slings, 6 steel helmets & 5 pouches. The total not to exceed £7.

Mr North was having difficulty in obtaining the oak for the Rec posts, but he had some 4×4 deal. Agreed that this be used.

The Chairman presented the Requisition issued by the WD to cover taking over the Rec. It was agreed that the offer of half the cost of the renewal of the gatepost &c, ie £1/9/3, be accepted. It was agreed to hold a further meeting on 28 May to discuss the question of salvage'. [PCM]

17 '**Baptist Church**. In order to emphasise the value of service of the community the various ARP & RC Units had been invited to attend the service next Sunday evening to be conducted by Mr FM Dupont'. [CIPC]

19 Baptism of Peter John Trewren. [DM]

24 '**GDNA**. Increased membership reported at the AGM. At a meeting of the new committee the Chairman reported the names of those elected for the 3 years 1940–43 and he welcomed Mrs Bowyer as President of IWC in place of Mrs Vellacott. After a ballot the following were co-opted for the ensuing year: Mrs Betson, Mrs Goodchild & Mr Skinner. President: Mr Sharp, Treasurer: Mr Bowyer, Hon Sec Mrs Turner, Vice-Chairman Mr Pease, Assistant Treasurer Mrs Bowyer, Assistant Secretary Mr Lennard-Jones. Mr Skinner & the Bursar of Girton College were

Beaverbrook appointed Minister for Aircraft Production.

Coastal towns from Great Yarmouth to Folkestone declared evacuation areas.

'Enigma' code cracked at Bletchley Park.

10 German troops invade Holland, crossing Yssel & Meuse rivers at several points.

10 Germany invades France & the Low Countries.

10 Churchill becomes Prime Minister in a coalition Govt including Attlee & Ernest Bevin.

11 Whitsun Bank Holiday cancelled.

14 Formation of LDV.

18 Pétain becomes French Vice-Premier.

20 German troops reach English Channel at Noyelles.

21 British & French tanks counter-attack near Arras, stalling German advance.

22 All citizens at disposal of Govt by new Emergency Powers Act.

24 Hitler orders Guderian to halt before Dunkirk, & the German advance continues towards Paris.

25 Allies fall back to Dunkirk with fall of Boulogne.

26 May – 4 June Operation Dynamo: over 330,000 Allied troops evacuated from Dunkirk.

27 Germany takes Calais.

27 Men aged 26 called up.

28 Belgian Army capitulates; cabinet-in-exile repudiates King Leopold's surrender.

30 BEF begins withdrawal W of Brussels.

31 'Signposts & direction indicators to be removed, which would be of value to the enemy in case of invasion.

TG Impey of the FA Party in HG uniform

elected auditors. It was agreed that the officers together with Mrs
Leakey should be the existing committee for the ensuing year'.
[CIPC]

28 'Mr Radford had received 9 volunteers for the Utility Squad and
Messrs Thompson Ltd had offered to lend various equipment to
be kept stored at their premises at Thornton Rd. He undertook
to let the Clerk have an inventory of articles used. Resolved to
thank Messrs Thompson for their offer and undertake to replace
anything lost or damaged. Mr F Piggott offered to lend other
equipment and also to act as Deputy Leader. It was agreed that
the PC provide Civilian Duty Respirators for the use of members
of the Squad and also to ask the Council to lend 12 hurricane
lamps and to provide 2gal of petrol to be held in reserve by Mr
Fletcher.

The FAP splints, calico & tannic jelly had been provided and that
the pouches & helmets would follow as soon as available.

After discussion on the Clacton crash, Dr Walton agreed to
attempt to get volunteers with bicycles to act as messengers.

Mrs Green representing the WVS reported on the arrangements
for salvage. After discussion it was agreed to let the LHS boys
continue with the collection of waste paper assisted in the sorting
by the WI, and to ask Mr Bradfield to organise the collection of
bones from receptacles about the village through the YMG, and
to ask the public through the Press to put out for collection with
the tins all types of scrap metal.

The Chairman undertook to see about getting the Fire Hydrants
repainted'. [PCM]

June 1940

7 Wedding at Girton Chapel of Miss E Hancock, 72 High St, & Mr
J Ryder, Chorley Wood. [CIPC]

7 '**YMG**. By courtesy of the Secretary of Addenbrooke's, members
were shown over the hospital last Saturday afternoon. The
operating theatre, X-ray Dept & dispensary proved particularly
interesting. The visitors saw a blood test being carried out.
Members left with a clearer conception of the very valuable work
Addenbrooke's is doing and much admiration for the manner in
which those responsible carry out a difficult task'. [CIPC]

11 'Dr Walton reported on the mobilisation of the various ARP
Services under actual raid conditions and stated that the warning
would be given by whistles, and the all-clear by hand bells. He
was given authority to purchase 7 FA pouches.

9 steel helmets & 9 Civilian Duty Respirators had been

Bicycle Messengers turned out to be a valuable means of communication

Elsewhere

336 civilians killed, 476 injured.

3 Germany bombs Paris.

4 Churchill speech: 'We shall fight them on the beaches ...'

5 Creation of 'Ironsides', small mobile armed groups for defence against parachutists.

5 Strikes banned.

6 Air-raids take place along much of E coast of England.

7 King Haakon & his Govt leave Norway for London.

8 Aircraft carrier *Glorious* plus 2 destroyers sunk off Narvik by *Scharnhorst* & *Gneisenau*.

8 Last Allied troops leave Norway.

14 German army enters Paris.

15 Operation 'Ariel' evacuation of British & French troops from Cherbourg, Brest, St Nazaire.

distributed to members of the Utility Squad and a receipt secured in each case.

Miss Hibbert-Ware undertook in conjunction with Mrs Green to canvass Thornton, St Margaret's & Huntingdon Rd & Pepys Way in order to get one householder in 10 or 12 to be responsible for collecting newspaper from others in the group, and Mr Pease undertook to ask Mr Newton & Mr Chandler to provide the necessary collections from these houses at regular intervals. LHS boys would still undertake the collection from the rest of the village and 3 lads from the YMG had undertaken to clear the "Bones Salvage" receptacles each week.

A circular was received from the RDC regarding the collection of scrap metal and the establishment of a dump in the Parish, and Mr Elwood undertook to organise this.

The Claim Form for compensation for use by the WD of the Rec having been received, it was decided that no compensation be asked beyond an undertaking to reinstate the ground to its pre-war condition at the conclusion of hostilities.

The Chairman undertook to report on a circular on the establishment of a Pig Club at the next meeting.

It was agreed to ask the Bus Co to supply a timetable of services and to mention the irregularity of service No 102'. [PCM]

13 'A proposal for conscription for ARP was rejected by SC RDC.
WI. Miss Gaskell (Shelford) gave a talk on household jobbing in the course of which she showed how to join carpets, put tin handles on saucepan lids &c. Miss Warrington then talked about the Produce Guild and urged members to join'. [CIPC]

23 Baptism of Patricia Elfrida Pauley. [DM]

28 '**YMG**. Owing to so many of the members either serving in HM Forces or being employed on war work, the Committee decided to discontinue the Sunday morning meeting until further notice'. [CIPC]

July 1940

4 Wedding of Leslie Albert Baker & Doreen Alpha Henderson. [DM]

6 Baptism of Veronica Gawthrop. [DM]

9 'An expression of sympathy was offered to the Clerk on the loss suffered by his family during a recent air attack on Cambridge.
The Clerk had prepared a list of bus times and it was agreed that this should be posted on the Notice Board.
Dr Walton reported on the present ARP position and it was agreed that a revised pamphlet be distributed.

16 Italy declares war on UK & France.
16 Pétain replaces Reynaud as Premier & negotiates armistice resulting in the Vichy Govt.
17 Pétain asks for armistice terms.
17 *Lancastria* sinks off St Nazaire, with loss of 3,000 lives.
21 First commando raid on Le Touquet.
22 Completion of 2nd LCC evacuation scheme; 100,000 children move to West Country & Wales.
25 First early morning air-raid alarm in London.
27 De Gaulle broadcasts first message to French from London.
28 UK recognises de Gaulle as Free French leader.
28 Demilitarisation & partial evacuation of CI. German aircraft bomb Jersey.
30 Germany occupies CI.

Littleton House, at the time a school for boys with learning difficulties, whose pupils played an active part in Salvage collection

Elsewhere

'Women of Britain, give us your aluminium pots & pans. We will turn them into Spitfires, Hurricanes, Blenheims & Wellingtons' (Beaverbrook).
258 civilians killed, 121 injured.
2 Hitler orders 'Operation Sea Lion'.
3 RN attacks French sqn at Oran. *Strasbourg* escapes, rest sink or ground with 1,147 casualties.
5 Vichy Govt breaks off diplomatic relations.
8 Swordfish aircraft damage battleship *Richlieu* at Dakar after

A manual Fire Engine was now situated in Girton, together with lengths of hose, and that 4 men, Messrs I King (Leader), Matthews, Watson & Whitehead, were being trained. Mr Searle undertook to build a trailer and it was decided to ask the Rev Hibbert-Ware if he would garage it. It was agreed to ask the RDC to provide training for 2 additional men.

A letter was received asking if a siren could be provided; the Clerk was instructed to point out that a Parish Meeting had decided against a siren, and that an additional ARW had now volunteered for duty in the sector covered by the complaint.

Miss Hibbert-Ware reported that the salvage of waste paper was proceeding and that Mr Newton & Mr Chandler were providing necessary cartage & collection.

The Parish had been circularised about scrap metal and a dump started in Mr Searle's yard. Mr Sharp had offered his garden as a dump to which the public could take their scrap. It was agreed that the metal should be sold by Mr Elwood and a grant made to the Housing Association'. [PCM]

12 '**GDNA** held a Whist Drive at 1 Reynolds Close.

WI. The 21st Birthday party was celebrated on 3 July in the garden of the President, Mrs Stewart. Miss Hibbert-Ware spoke about salvage and asked for volunteers. Miss Warrington gave an interesting talk on the Produce Guild, which has been formed for dealing with surplus fruit in the villages. Miss Fegan spoke on her work in a leper colony. The party concluded with an entertainment'. [CIPC]

14 Children's Service 3pm. [DM]

26 'Herbert Arthur Harvey of 18 Woodlands Park, Girton summoned for leaving a car without lights. Frank Fairey, a sergeant in the Girton Special Constabulary told the court that about midnight he found a car parked on the thoroughfare with no lights. Defendant was fined £1 with costs.

One of the most enjoyable concerts for some time was given last Friday evening by local talent trained by Miss Frost, LRAM, MRST, the entire proceeds, £4/3/-, were devoted to sending Postal Orders to the men on active service.

Baptist Church. "Faith & Courage" was the theme of the service last Sunday evening. At the quarterly Deacons' Meeting arrangements were made for the Harvest Thanksgiving services and the Secretary was requested to arrange co-operation in any united service that might be held on 10 Nov. It was also decided to contribute £5 to the Service Men's Canteen Fund'. [CIPC]

French reject demilitarisation proposals.

8 Metropolitan Police to be armed for some guard duty.

9 Tea rationing of 2oz per head per week introduced.

10 German aircraft begin bombing English ports & Channel shipping.

10 Union of Fascists banned.

10 Heavy German bombing of Britain marks start of first phase of the Battle of Britain.

10 'Stricter Black-Out Needed. A renewed appeal to the Public. All householders, shop keepers, factory owners & occupiers of other premises must remember once again the important need of complying strictly with the lighting regulations. Black-out is part of the national Defence and a most important part. DURING AIR-RAIDS – Beware of flying glass. As a result of an investigation into certain casualties caused by recent air-raids it has been established that about 60% were due to flying glass. In a statement issued by the Ministry of Information on Wednesday, it is pointed out that many people were caught by flying glass as they were preparing to go to their Anderson shelters. Many people spend far too long dressing in front of their bedroom windows. When they decide to dress the public should do so quickly. Clothes should be left ready on the previous night and should be placed in those parts of the room not exposed to the full impact of in-rushing glass'. [CIPC]

15 Home Office bans fireworks, and kite & balloon flying.

15 Unemployment up at 827,266, but down by half a million on June 1939 figures.

17 Troopship *Lancastria*, evacuating British forces from France, sunk by German aircraft off St Nazaire; over 3,000 killed.

19 Brooke replaces Ironside as C-in-C Home Forces. Ironside appointed Field Marshal.

19 Special Operations Executive formed to obtain secret information from the enemy.

20 Buying or selling new cars banned.

21 Czechoslovak Govt-in-exile formed in London.

23 In the third War Budget income tax up to 8/6, beer up 1d, purchase tax introduced for first time – 33% on luxuries; war expenditure for the next year estimated at £3,470M.

23 LDV renamed HG with more than 1,300,000 now enrolled.

25 Compulsory evacuation of women & children from Gibraltar.

29 Air attack on Dover; British claim 17 down. Germany accused of using RC aircraft for reconnaissance.

August 1940

13 'Mr I King, Leader of the Girton AFS reported that much of
the equipment had been provided and that 6 men, Messrs King,
Hales, Vic Watson, Ray Watson, Whitehead & Matthews, had
received some training. The DC having authorised training for
10 men, it was agreed to try to get a further 4 volunteers.

A circular was received from the DC regarding the prevention of
landing by aircraft on land under the jurisdiction of the PC. The
Clerk had replied that no such land in Girton was affected, but
had raised the point about agricultural land around the Parish.
The reply was that the owners of such land were to be approached
through the WAEC.

The Chairman had attended a Conference on Salvage from which
it emerged that no money was forthcoming from the sale of scrap
metal through the Govt Scheme. It was agreed that Mr Elwood
continue with the arrangement for selling the scrap privately.

The sum so far raised from the sale of waste paper was £6/8/7 &
from bones 17/6. It was agreed that a special account be opened at
Barclays Bank, and a decision made later as to how to use such
money. The very best thanks of the PC were tendered to Miss
Hibbert-Ware for all the work she has done and continues to do
for the Salvage Campaign.

The RCC circular about Food Production was received.

The Chairman was authorised to call a Conference of all
organisations in the village to discuss the question of securing
the use of areas of the Village Halls now occupied by the Military
Authority, for entertainment during the winter'. [PCM]

23 'Mr & Mrs Ebenezer John Farrow of "Long View" Cambridge
Rd celebrated their Golden Wedding on Monday. Mr Farrow is
a Deacon of Girton Baptist Chapel and Mrs Farrow has been
associated for many years with the Sisterhood Movement.

Baptist Church. The services were conducted by Mr Gayton.
Arranged by Mr FM Dupont a musical hour followed the evening
service. Several members of the Forces contributed to the
programme after which light refreshments were served. it is
hoped to make the musical hour a regular feature'. [CIPC]

30 '**YMG**. By courtesy of the managers, the school has been made
available for the meetings which will re-commence at 11am next
Sunday. Mr Michael Pease having kindly offered accommodation,
it is hoped also in the near future to recommence the Social Club
on Friday evenings. During recent weeks several group members
serving with the Forces have been welcomed home on leave'.

Elsewhere
 1 RAF bombs Krupps works at Essen.
 1 Maximum price of milk raised to 4d a pint.
 2 French military court sentences de Gaulle to death in his
   absence.
 2 August Bank Holiday cancelled.
 2 Beaverbrook appointed to War Cabinet.
 3 Churchill warns nation against believing rumours that invasion
   threat is over.
 5 Churchill & de Gaulle agree on organisation of Free French
   forces.
 5 German Govt announces that all citizens will need a Certificate
   of Ancestry proving their racial purity back to 1800.
 8 Forces pay increases by 6d per day; private's pay 17/6 per week.
 9 British troops withdraw from Shanghai & N China.
12 Dortmund–Ems canal blocked by low-level bombing; pilot
   awarded VC.
12 Portsmouth bombed & radar stations hit in southern England.
12 Wasting food becomes illegal.
14 Ministry of Home Security announces that parachutes had been
   found in Derbyshire, Yorkshire & Scotland, but no evidence of
   Germans discovered.
15 Heaviest attack so far: more than 1,000 German aircraft.
17 Germany announces total blockade.
20 Churchill: 'Never in the field of human conflict ...'
23 Battle of Britain begins in earnest with heavy air battles and the
   bombing of central London & RAF command centres.
23 LDV renamed HG.
25 First RAF raid on Berlin.
26 Germany apologises for Wexford bombing.
28 Vichy radio announces dropping of laws protecting Jews.
29 Butter ration cut from 6oz to 4oz; margarine ration unchanged.
29 Eastern Regional Commissioner urges parents to keep children
   away from where delayed-action bombs have fallen.
29 Signs similar to pre-war AA signs indicating points of the
   compass begin to be erected on roads used by military convoys.
29 Subscriptions to $2\frac{1}{2}$% National War Bonds in the week ending
   Tue 27 Aug were £10,116,120, making a total since 25 June of
   £181,679,540.
29 'ENSA plans more shows. Plans to double concerts, sports and
   studies for the Services will be in operation by the autumn. 600
   jobless actors & actresses will help ENSA give every soldier at

[CIPC]
30 Organ recital by Miss Frost. [DM]

September 1940

 1 MU Quarterly Service in Church 3pm. [DM]
 6 'Music at Girton Church. The organ, violin & vocal music given
   by Miss Frost & a choir of local voices on Friday evening was
   greatly enjoyed. The collection amounted to £2/11/6 & is being
   used to send gifts to men serving in HM Forces.
   Baptist Church. The Young People's Service was conducted by
   Mr K Marshall, the address by Mr K Bailey. Mr Hughes was
   the soloist at the evening service which was followed by the usual
   musical hour.
   YMG. There being a small attendance last Sunday morning the
   topic "Vision" was briefly discussed, after which there was a short
   discussion as to the best ways of maintaining interest under
   difficult war time conditions'. [CIPC]
10 'Mr Chandler & Mr Newton would be unable to continue to
   collect waste paper and it was decided to thank them for their
   co-operation. Mr Elwood & Mr Skinner undertook to collect from
   Pepys Way and Mr Searle from Girton College: Rev Hibbert-Ware
   & Miss Hibbert-Ware to continue to collect from Huntingdon Rd
   and the LHS boys to take over Thornton Rd.
   The Chairman reported that the Conference he had called to
   consider the question of Village Halls during the winter had
   agreed to form a Committee to organise entertainment one night
   a week with the Military detachment stationed in the village. Mr
   Palmer was appointed to the Committee from the PC.
   Dr Walton reported that the Wardens scheme was proving
   unsuitable and that the Military were providing an all-night
   watch at 3 points in the village. Householders in Thornton
   Rd were providing their own rota. A few stirrup pumps had
   come to hand and a demonstration of them together with the
   Manual Engine had been arranged for Sat 14 Sep. He promised
   to re-establish contact with Girton College on the question of
   temporary accommodation for those who might be rendered
   homeless by an attack'. [PCM]
13 '**RC**. The sewing party at Girton have now completed one year's
   voluntary service. The review of the year was that 283 articles for
   the Central Hospital Supply Service and 105 articles have been
   knitted for the Cambs Comforts for the Troops. The members of
   the Working Party qualified for a badge when they have given 100

least one show a fortnight. Bigger libraries, lectures by
schoolmasters & professors of first-class qualifications, optional
lessons for all ranks, will cater for every soldier'. [DS]

Elsewhere

6,954 civilians killed, 10,615 injured.

7 Start of the Blitz. Massive bombing raids.

12 Co-ordination of searchlights & AA guns improves protection of
London from air attack.

15 Luftwaffe suffers heavy losses on what becomes known as
'Battle of Britain' day.

17 Hitler delays his invasion plan.

17 Liner *City of Benares* evacuating children to Canada sunk with
77 out of 99 children lost, total killed 260.

17 Churchill announces 2,000 civilians killed & 8,000 seriously
injured in air-raids in first half of the month; service casualties
for same period was 250.

19 RAF continues attacks on invasion fleet in Channel ports.

19 Bevin announces that by the end of August 51,261 men register
as conscientious objectors.

22 Moscow radio reports RAF bombing has largely destroyed
invasion fleet.

24 18th successive night raid on London, with Southampton &
Brighton also attacked.

24 Plans announced to evacuate mothers as well as children from
Blitz areas; 444,000 children already evacuated from London
area.

24 Price of petrol up to 2/$\frac{1}{2}$ per gallon.

25 All Norwegian political parties except Quisling's National
Samling dissolved.

27 Germany, Italy & Japan sign Tripartite Pact.

28 First US destroyers arrive.

hours work, in return for which they contribute 1/- to the funds. A penny-a-week fund is contributed to by the members and to date 2 donations of 10/- each have been given to the Comforts Fund. A fund is now being started for 6 weeks for a collection towards a Spitfire.

Harvest Thanksgiving. The Baptist Church was crowded to its utmost capacity for the Harvest Thanksgiving service held last Sunday evening. The address was given by Mr AD Rayner. Pte D Hughes was at the organ and the choir augmented by members of the Forces under the leadership of Pte G Shaw led the hearty singing.

WI. Members met at Reynolds Close for their monthly meeting by kind permission of Mrs Pease. A smaller number than usual was present. After routine business, Miss Hibbert-Ware explained her scheme for collecting salvage paper. She was trying to reorganise it so to make it much easier for the collectors, and asked the members to help. After light refreshments, some round games were thoroughly enjoyed.

YMG. "After War, What?" was opened by Mr FG Evans. Several members took part. It was felt generally that a quickened sense of personal responsibility and a fuller appreciation of life's true values would do much towards removing the artificial standards that prevailed nowadays. Also that secret diplomacy in international affairs should be definitely abolished'. [CIPC]

19 & 22 Harvest Thanksgiving & Service. [DM]

27 'YMG. "The Colour Question" was keenly discussed. Mr George Young spoke of the prejudice & injustice associated with the question and pointed out ways in which true values could be recognised, in accordance with true Christian principles. "The Ideal Radio Programme" will be the topic for discussion next Sunday morning.

   Labour Party. The Women's Section heard the first-hand account of the situation in Whitechapel'. [CIPC]

October 1940

6 Baptism of Michael William Evans, Margaret Suzanne Evans, Valerie Dawn Collison. [DM]

8 'Dr Walton reported that a night watch had been organised and that it was proposed to use the Cookery Room as a centre. The CC had agreed to have a telephone installed. Girton College had offered to provide temporary accommodation for those who might be rendered homeless by air-raids and the WVS were making 2 dozen palliasses.

*Members of the RC pledged themselves to raise the
£5,000 necessary to buy a Spitfire*

Girton Home Guard marching through the Village

Elsewhere

Between July & Oct 217 merchant ships sunk in Atlantic by
U-boats.

BST continues throughout the winter.

Ministry of Food subsidises fish & chip shops to encourage
potato consumption.

6,334 civilians killed, 8,695 injured.

15 64 killed when Balham tube station, used as an air-raid shelter,
is hit.

Some discussion took place on the question of accommodating the Utility Squad when they reported for duty and Mr Pease undertook to speak to the leader of the TA Party with a view to their sharing the TA Hut: as an alternative, Dr Walton offered the use of the Cookery Room. It was agreed that Dr Walton, Mr Radford, Mr Piggott & Mr Tingey should confer on the location of the Squad equipment and that application be made to the CC for 4 electric lamps of Home Office Pattern.

Miss Hibbert-Ware reported that the collection of waste paper & bones was continuing'. [PCM]

13 Leading Stoker Bertie Frederick Hullyer killed, the first confirmed casualty from Girton. [DM]

20 Mr Searle organises CD Parade Service. [DM]

21 Funeral of Mary Ann Jarman (69). [DM]

26 Wedding of George Victor Barnes & Barbara Ruth Shead. [DM]

26 Wedding of Leonard Frederick Hills & Vera May North. [DM]

November 1940

12 'The Post Office was about to install a telephone at the Cookery Room and as soon as this was done the ARP Night Watching Scheme would come into operation.

Some discussion took place about the desirability of sending schoolchildren home on an Air-Raid Alert, the RDC had sent a resolution to the CC asking that school shelters be provided. LHS had offered to provide accommodation to any rendered homeless by air attack.

Mr Elwood reported on the continued salvage of scrap iron and Miss Hibbert-Ware reported that the LHS boys were not now collecting waste paper and that depôts had been established at various houses in the Parish. Mr Cole was to pick up from these depôts once a fortnight. The children were going to bring their paper to school on one afternoon each week.

The Agreement with the CC for exterminating rats at the Refuse Dump to be continued subject to DC approval.

A letter having been received from LHS asking for rubbish to fill in a Pond, it was agreed to provide as much as required.

Bus Service No 152 had been reinstated & would operate hourly 8.30am to 8.30pm.

It was agreed to ask the officer in charge of the Searchlight Post to co-operate in keeping Army lorries to the roadway'. [PCM]

16 Wedding of Robert Coe & Olive Rudd. [DM]

17 Baptism of George Brooks Reade, Christine Elsie Whitehead. [DM]

18 British re-open Burma road.
22 Expulsion of Jews from Alsace-Lorraine & Rhineland begins.
24 Hitler & Pétain agree on collaboration.
24 The Belgian Govt-in-exile sets up in London.
28 Ministry of Health announces evacuation of 489,000 more children from London area.
29 British troops land in Crete.

Elsewhere
   4,588 civilians killed, 6,202 injured.
 3 RAF units arrive in Greece.
 5 Roosevelt re-elected President for third term.
 6 Under-Secretary for War announces measures to give HG more permanent shape & better equipment without changing its 'local & friendly' character.
11 3 Italian battleships sunk at Taranto by Fleet Air Arm aircraft from carrier *Illustrious*.
12 Heavy bombing raids take place on Bristol, Sheffield & Liverpool.
14 German raid on Coventry kills 568 people & destroys cathedral & much of city centre, making thousands of people homeless.
19 RAF bombs Škoda armament works in Czechoslovakia.
24 Treasury cancels Boxing Day Bank Holiday.
29 Liverpool severely bombed.

28 Confirmation by the Bishop of Ely of Margaret Ann Ding & Freda
    Kate Ding. [DM]

December 1940
   North Stowe Deanery Magazine forced to cease publication. [DM]
 8 Baptism of Daphne Alice Coxall. [DM]
10 'The CC had conceded on the question of the provision of school
    air-raid shelters.
    The lamp at Girton Corner had been damaged by an Army car
    and in accordance with the DC Lighting Committee's suggestion
    the standard had been removed & stored for the duration of the
    War. The Clerk had secured an estimate for repairing the damage
    and forwarded it to the responsible Authority.
    The VI was about to be vacated by the Military and would again
    be free for use in the evenings.
    The ARP Night-Watchers' Scheme was in operation and the
    palliasses were now available. Mr Radford reported on the
    present availability of the members of the Utility Squad and
    the difficulty he was having in turning them out, and it was
    generally agreed that further recruits were urgently required. It
    was therefore decided that a Public Meeting be called soon after
    Xmas to discuss ARP problems and to attempt to secure recruits.
    The Clerk was asked to remind the Searchlight Unit to turn off
    the water on the Rec at night during the winter months and Mr
    Searle was asked to bind up the tap & service pipe.
    The Chairman kindly undertook to replace the tree on the green
    at the top of Woodlands Park, which had been broken off &
    destroyed. It was agreed to ask the RDC to arrange for repair
    to be carried out to the electric lamp standard at the top of
    Woodlands Park.
    The ARP Service using the Cookery Room were badly in need of
    beds and it was agreed that the Chairman & Dr Walton arrange
    for the palliasses, which it was previously decided should be
    located at Girton College, to be filled & kept at the Cookery Room.
    It was suggested that blankets be purchased by funds raised by
    means of some entertainment & other functions. Miss Hibbert-
    Ware kindly offered to provide the money for these comforts'.
    [PCM]
14 Baptism of Gareth Clifford Grant Mason. [DM]
16 Bishop of Ely resigns on health grounds. [DM]
21 Funeral of Elizabeth Plumb (80). [DM]
21 Funeral of John Hancock (73). [DM]

Elsewhere

Introduction of 'Utility' clothing & furniture.

Start of WRNS overseas postings.

Girls' Training Corps set up by the Mechanised Transport Corps for 16–18 year olds, giving them basic training before conscription into the women's services.

3,793 civilians killed, 5,244 injured.

6 Hitler sends *Fliegerkorps X* to Sicily to increase attacks on Malta & Mediterranean Fleet.

9 British take 40,000 Italian prisoners in Wavell's offensive in the Western Desert.

16 RAF bombs Mannheim, Cologne & Düsseldorf.

17 Rations temporarily increased for Christmas week.

17 Winchester housewife sentenced to death for spying.

23 Eden replaces Halifax as Foreign Secretary.

29 City of London suffers heavy incendiary raid.

The Village Institute was an important meeting centre. The end in December of its brief military occupation was welcomed.

January 1941

First issue of *Girton Church Magazine*: 8 pages with *Ely Diocesan Gazette* & *Home Words* inset; price 2d. [CM]

Flying Officer NAL Smith declared dead. [CM]

Wedding of Lloyd Weston & Caroline Lamb (no date given). [CM]

1 'Siren 11pm–4am & 4.30–7pm'. [PD]

2 'Siren at 11am, 11.20am & 8.30pm, 11.45pm'. [PD]

3 'Siren 11.45pm, 3.45am'. [PD]

5 'Siren 1.30pm, 2.15pm'. [PD]

7 'Siren 1pm, 2.45pm, 4.30 5pm, 5.15–5.30'. [PD]

7 Sgt William Henry Harper Johnson killed. [CM]

14 'The CC were unable to provide electric lamps for the Utility Squad, but Dr Walton was authorised to purchase 4 lamps. He thanked Miss Hibbert-Ware for her generosity in purchasing blankets & other comforts. Dr Walton said he would provide the Clerk with an inventory.

It was suggested the WI be approached to organise a Whist Drive to raise funds to supplement the allowances for refreshments for Night Watchers & others on duty.

Consideration was then given to the number of Trustees of the VI appointed by the PC. The Institute having become available to members of the Public, Mr Lilley contended that a full quota of resident Trustees was desirable, and as Messrs Elwood & Impey were on War service, it was agreed they retire. Mr Lilley & Mr Pease also retired, and were reappointed, Frank Skinner & Reg Gawthrop were appointed in place of Messrs Elwood & Impey to whom the PC expressed sincere thanks.

Mr Palmer agreed to take over the salvage of iron scrap.

It was agreed to make a further request to the County Surveyor for reflectors to be fitted to the posts at Girton Corner, and to send another letter to Histon PC asking them to carry out some improvements to the Histon end of the Girton–Histon footpath.

The account for exterminating rats at the Refuse Dump for the first occasion under the new contract was certified.

The Clerk reported the completion of Audit of Accounts for the year ending 31 Mar'. [PCM]

15 'Siren 11.15pm, 1.30am. Incendiaries on Cambridge. Up most of night'. [PD]

16 Mrs Nightingale & Mrs Pinder represent the PCC in Caius College at a Missionary Exhibition Committee Meeting. [CM]

18 'Siren 12pm, 1.20pm, 2pm, 4.30pm'. [PD]

19 'Siren 11.30, 12pm'. [PD]

Weather

from CG Pluck's diary

1 Cold, with frost
2 V cold, frost, snow showers
3 Frost, NE wind. V cold, sun shone
4 Frost with cold E wind
5 Frost, roads bad
6 Snow & frost. V cold, snowing most of day
7 Sleet & frost
8 Thawing a little
9 Frost, v cold
10 Thawing rain
11 Rain, cold. Snow nearly all gone
12 V nice & mild
13 Fair, frost
14 Weather fair
15 $2\frac{1}{2}$" snow, v cold
16 V cold
17 Frost, v cold
18 Cold, frost. Snowed most of day. 3" snow
19 Cold, snow showers
20 Cold, frost. Turned to rain at times
21 Thawing
22 Snow nearly all gone
23 V muddy everywhere. Cloudy & fog
24 Cloudy & fog
25 Rain all afternoon
26 Cold
27 Fair, turned to rain in evening. Cloudy. Rained all night, cold
28 Fair to showery, fog
29 Cloudy, cold
30–31 Cloudy

Elsewhere

1,500 civilians killed, 2,012 injured.
1 RAF bombs Bremen 3 nights running.
8 96,000 people sleep in Tube stations, 40,000 fewer than in Oct.
10 Carrier *Illustrious* & convoy reach Malta. Heavy air-raids on Malta.
19 British & Empire troops invade Eritrea under command of Platt.
21 *Daily Worker* banned.
22 Italian garrison in Tobruk surrenders.
22 Compulsory fire-watching duty introduced.
30 Derna, N Africa, occupied by British & Empire forces.
30 Roosevelt outlines Lend-Lease Programme.
31 Cardiff severely bombed.

The first issue of the Church Magazine

20 Baptism of Alan James Garmant. [CM]

21 '4 sirens: 2 in morning, 2 in afternoon'. [PD]

22 'Started making blackout for labs'. [PD]

23 'Siren 11am, 11.20am'. [PD]

24 'Blackouting labs most of day. Went on fire-watching all night'. [PD]

28 '2 sirens'. [PD]

30 '2 sirens. Bombs on Mill Rd at 4pm. Killed 3 people'. [PD]

30 Funeral of Josiah Gane. [CM]

31 'Did fire-watch all night'. [PD]

February 1941

 1 'Siren 11.45–12.30. Did fire-watch all night'. [PD]

 2 Baptism of John Varnam Edwards. [CM]

 9 'Siren 7.15–8.44, 1–2am'. [PD]

10 'Siren 7.30–9.30'. [PD]

11 'The Clerk reported that he had asked Messrs Wheatley to make an offer for the iron scrap collected in the village, and it was agreed that Messrs Shooter be asked to quote also. It was agreed that labels be printed to attach to the sacks of waste paper sent to London each month, and that a triplicate receipt book be purchased to record the number of sacks of each class sent.

The date of the APM was fixed for the 28 Mar and it was agreed the usual type of Agenda be prepared.

It was resolved to submit an estimate of £75 to the RDC to meet the expenses of the PC during the next Financial Year.

The Clerk reported the receipt of a letter from the CC asking if the WI was still available for housing Air-Raid Homeless & Refugees, and that after consultation with the Chairman & Head ARW, he had replied that the WI was no longer available, and that the Head ARW had accepted offers of hospitality from Girton College & LHS.

Mr EH Barber of the AFS was joining HM Forces and it was agreed to express to him the PC's sincere thanks for his help in this Service'. [PCM]

11 Funeral of Charles George Coe. [CM]

13 'Siren 7.30–9.20'. [PD]

14 'Siren 7.30–11pm'. [PD]

15 Funeral of Harry Christopher Strugnell. [CM]

17 'Fire-watching all night. Siren 7.45–10.10pm, 2.15–6am'. [PD]

18 'Siren 7.45–2pm, 4–5pm'. [PD]

20 SS Tea & Prize-Giving. [CM]

22 Wedding of Eric William Charles Rowney & Lilian Jean Evans.

The Rowneys on their wedding day (22 Feb)

Weather

1 Cold wind
2 Cold
3 V cold, snow showers
4 Cold. Sun shone
5 Snow, v cold. V windy night
6 Snow drifts 1' 6" deep. Cold
7 Fair, warmer. V wet everywhere
8 Milder
9 Milder, some wind
10 Fair, sun shone
11 Nice, milder, frost
12 Fair, cloudy
13 V nice, milder
14 Fair
15 Fair, milder
16 Showery, cooler
17 Showers most of day
18 Fair, cloudy
19 Snow showers, not v nice day
20 Cold. Snow showers all day
21 Cold, $2\frac{1}{2}$" snow
22 Fair, frost. Too wet for any gardening
23 Cool but fair. Frost
24 Frost but turned out nice

Elsewhere

789 civilians killed, 1,068 injured. All Cyrenaica in British hands.
3 *Scharnhorst* & *Gneisenau* slip through Skagerrak.
6 Commons votes for War Credit of £1,600M.
8 Food News. There is slightly more offal, but rabbits are not so plentiful. Sprats are an excellent substitute for herring, containing Vitamins A & B. Eggs: A little more plentiful. Poultry: Fairly good supply. Fruit: Cooking apples generally plentiful, rhubarb slightly cheaper. Vegetables: spring greens coming in, Sprouts a little dearer. Carrots, potatoes, parsnips, swedes & turnips all plentiful. Jerusalem artichokes make a nice change. [From NC]
8 Delivery of bunks for Anderson shelters will begin soon. Where shelters are issued the bunks will also be free. [From NC]
11 Cunningham's troops invade Italian Somaliland from Kenya.
12 Rommel arrives in Tripoli with the *Afrika Korps* & German units in Tripoli.
22 UK agrees to send forces to Greece.
25 Mogadishu falls to British African troops.

[CM]

22 Wedding of Kenneth Stienman Fensom & Sylvia Betty Evans. [CM]

23 Annual Parochial Church meeting. [CM]

23 Baptism of Trevor William Freeborn, Maureen Betty Rowney. [CM]

24 'Siren 8.30'. [PD]

25 'Siren 8.30–12.45am. Fire-watching in evening'. [PD]

26 'Siren 8–10.15pm'. [PD]

27 '4 sirens in day time. Fire-watching'. [PD]

March 1941

 1 'Siren 5–9.15pm'. [PD]

 2 'Siren 9.5–10.15pm'. [PD]

 2 Evensong moves to 6pm (has been 3pm during winter). [CM]

 3 'Siren 11.45pm–1.45am'. [PD]

 5 'Fire-watching in evening'. [PD]

 6 'Siren 12.10–2pm. Machine gun'. [PD]

 6 A letter from Church House acknowledges PCC payment of quota for 1940 and arrears for 1938 & 1939. [CM]

 7 '3 sirens in daytime'. [PD]

 8 'Siren 8.20–11.5pm'. [PD]

 9 'Siren 11.40pm–1.20am'. [PD]

 9 Baptism of Robert Leslie Dean. [CM]

10 'Siren 9pm–12.15am'. [PD]

11 'Siren 8pm–5.30am'. [PD]

11 'The Charity Commissioners having ruled the appointment of Messrs Pease & Lilley as Representative trustees of the VI at the Meeting on 14 Jan to be out of order, it was necessary to confirm the appointment at this meeting.

The ARP canvass was successful, and the night watch posts were now completely manned, also other private watching posts at St Margaret's Rd, Bandon Rd, Girton College, the Laundry & Mr Oxley's house had been established. Mr AGG Marshall had presented the Wardens with 10 stirrup pumps and it was agreed that the thanks of the PC be conveyed to Mr Marshall.

Mr Nightingale suggested that Mr Radford should be invited to call a meeting of the Utility Squad to consider the best method of arranging duties. The Head ARW agreed that this might be done, and Messrs Pease, Nightingale & Searle were appointed to attend the meeting.

It was agreed that the question of the provision of a siren in the Village should be put to the APM.

25 V nice day
27 Showers
28 Milder. Windy

Weather

 1 Windy, showers
2–3 Fair
 4 Frost. V nice, dry
 5 Fair
 6 Showery, cool. Plenty of mud about everywhere
 7 Snow $1\frac{1}{2}$". Turned to rain. Everywhere covered with water
 9 Cloudy, fog, turned out then to sleet & snow
10 Fair, drying a little
11 Fair, cold
12 Cool to fair
13 Fair, drying
14 V nice, warmer, more sun
15 V nice day, cool
16 Frost, cool, turned out fair
17 Cool, turned out Fair
18 Frost & fog
19 Frost & fog. Cold
20 Fair, cool at first
21 Cool, showers at times
22 Fair, showers in afternoon
23 Snow & sleet in

Elsewhere

4,259 civilians killed, 5,557 injured. Ernest Bevin's 'Essential Work Order' allows him to send labour to wherever it is required.
Start of registration of women for work. Any woman whose children are over 14 is liable for work.
 4 Commando raid on Lofoten Islands.
11 Roosevelt signs Lend-Lease Act.
24 Rommel launches first offensive; his troops re-occupying El Agheila.
29 RAF attacks *Scharnhorst* & *Gneisenau* in Brest.
30 Rommel launches offensive in Cyrenaica.
31 Severe air attacks on London, Portsmouth, Merseyside, Clydeside, Bristol & Plymouth.

Stan Reader, Queen's Regiment

Reporting on waste paper, Miss Hibbert-Ware said that labels for the sacks had now been procured, but that the Receipt Book system would prove too difficult to operate. Mr Shooter had offered £2 for the iron scrap deposited in his yard.

The Parish, Charity & Salvage accounts were approved and it was agreed that they be embodied in the APM Agenda, together with those of the VI. Mr Cole's account for refuse collection and the account for exterminating rats were passed for payment. The Clerk reported the receipt of 10/- from Mr Green for 6 months rent of the Smithy to 31 Dec.

Mr Nightingale stated that the organisations using the Cookery Room, whilst thanking Miss Hibbert-Ware most sincerely for her offer to provide the funds for extra comforts, thought that the money should be raised by some function or otherwise. Mr Lilley said that a Committee was being formed to organise entertainment &c for the Girton Comfort Fund and he thought that the Committee would be prepared to help'. [PCM]

13 'Fire-watching all night. Sirens 8.30pm–5.5am'. [PD]

14 Funeral of Kate Alice Aworth (77). [CM]

14 'LADIES HOME MISSION UNION: A MUSICAL PROGRAMME is being arranged by Mrs Burrows & Miss Frost, LRAM, MRST in aid of Home Missions, and is to be given in the VI on Friday, 14 Mar, commencing at 7.30 prompt. Tickets will be available at 6d each' (a report in April said it raised 'a good round sum'). [CM]

15 'Siren 9.20–11.25pm'. [PD]

15 Wedding of William Peter Wey & Esmé Margaret Pullan. [CM]

16 Evensong moves to 6.30pm. [CM]

17 'Siren 9.15–5am'. [PD]

18 'Siren 12.30–5.30am'. [PD]

19 'Siren 9–11pm, 2.20–3.30am'. [PD]

21 'Fire-watching in evening'. [PD]

23 'Siren 3pm, 3.10pm'. [PD]

23 Baptism of Anthony James Boardman. [CM]

23 Day of Prayer. [CM]

24 Funeral of Berenice Trillwood (2 weeks). [CM]

April 1941

3 'Siren in evening again'. [PD]

6 'Fire-watching'.[PD]

6 Baptism of Richard Kempton Broad. [CM]

7 'Siren 9pm–4.45'. [PD]

8 'Siren 9pm'. [PD]

9 'Siren 9pm–5.10am'. [PD]

morning, cleared in
afternoon, v cold
24 Fair at first, turned to
   rain
25 Showers most of day
27 Fair, rain in evening
28 Fog in morning.
   Showers & v cold in
   evening
29 V cold, showers
30 Snow at times, v cold
31 V cold, SE wind

The Cookery Room was built in 1910 as an extension to the School, for teaching Domestic Science. The ARP used it as a Night Watch centre

Weather
  1 Rain at times, cool
  2 Rain in evening
  3 Showers at times
  4 Showers
  5 Showers, v cold
  6 V cold E wind is

Elsewhere
  6,065 civilians killed, 6,926 injured.
  ATS given equal military status with
  men & comes fully under the
  provisions of the Army Act.
  1 British driven from Benghazi,
  beginning of Rommel's

9 American Tea raises £6/2/9 for overseas missions. [CM]

10 'Siren 10.15–4.30am'. [PD]

13 Baptism of Rosemary Ann Matthews, Gillian Ruth Harper. [CM]

14 'Fire-watching. Siren 3.30–4.15pm'. [PD]

15 Funeral of Sampson Lofts (92). [CM]

16 'Siren 9.45pm–4.45am'. [PD]

18 'Mr Pease was elected Chairman at the APM & Mr Lilley Vice-Chairman for the ensuing year.

The Head ARW had arranged a meeting of the Utility Squad at which it had been decided that one member of the Squad should be on duty during each "alert" to collect the rest of the Squad.

As a result of the resolution passed at the APM, the supply of petrol for the AFS car had been continued.

An application for the grazing of the Rec was received from Mr Chandler but the PC decided against letting the ground, it being felt that the many children now in the village should have first call on it. Mr Searle has asked to cut the ground as last year and he gave an undertaking that the grass would be used as feed.

A schedule of the Conditions of the Rec when taken over by the Military Authority was agreed.

A request having been received from the WAEC to clean out the ditches on the land rented from the Charity Trustees and used as a Refuse Dump, it was decided to clear out the tins which had been dumped in the near ditch in error, and pass on the letter to the Charity Trustees.

In response to a letter received from the RCC asking the PC to appoint a Local Food Production Committee and an Honorary Food Production Officer, it was resolved to call a Parish Meeting and invite Mr Cramp, CC to address it, and to circularise every house in the Parish.

In response to a letter from the RDC asking for the names of 2 persons who would be willing to act as Emergency Food Officers, it was decided to submit the names of Mr Pease & Prof Green, subject to his being willing to act.

The Chairman & Miss Hibbert-Ware reported on the Conference on Salvage. £2 had been received for the iron scrap collected in Mr Searle's yard.

A Committee was appointed to meet the Rev Hibbert-Ware, local War Savings Group Secretary, to discuss the action to be taken during the District War Weapons Week.

The HG, through Mr Jane, were given permission to use the Refuse Dump as a miniature rifle range, subject to an

drying up now

7 V cold E wind

8 Much better day, frost in evening

9 Fair, cool wind

10 Fair, cold

11 Cloudy

12–13 Fair

15 Fair

16 Nice day

17 Fair

18 Showers in evening

19 Showers at times

20 Showers

21 V nice day

22 Fair

23 V cold, E wind

24 Cold, E wind

25–27 V cold, E wind

28 Fair, v cold

29 Fair, cool

30 Fair

counter-offensive from Agedabia.

1 British & Indian troops capture Asmara.

5 Addis Ababa taken by British & Ethiopian forces.

6 German forces invade Yugoslavia & Greece.

7 Standard rate of income tax raised to 10/-.

9 RAF raid on Berlin; Luftwaffe raid on Birmingham.

12 Beginning of Rommel's siege of Tobruk (relieved on 10 Dec).

12 British & Empire forces form front at Mt Olympus.

13 Rommel attacks Tobruk.

17 Yugoslavia surrenders.

22 British troops begin withdrawal from Greece.

23 Greek king & Govt fly to Crete.

24 Germans defeat British & ANZAC forces at Thermopylae.

26 German paratroops & glider-borne forces land at Corinth.

27 Germans enter Athens.

30 Iraqi troops attack British bases & embassy in Baghdad.

30 RAF begins daylight sweeps over Europe.

30 Birmingham, Bristol, Belfast, Coventry, London & Portsmouth badly hit.

Iris Mayes ATS

undertaking to accept responsibility for any damage'. [PCM]

19 Funeral of Walter Harpley (82). [CM]

20 'Siren 3–5am'. [PD]

20 Funeral of Ernest William Dupont (75). [CM]

21 'Heard the cuckoo for the first time'. [PD]

22 'Fire-watching all night. Siren 10.20–11.40pm'. [PD]

23 'Siren 8.30–8.45pm'. [PD]

24 'Siren 12pm–1.45, 2.15–4.30am'. [PD]

25 'Siren 2.30–3.30am'. [PD]

26 'Siren 9.45pm–1.45am'. [PD]

26 Wedding of Leonard Charles Day & Peggy Laura Asplen. [CM]

28 'Light on in loft. Warden called'. [PD]

May 1941

1 'Fire-watching'. [PD]

2 'Siren 9.45–1.30pm'. [PD]

4 'Clocks on 1 hr. Siren 10.30pm, 4.45am'. [PD]

4 United Youth Service: St Andrew's, Baptists & YMG. [CM]

5 'Siren 11pm–4.30am'. [PD]

6 'Siren 11.15–4.40am'. [PD]

7 'Siren 10.45–12am, 2–4.45am'. [PD]

8 'Siren 12pm, 4.45am'. [PD]

10 'Siren 11.5pm–5.10am. Fire-watching at night'. [PD]

11 'Siren 11.30, 2.30, 3.15–5am'. [PD]

11 Baptism of Terence Roy Bartrip. [CM]

13 'Played cricket v RAMC. Lost 57 to 90 runs'. [PD]

13 'The Chairman reported that as Prof Green had been unable to undertake the post of Emergency Food Officer, he had asked Mrs Leakey to do so and she had agreed. His action was confirmed.

Mr Pease also undertook to ask Mr Tingey to surrender 4 of the helmets purchased for the FAP, as further supplies had been received from the CC. The 4 helmets should be re-distributed to the new members of the Utility Squad.

After examining the electric hand lamp which Dr Walton had secured for the use of the Utility Squad, it was agreed that the account for it should be met.

It was decided that a new edition of the ARP Bulletin should be prepared & distributed.

The Head ARW observed that although there appeared to be an adequate supply of stirrup pumps in the retail shops at up to 30/-, he was unable to get the pumps ordered through the RDC at the Govt advertised price of £1. The Chairman undertook to take up the matter.

Weather

1 Fair
2 Fair, cool wind, rain in morning
3 V cool wind. Fair
4 Fair
5 Frost, E wind, cool
6 Frost, E wind
7 Fair, frost, E wind
8 Fair, frost, cool E wind
9 Frost, E wind
10–12 Fair
13 Fair, cool
14 Fair, but cool
15 Showers, cool
16 Fair. Warmer, not too bad
17 Fair
18 Fair. Turned out nice
19–20 Showers
21 Fair
22 Showery, cool
23 Fair, cool wind
24 Fair
29 Rain most of day
30 V wet. Turned out cloudy
31 Cloudy, cool

Elsewhere

5,394 civilians killed, 5,181 injured.
1 Axis attack on Tobruk repulsed.
2 British complete evacuation of Greece. British occupy Basra.
5 Haile Selassie returns to Abyssinia.
9 RAF raid on Mannheim.
9 Raids on Clydeside & Humberside.
9 Liverpool suffers 7th successive raid.
10 Rudolf Hess flies to Scotland.
10 House of Commons hit in heavy raid.
11 RAF raid on Hamburg & Bremen.
12 'Tiger' convoy docks in Alexandria with 236 tanks for Desert Army.
15 Ernest Bevin says he will not negotiate with 'murderer' Hess.
15 Miners' Federation claims £4 a week national minimum wage.
Dame of Sark reported to be deported to a concentration camp as reprisal for civil disobedience.
Italians surrender at Amba Alagi.
20 German paratroops invade Crete.
20 *Hood* sunk by *Bismarck*, itself sunk by RN a week later.
'War Weapon Week' collects £124M: £21 per head.
King makes Smuts a Field Marshal, the first colonial to attain that rank.
28 Woolton announces experimental egg

A report on the Home Food Production Meeting was received; the Committee appointed by the PC to consider the War Weapons Week had discussed ways of extending the activities of the Village Savings Group. Mr Skinner reported on the Conference on War Weapons Week, and offered to give a prize for the best Poster designed by one of the school children. It was agreed to call a meeting on 19 May to consider the action to be taken to support War Weapons Week.

The balance on the Salvage account stood at £28/19/1 and it was agreed that the bills for the blankets &c purchased by Mr Nightingale should be met and 2 grants made: £5 to LHS Holiday Fund & £2/2/0 to GDNA'. [PCM]

14 '**GDNA**. Subscriptions to be 5/-. Mrs Betson, Mr Skinner, Mr Sharpe & Mrs Wilderspin to serve on Committee'. [CIPC]

15 'Siren 3–5am'. [PD]

16 'Siren 12pm–4.5am'. [PD]

17 'Siren 12.30–3.15am'. [PD]

18 'Went for walk across the fields'. [PD]

18 Cantata 'Rock of Ages' (Whitty) in aid of Comforts for Men on Service from Girton: £1/18/2 collected. [CM]

19 'Siren 1.5–1.25. 1.20–1.45pm'. [PD]

21 'Plane crash over field 3.20'. [PD] [Map site E]

23 Funeral of Janet Mary Piggott (6). [CM]

28 'Ill in bed'. [PD]

June 1941

Miss Bonsor, SS Teacher, is called up: the Rector appeals for volunteers [CM]

 1 Baptism of Frederick George Schick. [CM]

 4 'Siren 12.35, 3.45'. [PD]

 7 Baptism of John Edward Stearn. [CM]

 7 Wedding of Thomas Johnston Park & Doreen Lambard Nightingale. [CM]

 8 Death of Sgt Josef Kominek (see p225). [Map site B]

10 '3 helmets had been returned by the FAP and redistributed to the Reserve Party, the 4th would be returned in the near future.

The Head ARW reported that a meeting of the CD & other Services was being held to consider co-ordination in the event of invasion, and suggested that the publication of the ARP Bulletin should be deferred until after that meeting. It was agreed that the Bulletin be printed. A Committee had been formed from the various services using the Cookery Room to manage internal discipline.

Sgt Josef Kominek, who died in a crash at Manor Farm on 8 June

rationing, further restrictions on fish & milk. Successful prosecutions under Food Control Orders during the war so far total 17,319.

28 The ban on sugar for hot drinks in restaurants is postponed until further notice. Demand for & supply of wheatmeal bread increasing; Carrots: no case at present for making a Maximum Price order; Milk: further cut in the domestic supply not under consideration; Sausages: not to be rationed. Under the second reading of the Landlord & Tenant (War Damage) Bill if part of a house has been made unfit for habitation, there will be a reduction in rent. [NC]

31 Evacuation of Crete.

31 Unemployment figures for May lowest yet. 243,656 out of work, 400,000 less than a year ago.

Weather

2 Cold
3 Cloudy & cool
4 V warm
5 Cloudy & cool with showers
6 Showery most of morning
7 Cloudy, thunder
8 Showers, thunder at times, rain in afternoon
9 Showers
10 Rain
11 Fair. Cloudy, rain later
12 Fair, thunder
13 Fair

Elsewhere

1 British troops enter Baghdad.
1 Clothes rationing introduced.
3 Attlee memorandum approved at Labour Party Conference.
4 New pro-Allied Govt in Iraq.
8 Allied troops & Free French invade Syria & Lebanon.
10 Egg ration prices: 2/6 per dozen (large).
12 Allied Govts pledge no separate peace with the Axis.
14 US freezes Axis assets.
15 Wavell launches 'Operation Battleaxe' to relieve Tobruk.
16 Under-14 convictions up 41% in the first year of war.
17 Rommel forces British back towards

The final figure of the savings in Girton during War Weapons Week was £10,934. Among the investments was one of £480 from Trinity College. It was agreed to send a letter of appreciation.

It was resolved that the Clerk send out a letter to secure more scrap metal of the heavier type in response to the RDC's appeal for more iron salvage.

It was decided to ask the Military Authority if there is any possibility of the Rec being de-requisitioned'. [PCM]

12 First IC meeting (see Chapter 2).

21 Funeral of Arthur Croydon Naylor. [CM]

July 1941

1 Service of Intercession at 3.15 followed by tea in the Rectory garden [CM]

7 'Fire-watching'. [PD]

7 Baptism of Gillian Ann Coe. [CM]

8 'Mr Nightingale was authorised to attempt to secure a second-hand wireless set for the Cookery Room. Permission was given for the storage of a quantity of coal in the building.

Difficulty was being experienced in the Paper Salvage Week. It was agreed that an attempt be made to dispose of the paper locally and arrange for haulage into Cambridge by Mr Fletcher's lorry. The Chairman undertook to try to secure more helpers.

Mr Barrett had undertaken to accept responsibility for the reasonable usage of the Pavilion by the Young Men's Cricket Club and the Clerk was asked to secure a letter to this effect.

An application for the use of the Rec on August Bank Holiday for a Children's Sports was granted and Mr Searle was asked to cut the ground. It was agreed that a grant of £1 be made towards the cost of prizes; this to come from the Salvage Account.

It was resolved to ask Mr Elwood if, in view of his absence from the Parish on service with HM Forces, he was still desirous of retaining his membership of the PC.

The Chairman reported that after a joint meeting of the CD, an Emergency Committee had been set up to consider supplies necessary to the life of the village if it were to be isolated during an invasion of the country. He & the Vice-Chairman had been elected to serve, subject to the approval of the meeting. It was agreed that the appointments be confirmed'. [PCM]

13 Baptism of Peter Nigel Huke. [CM]

14 Fair, cloudy
15 Fair
16 Warmer
17 Warm
18–19 V warm
20 V hot
21–22 V warm
23 Still warm
24–26 V warm
27 Fair
28 Fair, cloudy
29 Fair, cooler
30 V warm

Weather

1–2 V warm
3 Warm
4 V warm
5 Fair
6–7 V warm
8 V warm, thunder storm
9–10 V warm
11 V warm, thunder
12 V hot again
13 V warm
14 Fair
15 Rain
16 Showers
17 Fair, warm
18 Showers
19 Warm, rain in evening
21–23 Warm
24 V warm
25 Fair
26 Showers
27 Fair
30 Showers
31 Fair, rain in evening

Egypt.
18 Press give details of development of 'radio location' (radar).
21 Damascus captured by Allies.
22 Operation 'Barbarossa'.
24 'Commons votes for £1,000M war credit; war expenditure now £10,250,000 per day'. [WD]
27 British military mission to Moscow.
29 Beaverbrook made Minister of Supply.

Elsewhere

501 civilians killed.
1 Auchinleck replaces Wavell as C-in-C ME. Wavell appointed C-in-C India.
3 Stalin orders 'scorched earth' policy.
4 Communists officially back the war.
5 Eden rules out negotiation with Hitler.
7 US marines take over UK bases in Iceland, Trinidad & British Guiana.
12 UK–USSR mutual assistance pact.
16 Germany captures Smolensk.
19 BBC announces the 'V' Army, resistance movement in Occupied Europe.
20 Stalin becomes People's Commissar for Defence.
21 First German air-raid on Moscow.
21 Japan begins occupation of S Indo-China, with Vichy consent.
26 Japanese assets in US frozen, all financial & trading relations suspended. UK & Dutch Govt-in-exile follow suit.
27 First air-raid on London for 10 weeks.
31 Goering orders Final Solution.

15 'Fire-watching'. [PD]
25 Consecration of Harold Edward Wynn as Bishop of Ely. [CM]

August 1941

 7 Harold Edward Wynn installed as bishop at Ely. [CM]
 8 'Fire-watching. Siren 11.45pm–1.5am & 3.45–4.50'. [PD]
10 'Went fishing, rained all the way home'. [PD]
12 'Siren 11.30pm–2.10am'. [PD]
12 'Dr Walton expressed thanks to the PC for offering to provide a
    wireless set for the use of the Cookery Room personnel, and spoke
    of the measures to be taken for crop protection. He also gave a
    résumé of the work undertaken by the IC, mentioning that Miss
    Robertson was taking charge of medical supplies and Dr Hertz
    the actual medical work. A list of wells & pumps in the village
    had been made. Dr Gane was making inquiries into available
    transport and Mr Pease into the legal position as affecting any
    area which might become isolated.
    A letter of resignation was received from Mr SA Elwood, and the
    Clerk was asked to convey to him the sincere thanks of the PC for
    his work during his period of office.
    A new arrangement had been made for the disposal of waste
    paper in that Mr CL Fletcher had undertaken to haul it into
    Cambridge once a fortnight. Mrs Green had undertaken the
    collection & sorting from the southern part of the Parish and
    several new helpers had come forward for sorting.
    A letter was received from Mr Barrett undertaking responsibility
    for the proper usage of the Pavilion by the Young Men's Cricket
    Club.
    Mr Skinner reported on the meeting held in Cambridge by the
    RC & St John Organisations with a view to extending the penny-
    a-week fund to the Rural areas, and the Chairman undertook
    to see whether the representation of the local Detachment had
    any suggestions to offer regarding the collection of the money
    throughout the village'. [PCM]
13 'Fire-watching'. [PD]
14 'Siren 3.15–4.10am'. [PD]
16 'Fire-watching'. [PD]

September 1941

 7 Day of Prayer. [CM]
 9 'The local RC Detachment were undertaking the arrangements
    for collection for the penny-a-week fund.
    Mr Pease in a brief report of the work of the IC mentioned that
    the DC had taken in hand the work of repairing pumps to ensure

Weather

1 Rain at times
2 Fair
3 V nice day
4 Cloudy, showers
5–6 Showers
7 Fair
8 Showery
9 Fair
10 Fair, windy
11 Showery
12 Fair
13 Showers
14 Fair
15 Showery & rain most of day
16 Fair to showers
17 Windy, showers
18 Showery at first, fair afterwards
19 Fair
20 Showery most of day
21 Fair, better day
22 Fair
23 Rain all day
24 Fair
25 Rain in morning, fair afterwards
26–27 Fair
28–29 Showers
30 Fair

Elsewhere

49 women pilots in ATA are used to deliver new aircraft from the factories to the airfields. ATA pilots fly 6 days a week, with 2 weeks holiday *pa*.

5 USSR resistance in Smolensk pocket liquidated; 310,000 troops taken prisoner.

7 Stalin becomes Supreme Commander.

17 Germany takes Novgorod.

18 Fire Service nationalised: 1,400 local brigades merge into 32 regions under NFS.

20 Beginning of 800 day siege of Leningrad.

25 Raid on Spitzbergen by British commandos, Canadians & Norwegian troops.

27 Govt takes over railways for the duration, paying £43M *pa* compensation to private operators.

Weather

2 Fair
3–4 V warm
5 Fair, fog at first
6 Fair, turned to cool wind

Elsewhere

217 civilians killed.
Italian midget submarine attack on Gibraltar.
Woolton calls the black market 'a thorn in our side'.

an alternative supply of drinking water. It was unanimously
agreed to invite Dr Walton to the PC in place of Mr Elwood.

It was resolved to invite Messrs Skinner & Sons and Mr Mitham
to tender for painting 28 street lamps.

Mr Searle undertook to see Mr Mitham regarding repairs to the
Pavilion lavatory and to discuss putting barbed wire along the
edge of the roof to prevent boys climbing upon it.

The Rector having asked permission to put surplus soil from
graves on the old pond site, it was decided it might be put on
the piece of land adjacent to the Churchyard'. [PCM]

20 Wedding of Cyril George Clarke & Claudia Martin. [CM]

20 Wedding of John Lynn & Joan Marguerite Hawkes. [CM]

21 Evensong moves to 6pm. [CM]

23 & 25 'Fire-watching'. [PD]

25 & 28 Harvest Festival & Service. [CM]

27 Wedding of Ronald Gillman Born & Catharine Bawden. [CM]

28 'Siren 11.15. Bombs on Huntingdon Rd'. [PD]

28 Baptism of John Wiseman, Peter Frederick Boot. [CM]

29 'Siren 8.10–9pm'. [PD]

October 1941

 3 'Siren 9.15–10.15, 10.25–11.20'. [PD]

11 'Fire-watching. Siren 8.15–9.45 & 12.10–12.25'. [PD]

12 Evensong moves to 3pm. [CM]

14 'Dr Walton, having accepted the invitation to serve as a member,
was formally appointed and signed the Declaration.

One tender for painting the street lamps, that of Mr SF Mitham
for £5, having been received, it was agreed that this should be
accepted and passed to the RDC for approval. [The original
tender survives, in the Cambs Collection.]

Dr Walton, in a brief report on ARP activities, remarked on the
falling-off of Night Watch personnel at the Cookery Room, due
to the lack of air activity recently, and said that a meeting of
all Services would be called to discuss the situation. A meeting
of householders in Pepys Way & vicinity would also be called to
formulate a scheme of Fire-watching.

Miss Hibbert-Ware reported a decrease in the collection of waste
paper and difficulty by reason of shortage of petrol. It was
suggested that a pony cart might be used.

It was agreed to ask Mr Garner to organise through the
schoolchildren the distribution of leaflets on Water Purification.

An invitation by the County Agricultural Officer to renew the
agreement for the destruction of rats at the Refuse Dump was

7–13 Fair
14 Cloudy, showers
15–16 Fair
17 Fair, warm
18–19 Fair
20 Warm
21 V warm
22 Warm
23 Fair
24 Warm
25–26 V nice day
27 V nice day, warm
28 Showers
30 Showers, fair

Weather
1 Fine
2 V nice day
3 Fair
4–5 Showers
6 V nice day
7–8 Fair
9 Rain at times
11 Showers, windy
12 V nice day
13 Fair
14 Showers
15 V nice
16 V nice day
17 Windy, turned cool
18 Windy, showers
19 Fair, windy
20 V nice day
21–22 V nice
23 Fair, showers
24 Showery at times
25 Cool
26 Windy, cool

3 First use of Auschwitz gas chambers, on USSR prisoners of war.
6 Jews ordered to wear Star of David as 'mark of shame'.
11 US navy ordered to 'shoot on sight' any Axis vessel threatening shipping in waters under US protection.
19 Kiev falls.
26 'Bomb Berlin' Party comes second in Wrekin by-election.
27 First Liberty Ship launched.
28 First convoy to USSR leaves Iceland.
30 Guard at detention centre in Peel IoM strengthened after disturbances; 20 British Fascists moved to Liverpool.
30 Newcastle bombed for second time; only the second serious raid in a month.

Elsewhere
262 civilians killed.
1 Commons votes third £1,000M war credit of year.
3 Road deaths in second year of war up 65% on pre-war figure.
16 Odessa falls to German & Romanian troops after 9-week siege.
16 Soviet spy Sorge arrested in Tokyo.
20 Stalin proclaims state of siege in Moscow.
31 US destroyer *Reuben James* torpedoed off Iceland.

considered, and it was decided that in view of the fact that the
Dump is not at the moment being used, the Agreement should
not be renewed.

It was resolved to ask the Bus Co to provide adequate sanitary
accommodation for their staff at Girton Corner.

Some discussion took place on whether or not an attempt should
be made to secure back from the Military Authority the use of the
WI, but no decision was reached'. [PCM]

19 & 27 'Fire-watching'. [PD]

November 1941

 4 'Fire-watching'. [PD]

 9 United Remembrance Services: preacher M Charlesworth, the
   President of St John's College. [CM]

11 'In view of the letting of the VI to the Girton Youth Centre on
   Tuesday evenings, it was decided to hold future meetings on the
   second Wednesday in each month.

   The WI was again available for use on the condition that it is
   vacated on 24 hours notice.

   The meetings held by the ARP Service with the object of
   increasing the number of personnel to man the Night Post had
   brought no satisfactory result. The Chairman suggested that
   in the event of serious air activity volunteers would probably
   be forthcoming. On the question of static water supplies Mr
   Pease undertook to find out the positions prevailing now that Fire
   Service had been taken over by the Home Office.

   Mr Nightingale had secured a wireless set for the Night Post and
   it was agreed to meet the account out of Salvage Money. He also
   undertook to look into the purchase of beds & mattresses.

   Miss Hibbert-Ware & the Clerk were appointed to attend a
   Conference on Salvage to be held at the RDC Offices on 26 Nov.

   It was decided to ask the County Surveyor to provide reflector
   posts at the corner of Oakington Rd.

   Mr Searle was asked to remove the tins from the ditch on Town
   Charity land rented by the PC as a rubbish dump.

   Mr Adams raised the matter of fire-fighting equipment at the
   VI. The Chairman replied that this matter had been under
   consideration by the Institute Trustees.

   Mr Pease briefly outlined the functions & activities of the newly
   formed Entertainments Committee'. [PCM]

12 'Fire-watching'. [PD]

23 Baptism of Margaret Ellen Hankin. [CM]

24 Funeral of Flora Chandler (69). [CM]

27 Windy, cool
28 V cold, N wind
29 V cold NE wind. Hail
   & snow showers, rain
30 Fair, cold
31 Not quite so cool

Weather

 1 Fair
2–3 Showers, cool
 5 Cool
 6 Windy, cool
 7 Cold wind. Cold all
   day, wind v strong
 8 Fair, cold wind
 9 V sharp frost
10 Showers
11 Showers. Rained in
   evening & all night
12 Cloudy. V muddy
   everywhere
13 V cold
14 Fair
15 Cold, fair
17 Fair, showers
17 Showers
19 V nice
20–22 Fair
23 V nice day
24–25 Fair
26–27 Fair, cool
28 Drizzle all day
29 Dull, foggy
30 Fair, frost, cold

Elsewhere

 3 Germany captures Kursk (& Tikhvin
   a week later), cutting rail line to
   Leningrad.
10 Churchill's Mansion House speech
   tells Japan that war on US means
   war on UK; Japanese Foreign
   Minister replies their aim is to make
   US & UK retreat from E Asia.
13 *Ark Royal* torpedoed off Gibraltar by
   U-boat.
17 Fat ration increased from 8 to 10oz.
18 'Crusader' desert offensive opened.
25 HMS *Barham* sunk off N Africa by
   U-boat.
26 Ritchie replaces Cunningham as
   Eighth Army commander.

The Army put shutters up on the WI Hall
windows

28 'Lantern lecture on bee keeping at VI. Fire watching'. [PD]

December 1941

7 Baptism of Ann Rose Mansfield. [CM]

10 'The question of static water supplies for fire-fighting purposes was entirely out of the hands of the RDC.

The Head ARW reported that 8 bunks & one bed had been provided at the Night Post and matters appeared to be running more smoothly. He reviewed the recent ARP exercises and Mrs Pease, who had acted as an umpire, also gave a brief report. A general discussion on the exercises would be undertaken at a meeting of the IC to be held on 15 Dec.

Arising from the conference on salvage, the RDC had agreed to provide a periodic collection of waste.

It was agreed to call a Public Meeting during the early part of Jan to discuss Chesterton Rural District Warship Week.

It was agreed to suggest to the Entertainments Committee that an invitation might be given to the soldiers occupying the Rec to attend functions free of charge'. [PCM]

14 'SINGING TEST Mrs Tucker's sudden illness on 14 Dec was a test of the singing of both choir & congregation through which they came decidedly well. In the morning, my daughter, Margaret, took on at a moment's notice. Her apparent falling asleep at one point may, I hope, be excused as she had been on ward duty all night. The congregation carried on!' [CM]

29 Funeral of Frances Hardcastle of Girton College (75; descendant of Sir William & Sir John Herschel). [CM]

30 'Bag Tea' (described as 'a well-known & popular feature in our Church life') in aid of the Quota Fund. [CM]

January 1942

1 Funeral of Elizabeth Hertz (77), widow of Heinrich Hertz (taken largely by Pastor Hildenbrandt and partly in German). [CM]

2 'A Party was attended by 175 village children & evacuees given by the Entertainments Committee in conjunction with the Evacuation Officer, Mr Michael Pease. After tea there was an impromptu concert by the secretary Mr J Ison, Maureen Baker, Jill Nightingale, Pamela Cornell, Kathleen Cole, Jean Hawkes, Rosina Bartrip. Mr George Grimwood of Histon gave a Punch & Judy Show, conjuring & ventriloquism. The party ended with Santa Claus presenting each child with a gift'. [CWN]

7 'Fire-watching'. [PD]

8 Funeral of Lilian Beatrice Coe (32). [CM]

9 Funeral of Rachel Stonebridge (76). [CM]

Weather

1 Frost, cloudy, drizzle
2 Cloudy, fog
3 Cloudy
4 Cloudy, drizzle
5 Fair, cold
6 Cold all day
7 Cold
8 Cold, frost
9–10 Fair
11 Fair, milder
12 Showers, thunder
13 Fair
14 Rain all day
15 Better day, fair
16 Cold, but fair
18–19 Fair
20 Fog to cloudy
21 Fair
22 Cloudy, drizzle
23–24 Fair
25 V nice
26 Frost
27 Cool, frost
28 Frost in morning. V nice day. Frost lasted all day

Weather

1 Fair, cool
2 Cool
3 Fair, rain later
4 Showers. Turned out better later in day
5 Cold. Hail & snow
6 Frost. Cool all day
7 Frost
8 Cold
9 Cold, snow showers
10 Cold, snow
11 Cool, 12° frost
12 Cold. Frost 12°

Elsewhere

Heavy penalties for black marketeers.
Incendiary raid on E coast.
2 National Service Act: male call-up age 18; female 20–30.
7 Attack on Pearl Harbour.
9 China declares war on Axis.
10 Japan sinks *Prince of Wales* & *Repulse*.
10 Eighth Army relieves Tobruk.
10 German spy Richter executed.
13 War Office decides against Junior HG.
18 Italian midget submarine raid on Alexandria – 2 battleships sunk.
18 Japanese cross from Kowloon to HK.
19 Japan captures Penang.
22 Heavy Axis air-raids on Malta.
23 New Rubber Control Board urges economy in use of rubber.
23 Hospital rations for Servicemen halved to match those of others.
25 HK surrenders to Japan.
26 Churchill tells US Congress that Allied offensive must wait till 1943.

Elsewhere

40,000 WRNS serve in 80 trades in Navy's Fleet Air Arm.
ROC comprises a full-time force of 40,000 & 30,000 part time, of which 650 are women.
1 Representatives of 26 Allied nations sign Declaration of the United Nations.
1 57 men & boys die in colliery disaster near Stoke-on-Trent.
1 The average strength of beer reduced by 5%; whisky production cut by a tenth; gold jewellery manufacture

10 SS Tea & Prize-Giving. [CM]

14 'Arising out of a brief report on ARP from which it transpired that
   the Service had had lectures on the rescue of airmen from crashed
   aircraft, it was decided to ask that similar information be given
   to the general public.

   A regular collection of waste paper had not yet been undertaken
   by the RDC, it was agreed to write deploring this fact.

   A resolution was received from the WI asking for some
   improvement in the collection of paper, and it was agreed to
   thank the WI and say that efforts were being made to this end.
   The Chairman gave a short account of the work of the Salvage
   Committee of the RDC on the scheduling of iron railings.

   On a discussion on the Rec concern was expressed at the severe
   wear & tear of the ground caused by vehicles not using the
   proper roadway: it was noticed that several clearly defined tracks
   lead to Mr Irvine King's premises. If some improvement could
   not be effected than PC would have no option but to consider
   withdrawing his privilege of a private entrance.

   It was resolved that a Parish Meeting be called for 29 Jan to
   consider a programme of events &c for Warship Week.

   The date of the APM was provisionally fixed for 28 Mar'. [PCM]

15 'Fire-watching'. [PD]

15 Funeral of Martha Ann Amps (77). [CM]

16 **WI**. The subject of the New Year meeting attended by 30–40
   members was "Our Village As It Was" described by 2 members
   who had known it longest – Mrs Sadler & Mrs King. It was a
   surprise to many members to learn that under the squirearchy of
   Mrs Houblon (pronounced "Hubble") of The Close & the Rev Mr
   Potticary the village was still almost Elizabethan, complete with
   wakes, Maypole, bell-ringers & curtsying old ladies in cuckoo-
   bonnets'. [CWN]

23 'Fire-watching'. [PD]

23 '**War Effort**. £1/5/6 was raised by a competition for a sack of
   potatoes donated by Mr Hall and won by Mrs W Evans (senior).
   The money was handed to Miss Frost to distribute to villagers
   serving in the forces'. [CWN]

26 Mr EH Liveing presents plan of Churchyard to the Parish. [CM]

30 'A Whist Drive was organised by the Entertainments Committee.
   Mr WG Dixon resigned from the Entertainments Committee. Mr
   JH Garner was Chairman.

   Postal Orders are to be sent to all NCOs & men of the village
   serving with the Forces in alphabetical order of name taken from

13 Frost, snowed all afternoon
14 Frost, snow
15 V cold, dry. Roads bad, 13° frost
16 Cold, frost
17 Sharp frost. Roads much better now
18 V cold, frost
19 Frost, cold
20 Frost, v cold
21 18° frost, cold
22 Sharp frost
23 V cold. Snowed & rain all day, but thawing
24 Cold
25 Fair
26 V cold, frost. NE wind all day
27 Snow, v cold all day
28 Frost, cold
29 Frost
30 Frost, rain, snow, cold

banned except for wedding rings; standardised ring to cost 1gn.
3 American, British, Dutch & Australian Command set up in FE.
10 Japanese enter Kuala Lumpur.
11 USSR re-opens narrow supply corridor to besieged Leningrad.
12 Sugar & fat rations both reduced to 8oz per person weekly.
13 U-boat offensive along US E coast begins.
13 Constitutional crisis in IoM as House of Keys rejects extension of National Service.
14 *Tirpitz* moves to Norway.
16 Japan begins main attack on Burma.
24 Battle of Makassar Strait, first US surface action since 1898.
26 First US troops arrive in UK.
28 Miners at Kent colliery return to work after unsuccessful 19-day strike.
29 Rommel recaptures Benghazi.
31 Last British & Empire troops withdraw from Malaya to Singapore.
31 USSR winter offensive begins on all fronts.

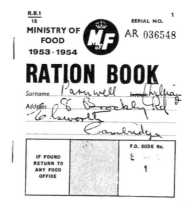

Food and clothing were strictly rationed

the Roll of Honour in the Church porch. [CWN]

31 'Fire-watching'. [PD]

February 1942

1 Evensong moves to 3.30pm. [CM]

6 'Waste Paper Salvage. 2 tons was collected as a result of a house-to-house canvass.

Warship Week. A drive was taking place for more members for Savings Groups. Dr Gane was asked to organise a parade on opening day. Miss Frost was to arrange a concert in the evening. The Entertainments Committee to organise 2 whist drives, social & dance. Mr Garner suggested an exhibition of schoolchildren's work & a poster competition. Mr Monkman suggested that the HG could arrange an exhibition of equipment. The village target was set at £5,000'. [CWN]

10 'The Pantomime "Red Riding Hood" took place, produced by Mrs L Cornell and acted by village & evacuee children. Actors: Robin Marthen, Betty Amps, Kathleen Cole, Mrs Cornell, Lily Seymour, Rita Benwell, Barbara Goldbourne. A musical play followed. Actors: Pamela Cornell, Z Teff, F Hill, S Wagstaff, P Hill, V Whybrow, J Foster, B Nightingale. Acrobatic dancing by Betty Amps. Piano solo by Pat Hill; accompanist for the evening was Miss Jameson'. [CWN]

11 'A report was made on the Parish meeting held to consider Warship Week and it was decided to take up the question of selling stamps &c on the afternoon and submit a requisition to the RDC for the necessary supplies.

It was decided to alter the date of the APM to 30 Mar subject to the concurrence of the Youth Centre.

A letter was received from Mrs Green of the WVS regarding the collection of ashes with the tins at the monthly collection of unburnable rubbish, and after consideration it was agreed to make an appeal to the public to dispose of this type of refuse themselves on their gardens & paths.

An application was received from the Billposting Co (Messrs Mills & Rockley of Coventry) for a reduction in the rental of the Smith hoarding site. It was decided in view of the curtailment of advertising to terminate the agreement'. [PCM]

15 Baptism of Jennefer Dean. [CM]

15 Pte Cyril Andrews killed in action in Singapore. [CM]

16 'Fire-watching'. [PD]

19 Funeral of George Nightingale (75). [CM]

20 Funeral of Charles Henry Hankins (92). [CM]

Weather

1 Snow most of day, 3"
   deep
2 Cold. Heavy snow
   fell. Frost
3 Snow, snow in night,
   about 4", thaw in
   afternoon
4 Cold, freezing most of
   day. Snow not going
   away quickly now
5 Sharp frost. V cold,
   NE wind & snow
   drifts
6 Cold, frost. Snow still
   covers the ground
7 Cold wind. Snow
   covers the ground
8 Fair, but cold
9 Snow still covers the
   ground. Cold
10 Cold, thawing slowly
11 Cool
12 Cool, rain
13 Fair
14 Cool wind
15 Fair
16 Cool, frost
17 Frost, v cold wind
18 Frost
19 Fair, frost. Sun shone
   nicely
20 Fair, frost
21 V cold, snow at times
22 Cold
23 V cold, frost
24 Frost, v cold wind
25 V cold all day. E wind,
   frost
26 Frost, v cold

Elsewhere

Attlee becomes Deputy Prime
Minister.
Ministry of Production established.
1 Quisling becomes Prime Minister of
   Norway.
9 Soap rationing begins.
10 First meeting of Pacific War Council
   in London with UK, Australian, NZ
   & Dutch representatives.
10 Police given wider powers to curb
   'gambling parties'.
11 Anti-conscription riots in Montreal.
12 *Gneisenau* crippled by bombing in
   dock at Kiel.
14 Air Ministry issues 'area bombing'
   directive.
15 Singapore falls, with capture of
   130,000 troops.
17 Japan bombs Darwin.
22 Harris appointed C-in-C Bomber
   Command.
27 Paratroops raid Normandy to
   capture 'Würzburg' radar.
27 Battle of Java Sea. Allied force
   destroyed.
28 Japan invades Java.
28 Battle of Sunda Strait.

27 'A Whist Drive with 18 tables took place in Feb organised by the local platoon of the HG. This raised a sum of £6/7/-'. [CWN]

March 1942

1 Evensong moves to 6pm. [CM]

4 'Fire-watching at night'. [PD]

6 'A Concert at Girton VI took place in aid of local ARP funds. Mr Palmer was in the chair, supported by Dr Walton'. [CWN]

7 Wedding of Douglas Clifford Pearce & Edith Joan Pauley. [CM]

11 'Dr Walton briefly reported on the work of the IC and said that most of the recommendations made in the memorandum had been accepted by the CC. He also outlined the address on Invasion problems given recently in Cambridge by General Anderson: the Govt's policy for the civilian population was active collaboration with the Military Authority as against the passive "stay put" doctrine previously recommended. In view of the necessity for informing the public of the action to be taken it was agreed to put down the matter as an item on the Agenda for the APM.

Mrs Green said that residents were desirous of having their tins kept separately from the other unburnable rubbish. The Chairman said that the Ministry of Supply was to discuss the question of salvage with the RDC in the near future and he would report on the outcome at the APM.

Mr Garner had organised the schoolchildren into groups for collecting waste paper.

Reference was made to Warship Week and the Clerk has submitted a requisition to the RDC for stamps & certificates.

The items for the APM Agenda were agreed and it was decided to print 50 copies. It was agreed to ask Mr Barrett to report on the Youth Centre and Dr Gane on the HG'. [PCM]

12 'Fire-watching'. [PD]

15 Dedication of Children's Banner. [CM]

15 Evensong moves to 6.30. [CM]

18 Funeral of Alice Watson (60). [CM]

20 'Fire-watching'. [PD]

21 Wedding of Frederick Ernest Benstead & Sheila Daisy Watson. [CM]

27 'A Concert given by Shrubbery School children, Thornton Rd, raised £10 as a contribution to Warship Week'. [CIPC]

27 'A villager was fined 10/- for allowing a light to be seen after blackout on 7 Mar'. [CIPC]

27 Fair, frost. Sun in
   afternoon
28 Cold but fair, frost

Weather

 1 Fair, frost
 2 Cold
 3 Fair
 4 Cold rain all day
 5 Snow $\frac{3}{4}$"
 6 Snow, frost
 7 V sharp frost
 8 Fair, much better day
 9 Fair
10 Fair but cool
11 Fair, showers
12–14 Fair
15 V nice day
16–18 Fair
19 Showery
20 Fair, some fog
21 Fair, but cold
22 Cold
23 Fair, much better day
24 Fair, warmer
25 Fair, dry
26 Nice day, frost
27 Turned cooler, frost
28 Fair
29 V nice day
30–31 Fair

Elsewhere

   189 civilians killed, 149 injured, in
   last 4 months.
   Annual debt £2,701M
   'Dig for Victory' Campaign
   intensifies.
 1 USSR offensive in the Crimea.
 2 Japanese land on Mindanao.
11 White bread banned.
16 USSR ends Moscow
   counter-offensive.
17 25% cut in clothes ration.
   Double-breasted jackets & turn-ups
   banned.
18 Mountbatten appointed Chief of
   Combined Operations.
22 Battle of Sirte.
24 Govt refuses Lords an inquiry into
   loss of Singapore.
25 Govt suffers first defeat of war in
   Grantham by-election. Independent
   wins with 'Production for Victory'
   slogan.
26 Churchill tells Tories: 'It now seems
   very likely that we & our allies ...
   cannot lose this war ... except
   through our own fault'.
27 RN & Commando raid on St Nazaire
   docks.
28 RAF destroys Lübeck.
28 First group of Parisian Jews sent to
   Auschwitz.
30 MacArthur appointed C-in-C SW
   Pacific.

28 'Fire-watching'. [PD]
30 'A Variety Performance in aid of the YWCA organised by Leonard
   Cornell raised £5/2/6.
   The Warship Week programme was completed. Itinerary –
   Sun: Parade of defence services. Mon & Thurs: Whist Drives.
   Tues: Exhibition of children's posters & handiwork. Wed: Dance.
   Fri: concert. Sat: Social & Dance. Darts tournament during the
   week. The Cookery Room open for the sale of savings stamps &
   certificates'. [CWN]
31 Funeral of Young Prior Asplen (74). [CM]

April 1942
 1 'ARP blankets sterilising & bed ticks wash'. [PD]
 2 Wedding of Clifton Wilson Nicholls & Muriel Morton Thompson.
   [CM]
 3 'Driver Alex Ulyatt, aged 26, of St Margaret's Rd, reported
   missing'. [CWN]
 4 Wedding of Cyril Stephen Wilson & Mary Morris. [CM]
 8 MSL American Tea (£7/19/4 raised). [CM]
10 'Pte Cyril Andrews, Cambs Regiment, aged 28, reported missing,
   the youngest son of Mrs Andrews of Ladysmith Cottages. Before
   being called up he was employed by Cambridge Scientific'. [CWN]
12 Baptism of Terence Leslie Farr, Margaret Rose Neep. [CM]
13 'Fire-watching'. [PD]
16 Baptism of Yvonne Gwendoline Melbert. [CM]
17 £14/4/- was raised by Miss Frost's concert for Warship Week
   (£14) with 4/- raised by Helena Wright from the sale of "woolly
   favours"'. [CWN]
19 Bishop's visit to Girton. [CM]
22 'Mr Pease & Mr Lilley were re-elected Chairman & Vice-
   Chairman respectively for the ensuing year.
   The Clerk was instructed to write to Mr Gordon asking if he
   still wished to continue as a member of the PC. Mr Nightingale
   undertook to see Mr Gawthrop on the same subject.
   Following representations made after the APM regarding the
   inadequacy of the fire-fighting equipment the Chairman & Mr
   I King were meeting the DFO. Dr Walton also signified his
   willingness to attend the interview.
   A meeting of the Heads of the various Services had been held at
   which it was decided that a joint Watch Committee was desirable.
   It was agreed that the PC would arrange a full meeting of all the
   Services to discuss the matter.
   The Ministry of Supply now required dumps of empty food tins

Weather

1 Fair, showers at times
2 Fair
3 Rain in morning, turned out fair
4 Showers
5–6 Windy & showers
7 Windy & showers, heavy rain & hail showers
8–9 Windy, showers
10 Windy
11 Fair
11 Fair, cool wind
11 Fair, windy
15–19 Fair
20 Cloudy, showers
21 Fair, cloudy
22 Fair
24–27 Fair
28 Fair, cool wind
29 Cool, E wind
30 Cool, E wind, sharp frost

Elsewhere

938 civilians killed, 998 injured.
9 US forces on Bataan surrender, siege of Corregidor begins.
9 Japanese aircraft raid Trincomalee, sinking carrier HMS *Hermes*.
14 Purchase Tax on luxuries doubled; beer up 2d, whisky up 4/8 to 22/6 a bottle; cigarettes up $2\frac{1}{2}$d to 9d for 10.
15 King awards GC to Malta after more than 2,000 air-raids.
17 Low-level daylight attack by Lancaster bombers on Augsburg.
18 'Doolittle' Raid: US bombers attack Tokyo.
21 Fuel rationing introduced to save 10M tons of coal *pa*.
23 Luftwaffe raid on Exeter, beginning 'Baedeker' raids.
29 More Govt defeats, at Rugby & Wallasey; independents favouring more vigorous war effort elected.

to be established. It was agreed to ask the County Surveyor for permission to put a dump on the waste land near Chestnut Farm (Mr Hardwick's), and Messrs Ralph Thompson Ltd for similar permission for No 1 Thornton Rd. It was agreed that a circular be distributed to each household giving the following details:

Householders to wash, strip off wrappings & take their tins to the dump themselves.

The PC not to undertake the collection of any tins.

Any receptacle containing tins to be left unemptied.

Mr Searle & Mr Nightingale suggested that this should be tried for 3 months. It was decided to ask the WVS to undertake distribution of the circular.

Miss Hibbert-Ware suggested that as recognition of the work of the schoolchildren in collecting waste paper the PC should consider equipping the School with radio and it was unanimously decided to do this'. [PCM]

24 'A villager was fined £1 for failing to immobilise his car'. [CWN]

26 Baptism of John Thomas Pauley. [CM]

29 'Fire-watching'. [PD]

May 1942

Girton College photographic archive of St Andrew's Church organised by Miss Murray. [CM]

4 'ARP washing'. [PD]

9 Baptism of Hilary Grace Marsdon, Stanley William Snell. [CM]

10 Easter Play 'In the House of the Other Mary'. [CM]

10 Wedding of Dennis High & Pauline Mary Hall. [CM]

13 'A letter having been received from Mr Gordon tendering his resignation, it was resolved to accept it with regret.

As a result of the interview with the DFO a trailer pump was to be stationed at Girton College. The officer has suggested that Washpit Brook might be cleaned out to serve as a static water supply and that the Laundry supply could also be used.

In connection with the proposed Village Watch Committee, the Head ARW reported that under the present conditions of enemy attacks on smaller towns, no change in arrangements would be made for the time being. An Invasion Exercise was being held on 16–17 May and the PC would be expected to co-operate with the CD & Military Services.

A draft circular on Salvage was agreed, and since the WVS could not undertake distribution it was decided to ask Mr Garner if he would kindly organise its distribution by the schoolchildren.

It was agreed to allow the Entertainments Committee to use the

Part of the photographic archive of St Andrew's Church, produced by members of Girton College to aid restoration in the event of bomb damage: L the 13th century rood screen, R the roof

Weather

1 Fair
2 Warm
3 Fair
4–5 Warmer
6–7 Warm
8 Some rain
9 Frost
10 Fair, cool wind
11 Rain, cloudy
12 Cooler
13 V cold
14 Fair
15 Frost
16 Warm
17 Fair
18 Showery
19–20 Fair
23 Fair
24 Windy
25 Windy, showers, rain in evening
26 Showery. Good rain in

Elsewhere

339 civilians killed, 425 injured. Luftwaffe strikes Exeter, Hull, Canterbury & S Coast.
1 Mandalay falls to Japan.
1 U-boats sink many Allied ships in Gulf of Mexico.
2 British withdrawal from Irrawaddy.
4 Battle of the Coral Sea – first naval battle fought entirely with aircraft from carriers out of each other's sight.
5 British force lands on Vichy-ruled Madagascar.
12 First contingent of US Eighth Army Air Force arrives.
20 Last British troops retreat from Burma into India, leaving Japan in almost complete control.
23 USSR encircles E of Kharkov: 70,000 killed, 200,000 captured.
25 Labour Party Conference overwhelmingly welcomes UN

Rec on Whit for a children's sports gala. Mr Searle undertook to repair the swing chains and cut the ground.

A circular was received from the PCs' Advisory Service on Food Production and Mrs Stewart reported that the WI had already arranged a meeting in May to inaugurate a Produce Centre.

The Chairman & Mr Skinner undertook to attend the PCs' Advisory Service Meeting in May'. [PCM]

15, 23 & 31 'Fire-watching'. [PD]

27 Funeral of Josephine Palmer (2 weeks). [CM]

31 Baptism of Maureen Gathercole. [CM]

June 1942

Church railings removed by the Ministry of Works, without consultation [CM]

8 'Fire-watching'. [PD]

10 'The Chairman & Mr Skinner reported on the PCs' Advisory Service Meeting in May and Mrs Stewart reported that 2 further meetings on Food Production had been arranged by the WI and that a Rabbit Club had been formed.

It was unanimously agreed to invite Mr Tingey to fill the vacancy on the PC caused by the resignation of Mr W Gordon.

Watchers at the ARP Night Post were now being called up for the HG and a scheme was under consideration whereby trained HG should undertake watching duties whilst the regular watchers were undergoing training, during which time they would be exempted from duty.

Dr Walton submitted an application from Mr Tingey, Leader of the FAP, for a supply of medical stores & equipment to supplement the present stocks which in the light of the recent exercise were inadequate. It was agreed to meet the cost and the Head ARW undertook to secure them & attend to their proper storage. Dr Walton also reported on the recent Defence Exercise.

The Emergency Food Officer reported that stocks of food had now been received & distributed at 6 points.

The RDC proposed to requisition from Messrs Ralph Thompson Ltd the plot of land at No 1 Thornton Rd on which it was desired to establish a dump of tins for salvage purposes. The PC agreed that the circular on Salvage should now be distributed.

It was resolved to send a letter of thanks to the various services for their part in the recent Exercise'. [PCM]

16 'Fire-watching'. [PD]

20 Wedding of Stanley John Davis & Rosalie Norma Baynes. [CM]

24 'Fire-watching. Siren for 1 hour & 2–5.45pm'. [PD]

afternoon
27 Fair
28 Showers
29 Showers, thunder
30 Showers
31 Fair

Alliance.
26 UK & USSR sign 20 year treaty of mutual assistance.
26 Start of Rommel's offensive against Gazala Line.
28 Mexico declares war on Axis powers.
30 First RAF 1,000-bomber raid on Cologne.

Weather

1 Cloudy, showers
2 V warm
3 Fair, v warm
4–6 V warm
7 Cooler
8 Cool again, more wind
9 Cool
10–11 Fair
12 Rain in morning
13 Cloudy, showers
14 Fair, thundery
15 Showers, cool
18–19 Warm
20 Warm, stormy
21 Warm
22 Warmer
23 Warm again
24 Warm
25 Warm, v cold night
26–28 Fair
29 V warm

Elsewhere

300 civilians killed, 337 injured.
4 Battle of Midway; Japanese fleet crippled.
5 US declares war on Bulgaria, Hungary & Romania.
9 Czechoslovak villages of Lidice & Ležáky wiped out in reprisal for assassination of Heydrich.
12 Withdrawal of basic petrol ration; licences issued instead.
15 Unemployment below 100,000.
16 Supply convoy reaches Malta.
17 Heavy fighting at Sidi Rezegh.
18 Second Axis siege of Tobruk.
20 Rommel drives British back beyond Tobruk.
22 Defence Regulations to ensure black marketeers 'disgorge their ill-gotten gains'.
23 Miners accept national minimum wage for face workers of 83/- per week.
25 Auchinleck takes direct command in desert.
28 Operation 'Blau': German summer offensive on oil-rich Caucasus.
30 Rommel reaches El Alamein.

July 1942

1 Miss KT Butler succeeds Miss HM Wodehouse as Mistress of Girton College.

2 'Fire-watching'. [PD]

2 Funeral of Frederick Stearn (74). [CM]

7 Whist Drive & Jumble Sale raise £16/11/3 for repair of the Churchyard wall. [CM]

8 'It was agreed to make a donation of 30/- to the local RC Detachment out of the Salvage Account.

Mr L Tingey signed the Acceptance of Office as a Parish Councillor and was warmly welcomed by the Chairman.

Dr Walton reported on the continued calling-up of CD personnel for HG duties and it was resolved to apply to the CC to secure exemption from HG duties for the Utility Squad thus placing them on the same footing as other services. He also gave a brief account of the recent local Exercise.

Mr Pease & Mr Lilley were elected to represent the PC on the IC for the ensuing year.

The Clerk would shortly become liable for military service and tendered his resignation. It was resolved to advertise for someone to fill the vacancy under the following terms: Either male or female; not liable for military service; to provide own office accommodation; the PC to provide typewriter; salary £20 *pa*, payable quarterly in arrears; the post to be of a temporary nature'. [PCM]

10 'Fire-watching'. [PD]

11 Funeral of Alice Elizabeth Bass (72). [CM]

19 Baptism of Beryl Joan Lawrence. [CM]

23 'Siren 12.5pm–1.10am'. [PD]

23 Baptism of Michael Leah Hayes. [CM]

25 SS Tea & Games in Girton College (about 50 attended). [CM]

27 'Siren 7.30–7.45am & 1.15–3.30'. [PD]

28 'Siren 1.30–3.45. Bomb on Cambridge. Shot at plane over here'. [PD]

29 'Siren 1.45–3.30'. [PD]

August 1942

3 'Siren 4–4.30am & 6.30pm. Shot at plane'. [PD]

5 'Ivy had son this morning $8\frac{1}{2}$lb about 5.35am, going on well. Siren 2.30–3.00am'. [PD]

6 'Sharp raid on town about 1–2am dropping 2 incendiary bombs'.

Weather

1 Warm
2 Fair, cooler
3 Cooler
4–8 Fair
9 Fair, warm
10 Showers, rain most of night
11 Showers
12 Fair
13 Fair, showery at times
14–15 Fair
16 Showers
17 Cloudy
18 Rain all day
19 Fair
20 Showery
21 Fair, warmer
22 Showery
23–24 Fair
25 Fair, warmer, much better day
26 Fair
27 Rain most of day, heavy rain all morning
28 Fair
29 Warm
30–31 Fair

Elsewhere

41 civilians killed, 871 injured.
1 Auchinleck stops Rommel's advance.
1 First Battle of El Alamein.
2 Churchill wins vote of confidence following fall of Tobruk.
5 Much of Convoy PQ17 sunk by U-boat & Luftwaffe attacks.
9 German forces move on Stalingrad.
12 Australian force arrives at Kokoda.
14 Congress Party passes 'Quit India' resolution.
16 Mass round-up of French Jews begins.
16 Widows' & pensioners' allowances increase by 2/6 per week. Labour says it is not enough.
22 Treblinka extermination camp opened.
23 German army takes Rostov & pushes on to the Caucasus.
31 Motoring for pleasure banned.

Tom Nightingale, RAF Transport Command. Based at Biggin Hill transporting gas for barrage balloons.

Weather

2–4 Showery
6–7 Fair
8 Showery
9 Fair, showery

Elsewhere

403 civilians killed, 509 injured.
3 Churchill goes to Cairo to reorganise command structure in N Africa.
8 Alexander C-in-C ME; Montgomery

[PD]

7 'Fire-watching'. [PD]

12 'It was agreed to purchase 6 Hurricane Lamps for use as emergency lighting at the ARW Posts, FAP &c.

The Clerk reported correspondence regarding the provision of a static water supply near LHS in which Dr Turner agreed to take up the matter direct with the DFO.

The Chairman undertook to make contact with the DFO regarding the provision of a trailer pump at Girton College to serve the Village as promised.

Dr Walton reported that the the CC were unable to take any action regarding the deferment of calling-up of members of the Utility Squad for service with the HG, but promised to pursue this matter further.

4 applications were received for the post of Clerk of the Council and it was decided to interview all the candidates at the next meeting of the PC'. [PCM]

19 Cpl Thomas Cecil Gerrard killed. [CM]

20 Funeral of Margaret Gwendoline Porter (21). [CM]

20 Wedding of Creighton Austin Harrison & Georgette Valerie Schutz. [CM]

23 Baptism of Christopher James Smith. [CM]

27 & 29 'Fire-watching'. [PD]

27 Funeral of Rose Annie Houghton (47). [CM]

September 1942

Cpl TC Gerrard posted missing after Dieppe. [CM]

1 RSM AH Wagstaff (LtAA) killed in action. [CM]

3 National day of prayer. [CM]

6 'Went gleaning in evening. ARP washing'. [PD]

8 'Siren 10.40–11.30. Had bombs in our field about 11.20, 10 altogether, some not gone off. Lots of flares about'. [PD]

9 'Lots of people to see bomb holes'. [PD]

11 'Fire-watching'. [PD]

16 'After interviewing Messrs LJ Dixon & CE Lintott for the post of temporary Clerk it was agreed to appoint Mr Lintott on the following terms: The post to be taken up when the present Clerk is called up and to be temporary, in the first place for a probationary period of 3 months. Salary at £20 *pa* payable in arrears. The PC to provide a typewriter for PC or other public work, to include the post of Salvage Officer.

The Chairman & Dr Walton had written to the DFO regarding the pump at Girton College but no reply was yet to hand.

10 Cloudy
11–12 Showery
13 Fair, some showers
14 Warmer
15 Fair, warmer
17 Fair, warm
18–19 Warm
21 Cooler, windy
22 Showery
23 Fair
25 Rain all morning
27–28 Warm
29 Fair
29 Warm
30 Fair
31 Showers

commands Eighth Army.
9 Arrest of Gandhi, Nehru & other Indian leaders.
12 First Moscow Conference. UK, US, USSR & Free French representatives discuss opening of second front.
13 Siege of Malta broken.
17 Unemployment rises for second month running to 107,534.
18 First use of RAF's Pathfinder Force.
19 Disastrous raid on Dieppe.
22 Brazil declares war on Germany & Italy.
23 German troops reach Volga; air-raid devastates Stalingrad, killing 40,000.
31 Battle of Alam Halfa.
31 Luftwaffe attacks limited mainly to coastal areas.

Weather

1 Showery
2 Fair
3 Fair, turned to rain
4 Fair
5 Showery
6–9 Fair
10–11 Warm
12–14 Fair
15 Windy, fair
16 Fair
17 Windy, fair
18 Fair
19 V nice, warmer
20 Windy, showers
21 Showery
22 Fair, warm
23 Fair, cool wind,

Elsewhere

207 civilians killed, 238 injured.
9 War expenditure £12.5M per day.
10 Further Allied landings on Madagascar.
10 Servicemen get 6d-a-day pay rise.
12 Battle of Bloody Ridge on Guadalcanal.
13 Battle of Stalingrad begins.
14 Unemployment drops below 100,000 again after summer rises; now 98,662.
21 British & Indian troops open offensive into Arakan.
21 British land on E coast of Madagascar.
23 Heavy Japanese attacks on Guadalcanal.

Dr Walton reported on the recent bombing incident in the village and questioned whether the duplication of effort by the Police & ARP should be taken up with the Commissioner. He expressed his appreciation of Police Reserve Smith. He also reported that he had interviewed the local representatives of the Ministry of Labour & National Service regarding the calling-up of members of the Utility Squad and had learned that there were no automatic exceptions, the final decision being left to the local HG Commander. In view of the fact that members of the Squad were now assisting in Night-Watching, he considered that these men, if called into the HG, should be placed in Category "B". The PC endorsed this view, and also suggested that the IC might secure for CD Duties those who at present are not doing such work.

It was agreed to make the following grants from the Salvage Account: LHS £5; Aid to China Fund £2/2/-; Aid to Russia £2/2/-; Baden-Powell Dinghy Fund 10/6; and to purchase 2 more blankets for the ARP Post.

The Salvage Officer asked that Mr Cole might pick up full bags of waste paper from the depôts and this was agreed.

The Clerk undertook to see to the clearing up of the tin dumps. Thanks were expressed to the Clerk for his work during the past 6 years'. [PCM]

20 Baptism of Norman Eric Sales, Ann Rosemary Cartwright, Isabel Mary Bonny, Judith Anne Clarke. [CM]

27 Evensong moves to 6pm. [CM]

October 1942

 5 'Fire-watching'. [PD]

 7 Funeral of Kathleen Isabel Hodder (32). [CM]

11 Evensong moves to 3.30pm. [CM]

14 'Dr Walton reported that the matter of available manpower for the CD had been discussed by the IC and he had been asked to see the National Service Officer as to the allocation to the various services of the men now being called up; the matter was still in hand. He also reported that the DFO had now indicated that he was unable to provide a trailer-pump at Girton College.

The IC had decided therefore to press very strongly for more adequate equipment to be provided for the local Fire Squad.

With regard to the medical services in the Village the IC felt that the different organisations operating these services in the village required co-ordination and had decided that a sub-committee of the IC should meet the heads of these organisations to discuss the matter. Mrs Leakey & Mr Porter had been asked to try to

thunder storm
24–26 Fair
27 Warm
28 Showery, rain most of
day
29 Showery
30 Rain at first

26 Germany captures main Volga ferry
landing in Stalingrad.

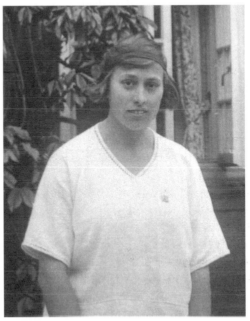

*Mrs HW Leakey, née Averne, an
indefatigable worker for the Village for
most of her long life, as an undergraduate
at Newnham*

Weather
1 Fair
2 Fair, v nice day
3 Fair, turned out nice,
heavy fog at first
4 Fair
5 Fair, but dull, turned
to rain
6 Fair
7 Cloudy, turned to
rain, v mild
8 Showery
9 Windy
10 Fair, some wind
11 Fair, turned out nice
12 Fair, frost
13 Fair

Elsewhere
229 civilians killed, 370 injured.
3 Commando raid on Sark.
6 Montgomery launches the Battle of
El Alamein.
9 Systematic air attacks on Axis
supply routes & bases in Italy &
Libya.
11 Battle of Cape Esperance.
15 Japan lands further reinforcements
on Guadalcanal.
18 Hitler issues Commando Order – all
commandos taken prisoner to be
executed.
22 Clark arrives in Algiers by
submarine for secret talks with
pro-Allied Vichy French.

organise a messenger service.

It was decided that a further edition of the ARP Bulletin should be prepared & distributed.

It was agreed to ask Mr Mitham to procure & fit new chains to the children's swings as required.

An entry had been forced into the Smithy; it was resolved to put the matter in the hands of the Police.

It was resolved to make representations to the CC asking for a more effective clearance of snow from the village during the coming winter'. [PCM]

21 'Fire-watching'. [PD]

24 Wedding of Arthur Frederick Carr & Doris Constance Isabella Cox. [CM]

25 Baptism of Penelope Ann Ryder. [CM]

29 Wedding of Stanley Reginald Dixon & Joyce Marguerite Bonsor. [CM]

November 1942

Mr Ison presents a Roll of Service to the Parish Church. [CM]

11 'The position regarding manpower had been made clearer by a circular from the County ARP Authority in which Wardens are urged to join the HG in Category 2. The HG would help the Wardens' Service during the period in which Wardens were under training, acting whilst carrying out CD duties under the instruction of the Senior ARP Officer. Dr Walton thought that with the co-operation of the HG the manpower problem would largely be solved.

A Trailer Pump had now been delivered into the Parish and was housed at the Pump House at the top of Woodlands Park. The local NFS Squad would immediately receive the necessary training. It was decided that the old trailer should be put in the charge of the ARP Utility Squad on the understanding that it is available if necessary for other Parish work.

It was decided to endeavour to check the mis-use of the Rec Pavilion.

A Precept for £25 was made'. [PCM]

15 Baptism of Monica Grace Fairley. [CM]

15 United Remembrance & CD Sunday Service overwhelms the seating in the Church. [CM]

14 Cloudy
15 Rain at first, turned
   out v nice
16–17 Fair
18 Fair, cloudy
19 Cloudy at first,
   brighter
20 Fair at first, rain in
   afternoon
21 Cloudy
22 Rain at first, fair but
   cloudy
23 Fair, some showers
24 Windy, fair
25 Fair, rain in evening
26 V wet

Weather

1 Rained all afternoon,
  very heavy
2 Cloudy, turned out
  fair
3 Rain all day
4 Fair
5 Rain most of day
6 Fair, brighter day. V
  muddy everywhere
7 Cloudy
8 Cloudy, fair
9 Nice day
10 Fair, fog at first
11 Fair
12 Foggy, cloudy
13 Fog at first, turned
   out much better
14 Fair
15 Cold, cloudy, turned
   out fair
16 Fair, but cold
18 Cold, but fair, cloudy
19-20 Fair, cloudy
21 Fair, cold
22 Fair

22 Royal Proclamation reduces call-up
   age to 18.
23 Battle of Santa Cruz.
23 Second Battle of El Alamein.
26 Intense air attacks on Malta.
31 Luftwaffe 'hit & run' raids on coast
   damage Canterbury.

Elsewhere

Cripps replaced by Morrison in
Cabinet.
2 Operation 'Supercharge' at El
  Alamein.
3 Merchant seaman hanged for
  treason.
5 Vichy French forces on Madagascar
  surrender.
8 Operation 'Torch': Allied landings in
  N Africa.
11 Axis troops march into unoccupied
   Vichy France.
11 Last Axis forces driven out of Egypt.
11 New VD regulations after steep
   increase in cases of syphilis.
12 Battle of Guadalcanal.
15 Production of private cars banned.
19 Heavy RAF raid on Turin.
19 USSR opens counter-offensive N & S
   of Stalingrad.
27 French fleet in Toulon scuttled.

December 1942

9 'Resignations from the PC were received from Mrs JG Stewart &
Mr S Gawthrop and the Chairman was asked to express to them
the sincere thanks of the PC.

Discussion took place on the housing of the new Fire Pump and
the Chairman undertook to find out the sleeping duties required
by the NFS to be undertaken by the local Squad. The Clerk was
asked to enquire whether Dr Hallam would continue to house the
old trailer when this is used by the ARP Utility Squad.

Miss Hibbert-Ware complained of filthy stuff in the wastepaper
bags and the Clerk was instructed to prepare a circular.

The RDC was taking no action regarding the collection of non-
ferrous metals.

Arising out of a suggestion by Mr Lilley, the Clerk was instructed
to give public notice of future meetings of the PC.

Some discussion took place on the inconvenience caused by the
shortage of cycle lamp batteries and it was agreed to write to the
President of the Board of Trade asking if either the production
could be increased or the distribution improved.

Mr Pease was appointed to act as Citizens' Adviser'. [PCM]

3d note, used by British Forces in NAAFI Canteens; above: front, below: back

23 Cloudy, cold
24 Cloudy, not very nice
25 Drizzle, cold, Fair at
   times
26 Showers & drizzle
27 Cloudy
28 Drizzle, cold, fair at
   times
29 Cold, fair, showers
30 Cold, frost

Weather

 1 Frost, rain later
2–3 Frost
 4 Cool, raw, frost
 5 Rain, cold
 6 Cold, turned nice
 7 Fair, cloudy
 8 Fair
 9 Wind, cool
10 Wind, fair
11–12 Fair
13 Windy, fair
14 Fair
15 Cloudy, cool
16 Cool, windy
17 Fair
18 Showers at times
19 Showers
20–22 Fair
23 Nice day
24–25 Very nice day
26 Foggy
27 Fair
28 Fair, cool wind
29 Cool NW wind
30 Snow in morning,
   cleared up, sun
   during day
31 Some more snow in
   night, not quite so
   cold

Elsewhere

109 civilians killed, 201 injured.
Women permitted into Anglican
churches without head-coverings.
[CM]
71,000 Girls in the WLA.
Nuffield Foundation formed.
Women admitted to AEU.
 2 Fermi activates first atomic pile.
 4 First US air-raid on mainland Italy.
11 'Cockleshell Heroes' raid.
11 3 destroyers sunk in 1 week.
12 Axis retreat at El Agheila.
14 5/- pay rise for railwaymen.
14 Unemployment hits new low of
   81,943.
17 Eden gives first official Allied
   statement about extermination of
   Jews.
20 First use of 'Oboe' by RAF.
22 War Graves Commission announces
   roll of honour for civilians.
25 Eighth Army occupies Sirte.
25 Bell-ringing ban lifted for Christmas.
31 Battle of Barents Sea.
31 RC spend £375,000 per month on
   food parcels for PoWs.

January 1943

2 'Fire-watching. Went to Bird Sanctuary, got rabbits'. [PD]

5 Funeral of Mr C Lofts. [CIPC]

7 'Went to Rabbit Club at Wheatley'. [PD]

13 '5 nominations were received for the 2 vacant seats on the PC caused by the resignation of Mr Gawthrop & Mrs Stewart and upon a vote being taken it was agreed to invite Mr SA Lawrence & Mrs BM Turner to accept the appointments. Under the terms of the Order by which the PC appoints 7 Trustees of the VI, Messrs Garner & Betson & Mrs Leakey were due to retire in Jan. The Clerk was instructed to ascertain if they would be willing to stand for election for a further term of 4 years. In the event of Mrs Leakey not being willing to do so it was decided to invite Mrs Thompson.

Dr Walton reported that some members of the Utility Squad had been conscripted into the HG and others had joined the ARP Services in the Village and suggested that the Squad be disbanded. It was decided to thank the members of the Squad for their service and invite them to join one of the other ARP Services: their equipment to be handed back to the Clerk as soon as convenient. It was decided to hold over the publishing of the ARP Bulletin for the time being.

It was decided to give an Honorarium of £1 each to Mr Cole & Mr Gunn for their work in collecting wastepaper. Some difficulty was being experienced in the collection of refuse from Girton College because unburnable refuse was being mixed with the tins; it was decided to write to the College.

The ditch along the land rented from the Trustees for disposal of refuse required clearing and under the agreement with the Trustees the PC was liable for this work. It was decided to put the work in hand and notify the RDC.

It was agreed to write to Trinity College regarding an obstruction placed by their tenants across the Bridleway leading from the Five Bells PH to Madingley, and to ask Mr Hardwick to cut back his hedge on Girton Rd'. [PCM]

15 'Siren 8.50–9.10'. [PD]

15 Visit from Sir Sydney Nicholson MVO, Director of the School of English Church Music. [CM]

17 'Siren 7.50–9.25'. [PD]

20 'Siren 10.10–10.45'. [PD]

23 SS Tea & Prize-Giving. [CM]

25 'Fire-watching'. [PD]

Weather

1 Rain & wind. V heavy showers at times especially in afternoon
2 Slight frost, wind cold. Turned out fair but cold
3 Frost
4 Cold, frost
5 Frost, cool
6 Snow in morning, turned to rain
7 Rain at first, turned cooler later on in day
8 Frost
9 Frost. V cold N wind
10 Rimey frost. V bad morning, roads all ice
11 Fair, cold
15 Fair
16 Frost
17 Windy
18 Fair
19 Showery
20 Fair, some showers
21 Fair. Rain in morning
22 Fair
23 Showers at times
24 Fine
25 Showers
26–28 Fair
29 V nice day
30 Hail storm & rain, cooler
31 V windy, storms

Elsewhere

328 civilians killed, 507 injured.
1 Hitler scraps most of German surface fleet.
2 German withdrawal from the Caucasus begins.
10 USSR offensive on Germans in Stalingrad.
12 USSR breaks worst of siege of Leningrad.
12 USSR launches offensive towards Rostov.
13 Call-up for single girls lowered to 19.
14 At Casablanca Churchill & Roosevelt agree on unconditional surrender of Germany & Japan.
16 Iraq declares war on Axis powers.
19 Churchill & Roosevelt agree to prepare for invasion of France.
20 Daylight raids over SE England include bombing of school in London, killing 44 children & one teacher.
22 Japanese resistance in Papua collapses.
23 Tripoli taken by Eighth Army.
30 First use of H2S radar by RAF bombers.
31 Von Paulus surrenders at Stalingrad. Stecker surrenders 2 days later.

M Ellis, injured by a propellor blade early in the War

26 Baptism of Prudence Margaret Hales. [CM]

February 1943

  1 'Fire-watching'. [PD]

  8 'HG at Drill Hall, E Rd. Fire-watching'. [PD]

10 'Mrs BM Turner & Mr SA Lawrence signed their Acceptances of Office as Parish Councillors and were warmly welcomed by the Chairman. Mr JH Garner, Mr S Betson & Mrs HW Leakey were re-appointed Trustees of the VI for a further term of 4 years.

On discussing a circular from the RDC regarding "Wings for Victory" Week it was agreed to include this on the Agenda for the APM, the date of which was fixed for 31 Mar.

The Chairman & Dr Walton agreed to take up with the DFO the question of the housing of the Fire Pump which it was considered should be kept near the ARP Post in order that members of the Fire Squad could share the Night Watches with the Wardens and not have to man a separate Post.

An estimate of expenses for the ensuing year of £85 was agreed. A letter was received from a joint Committee of the WVS & WI regarding the cessation of the Pies for Rural Workers Schemes and it was agreed to include this on the Agenda for the AGM'. [PCM]

12 Funeral of Mary Ann Aldridge (76). [CM]

15 'Had note to return HG kit'. [PD]

18 'Returned HG kit in morning'. [PD]

19 '**WI**. At the Feb meeting, Mrs Leakey presiding and about 30 members being present, a lecture on Joan of Arc was given by Mr HF Stewart, illustrated with lantern slides, Miss Hibbert-Ware kindly providing the lantern. Nominations were received for the next year's committee which will be elected at the AGM in March and members were urged to attend. The programme committee was elected, and included the president & secretary (ex officio), Mrs Noel Jackson, Mrs Crabbe & Mrs Lintott. It was decided to send any books brought to the next meeting to the Merchant Navy'. [CIPC]

23 'Fire-watching in evening'. [PD]

March 1943

H Bradfield & FC Barrett begin their circular letters to members of the YMG on active service.

  3 '8.40pm & 4.40am. Fire-watching for C Andrews'. [PD]

  6 'Fire-watching'. [PD]

  6 '**WI**. The members of Girton WI are grateful to the Ministry of Information for the enjoyable & instructive show of films at the

Weather

1 Windy, fair. Plenty of water about everywhere
2 Showers, Windy
3 V nice day
4 Fair
5 Showery
6 Fair. Showers
7 Fair, cool
8 Fair
9 Windy & rain
10 Fine in morning, rain later all afternoon
11 Fair, mild
12 Fair
13 Fair, drying up
14 Windy, fair
15 Fair, cool, showers
16 Fair
17 V nice day
18 Fair
20 Fair, cool
21–25 Fair
26 Nice day
29 Fair

Elsewhere

1 Japan evacuates Guadalcanal.
4 Eighth Army enters Tunisia.
8 Kursk retaken by USSR.
14 Battle of Kasserine Pass. Rommel delays Allies.
15 Voroshilovgrad retaken by USSR.
18 Goebbels' 'Total war' speech.
25 UK & US bombers begin round-the-clock bombing of German cities.
27 Telemark Raid on heavy-water plant. Common Wealth Party does much better than expected in Ashford by-election.

Mr FC Barrett, who with Mr H Bradfield began the letters to service men this month

Weather

1 Fair, cool wind
2–3 Fair
4 V nice
5–6 Fair
7 V nice day
8–9 V nice day, frost

Elsewhere

293 civilians killed, 439 injured.
1 Battle of Bismarck Sea.
3 173 Londoners killed in crush at Bethnal Green Tube station shelter, caused by panic at new AA weapon noise.

monthly meeting in April. Of all the programme "Soviet School Child" was most appreciated. Exquisite scenes of children of all ages, learning in model schools, playing & swimming, drew the comment from one child in the audience, "Oh, I wish I was a Russian". Miss Hibbert-Ware presided during the business half-hour, and she & Mrs GA Hall were elected Vice-Presidents'. [CWN]

6 Wedding of Gilbert William Warner & Gwendoline Grace King. [CM]

10 'The question of the housing of the Fire Pump was still under consideration by the DFO. It was suggested that to economise in manpower the ARW should share night watches with the FAP. A request was received from the DFO to install a static water tank on Smithy Green'. [PCM]

11 Funeral of Kate Florence Brind (41). [CM]

13 'Went to Bee lecture'. [PD]

14 'Fire-watching'. [PD]

14 Evensong moves to 6.30pm. [CM]

18 Baptism of Richard Anthony Gwillam. [CM]

20 Wedding of Kenneth William Childs & Agnes Mary Kidman. [CM]

22 'Fire-watching'. [PD]

26 '**WI**. Questions of education & planning were discussed at a special meeting on Wednesday. The presence of experts & teachers gave value to the conclusions reached in answer to the questionnaire sent out by HQ. If the school leaving age is put off till 15 or 16, it was felt strongly that no differentiation should be made between town & country children in the range of subjects taught during the additional years; that the time should be devoted to an extended curriculum of studies. It was the consensus that a period of boarding school life would be of great value in teaching the child independence and fitting him to take part in community life. 14 was suggested as the most suitable age. For the years 16–18, cultural classes and training in citizenship, as well as vocational studies, were advocated. The weekly day of general education (as provided by Bournville for young employees, and in pre-war days by Messrs Chivers) should be supplemented by a short yearly residential period of more intense study. Town & country teachers should have equal pay since the highest qualifications are required for all. Meetings of teachers & parents should occasionally be held to discuss educational questions, and a closer contact established between

12 Fine
13 Fair
14 Fair, nice day
15–17 Fog, rain
18 Fog
19–20 Fair
21 Heavy fog at first.
Fair
22 Heavy fog, turned out
fair
23 Fair
24 Fair, rain at first,
cleared up afterwards
25 Showery at times
26 Turned colder, wind
in W
27–28 Fair
29 Fair, some showers
30 Windy, fair
31 Showery at times

5 Bombing of Essen begins Battle of
the Ruhr.
6 Battle of Medenine.
13 Time-bomb in Hitler's aircraft fails
to explode.
16 During Battle of the Atlantic 38
U-boats attack 2 convoys sinking 21
merchant ships.
20 Battle of Mareth Line.
23 Viscount Samuel reports on
'Holocaust'.
25 Wingate orders Chindits to retire to
India.

Girton AFS with their pumping engine
Top: Stan Nightingale, Les King, Neville King, Ron Foster, 'Fag', Vic Watson
Middle: Irvine King, Hubert Whitehead, Ray Nightingale
Front: Sid Matthews, Bob Watson, Bernard Watson

the school & the home. All these improvements were dependent on the parents obtaining the family allowances and the measure of social security advocated in the Beveridge plan'. [CWN]

27 Funeral of Maria Cole (72). [CM]

30 'Fire-watching'. [PD]

31 '100 residents were present at the APM. A target of £6,000 was set for Wings for Victory Week'. [CWN]

April 1943

4 Baptism of Robert Vernon Secker. [CM]

7 'Fire-watching'. [PD]

21 'The APM was held on 21 Apr at which were present Messrs Adams, Lawrence, Nightingale, Pease, Searle, Tingey & Mrs Turner. Mr Pease was re-elected Chairman & Mr Geo Lilley Vice-Chairman for the coming year.

The Head Postmaster regretted that he was unable to provide an additional posting box near Dodford Lane, but an early morning collection of mail would be resumed.

GDNA asked that the Association might be considered at the next allocation of salvage money.

Mr SA Lawrence was elected to the Rec Committee. Mr Pease & Mr Skinner were re-elected to the CPCC'. [PCM]

23 'A sum of £34/17/6 was sent to the British Sailor's Society, raised from a house-to-house collection in Girton'. [CIPC]

23 'The Rec Committee met on the Ground to examine further damage to the Pavilion. It was decided to put the matter into the hands of the Chief Constable'. [CIPC]

23 'A dance for "Wings for Victory Week" raised the sum of £10'. [CIPC]

23 '**HG** held a concert in the VI which raised a sum of £7/0/6. for Girton Services Fund'. [CIPC]

23 'On Sunday a service was held conducted by the Rector. Pte Blott of the HG read the lesson. Mr Bradfield offered a prayer. A realistic HG demonstration followed during which the playing field was dive-bombed by an RAF plane. Flying Officer Boyes DFM made a special visit to the village. He remarked that a bomber could be purchased for £40,000 and a tyre for a fighter aircraft for £3. The cost of 16 Spitfires in May 1943 was £80,000'. [CIPC]

May 1943

Mr Dennis High posted as missing. [CM]

8 'Rabbit Show in afternoon'. [PD]

9 'Fire-watching'. [PD]

Weather

1–2 Fair
3 V nice, warm day
4–5 Fair
6 Fair, showers
7 Fair, v windy
8 Fair
9 Fair, v windy
10–12 Fair
13 V nice, warm
14 Fair, v warm
15–16 V warm, heat
  wave
17 V warm again
18 Warm again
19 Showers at times
20 Warm again
21 Warm
22 Fine
23 Showers most of day
24–26 Windy
27 Fair, cool wind
28 Fair
29 Shower, warm
30 Showers

Elsewhere

172 civilians killed, 205 injured.
First Army takes Kalrouan.
German attack on Warsaw Ghetto.
First plans announced for NHS after
the war.
Common Wealth Party wins
Eddisbury by-election.
6 Eighth Army night attack on Wadi
  Akarit fails. Axis retreats to
  Enfidaville. UK & US forces link up;
  First Army progress in N Tunisia.
12 Eighth Army takes Sousse. 20,000
  prisoners taken in Tunisia since
  March.
14 Slim takes over command in Arakan.
16 *Pakenham* & Italian destroyers sunk
  in Sicilian Channel.
20 Limited recruitment of women for
  HG announced.

Weather

1 Showers
2 Fair
3 Windy, cool

Elsewhere

584 civilians killed, 733 injured.
Compulsory arbitration introduced
in the coal industry.

12 'After further consideration the CD Committee of the CC had been unable to alter its decision to disband the Girton FA Party. 6 members of the Party had now joined the ARW in order that FA should still be available in the Village. Dr Walton said that the enrolment of 6 trained FA men would relieve the Wardens of the great onus which had been placed on them by the disbandment of the FA party. The Wardens were to receive some reserve training and certain equipment was to be provided. The FA Hut would become the official ARP Post and the Cookery Room vacated. Some discussion took place on the return of blankets belonging to the PC by the members of the NFS now that they had been provided with a separate post & equipment; it was agreed to ascertain the exact quantity of equipment before definitely pressing for the return of the PC's blankets. [PCM]

The Clerk had written again to Mr King regarding the footpath. It was agreed to refer to the Transfer Deeds to see the exact terms of the CC's right of entry into the ground from Mr King's side'. [PCM]

12 Funeral of Sarah Maria Smith (84). [CM]

16 'Wings for Victory' Parade & United Service. [CM]

17 & 25 'Fire-watching'. [PD]

20 'Went to Rabbit Show'. [PD]

26 Funeral of Lily Osborne (50). [CM]

27 Confirmation at GSM of Peter Alton, Elizabeth Amps, Brian Betts, Maureen Cranfield, Barbara Mitham, Brenda Nightingale. [CM]

28 Pte Walter Philip Arthur Dixon dies in Thailand (PoW). [CM]

June 1943

 2 'Fire-watching'. [PD]

 4 'Woodlands Park "Wings for Victory" target was £75. The sum saved was £428/14/6'. [CWN]

 9 'The ARP Services were now installed at the FA Hut and it had been suggested that the timber &c which the PC had purchased for bunks &c at the Cookery Room might be utilised for a cycle shed &c at the Hut. The PC agreed and offered to meet the cost of roofing.

3 blankets had been returned from the NFS members by Mr King and it was agreed that they be stored at the Hut. A census of Gas Masks would be taken in June.

A letter was received from the DFO stating that a towing vehicle would be allocated as soon as available.

Mr Nightingale said that he was endeavouring to secure an

4–5 Fair
6 Cool wind at times
7 Cool wind
8 Rain most of day
9 Windy
10 Rain most of day
11 Fair
12 Fair, windy
13 Warm
14 Warm again
15 Fair, warm
16 Warm again
17–19 Warm
20 V warm
21 Warm
22 Warm, some showers
23 Fair
24 Rain most of day
25 Fair, drying up again
26–29 Warm
30 Rain, thunder, warm.
   Turned out fair
31 Warm

Part-time work made compulsory for women aged 18–45.
6 Enfidaville Line breached.
7 Tunis & Bizerta fall to Allies.
13 Churchill & Roosevelt set provisional date of May 1944 for invasion.
13 Axis troops in N Africa surrender.
16 RAF Dambuster raids.
16 Warsaw Ghetto destroyed.
18 Heavy bombing of Pantellaria.
20 First Tory Party Conference since 1939 in Central Hall. Beveridge proposals accepted 'in principle'.
23 Heavy RAF raid on Dortmund.
30 BBC reintroduces 'Bow Bells' call-sign.
30 Bomb on Torquay church kills 20 children.

Weather

1 Showers
2 Showers, rain most of day
3 Thunder storm
4 Fair
5 Showers
6 Windy, fair
7 Fair
8 Fine afternoon
9–10 Fine
11 Fair
12 Showery
13 Fair, showery
14 Showery, thunder,

Elsewhere

201 civilians killed, 284 injured.
1 Allied Tactical Air Force formed.
3 First allocation of Algerian wine retails at 8/- a bottle.
10 Combined Chiefs of Staff issue 'Pointblank' directive.
11 Himmler orders liquidation of all Polish ghettos.
18 Wavell appointed Viceroy of India.
18 'Radiolocation' officially renamed 'RADAR'.
21 Allies take New Georgia.
28 Cologne Cathedral badly damaged.
30 Aircraft losses to date: Axis 18,031,

exchange of the Wireless Set for a Battery model as the new Post had no electricity.

The reference in the Deed of the Rec to the CC's right of entry on Mr King's side of the Ground was not very helpful. Mr King had put up a notice at his gate asking the public to keep to the proper roadway.

It was agreed to accede to a request from Mr Maw, 32 Thornton Rd, to use the Rec in July for a Religious Service.

Mr Pease said that a Special Service was being held at Girton in June under the auspices of the RC & St John and the local detachments cordially invited the PC to attend'. [PCM]

9 Baptism of Robin Charles Huddlestone. [CM]

13 Baptism of Bernard John Scott, Michael James Dean, Rona May Plumb. [CM]

18 'Fire-watching'. [PD]

20 Baptism of Michael James Coe. [CM]

23 Funeral of Winifred Doris Jones (33). [CM]

Dennis High confirmed killed. [CM]

July 1943

Mr Austin & Mr Dixon reported taken prisoner. [CM]

10 Wedding of Walter Bernard Scott & Marjorie Chandler. [CM]

14 'Some discussion took place on Salvage and the Clerk had purchased 100 sacks for the collection of waste paper. The RDC are to purchase a lorry for the collection of salvage. The costs would absorb all money received by the sale of the salvaged material. It was decided to await the RDC's official notification before finally deciding what attitude to adopt.

It being understood that the Ambulance allocated to the former ARP FAP was to be disposed of, the PC decided to make an offer. Mr Nightingale & Dr Walton undertook to confer on building a suitable garage for the Utility Squad trailer.

Mr Pease put forward a letter setting out a proposal to extend Bus Service 152 to Oakington and alter the route of County Services 107, 123a to the main Hunts Rd, the times of Service 152 to remain the same as at present. It was decided to point out that the present bus used on Service 152 was often inadequate and ask that steps be taken to see that when the Service starts from Oakington, adequate accommodation is provided: the PC to reserve the right to raise the matter again should the times prove unreliable or the accommodation inadequate.

The local Military detachment had temporarily taken over the Rec Pavilion. It was decided to put up a Notice Board requesting

rain afternoon
15 Fair
16 Showers
17 Showery, rain most of
   day
18 Fair
20–21 Fair
24 Warm
25 Fair, cloudy, warm
26–27 Warm
28 Warm again
29 Fair
29–30 Warm

RAF 9,908.

Victor Pauley, Royal Signals, India, July 1943

Weather
 1–5 Warm
 6 Fair, thunder storm
 7 Cooler, thunder storm
 8 Showers
 9–10 Showery
11 Fair, showers
12 Showers
14–15 Fair
17 Warm
18–22 Fair
25 Warm
26 Fair
27 Warm
28–30 V warm
31 V warm, thunder
   storm, some rain

Elsewhere
   167 civilians killed, 210 injured.
 5 Operation '*Zitadelle*' starts Battle of
   Kursk.
 9 Allies land on Sicily.
 9 At least 12 die as 'hit-&-run' raider
   hits E Grinstead cinema.
13 Hitler's calling off attack on Kursk
   begins retreat on the Eastern Front.
19 Hitler & Mussolini meet at Feltre.
19 Rome heavily bombed: about 2,000
   killed, Basilica of San Lorenzo
   destroyed.
22 US Seventh Army captures Palermo.
24 First use of 'Window'.
25 RAF raid on Essen.
25 Mussolini overthrown & arrested.
   New Italian Govt under Badoglio.
25 King Victor Emmanuel III dismisses
   Mussolini as Prime Minister.
26 Italian Fascist party dissolved.
27 Heavy bombing of Hamburg causes
   firestorm.

the public to keep to the roadway when going to Mr King's house. At the request of several residents in Thornton Rd, Mr Lilley asked if the PC would consider making a collection of unburnable rubbish once a fortnight in winter instead of once a month. Mr Nightingale undertook to examine the type of refuse put out there next month, and it was decided to defer discussion'. [PCM]

17 Funeral of Adrian Clive Trillwood (2 days old). [CM]

18 Baptism of Maureen Elizabeth Collison. [CM]

25 Baptism of Rosalind Judith Sharp. [CM]

29 Sgt Reginald George Cecil Austin dies of cholera in Thailand (PoW). [CM]

August 1943

5 'Fire-watching'. [PD]

11 'The CC could not entertain the offer to purchase the Ambulance. A FA Point was to be set up at the ARW Post and those Wardens who were formerly members of the FA Party would take charge of the Point should an incident occur: all the FA Equipment would be kept there. Mr Searle kindly offered to store the trailer pending the building of a shelter.

In answer to the PC's letter regarding Bus Service 152 the Regional Transport Commissioner stated that the points raised would be given consideration.

It was decided to purchase a load of gravel for the entrance roadway and also to creosote the woodwork of the Smithy and point up the brickwork. Mr Nightingale undertook to ascertain if the members of the Military Unit would do the work.

The following grants were made from the Salvage Account: LHS £5; Local Forces Comfort Fund £5; GDNA £2/2/-; IWC £2/2/-; Aid to Russia Fund £2/2/-; Aid to China Fund £2//2/-.

Some discussion took place on the collection of unburnable rubbish and it was decided to make a collection twice each month for an experimental period of 6 months. The Clerk was instructed to post notices'. [PCM]

11 Baptism of Ralph John Nicholls. [CM]

21 'ARP washing'. [PD]

September 1943

Announcement that the Church had paid £6/12/3 towards diocesan quota (1942: £23/7/-). [CM]

1 Bag Tea towards quota. [CM]

3 4th anniversary of war: Day of Thanksgiving, Prayer & Dedication.

8 The Salvage officer reported that a circular had been received

Mr Irvine King

Weather

1–2 Warm
3 Warm, fair
4–6 Fair
7 Showery, fair
8 Fair, windy
9–10 Fair
11 Showery
12 Fair
13–18 Warm
19–20 V warm
21 Showers
22 Fair, showers, windy
23 Fair
24 Warm
25 Showery
27 Fair, windy, showers.
   Turned out fair later
28 Rain all morning
29 Windy
30–31 Fair

Elsewhere

1 54 US bombers lost in raid on Ploesti
   oil refineries.
15 Portsmouth suffers heaviest raid for
   2 years.
17 RAF raid on Pennemunde.
17 First US raid on Regensburg &
   Schweinfurt: 60 aircraft lost.
17 CD casualties so far: 1,211 killed,
   over 2,000 seriously injured.
19 Quebec Conference.
24 Himmler appointed Minister of
   Interior.
24 Mountbatten appointed Supreme
   Commander SE Asia.
27 Minister of Information says Hess
   came to find quislingites to
   overthrow Churchill.
29 Martial law in Denmark, King
   Christian X becomes virtual prisoner.

Weather

1–5 Fair
6 Fair, warm
7–8 Fair
9 Warm again
10 Showers in morning
11 Showery

Elsewhere

5 civilians killed, 11 injured.
Anderson appointed Chancellor of
the Exchequer on death of Wood.
3 Allied landings near Lae.
3 Italy signs secret capitulation.
Eighth Army lands at Reggio di

from the RDC setting out the DC's scheme for collecting salvage. In accordance with the PC's previously expressed desire he had written to the RDC stating that Girton saw no reason to change its present arrangement.

On a request from the RDC for a list of areas infested with rats it was resolved to submit the following: Major Infestations: NIL; Minor Infestations: Wellbrook Laundry and precincts during winter months only; Messrs Chivers sewerage beds: No 68 Thornton Rd. It was resolved to ask the RDC to make a bylaw for the compulsory use of sanitary dustbins.

The Rector had asked the views of the PC on the question of putting up a wall or hedge along the Churchyard. Mr Pease was asked to thank the Rector for giving the PC the opportunity of expressing its opinion and suggest that when the matter came to be discussed by the PCC the PC should be invited to send representatives.

It was agreed that public meetings be held at 7.30pm.

The news of Italy's capitulation having been received that evening the PC decided to send a telegram of congratulation to the Prime Minister'. [PCM]

14 & 30 'Fire-watching'. [PD]

22 Funeral of Ann Heinrich. [CM]

October 1943

Urgent Church roof repairs needed: Rattee & Kett quote £34. [CM]

 2 'Siren 12.45–1.45. Bombs at Histon'. [PD]

 3 Baptism of Lyn Lane. [CM]

10 Baptism of Ivor Paul Mansfield. [CM]

13 'The DC were not prepared to make a bylaw for the compulsory use of sanitary dustbins. Some discussion took place on the use of a pit at the back of Woodlands Park for tipping unburnable rubbish. In view of the proximity of dwelling houses it was decided to take no action.

The Trustees of the Town Charity Messrs Pease, Adams, Lilley, Searle & Wilderspin, were re-appointed for a further term.

It was decided to notify the WD LA of the damage to the Rec gate & fence caused by an Army lorry and to ask for them to be reinstated.

Messrs Lawrence & Lilley undertook to site the notice Board about the footpath across the Rec and it was decided to ask the County LA to make up the roadway.

It was resolved to repaint the Notice Board asking the public to

12 Fair
13 Showers, warm, thunder storm in the night
14 Fair
16–26 Fair
27 Fair, cold wind
28 Showers, cold again
29 Showery, warm
30 Warm

Weather
1 2 Fair
3 Fair, cold wind
4–8 Fair
9 Nice day
10 Fog then v nice
11 Foggy, warmer
12 Fog at first, cleared up later
13 Warm
14 Cloudy
15 Fair, mild
16 Fair
17 Rain in morning
18 Fair
19 Fair, windy, showers
20 Fair
21 Showery. Rain in morning
22 Fair, mild

Calabria.
6 TUC Conference opens in Southport. Bevin says demobilisation would be much harder than mobilisation.
8 Eisenhower announces unconditional surrender of Italy.
9 Persia declares war on Germany.
10 Allied landings at Salerno.
11 German forces occupy Rome.
11 Italian fleet surrenders at Malta.
11 Kesselring declares Italy now under military Govt.
12 Mussolini rescued by German paratroops.
14 Free French liberate Corsica.
15 British forces land on Dodecanese.
21 USSR troops cross Dniepr at Bukrin, soon establishing several small bridgeheads.
22 Midget submarines attack *Tirpitz* in Altenfjord.
25 USSR recaptures Smolensk.

Elsewhere
118 civilians killed, 282 injured. UK & US announce a UN War Crimes Commission.
1 Allies enter Naples.
3 Germany takes UK garrison on Kos.
4 Round-the-clock air attacks on Frankfurt.
13 Italy declares war on Germany.
13 US Fifth Army crosses Volturno.
14 60 US bombers lost in second raid on Schweinfurt.
19 Second Moscow Conference of Allied ministers sets up commission to look at post-war problems and suggests foundation of United Nations.
26 Hospital ship repatriates 700 wounded PoWs to Liverpool from Germany.
27 Montgomery issues final El Alamein

keep to the roadway and have the tree upon which it had been fixed felled.

The Clerk was instructed to purchase 4yd shingle for the Woody Green Path'. [PCM]

14 Baptism of Barry John Edmunds. [CM]

16 'Fire-watching'. [PD]

16 Wedding of Walter William Halls & Ivy May Windmill. [CM]

22 'Siren 7.44–8.40'. [PD]

24 'Fire-watching'. [PD]

24 Baptism of Carole Ann Chaplin, Eileen Mary Cundell. [CM]

November 1943

1 'Fire-watching'. [PD]

6 Funeral of Esther Priscilla Hardwick (73). [CM]

7 Baptism of Helen Angela Palmer. [CM]

7 Evensong moves to 3pm. [CM]

10 'Mr McGorian was no longer able to collect waste paper from the village and after discussion it was resolved to ask Mr Cole to haul it into Cambridge for disposal. It was decided to move the tins from the Thornton Rd dump to Chestnut Farm.

The County LA had provided a supply of ashes for the Rec roadway and would meet the cost of spreading them.

The PC learned with regret of the continued illness of Mr Chas Nightingale and it was unanimously decided to convey to him the condolences of the PC and best wishes for a speedy recovery.

It was agreed to ask the County Surveyor to attend to the footpath on Girton Rd near Pepys Way.

A Precept for £30 was made'. [PCM]

20 Baptism of Neil Roderick Slater. [CM]

26 'Fire-watching'. [PD]

27 Funeral of Edmund Bailey (70). [CM]

29 Baptism of Phyllis Isobel Jane Bailey Crawford, Alastair Stewart Bailey Crawford. [CM]

December 1943

Influenza outbreak. [CM]

8 'The ARP mattresses had now been removed to Girton College and the FA Equipment supplied by the PC had now been taken to the ARW Post.

The gravel for the Woody Green Path & Dovehouse Close Path had been delivered and would be spread as soon as possible'. [PCM]

23 Showery in morning
24 Fair
25–27 Fog, turned out fair
28 Foggy
29 Foggy again
30 V fair
31 Fair, some showers

plan.
31 Admiralty reports 26 U-boats sunk.

Weather

1 Fair, rain at times, v mild
2 Fair, showers, mild
3–4 Foggy, turned fair
5 Fair
6 Fair, showers, cold
7 Fair, cold wind
8–12 Fair
13 Showers
14 V cold wind & showers, some snow
15 V cool, wind N
16 Fair, cold wind
17–19 Frost
20 Foggy
21 Foggy, drizzle
22 Fair, cloudy at first
23–25 Fair
26 Fair, cool
27 Drizzle most of day
28 Showers
29 Fair, cold
30 Cold wind, fair

Elsewhere

119 civilians killed, 238 injured.
Allied Expeditionary Air Force formed for invasion of Europe.
First NAAFI women posted to N Africa soon after El Alamein victory.
Woolton appointed Minister for Reconstruction.
Mosley released on health grounds amidst storm of protest.
4 Fifth & Eighth Armies link up in Italy.
8 Hitler in last speech to National Socialist Party pledges to go on fighting past 12 o'clock.
20 4,800 British PoWs taken on Samos.
20 Eighth Army crosses the Sangro for the first time.
22 Cairo Conference: UK, US & China.
22 Battle of Berlin: RAF drops 700 tons in biggest operation yet.

Weather

1 Fair
2 Rain in morning, turned out nice
3 Fair, cold
4–5 Foggy, frost
6 Foggy, cool
7–9 Fog

Elsewhere

10 civilians killed, 41 injured.
168,524 tons shipping sunk, 8 U-boats.
Structure of the UN decided at Dumbarton Oaks.
Bretton Woods: World Bank, IMF & fixed exchange rate system.

24 Wedding of Frank Sheffler & Florence Nightingale. [CM]
27 'Fire-watching'. [PD]

Miss Alice Hibbert-Ware died on 29 Jan

January 1944

2 Baptism of Richard Edward Dean. [CM]
4 'Fire-watching'. [PD]
12 Mr Palmer had now been called to join HM Forces. This had been expected and was provided for by the appointment of Mr Lintott in August 1942.

Dr Walton reported considerable illness among the Wardens, particularly Mr Duckett who met with an accident on Christmas Eve, and had for the time being to give up duty. Mr Baguly agreed to take charge of the Thornton Rd section.

Mr Lilley suggested that the Committee form a Post-War Planning Committee to undertake the policy of re-construction.

A fresh infestation of rats was reported by Dr Walton between Bandon Rd & Girton Rd, also the infestation behind the laundry was getting worse, and the Clerk was instructed to notify the Sanitary Inspector.

It was agreed to make an honorarium of £1 to L Cole, 10/- to J Gunn & 10/- to B Cole for their work in collection of waste paper. The Salvage Officer was instructed to ascertain if a return of Salvage had been made to RDC for Dec'. [PCM]
16 Baptism of Veronica Matthews. [CM]
17 Funeral of Naomi Florence Skeel (87). [CM]
20 'Fire-watching'. [PD]
21 'Siren 9.15–10.10'. [PD]

10 Snow showers, cold, frost
11 Cold but fine
12 Cold
13 Frost
14 Frost, fog, v cold, raw
15 Frost, fog. Thawed out again, cold
16 Fog again
17 Fair, but fog
18 Cool, showery
19 Cool, rain earlier
20 Cold
21 Cool
22 Fair, cool
25 Fair
27–28 Fair, cool
29–30 Cold, fair

Weather

1 Fair, cool
2 Nice day
3 Showers, fair
4 Fair, cold wind
5 Frost
6–8 Fair
9 Fair, mild, turned to rain
10 Cold, but fair
11 Fair, hail, sleet, cold
12 Milder, fair. V wet about everywhere
13–14 Fair
15 Fair, turned v foggy
16 Foggy
17 Cloudy
18 Milder
19 Showery
20 Showers
21 Fair
22 V windy
23 Strong wind, cool
24 V strong wind, gale

Govt promises house building target of 300,000 a year.
2 Luftwaffe raid on Bari; ammunition ship explodes sinking 17 others.
2 'Bevin Boys' conscription begins.
3 Second Cairo Conference: UK, US & Turkey.
4 Bolivia declares war on Axis.
4 Partisans set up Provisional Govt in Yugoslavia.
12 Rommel becomes C-in-C Army Group B.
16 Education Bill reforms.
24 Eisenhower appointed Supreme Commander AEF.
28 *Scharnhorst* sunk.

Elsewhere

107 civilians killed, 260 injured. 130,635 tons shipping sunk, 15 U-boats.
Indian troops retake Maungdow.
Konev launches offensive in southern Ukraine.
Malinovsky & Tolbukhin launch offensive aimed at Odessa & Crimea.
3 Montgomery takes command of British contingent of AEF.
12 Churchill & de Gaulle meet in Marrakesh.
15 Cabinet committee suggests partitioning of Germany.
16 Eisenhower becomes C-in-C AEF at Second Front HQ.
17 First offensive against Monte Cassino.
19 Arrest of 2 quislingite Irishmen parachuted into County Clare.
19 Novgorod retaken by USSR troops.
22 Allied landings at Anzio.
22 Miners win pay rise with face

22 'Siren 5–5.45am'. [PD]

26 Funeral of Louisa Emily Brown (54). [CM]

28 'Fire-watching'. [PD]

29 'Car turned over 10.35pm on roadway'. [PD]

30 'Helped RAF officer with car'. [PD]

February 1944

3 ' Siren 8.55pm, Siren 4.45am'. [PD]

3 Funeral of Alice Hibbert-Ware (74); see *KiT* p56. [CM]

4 Funeral of Maggie Dean Horrocks (71). [CM]

5 'Fire-watching'. [PD]

6 'Siren 5.55–6.30am'. [PD]

7 'ARP washing'. [PD]

9 'At the request of the Chairman the PC stood in silence as a
mark of respect to the late Miss Hibbert-Ware. The Chairman
undertook to write a letter of condolence from the PC to Mr
Hibbert-Ware. It was resolved to make an appointment to fill
the vacancy on the PC at the next meeting.

A letter was received from Mr Garner suggesting that the
various organisations in the Village should combine in some
suitable memorial; the Chairman agreed to call a meeting of
representatives to discuss the matter.

The Rec Committee hoped to give a report of the general condition
of the children's corner at the next meeting.

Some discussion took place on the APM, the date of which was
fixed for 29 Mar.

The Clerk reported that Mr Bennett was spreading gravel on
Histon footpath and was asked to see Mr Bennett to make certain
he completed this work as far as the Girton boundary.

The Audit of the accounts for the year had taken place without
comment. An estimate of £80 for expenses for the ensuing year
was approved.

The Clerk reported the receipt of 10/- being half year's rent on the
Smithy.

Mr Hibbert-Ware had kindly agreed to the continued use of the
garage at "Hilary" as a depôt for waste paper.

The RDC had objected to paying the account for removal of tins
from Thornton Rd to Chestnut Farm. It was agreed the Chairman
write again for re-consideration, pointing out that the PC had
received no financial benefit from previous collection of scrap'.
[PCM]

17 Funeral (at Attleborough) of Anna Frances Chaplin. [CM]

20 Evensong moves to 6pm. [CM]

most of day

25 V strong wind, cold

26–29 Fair

30 V nice day

31 Fair, cool

Weather

1 Fair, milder

2 Fair, milder, windy

3 Cooler, windy

4 V cold wind

5 V cold

6 Fair, cold, snow, rain

7 Fair, cool

8 Fair

9 V cold wind but fair.
   Showers at times

10 V cold NW wind.
   Snow showers

11 Fair

12 Nice day, cold

13 Fair, cold

14 Fair, but cold

15 Nice day

16 Rain all morning

17 V cold, snow showers

18 V cold again

19 V cold, snow showers

20 Cold

21 V cold

22 Cold again

23 Fair

24 Frost, fair

25 Cold

26–27 Fair

28 Cold, snow showers

29 Frost

workers earning £5 a week.

26 Red Army lifts siege of Leningrad.

29 Direct bomb hit on cinema in
   Croydon, but only 7 killed of 1,250
   audience.

Elsewhere

961 civilians killed, 1,712 injured.
116,855 tons shipping sunk, 20
U-boats.
S Wales miners on strike.

1 US marines capture Kwajalein Atoll.

5 USSR takes Rovno, Aopolostovo &
   Nikopol.

7 India Division holds out at Sinsweya.

13 Allies counter-attack in Arakan.

15 Heaviest RAF raid yet on Berlin.

15 Freyburg's massive aerial attack
   destroys monastery on Monte
   Cassino.

16 NZ troops land on Nissan.

17 Japanese base at Truk destroyed by
   US carrier-borne aircraft.

17 Common Wealth Party candidate
   wins W Derbyshire by-election from
   Govt by 4,561.

17 Butler's NHS Proposals published.

18 RAF bombs Amiens prison, allowing
   Resistance prisoners to escape.

18 Heaviest night raids on London since
   1941.

18 Road deaths for 1943 total 5,796,
   over 50% in blackout.

29 Germany counter-attacks Anzio
   beach-head.

March 1944

3 Funeral of Sarah Ann James (84). [CM]

5 Baptism of Brian Stanley Porter, Christopher John Blatchford Reddall, Susan Elizabeth Jessie Reddall. [CM]

6 & 8 'Fire-watching'. [PD]

8 'The Chairman welcomed the return of Mr Nightingale after his long & painful illness, also extended to Mr Tingey condolence of the PC in his recent loss.

It was agreed that the ARP Bulletin be published again & distributed as soon as possible.

Mrs Leakey had agreed to accept the vacant seat on the PC, and on the proposition of Mr Adams she was elected.

Some concern was expressed at the repeated damage to the Pavilion, the Committee reporting that the lock had again been forced. It was agreed to have the necessary repairs put in hand and the Clerk was instructed to notify the Police.

Some discussion took place on the Agenda for the APM and it was decided to include a proposition to institute a Post-war Planning & Reconstruction Committee, which Mr Lilley agreed to introduce to the meeting.

A request was received from Mr Booth that the refuse dump in LHS, now being full, should be sealed off. The Clerk was directed to notify the RDC'. [PCM]

15 ' Fire-watching'. [PD]

15 Funeral of Ann Delys Price Jones (54). [CM]

17 Funeral of Eliza Jane Kidman (84). [CM]

18 Baptism of Eileen Rose. [CM]

19 Evensong moves to 6.30. [CM]

24 'Fire-watching'. [PD]

29 APM

April 1944

9 Baptism of Joan Elizabeth Matthews. [CM]

14 Baptism of David Charles Hind. [CM]

15 Baptism of Marguerita Cunningham. [CM]

19 'The APM was held on Wed 19 Apr at which were present: Messrs Adams, Lawrence, Lilley, Nightingale, Pease, Searle, Skinner, Tingey, Mrs BM Turner & Mrs Leakey.

Mr Pease was re-elected Chairman & Mr Lilley Vice-Chairman for the ensuing year.

Mrs Leakey signed acceptance of Office.

It was decided to arrange a meeting of the special committee to discuss further the suggested memorial to Miss Hibbert-Ware.

Weather
3 Cold wind
4 Frost, cold wind
5–6 Frost
7 Frost, cold
8 Fair, cool
9–11 Fair
12 Fair, rain at first
13 Frost, v cold
14 Frost, cold wind
15 Frost
16 Fair
18 Fair, milder
19 Fair
20 Cooler, fair, shower
21 Fair
22 Fair, cold wind
23–25 Fair
26 V nice, warm
27 Fair, warm
28 Warm
29 Showers
31 Fair

Elsewhere
279 civilians killed, 633 injured.
Totals to date 50,324 civilian, 50,103
military.
157,960 tons shipping sunk, 25
U-boats.
4 Chindits cross Chindwin into Burma.
4 USSR offensive on Byelorussian
front.
4 US begins daylight air-raids on
Berlin.
9 Miners' strike spreads to Scotland.
0.3M tons lost per week. Welsh
miners return to work by 12th.
15 Japan launches offensive towards
Imphal & Kohima.
16 Oswald Job hanged for spying.
18 RAF raid on Frankfurt.
20 German troops occupy Hungary.
24 Wingate killed in air crash.
25 USSR reaches Romanian frontier.
30 RAF raid on Nuremberg, 95 out of
795 bombers lost.
31 RAF losses after 35 major attacks
since 18 Nov: 1,047 aircraft
destroyed, 1,682 damaged.

Weather
1 Fair
2 Rain in morning
3 Showers, rain in
evening again
4 Shower at first
5 Shower, warm,
thunder
6–8 Fair
9 Fair, shower
10 Easter Monday. V
nice

Elsewhere
146 civilians killed, 226 injured.
82,372 tons shipping sunk, 21
U-boats.
US pays Swiss $1M compensation for
bombing Schaffhausen.
Bevan urges end of Govt
intervention in strikes.
1 RAF hits Gestapo HQ in The Hague.
1 'Salute the Soldier' week raises
£166M.
1 Visits to within 10 miles of S & E

The Chairman read a letter from Mrs Sharp stating that a Parents' Organisation had been formed in the Village to study questions of education, also requesting that a Parish Meeting be called. It was agreed that the matter be left with the Chairman to confer with Mrs Sharp.

Mr Lilley agreed to draw up an Agenda on re-construction for presentation at the next meeting of the PC.

Concern was expressed at the removal of the road name plate at Hicks Lane and the Clerk instructed to notify the Police.

Dr Walton hoped to present the ARP Bulletin at the next meeting. Some FA equipment delivered to the Depôt did not correspond with the invoice: the Chairman asked Mrs Turner to take charge of all FA equipment in the Village in consultation with Dr Walton. The Salvage Organiser was asked to write to the RDC reminding them of our previous letter, asking for their further consideration regarding the account for £4. Thornton Rd be cleared, and to write to Messrs Thompson to ask them to wire off this piece of ground and to thank them for their accommodation'. [PCM]

23 Pte Cyril Stephen Wilson killed in action in Rangoon. (For a photograph see p199.) [CM]

30 Baptism of Clifford Fitness Rule. [CM]

May 1944

6 Pte Thomas Alfred Pauley killed in action in Egypt. [CM]

10 'Mr Lilley reported he had drawn up an agenda on re-construction. After some discussion & alterations it was decided to present the agenda at a meeting of the Re-construction Committee in June.

Mrs Leakey reported that the recently formed Parents' Organ-/newline isation was obtaining all possible information on child population &c to make a report to the proper authority.

It was decided to write to the CC to ask them to make up the roadway from the end of the Rec to Mr King's bungalow, as the track still appears to be used. The Clerk was also instructed to write to the Surveyor asking if he could arrange to do the tarring around the swings & see-saw, when next his men are working in this district.

Dr Walton reported that owing to various alterations in personnel, he was not yet able to present the new ARP Bulletin;

11 Fair
13–14 Fair
15 Showers
16 Fair
17 Fair, cool
18 Warm. Frost in
   morning
19 Frost in morning
20–24 Fair
26 Fair, warm
27–28 Fair
29 Cloudy, fair
30 Fair, warm

*Pte TA Pauley, died
6 May*

Weather
1 Fair
2–4 Colder, windy
5 Showers, cold wind
6 V warm
8–10 Fair
11–13 Warm
14 Fair, showers
17 Rain
19 Fair
20 Fair, cool wind
21 Fair, but v cold wind
22 Fair
23 Cooler
24 Windy, cooler
25 Windy
26 Warmer

coasts banned.
2 USSR troops enter Romania.
3 *Tirpitz* damaged.
3 Part-time work compulsory for
   women aged 18–45.
4 De Gaulle heads Free French.
5 Battle of Kohima.
6 Miners' leaders urge end of unofficial
   strikes.
6 PAYE introduced.
7 Goebbels takes control of Berlin.
10 Odessa retaken by USSR.
17 Japan launches Ko-go in China.
17 Quarterly unemployment 73,092.
18 USSR takes Balaclava.
18 Diplomatic bags & messages from
   foreign embassies censored.
21 Miners' pay agreement signed.
22 Allies land unopposed at Hollandia
   & Altape.
22 Tito's Partisans storm Korcula.
25 Budget: large tax relief for post-war
   reconstruction, prices up 28% in the
   war, wages up 40%.
27 Foreign travel banned.

Elsewhere
No civilian casualties.
27,297 tons shipping sunk; 22
U-boats.
Butler's Education Act comes into
force, introducing the 11-plus.
1 Successful 4th attack at Monte
Cassino.
1 Tito's army recognised after mission
to London.
4 British counter-attacks repelled at
Kohima.
8 Eisenhower chooses 5 June as D-Day.
9 Sevastopol retaken by USSR.
10 Chinese/US Yunnan army crosses
Salween into Burma.
10 Free French claim Resistance Army

he also gave a brief account of the night exercise held recently.

The Clerk was instructed to send a congratulatory letter to Mr Pease from the PC on his appointment to the Chairmanship of the RDC.

The Salvage organiser reported that all tin dumps in the Village had now been cleared by the Ministry and that correspondence shows that the fencing at the Thornton Rd dump was in good order when taken over by the PC. Mr Searle agreed to put this in order and to paint the road name plate'. [PCM]

10 Bring & buy sale (MSL) raises over £16. [CM]

11 Confirmation at GSM of Iris Hancock. [CM]

28 Baptism of Frances Alison Clarke. [CM]

June 1944

 2 Funeral of Sarah Jane Young (78). [CM]

 3 Wedding of Frederick Butler & Ada Elizabeth Hancock. [CM]

 6 First meeting of PRC postponed because of D-Day. [RCM]

10 Funeral of Edward Joseph Young (62). [CM]

14 'Mr Nightingale reported that the Rec roadway was now in excellent condition, but suggested more concrete posts should be erected for guidance of vehicular traffic. Mr Searle undertook to do this work, also to cut the grass.

The ARP Bulletin was now ready and could be printed & distributed in a few days.

The Chairman had received a request from a number of residents to call a further Parish Meeting for the purpose of forming a society to study educational problems. Agreement was reached and the date fixed for Fri 30 June.

Some discussion took place on the question of unburnable rubbish, and it was agreed to call the attention of residents to the fact that the PC could not undertake responsibility for collection of other than unburnable rubbish.

The Chairman brought to the notice of the PC the Book Drive to be held in the Village.

The Salvage Organiser was instructed to arrange for collection & sorting of books with the Headmaster'. [PCM]

20 'Fire-watching'. [PD]

July 1944

 4 First meeting of PRC.

12 'The PRC had formed sub-committees for Housing, Community Centre, Village Greens & Open Spaces.

A request from the Entertainments Committee to use the Rec on

27 Warm
28 V warm
29 V warm, hot
30 V hot
31 Cooler

Weather
1 V cool
2–3 Fair
4 Fair, cooler
5 Fair
9 Warmer
11–12 Fair, windy
13 Shower, fair
14 Fair
15 Fair
16 Cooler
17 Fair
19–20 Fair, windy
21 Windy
22 Fair, cool
23 Fair
25 Fair
26 Fair, some showers
27 Thunderstorm, hail
   like peas, & rain
29 Fair
30 Fair to showers

Weather
1 Fair
2 Showers, rain in
   evening
3 Rain all day

now 100,000 strong.
11 French N African troops break
   through Gustav Line by crossing
   Aurunci Mountains.
12 Germans in Crimea surrender.
15 Deportation of Hungarian Jews
   begins.
18 Polish troops capture ruins of Monte
   Cassino.
19 Eden reports 47 RAF officers shot
   escaping from *Stalag Luft 3*.
23 US Fifth Army attempts break-out
   from Anzio beach-head.

Elsewhere
1,935 civilians killed, 5,906 injured.
104,084 tons shipping sunk, 25
U-boats.
RAF drops 56,000 tons in support of
invasion.
2 Ammunition train explodes at
   Soham; railwayman tows blazing
   truck clear but explosion leaves 2
   dead, 20 injured & 500 homeless.
4 Allies enter Rome.
6 D-Day.
9 USSR assault on Karelia.
13 V1 attacks: first hit 4.18am on
   Swanscombe.
16 Eighth Army captures Foligno &
   Spoleto.
16 'Mulberry' harbours completed in
   Normandy.
17 Free French forces take Elba.
18 Eighth Army takes Assisi.
19 Storms damage 'Mulberry' harbours.

Elsewhere
2,441 civilians killed, 7,107 injured.
78,756 tons shipping sunk, 23
U-boats.
Churchill statement on Doodlebugs:

August Bank Holiday for a fête was granted, on condition that side shows &c were placed according to the instructions of the Clerk, no charge be made for admission, and the ground left tidy & in good order.

Correspondence from the Price Regulation Committee was read, regarding the granting of a licence to Mr LD Hills at 50 High St for Stationery. The PC agreed that there was need for additional facilities and the Clerk was instructed to write requesting that a licence be granted.

The Chairman had received a letter from Mr Hibbert-Ware, stating he would be leaving in August to take up residence in Cambridge, therefore he would no longer be able to carry on with Salvage work. The Salvage organiser was asked to write on behalf of the Salvage Committee thanking him for his past services. Mr Searle kindly offered to provide accommodation for Salvage, if no other place could be found. It was agreed to purchase 2 new bins for bones.

The question of evacuation was raised & discussed, and compulsory billeting was recommended'. [PCM]

14 The PRC was informed that the Community Centre plan had been welcomed by Mr Morris of the CC who was happy to meet the PRC [RCM]

15 Funeral of Harriette Mann. [CM]

22 'Fire-watching'. [PD]

23 Baptism of Judith Perry, Margaret Perry. [CM]

27 Mr Morris suggests approaching the Carnegie Centre for funds for the proposed Community Centre [RCM]

August 1944

9 'Mr Nightingale asked whether a letter had been sent to the newly formed Girton Education Association asking for their co-operation with the billeting problem – and whether a satisfactory reply had been received. In the absence of Mr Pease this could not be answered, but Mrs Leakey reported that help had been received from Mrs Armitage, a prominent member.

Miss McMorran at Girton College asked if the PC would, on completion of the memorial to Miss Hibbert-Ware, accept financial management. It was agreed to ask for fuller information regarding the cost of maintenance, and to discuss the matter at the next meeting.

Mr Lilley suggested that the road name plates should be cleaned & painted before the winter, and new ones erected at Thornton Rd & Hicks Lane corner. The Clerk was instructed to write to

5 Fair
6 Fair, warm
7 Fair, showers
8 Fair
9 Fair, rain, showers
10 Cooler, showers
11 Cooler again
12 Fair
13 Rain
14 Fair
15 Fair, rain in morning
16 V warm
17–18 Fair
19 Fair, turned cooler in
   evening
20–25 Fair
26–28 Warm
29 Showery, rain in
   morning
30 Fair, showers
31 Fair

2,754 launched, 2,752 dead & 8,000
injured.
3 Red Army takes Minsk.
9 Allies take Caen.
18 Tojo resigns following loss of Saipan.
20 Hitler survives bomb plot:
   conspirators executed.

*The Revd G
Hibbert-Ware*

Weather

1–3 Warm
4–18 V warm
19 Showery, rain at
   times
20 Rain all day
21 Showers
22 Warm, showers
23 Fair, warm
24 Rain at times
25 Warm
26 Showers, warm
27 Fair
28 Showers, warm again
29 Showery

Elsewhere

Polish Home Army rises against the
occupation.
7 weeks of non-stop V1 attacks:
5,540 launched, 4,735 people killed,
14,000 injured & 17,000 houses
completely destroyed.
9 Allies take 4,000 prisoners at
Falaise.
15 Operation 'Dragoon': Allies land on
French S coast.
23 Liberator crashes on school near
Preston: 38 children & 22 adults
killed.
26 De Gaulle enters Paris.

Mr Maw, 30 Thornton Rd, & Mr Mitham for tenders also to to Impington PC to ask if they would erect name plate at the Huntingdon Rd end of Thornton Rd, or allow GPC to do this & charge Impington.

Mr Searle asked that the PC give their permission to allow Parish organisations use of the trailer housed at Mr Searle's farm. Consent to this was granted.

Mr McGorian was unable to accept any more waste paper for the time being. It was hoped some solution would be forthcoming before the next meeting.

The fête held on August Bank Holiday had proved a great success, a total of £167/11/9 having been received, the approximate profit being £125'. [PCM]

14 Baptism of Allen James Davis. [CM]

17 Bag Tea towards Quota: £22/17/9 raised. [CM]

23 'Fire-watching'.[PD]

23 Cpl Leonard Maurice Johns killed in action in India. [CM]

23 Wedding of Allan John Larkin & Ethel Louise Marjorie Percival. [CM]

September 1944

3 Baptism of John Peter Rowney, Joan Ann Rowney. [CM]

4 Sadlers' golden wedding. [CM]

5 Wedding of Kenneth Charles Sellers & Ruth Sofie Hirsch. [CM]

7 Baptism of Audrey Maureen Green. [CM]

7 Received into the Church: Ruth Sofie Hisrsch. [CM]

7 PRC approves draft application to Education Committee for School & Community Centre. [RCM]

12 Memorial service for Mr Johns (killed 23 Aug 1944). [CM]

13 'A tender for new road name plates & the renovation of existing ones for £25 was received from Mr Maw. It was agreed this was too high. Impington PC agreed to allow GPC to erect a name plate at Huntingdon Rd end of Thornton Rd, charging the cost to Impington PC.

In view of the recent lighting order, it was agreed to request the proper authority to put the street lamps in order.

Mr Adams brought to the notice of the PC the poor condition of the roadway at the bus stop at Girton Corner and the Clerk was instructed to write to the County Surveyor requesting that some repair be effected at this point.

The programme for the weekend at Impington for Sep 23 & 24 under the auspices of the CPCC, was given some consideration and Mrs Turner agreed to go as representative of GPC'. [PCM]

30 Showery, warmer
31 Showers, warm,
    thunder

The Hibbert-Ware Memorial Garden

Weather

1 Showers
2 Rain most of day,
   strong wind, thunder
3 Showery
4 Rain most of day
5–6 Showery
7 Rain all day
8 Showery, thunder
   storm
9–10 Fair
11–13 Warm
14–15 Fair
17 Sun Fair
18 Fair
20 Cloudy
21 Foggy
22 Fair, showers
23 Fair
24 Wet & windy all day
25–28 Fair
29 Showers
30 Fair

Elsewhere

190 civilians killed, 360 injured.
Allies liberate Arras, Verdun, Dieppe
& Abbeville.
1 US troops enter Germany.
3 British troops liberate Brussels.
3 Ceasefire between Finland & USSR.
3 5th anniversary of start of war:
   National Day of Prayer. Empire
   casualties: 242,995 dead 80,603
   missing 311,500 wounded & 290,181
   captured.
5 Patton's troops cross Moselle.
6 Blackout & CD measures relaxed.
6 Compulsory HG drill ended.
6 Victory in the 'Battle of London' after
   80 days of V1 attacks: over 8,000
   launched, 2,300 reach London.
8 First V2 hits Chiswick.
12 'Octagon' Conference plans for UN.
17 Airborne assaults on the Maas, Waal
   & Rhine.
18 PLUTO becomes operational.

14 Harvest Festival. [CM]

October 1944

  1 Baptism of Roger Graham White, Michael Burdette Auger. [CM]

  1 Evensong moves to 6pm. [CM]

11 Miss HJ McMorran, treasurer of the Alice Hibbert-Ware Memorial Committee, asked if on completion the PC would be prepared to accept the garden. A proposition by Mr Lilley, seconded by Mr Searle was adopted, that the PC approve this scheme. The Clerk was instructed to reply stating the PC's approval, but pointing out that the acceptance could in no way bind their successors on the PC, also that the matter would be raised at the next APM.

The Clerk was instructed to write to the RDC in connection with the road name plates.

It was agreed to write to the WD asking if they would at an early date relinquish their occupation of the Rec, also to write to the Baptist Chapel authorities drawing their attention to the dangerous condition of their notice board.

A circular was received from RDC setting out the conditions regarding the restricted form of street lighting but suggesting that no action to be taken. The Clerk was instructed to write to the RDC asking them to reconsider their decision as it was felt that some form of street lighting was necessary.

Night watching at the hut had now ceased, but Wardens were on call if necessary. It was recommended that the wireless set be disposed of. A proposition by Mr Adams was adopted that a hearty vote of thanks be accorded on behalf of the PC & residents to all those who had served there under Dr Walton.

Mrs Chenery 34 Thornton Rd could no longer loan her garage as a depôt for waste paper. The Salvage Organiser was instructed to express the committee's thanks.

Mrs Turner reported on the CPCC at Impington on 23–24 Sep mentioning those who had spoken on the housing problem, and brought to the notice of the Councils a proposition which had been adopted, that PCs should be the authority for the allocation of Council houses and that all planning schemes should include a Rec'. [PCM]

23 'Went down town in morning & got oranges'. [PD]

November 1944

  8 'The wireless set, lately in the possession of the Wardens, had now been presented to LHS. Mrs Turner asked if any action should be taken regarding the disposal of FA equipment and it

Weather

1–2 Fair
3 Fair, cool
4 Rain in morning
5–7 Fair
8 Foggy in morning
9 Fair
10 V nice day
11 Showers
12 Fair, some showers
13 Fair, cool
14 Fair
15 V nice day
16 Rain all morning
17 Rain
18–19 Fair
20 Rain at times
21 Fair, some showers
22 Fair
23 Showers
24–25 Fair, v nice day
26 Showery
27 28 Fair
29 Showers at first,
    turned out fair
30 Fair, slight frost
31 Showers

25 Withdrawal from Arnhem.

Elsewhere

118 civilians killed, 282 injured.
Warsaw uprising finally crushed,
despite massive Soviet presence on
the outskirts.
Armistice signed by USSR &
Bulgaria.

2 Aachen falls to US First Army,
12,000 prisoners taken since Oct.

9 Allied 3rd Moscow Conference agrees
on 'spheres of influence'.

10 Massive tank battle near Debrecen.

12 First agricultural production figures
since 1939: wheat up 80%, potatoes
up 104%, cattle up 6.5%, pigs down
58%.

14 Rommel commits suicide.

16 Unemployment in last quarter up
16,379 to 79,235.

18 British capture supply depôt at
Mohnyin.

18 Establishment of *Volkssturm*. All
able-bodied males 16–60 drafted.

19 German forces raze Warsaw.

23 Decisive US victory at Leyte Gulf.

23 First organised *kamikaze* attacks.

Weather

1–2 Fair
3 Rain in morning
4 Windy

Elsewhere

716 civilians killed, 1,511 injured.
37,980 tons shipping sunk, 6
U-boats.

was proposed that Mrs Turner, Dr Walton & Mr Tingey, should make a survey of the stock & report to the next meeting. The RC Detachment were anxious to see a Homecoming Fund started in the Village. After some discussion it was proposed to call a meeting of representatives of all organisations in the Village to discuss the matter.

A tender was received from Mr Mitham for £4/4/- to renovate road name plates, and this was forwarded to Chesterton RDC.

The Chairman had received a letter from the Minister of Home Security & the Regional Commissioner, stating that ICs could now be disbanded, and expressing the thanks of the country to all those who had served on these committees, which was endorsed by the PC.

Mr Adams reported that palings on the Rec had been forcibly removed, and Mr Nightingale added that the barbed wire round the huts was in a dangerous condition. It was proposed that a letter be sent to the Youth Club & the Cadets asking for their co-operation in protecting Village property. Mr Searle agreed to enquire if it was possible to collect the wire & store it for the time being.

A letter was received from Mr Hibbert, OC Cadets, asking for permission to retain one of the Army huts on the Rec for their use. The Clerk was instructed to reply stating that the PC have no authority in this matter'. [PCM]

10 Baptism of Christopher Stuart Corbett Clark. [CM]

12 Baptism of Ruth Mary Lawrence. [CM]

19 Baptism of Jonathan Stanley Ingle. [CM]

December 1944

 3 Baptism of Richard David Taylor. [CM]

 3 Evensong moves to 3pm. [CM]

 6 'A letter was received from Mrs Mellish Clark asking if a representative could be appointed for the SSAFA. It was proposed that Mrs Lintott be asked.

In connection with the proposed formation of a Homecoming Fund, Dr Walton suggested the fund should take the form of a friendly society to be administered by temporary officers and handed over to service men on their return. It was agreed to make this proposal at the forthcoming APM.

It was resolved to write to the WD to bring to their notice the poor condition of the huts &c, also asking for the release of this site.

Histon PC were unable to obtain the necessary labour to repair the footpath. The Clerk was instructed to reply suggesting they

5 Windy, rain in
   afternoon
6 Fair, frost, rain later
8 V cool, windy
9 V cold, frost, v cold
   wind
10 Cold, but bright
11 Fair, turned out nice
12 Fair
13 Fair, cool
14 Showers
15 Fair
16 Rain, frost
17 V wet day
18 Showery
19–20 Showers
21 V nice day
22 Showers
23–24 Fair
25 Fair, frost in morning
26 Fair, turned to rain
27 Fair, much better day.
   Bright
28 Fair
29 Showery. Turned out
   nice
30 Fair

Weather
1 Fair
2 Fair, cold wind
3 Fair, showers
4 Fair, cool wind,
   showers at times
5 Cold wind, fair
6 Frost
7 Cold, but fair, rain in
   evening
8 V cold, raw, hoar frost
9 V cold, frost
10 Frost
11 Cold
12 Cool, v dark

First of 9,000 Japanese balloon
bombs launched against US. 6 killed
near Lakeview.
RAF sinks *Tirpitz* in Tromsø Fjord.
Second *Panzer* Army establishes line
W of Belgrade.
Roosevelt wins 4th term; Truman
Vice-President.
B-29s from Saipan make first raids
on Japan since 'Doolittle' raid.
1 HG stands down.

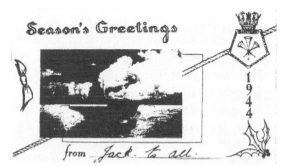

Christmas card sent to FC Barrett and the
YMG, December 1944. On the back is written
'With Best Wishes to all the Youth Club, and all
my old Pals, & yourself. Yours Sincerely, Jack.'

Elsewhere
367 civilians killed, 847 injured.
Greater London Plan published.
1 *Vanguard*, last & biggest UK
   battleship, launched.
9 Eighth Army suspends offensive in
   Italy.
16 Germany begins 'Battle of the Bulge'.
17 German massacre of US prisoners
   near Malmedy.
18 B-29 daylight incendiary raid on
   Hankow.
22 Call-up of 250,000 'to sustain &
   nourish our armies in the line'.
24 Restrictions on car lights lifted.

might approach the CC.

Dr Walton reported he had with Mrs Turner examined the FA equipment & found it in fairly good condition, and it was proposed that this stock should be handed over to GDNA, subject to the law being favourable.

A letter of thanks was being sent on behalf of the PC to all who had served on the IC.

Disposal of waste paper was now much easier, and it was agreed to bring to the notice of residents the recent broadcast on the continued necessity of salvage of all kinds of waste'. [PCM]

 8 Funeral of George Naylor (51). [CM]

18 Baptism of Nancy Mary Clark. [CM]

23 Funeral of Amelia Pike (62). [CM]

23 Funeral of Archibald John Mack (75). [CM]

23 Funeral of William Cranfield (82). [CM]

31 Baptism of Derek George Medlock, Rosemary Anne Booth. [CM]

January 1945

 7 Baptism of Rosalind Mary Gawthrop. [CM]

10 'A letter was received from the WD suggesting that the PC might be willing to purchase the huts on the Rec. It was resolved to pass on this letter to the RDC.

Complaints continued to be received about the condition of the Girton–Histon footpath, and the Clerk was instructed to notify the Histon PC that unless some assurance was forthcoming GPC would have no alternative but to draw the attention of the overriding Authority to the condition of this footpath.

A letter was received from Mrs Burrows asking if a grant could be made to her from the Salvage Fund to enable her to continue sending hampers of fresh vegetables to minesweepers. The Clerk was instructed to reply suggesting that the scheme might be made more widely known and that the question of a grant would be decided at the next meeting. It was agreed that Mrs Burrows' work should be brought to the notice of residents at the next APM.

A letter was received from Mrs Green stating that the Dr had ordered her to give up her outdoor activities for at least 2 months, and therefore would be unable to collect the bones for the time being. It was agreed to ask Mr Cole to do this when he is making the collection of unburnable rubbish.

The Gas Co had made enquiry about the lamp standards which had been taken down at the beginning of the war. The RDC had again taken up the matter of street lighting with the Gas Co.

13 Frost, foggy
14–15 Fair
16 Showers
17 Windy
18 Fair
19–21 Foggy
22 Drizzle all day
23 Fair, some fog, cool
24 Foggy, frost
25 Foggy, rime frost
26 Frost, fog, rime frost
27–30 Frost
31 Frost, cold wind

26 Red Army encircles Budapest.
29 Hungary declares war on Germany.
31 HG demobilised.

Weather

1 Frost
2 Cool, thawing
3 Cold, rain later
4 Frost
5 Frost, snow showers
6 Snow, frost
8 Snow, frost
9 Snowing, frost
10 Frost, snowing
11 Frost
12 Snow, thawing
13 Frost
14 Fair, but cold
15–17 Fair
18 Windy, thunder
   storm, heavy rain,
   stormy
19 Snow again, v cold N
   wind
20 Cold, frost
22 Frost, cold, snow
   showers
23–24 Frost
25 Frost, rime. V cold
   day

Elsewhere

585 civilians killed, 1,629 injured.
82,897 tons shipping sunk, 14
U-boats.
1 Operation 'Nordwind' against US
   Seventh Army in Vosges.
1 Last major Luftwaffe attacks in the
   W, against airfields in France & Low
   Countries.
2 Kamikaze attacks on US convoy in
   Lingayen Gulf.
2 Saboteurs wreck V2 factory in
   Copenhagen.
3 British take Akyab unopposed.
9 100,000 US troops land at Lingayen
   Gulf, largest Pacific operation so far.
14 British Indian Division crosses
   Irrawaddy.
17 Red Army takes Warsaw.
19 Hitler orders large attacks or
   retreats must have his approval.
27 Red Army liberates Auschwitz.
28 First convoy for 3 years reaches
   China, through Burma.
31 Owing to bad weather RAF drops
   only 32,000 tons of bombs.

Dr Walton handed over to the PC the minute book & documents relating to the IC.

In reply to a question by Mr Lilley as to the position of PCs under the proposed new Local Gov Act, the Chairman stated that up to the present no alteration was anticipated'. [PCM]

28 Evensong moves to 6.30. [CM]

February 1945

 3 Wedding of Charles William Jobson & Maud Amelia Crane. [CM]

 3 Wedding of John Reginald Anderson & Alice Rosemary Gauge. [CM]

 5 Funeral of Naomi Blanche Hoppit (47). [CM]

10 SS Party organised by Mr & Mrs Cornell. [CM]

11 Baptism of Elaine Scott Foster. [CM]

14 'A letter was received from the Cambs Cadet Battn asking for permission to rent one of the huts on the Rec. The Clerk was instructed to reply stating that subject to the site being released, the PC were prepared to enter into a yearly tenancy agreement on terms to be arranged later.

Work had commenced on the Histon section of the Girton–Histon footpath.

The FA equipment had been handed over to GDNA.

It was agreed that the Minute Book & documents relating to the IC should be deposited in the Council's strong box and an index be affixed in the PC's Minute Book.

The 4 Trustees of the VI, Mr Pease, Mr Lilley, Mr Skinner & Mr Gawthrop due to retire on Jan. 2 were asked to continue in office for a further period and agreed to do so.

In reply to a question by Mr Adams, Mr Lilley stated that with the growth of Village organisations only a very few dates were available for the letting of the VI, but with the release by the Army of the WI, it was hoped the position would be eased.

The RDC had recently purchased a motor vehicle for the collection of unburnable rubbish, and it is hoped this will be available shortly for a weekly collection in Girton.

The Homecoming Fund asked to use the Rec on August Bank Holiday for a fête. It was agreed to leave this for discussion till the next meeting.

An estimate for expenses for the next financial year was agreed at £80.

The following grants were made from the Salvage Fund: Alice Hibbert-Ware Memorial Fund 20gn; LHS 2gn; Entertainments

26 Frost, rime
27 Cold, frost, snow
   showers
28 Snow, frost
29 Frost
30 3" snow
31 Thawing

Weather

 1 Milder. V wet
   everywhere
 2 Milder
 3 Frost, fair
 4 Fair
 5 Fair, nice day
 6 Rain at times
 7 Fair
 8 Snowing
 9 Fair
10 Cooler
11 Rain most of day
12 Showers
13–17 Fair
18 V nice day
19–21 Fair
21 Frost, fine day
22 V nice day
23 Fair, showery
24–27 Fair

31 USAAF sends out 18,924 bombers &
   13,615 fighters, dropping 54,564
   tons.

Elsewhere

   483 civilians killed, 1,152 injured.
   Totals to Sep 1944: 57,468 killed,
   89,178 injured.
   95,316 tons shipping sunk; 22
   U-boats.
 1 US Seventh Army reaches Moder &
   Siegfried Line.
 4 Churchill, Roosevelt & Stalin agree
   at Potsdam to partition Germany,
   Austria & Korea.
 5 RAF Balloon Command disbands as
   air-raid threat lessens. 278 V1s
   claimed by balloons.
10 USSR captures motor vehicle dump
   in E Prussia.
13 Allies bomb Dresden: some 60,000
   dead.
13 Budapest surrenders to USSR
   troops.
16 US troops take Corregidor.
19 US assault begins on Iwo Jima.
22 Allied air attacks on German
   transport lines.
28 Admiralty claims more than 1,000
   enemy vessels sunk by mines since
   1939.
29 Indian Division crossed Irrawaddy.

Fred Evans, RA

Committee 3gn, Homecoming Fund 3gn; GDNA 2gn, IWC 2gn, L
Cole £1, W Stanford £1, Air-Raid Distress Fund £3. [PCM]

19 Pte Ernest Sidney Pigden killed in Netherlands. [CM]

20 Funeral of Kate Scott (70). [CM]

March 1945

 5 Memorial Service for ES Pigden (killed 13 Feb 1945). [CM]

12 Baptism of Rachel Lavinia Foster, Rebecca Foster. [CM]

14 'A letter was received from GDNA thanking the PC for the
FA equipment, some of which was found to be unsuitable and
permission was asked to pass this on to Addenbrooke's.

Some concern was expressed at the wilful damage done to the
Coronation Tree, and it was agreed that a notice board be erected,
requesting the public to see that their property is not allowed to
be destroyed.

A letter was received from the Battn Cambs Cadet Force,
together with a draft lease. After some discussion the Clerk
was instructed to reply, stating that the PC were still not able
to grant permission, but agree in principle, if they would accept
the following additions & alterations of the agreement: A yearly
tenancy with 6 months notice on both sides; lease to apply only to
the land on which it stands; Cadet Force to undertake to keep
huts in decent repair; The PC not to be held responsible for
damage; the PC would grant free access to the hut & the use
of the water tap; Cadet Force to undertake to use the hut only
for work in connection with Cadets; and to make no structural
alterations. The PC would, as soon as they learn that the site is
released, take steps to reach agreement with the Cadet Force.

It was resolved on receipt of a joint application from the
Homecoming Assoc & the Entertainments Committee to agree to
the letting of the Rec on August Bank Holiday.

The Agenda for the APM was agreed.

A weekly collection of unburnable rubbish would commence in
April subject to the RDC being able to obtain the necessary
labour.

A letter was received from Mr Peake & Mr Newman drawing
attention to the dump which had accumulated at Chestnut Farm,
and asking that this be removed. Mr Searle agreed to see that
this work was completed as soon as possible.

Mr Skinner, owing to failing health, wished to retire from the
RDC. The Chairman suggested someone should now be asked
to fill the vacancy and the Clerk was instructed to write to Mr
Skinner thanking him'. [PCM]

Weather

1 Cooler day
2 Frost, cool
3–10 Fair
12–13 Fair
14 Warm
15–24 Fair
26 Fair, showery
27–30 Fair

Elsewhere

792 civilians killed, 1,426 injured. Introduction of Family Allowance.
3 Luftwaffe attacks 27 airfields in last raid of the war, losing 6 aircraft & destroying 22.
5 Germany begins conscripting 15- & 16-year olds.
6 British & Indian troops enter Mandalay.
6 Strikers at London docks refuse to return to work. 3,000 troops handle essential cargo.
14 Bomber Command deploys 'Grand Slam' bomb, destroying Bielefeld viaduct.
20 Indian Division captures Mandalay.
22 League of Arab States formed.
23 French First Army crosses Rhine for the first time since Napoleon.
27 Last V2 lands on Orpington.
29 Last Air-Raid warning.

Chestnut Farm

14 MSL Sale raised £21/3/7. [CM]

23 Annual Parochial Church Meeting. [CM]

24 Baptism of John Richard Gane. [CM]

24 Wedding of Edward Ervine Keith & Doris Margaret Seymour. [CM]

April 1945

1 Baptism of Nicholas John Sedgwick, Kathryn Mary Monkman, Carol Ann Wiseman (Easter Day). [CM]

5 Funeral of Ann Rose Mansfield (3). [CM]

18 'The APM was held on Wed 18 Apr at which were present: Mrs BM Turner, Mrs HW Leakey, Messrs Adams, Lawrence, Lilley, Nightingale, Pease, Searle, Tingey & Dr Walton.

Mr Pease was re-elected Chairman, and Mr Tingey proposed a vote of thanks be accorded Mr Pease. Mr Lilley was re-elected Vice-Chairman. It was decided to hold a Parish Meeting on 9 May to accept nomination to fill the vacancy on the RDC.

Arising out of the APM the Chairman referred to the PRC, and the decision taken to uphold the proposal regarding the Community Centre. With the possibility of it becoming more active, it was agreed to enlarge this Committee and the following 6 residents: Mr Thomson, Mr Wilderspin, Mr Marshall, Mr H Kidman, Mr I Bailey, & Mr R Gawthrop were asked to serve. A meeting will be held on 16 May.

It was agreed to write to Mr Burkett confirming the PC's decision to allow the Cadets to rent a hut on the Rec.

Emergency food dumps in the Village had now been cleared.

A precept for £80 was made'. [PCM]

22 Baptism of Richard Biggs, Alan John Porter, John Hedley Davis. [CM]

24 Wedding of John Robert Snell & Frances Grace Auger. [CM]

26 Funeral of Frank Skinner (75). [CM]

29 Baptism of Glyn William Jackson, Graham Gary Grant. [CM]

May 1945

Exhibition: Girton – past present & future. [CM]

2 Funeral of Annie Nightingale (87). [CM]

2 Funeral of Archibald Major Wallaker (61). [CM]

3 Confirmation at GSM of Peter O'Connor Thomson, Peter Philip Graves, Joyce Olive Edwards. [CM]

8 'Victory Day, holiday'. [PD]

9 'On a motion by Mr Tingey, the PC expressed its thanks to Mrs

Weather

1 Fair
2 Fair, cool
3–4 Fair
5 Showers
6–7 Fair
8 Fair, cool
9 Fair
11–12 Warm
13 V warm
14 Fair, some showers
15–20 Warm
21 Turned v cold
22 Cooler
23–24 Frost
25 Frost, turned warm
26 Fair
27 Fair, cooler
28 Cool wind
29 V cold wind, some
  showers
30 2" snow, v cold.
  Snowed most of
  morning

Elsewhere

First woman Metropolitan Police
Court magistrate appointed.
Fisher succeeds Temple as
Archbishop of Canterbury.
1 US forces land on Okinawa.
3 MacArthur appointed C-in-C Pacific
  land forces.
7 Battle of E China Sea: US aircraft
  sink *Yamato* in 3-hour battle.
9 Eighth Army launches final offensive
  in Italy.
12 Truman succeeds Roosevelt.
15 British troops liberate Belsen.
16 Hitler's last Order of the Day to
  Eastern Front that anyone who
  orders retreat is to be shot.
20 Home Secretary reports 60,585
  civilians dead & 86,175 seriously
  injured in air attacks.
23 Hitler orders Goering's arrest.
28 German troops in Italy surrender.
28 Mussolini & his mistress killed by
  partisans.
30 Hitler marries his mistress in his
  bunker, where both are later found
  dead.
30 Total V1 & V2 casualties: 2,754
  killed, 6,523 seriously injured.

Weather

1–2 Frost, cool
3 Frost
4 Snow showers, frost
5 Showers, rain in
  afternoon
6 Fair
7 Fair, warmer

Elsewhere

2 German army in Berlin surrenders.
4 Montgomery reports to Supreme
  Allied Command that all enemy
  forces in Holland, NW Germany &
  Denmark have surrendered.
8 VE Day.
9 CI garrison surrenders to 30 UK

Leakey & Mr Pease for their work as Parish Food Organisers. Mr
Pease in reply proposed to send a note of thanks to all those who
had stored the Emergency Food, and the PC asked that its thanks
might be included in this letter.

Mr Tingey stated that as he was leaving the district he would
have to resign.   The Chairman remarked how the PC had
appreciated his past services, especially his untiring efforts in
the launching of the FAP under ARP.

This resulted in there now being 2 vacancies on the PC, and the
following names were suggested: Dr EJ Smith, Dr Gane, Mr
Fagg, Mr Booth, Mr Chaplin, Mr Thomson, Mr Wilderspin, and
the Clerk was instructed to write asking if they would be willing
to allow their names to go forward.

On a proposition by Mr Searle seconded by Mr Adams, Mr
Lawrence was appointed to the Trustees of the VI in place of Mr
Skinner.

Mr Pease agreed to attend the meeting of the CPCC. On receipt
of a complaint from Mr Garner that the huts on the Rec had
been broken into, the Chairman stated he had notified the Police,
and it was resolved to write again to the WD. Some concern was
expressed at the amount of barbed wire still lying about in the
Village. It was decided to contact the Military to get this cleared
up.

Letters were received from the Baptist Chapel Council & the
Girton Conservative Association asking for permission to use the
Rec for an open air service, & a meeting. Permission was granted
subject to the usual conditions.

Mr I King stated that the NFS HQ had asked him to make
application to retain the trailer which was lent to the AFS. After
some discussion the Clerk was instructed to reply stating that
the trailer had been bought by the PC & had only been lent to
the AFS up to the time when a trailer pump had been supplied
by the NFS and that the trailer now in question was the property
of GPC.

The weekly collection of unburnable rubbish was still being
delayed owing to difficulty in obtaining the release of the driver'.
[PCM]

11 Funeral of William Michael Brandon Reader (77). [CM]
16 PRC agrees to acquire the site for a new School. [RCM]
26 Baptism of Claire Mary Lilley. [CM]
30 Leslie Burgess RAF dies in an accident in Italy. [CM]
31 Funeral of Claire Mary Lilley (5 weeks). [CM]

8–10 Warm
11–12 V warm
13 Fair, cloudy
14–17 Warm
18 Fair, warm
19 Fair
20 Showery
21 Fair, some showers
22 Fair
23 Fair, turned v cold
24–25 Fair
26 Fair, showery
27 Showers, thunder
  storm
28 Fair
29 Fair
30 Fair, some showers
31 Fair

troops.
13 Bruning unconditionally surrenders all boats under his command at Felixstowe.
13 Royal Family & Allied military leaders attend Thanksgiving Service at St Paul's.
23 Himmler commits suicide at Second Army HQ.
23 Churchill resigns.
23 King announces the date of 15 June for dissolution of Parliament.
26 Churchill announces Caretaker Cabinet.

'German soldiers came in all sorts of conveyances to give themselves up' (p214). Roy Ellis' pictures of German troops surrendering at Lüneburg.

June 1945

3 Baptism of Timothy John Brading, Beverley Victoria Roberta Blott. [CM]

13 'The voting to fill the 2 vacancies on the PC resulted in Mr J Wilderspin, 26 Girton Rd & Mr JW Bailey, 53 Cambridge Rd being co-opted until March 1946.

Lt Monkman would deal with the barbed wire at Mr Hall's field as soon as possible but the slit trenches & wire at Girton Corner did not come within his area of operation. He referred the PC to Major Chapman OC Battn Cambs HG. It was agreed to write.

Further correspondence from the Cadet Force, making request to fence in part of the Rec and to retain 2 huts resulted in considerable discussion, and the Clerk was instructed to reply confirming the PC's previous decision.

Application for use of the Rec on August Bank Holiday was received from the joint committee of the Entertainments Committee & Homecoming Fund Association. This was granted subject to the usual conditions.

A letter was received from the PCC complaining of the inconvenience caused by the 152 bus drawing up at the Church during any funeral service. The Clerk was instructed to reply pointing out that the present stopping place had proved to be the best, and to suggest the PCC might come to some arrangement with the driver.

The Chairman on behalf of the PC expressed thanks to Mr Searle for his past service to the parish by virtue of his work in the collection of unburnable rubbish.

The Homecoming Fund Association applied for permission to erect a target indicator on the Rec. Subject to this meeting with the Council's approval permission would be granted.

As no further use could be found for the trailer purchased out of the Salvage Fund it was decided to advertise this for sale.

A letter of thanks was sent to Mrs Marshall for allowing her premises to be used for storage of paraffin for the ARP.

The Chairman undertook to arrange with Dr Walton for the collection of all ARP equipment ready for disposal'. [PCM]

24 Baptism of Richard John Osborne, Jennifer Dorothy Hodder, Owen John Hodder, Marion Elizabeth Hodder. [CM]

26 PRC told that grants may be available for expansion of Rec, and that the Rector agrees in principle to sell Glebe land for a School. [RCM]

31 Funeral of Ellen Irene Coe (40). [CM]

Weather
1 Fair
2 Fair, showers
2 Fair
3 Fair, showers
4 Fair
7 Fair
8 Fair, showers
9–10 Showers
11–12 Showery
13 Fair
14 Showery
15 Fair, showers
16 Fair
17 Showers, fair
18 V warm
19 Warm
20 Fair, showers, warm
21 Showery, warm
22–23 Warm
25 V warm
26 Cooler
27 Warm
28 Fair, cool
29 Fair
30 Showery

Elsewhere
4 Churchill says no socialist system can be established without political police.
5 Allied Control Council assumes Govt of Germany.
6 Brazil declares war on Japan.
7 King Haakon returns to Norway.
10 Australian troops land in Brunei.
14 Von Ribbentrop arrested in Hamburg.
15 4th longest Parliament ever dissolved after 9 years, 6 months & 30 days.
18 Demobilisation begins.
19 British & Indian troops invade Thailand from Burma.
22 US Tenth Army captures Okinawa.
26 UN Charter signed by 50 Allied nations.

Girton Glebe School, opened in 1951 and built on Glebe Land

July 1945

8 Baptism of Stephen Christopher Foster. [CM]

11 'On behalf of the PC, the Chairman welcomed Mr Wilderspin & Mr Bailey, the 2 new members co-opted at the last meeting and both signed the Declaration.

It was agreed to write to Mr Peak asking if he could arrange to have the slit trenches filled in & barbed wire cleared away at Girton Corner.

Some concern was expressed at the delay in securing the release of the site occupied by the Military and it was agreed to make further application and copy the letter to Lt-Col Drake Digby.

It was proposed to arrange with the CC for the use of the steam roller to level out the old pond site, with a view to having this made into a car park.

Dr Walton was authorised to offer for sale to the residents now holding the 10 stirrup pumps at 7/6 each. Also to collect the remaining ARP equipment and arrange for its sale. Mr Pease agreed to arrange for the sale of the 6 stable lanterns, and it was agreed to offer the table to the Trustees of the VI.

Mr Pease gave a brief report on the last meeting of the Community Centre Committee, outlining the proposal for a new School & Community Centre, and stated that the Committee & school managers had arranged to meet the General Purposes Committee of the Education Committee on 1 July to lay before them the requirements of the Community Centre Committee. Mrs Leakey, Mrs Turner, Mr Lilley, Dr Walton & Mr Pease agreed to attend.

Salvage was again raised by the receipt of a letter from Mrs Chaplin stating that considerable time had elapsed since the last collection and that her accommodation for waste paper was very limited. Mr Searle agreed to arrange with Mr Cole for a fortnightly collection and the Salvage organiser was asked to present the accounts at the next meeting.

The sale of the motor trailer realised the sum of £10'. [PCM]

16 PRC prepares for a meeting with the Education Committee, and receives a report from Mr Barrett re the Rec. [RCM]

August 1945

5 Baptism of Barry Lane, Anthony Brian Scott. [CM]

5 Baptism of Susan Caroline Fairley. [CM]

8 'Mr Pease gave an account of the meeting held on 1 July. The proposals for the new school were favourably received, but it would have to be included in the CC's Development Programme.

Weather

1 Showery
2 Fair, warm
2 Showery, cool
3 Fair
4 Warm
5 V warm
8 Fair, warm
9 Warm
10 Rain most of day
11 Showery
12–14 Warm
15 Warm, showery
16 Cooler, windy
17 Warm
19 Fair
20 Warm
21–23 Fair
25 Warm
26 Cooler, showery
27 Fair, cooler again
28 Warm
30 Warm

Elsewhere

4 'Desert Rats' establish British Sector in Berlin.
5 MacArthur announces victory in the Philippines.
16 Quarterly unemployment rises 22,856 to 111,825, up 40%.
17 Potsdam Conference demands Japan's unconditional surrender.
26 Labour wins Election by 399 to 213.

Mr MS Pease, for most of the War years Chairman of GPC

Weather

3 Warm
4 V warm
5 Thunder
6 Showery, cool
7 Cool, showery

Elsewhere

6 Hiroshima bombed.
8 USSR declares war on Japan & invades Manchuria.
9 Nagasaki bombed.
14 Japan accepts terms for ending the

As the pavilion could not be included in any educational scheme, this might have to be provided out of local funds. It was agreed that Community Centre business should be included on all future agenda for PC meetings.

Correspondence from the WD LA was read and as this was thought to be unsatisfactory, it was resolved to write again stressing the urgency of de-requisitioning.

Mr Pease was authorised to act for the Parish in negotiating the renting of one of the huts to the Cadet Committee.

Permission was granted to the WI for the use of the Rec for a demonstration van on 12 or 13 Sep.

Mrs Turner & Dr Walton were appointed to represent the PC at the CPCC at Impington on Sep 22.

Dr Walton was proceeding with the sale of remaining ARP equipment, 4 offers having been received for Stirrup Pumps.

The RDC requested information on vacant property in the Village and the Clerk was instructed to write to the effect that no property was available for requisitioning.

Some discussion took place on Salvage and it was considered this should now be discontinued. Mr Pease agreed to interview the Sanitary Inspector about the collection of waste paper'. [PCM]

11 Memorial Service for Leslie Burgess (died 30 May 1945). [CM]

12 Baptism of Elizabeth Anne Secker. [CM]

15 'VJ Day'. [PD]

20 Baptism of Desdemona Ishbel Coates. [CM]

25 Wedding of Malcolm Donald Jeeps & Desdemona Ishbel Coates. [CM]

25 Wedding of William Ernest Bacon & Joy Ellen Porter. [CM]

30 Quota Bag Tea with Sideshows & Entertainment. [CM]

September 1945

Groups of children raise £2/13/2 for the Church. [CM]

 2 Baptism of Barbara Johnson. [CM]

12 'A letter was received from the Parish Clerk, expressing the wish to resign from office owing to his having to leave Girton. The PC decided to excuse the 3 months' notice. The Clerk agreed to act until the next meeting of the PC, and was instructed to advertise the vacancy. It was decided to hold a special meeting of the PC on Wed Oct 3 to appoint a new Clerk.

The Military had now released the site on the Rec, and the huts removed and claim forms received from the Land Agent & Valuer. It was resolved to ask the RDC to survey the site to estimate the cost of restoring it.

8 Cooler
9 Showery
10 Warm
11 Coolish
13–14 Fair
17 Fair

Ken Blunt RN

war.

15 Details released of RADAR, one of the most closely guarded secrets of the war.

15 VJ Day. Enormous crowds cheer King & Queen at State Opening of Parliament.

19 National Day of Thanksgiving. Royal Family, Cabinet & foreign diplomats attend service at St Paul's.

23 Parliament ratifies UN Charter with all-party approval.

24 Truman orders end of Lend-Lease Programme.

24 Bevin says 700,000 homes in London need repair. 43,000 remain uninhabitable in London, 10,500 elsewhere.

29 Nuremberg War Trials announced.

Weather

3 Fair
4 Rain most of day
7 Fair
9–10 Fair
11–13 Showery
14 Fair, turned to rain
16–19 Fair
20 Showers, windy
21 Showers
22 Fair, windy
23 Fair, showers
24 Fair, some wind

Elsewhere

2 Vietnamese independence announced.

2 Japan signs surrender agreement aboard *Missouri*.

15 Anniversary of Battle of Britain: 300 aircraft in London flypast.

15 Princess Elizabeth suffers bruising after fall from horse. Princess Margaret makes first public speech in her stead.

19 Joyce sentenced to be hanged for treason.

Some discussion took place regarding the activities of Cadets at the hut on the Rec, as it was thought that firearms were being used there, and as there appeared to be no supervision of their activities, it was resolved that Councillors should note any untoward happening and report to the next meeting.

The Clerk was instructed to write to Mr Pease asking if he would report at the next meeting, on progress made regarding the housing problem as it was considered that housing would take priority with residents rather than a Community Centre.

It was agreed that the Committee sponsored by the PC to organise VJ celebrations should continue, and arrange a dinner or tea for Pensioners, and on a proposition by Dr Walton it was agreed that a grant for this be made out of the Salvage Fund.

The RDC & the Gas Co were conferring that day on the question of street lighting'. [PCM]

13 Funeral of Ethel Ada Sadler. [CM]

22 Wedding of George William Rogers & Gertrude Lillian Joan Smith. [CM]

24 Funeral of Alice May Golding. [CM]

27 & 30 Harvest Festival & Service. [CM]

October 1945

3 'Applications for the post of temporary Parish Clerk were received from Mr FJ Rule of 31 Woodlands Park & Mr BE Crabbe of 36 Church Lane. As Mr Rule is still serving in HM Forces and unable to attend for interview, it was resolved, on a proposition by Mr Searle, to appoint Mr Crabbe as Clerk for a probationary period of 3 months.

After considerable discussion between the RDC & the Gas Co a lower tender for street lighting had been agreed upon, and it was agreed to ask the RDC to introduce street lighting at once without restoring full lighting.

Mrs Turner, Mr Wilderspin & Dr Walton all agreed that the CPCC at Impington was very successful. Dr Walton in his report stated that the subjects chosen for the lecture were most suitable and mentioned in particular those on the Education Act, Playing Fields & Community Centres and the address by Dr Orwin on maintaining an interest in village life.

Mr Pease reported on the housing problem, stating that the Minister of Town & Country Planning had now agreed to allow the site at the end of Pepys Way to be used for building.

The Chairman reported he had asked Mr Burrows to negotiate with the Cadet Force to occupy the Hut on the Rec at £1 *pa*. Some

25 Windy
26–27 Fair
28 Showery, turned out v nice
29–30 Fair

26 National Socialist Party declared illegal.
28 School-leaving age raised to 15.

St Vincent's Close, Girton's post-war housing

Weather

1–3 Fair
4 Foggy & cloudy
5 V nice day
6 Warm
7–8 Fair
10 Fair
12–13 Fair
15 Fair
16–17 Nice, fog in morning
18–19 Nice day
20 Fair, rain later
21 Rain most of day
22 Fair
23 Showers
24 Showers
25 Rain most of day
26 Showery
27 Fair
28 Showery
29 Fog

Elsewhere

5 Duke of Windsor returns to England.
7 King visits bombed areas in East End.
8 Hess flown to Germany to stand trial.
9 Laval sentenced to death for collaboration.
11 Fighting breaks out in China between Nationalists & Communists.
18 First open session of Nuremberg Tribunal.
20 Arab League expresses hostility to formation of a Jewish state.
24 UN comes into being, 29 ratifications having been received.
24 Quisling executed by firing squad.
30 Parliament adopts a vote of thanks to all men & women in armed forces.

concern was expressed at the use of the Cadet Hut, and it was agreed to write to the OC asking for an assurance that if firearms were used, there would be no danger to the public.

Arising out of the Impington CPCC Dr Walton agreed to draft a village directory on the lines of the ARP Bulletin for presentation at the next meeting.

Arrangements should be made at the next meeting to organise some programme for the official Peace Celebrations & a stand-down Party for all War Organisations'. [PCM]

7 Baptism of Gillian Mary Sharp. [CM]

19 Funeral of Lily Mary Smith. [CM]

November 1945

4 Baptism of Richard John Huddlestone. [CM]

17 Wedding of Edward William Daniel & Doris Emily Pauley. [CM]

18 Baptism of Nicholas John Potter, Jennifer Mary Ford, Jennifer Rosemary Doggett. [CM]

18 Memorial Service for Walter Dixon (died in PoW camp 28 May 1943). [CM]

21 'A letter from the Chesterton RDC respecting the restoration of street lighting was noted, also that street lighting had now actually been restored.

A reply from the Chesterton RDC to the PC's request for surveying assistance was considered, and as the RDC were unable to help Mr Searle undertook to proceed with the work of levelling & ploughing &c as soon as possible and the cost would be claimed from the Military when the job was completed.

A reply had been received from the A Coy Cmdr in answer to the PC's complaint respecting the lack of discipline & use of firearms by the Girton Cadets. The reply was noted, no further action being considered necessary at present.

Dr Walton's report on the Village Directory met with general approval and as this was not quite completed it was agreed to discuss it more fully at the next meeting.

Peace Celebrations. After some discussion the PC decided that this subject should be included in the Agenda for the APM.

Stand Down Party. Members undertook to ascertain the views of the various interested bodies.

Appointment of Governor to IVC. Considerable discussion on this question took place and it was resolved that Mrs Leakey be asked to accept the appointment and in view of the urgency of the nomination alternative nominations (Mr Dark & Dr EJ Smith)

30 Fairish, fog at first
31 Fair, fog later

N Lewis RE

Weather

1 Fair, fog in morning
2–3 Fair
5 Fair
6 V nice day
7–8 Fair
9 Fair, turned colder & windy
10 Fair
12 Fair but cold
13 Fair, sun shone
14 Fair
15 Frost
16–17 Fair
19 Fair
20 Fair, cooler, fog
21 Fair, fog
22 Showery
23 Fair
24 Fair, cooler
26 Fair, turned colder
27 Frost, cold
28–30 Fair

Elsewhere

7 A Gloster Meteor regains world air speed record at 606mph.
11 King & Princess Elizabeth lay wreaths at resumed Remembrance Day service.
12 French Institute awards Churchill gold medal.
13 De Gaulle elected Head of provisional French Govt.
19 Labour announces nationalisation plans.
29 Yugoslavia declared a Federative Republic.

Pte Walter Dixon

were agreed if Mrs Leakey was unable to accept.

Road signs. The Clerk was instructed to inform the Chesterton RDC that the school sign at the Thornton Rd Corner was no longer required as the school no longer exists and to suggest that this sign should be replaced by a "Dangerous Corner" sign.

Salvage. It was agreed to continue the collection of salvage in view of the still serious shortage of paper'. [PCM]

23 Baptism of James Arthur Dean. [CM]

23 Memorial Service for RGC Austin (died in PoW camp 29 July 1943) [CM]

December 1945

 1 Baptism of Peter Richard Stock, Christine Johnson, Margaret Linda Burgess, Lesley Anne Burgess. [CM]

11 Funeral of Elsie Maud Nightingale. [CM]

12 'Arising out of the minutes it was noted that the hole & barbed wire at Girton Corner had still not been removed and the Clerk was instructed to again draw the Surveyor's attention to this and stress the added danger to the public owing to the prevalence of darkness & fog during this time of the year.

Dr Walton stated he had not been able to complete the draft of the Village Directory and it was agreed to postpone discussion on this until the next meeting.

Considerable discussion on the conduct of IVC took place and Mrs Leakey reported on her recent visit to the College. She also stated that it was probable that a meeting between Mr Parr (Warden) and the parents of the children attending the College would be arranged at Girton before the Spring Term commenced.

Dr Walton stated that a list containing the names of all residents who served in HM Forces during the recent hostilities would be posted on the Village notice boards in a few days and it was hoped that residents would check these lists to ensure that no names have been omitted'. [PCM]

23 Baptism of Mary Frances Chaplin. [CM]

Weather

 1 Cooler
 2 Showery
 3 Fair, cold
 4 Showers, cold, frost
 5 Fair, cold again
 6 V cold again
 7–8 V cold, frost
 9 Sharp frost, v cold
10 Fair, cool, fog
11–12 Fair
13 Fair, rained later
14 Fair
17–21 Fair
22 Fair, showery later
23 Showery, v muddy
24 Windy, showers
25 Fair, showery
27 Fair
28 Rain & snow
29 Fair, cold
30 Frost, fair but cold
31 V cold again

Elsewhere

 4 US votes to join UN & to permit use of US peace-keeping forces.
10 Minimum wage set at 10/- per day.
14 Convicted Concentration Camp personnel hanged.
15 UN HQ to be in US.
16 Unesco formed in London. Churchill addresses Belgian Parliament advocating United States of Europe.
25 King broadcasts Christmas message from Sandringham to Empire.
27 IMF & World Bank established.

Mr Gordon Pluck, whose diary provides the weather data

2: ARP and the Invasion Committee

DR de Lacey

By Sep 1939 preparations against the war in the air were already well under way, and Dr Walton was ARW. In May 1940 he presented a report to the PC, which agreed to circulate its 4 cyclostyled pages as a bulletin to every household.

In Jan 1941 the PC authorised the distribution of an appeal for volunteers and equipment. That May a revision of the ARP Bulletin was agreed, and an expanded, printed version was circulated in July. A further revision was recommended in Oct 1942, but this was not ready until June 1944, when the PC decided to turn it into a peace-time Directory of Services.

Also in 1941 an Invasion Committee was set up in line with Govt policy. With Dr Walton as Secretary it first met in June 1941 and the last recorded meeting is in Oct 1942. From then on presumably the Committee held itself in abeyance until 2 years later it was officially abolished. Its documents however provide a fascinating perspective on the Village.

The Committee's archives lodged in CRO with the Parish Records include the Jan 1941 appeal (p141–143); the 3 *Bulletins* of which we reproduce the third (p144–151); the IC Minutes (p152ff); the IC *Report* (p164ff); correspondence relating to ARP exercises and the abolition of ICs (including the letters on p173) and a number of printed documents circulated by central Govt, including 3 of 5 Public Information Leaflets on Civil Defence issued by the Lord Privy Seal's Office, a copy of *Consolidated Instructions to ICs in England and Wales* (London: HMSO, July 1942) with an addendum, and several letters relating to the abolition of ICs. Although extant versions of these appear to be very rare, space precludes our printing them here.

Our transcription is as accurate as possible consistent with a reasonable presentation preserving the text & format, though correcting obvious errors. *Italics* represent underlined text.

One further point may be noted. Although there are many Doctors mentioned in these documents, most of them are academics, not medical practitioners. There was no medical practice in the Village, and the obvious candidate in time of emergency was Dr Hertz, daughter of the German radio pioneer. Her nationality created interesting problems for the IC.

Appeal for Volunteers: January 1941

AIR-RAID PRECAUTIONS (GIRTON)

At a Parish Meeting held on Jan 15th 1941, it was decided that a personal invitation for closer co-operation with the ARP Services and an appeal for volunteers should be circulated to all residents. Not only are the existing Services in need of new recruits to replace men called up for military service, but ARP duties have become more frequent and may possibly increase still further. The recent extensive use of incendiary bombs has increased the risk of damage to life and property. This danger cannot be met entirely by the existing ARP personnel which is only a small fraction of the total population of over 2,000 in the Parish. The Minister of Home Security has appealed to the Public for active help in defence against fire. In certain areas registration of men and women between the ages of 18 and 60 for fire-watching and fire-fighting is to be made compulsory. In such cases the duty required is 48 hours per month. Duty at the places of residence exempts from duty at work premises and vice versa. Compensation is granted on the same basis as for CD personnel.

In Girton the risk of extensive fires is certainly not so great as in industrial centres and it should be possible with less exacting measures, to meet the increased danger. It is proposed to extend the system of Night Watches organised by the Wardens at Thornton Rd, and the Cookery School, so that an effective look-out can be kept over the whole Parish, and men will be available to give instant warning and deal with incendiary bombs should they be dropped,

> *In order that these precautions may be put into operation with the least possible delay, each householder is asked to fill in the form on the back of this circular and keep it until it is called for by a member of the ARP Services.*

Services requiring recruits

Night Watchers and Fire Fighters. About 40 additional men are required to take turns at the Night Watch Posts. Night Duty will not occur more often than once a week, and if sufficient volunteers join it may be less. Generally, only part of the watch is spent on patrol. Beds, tea &c are provided. Steel helmets are available for those on patrol.

Rescue Party. Men are urgently wanted for the Local Rescue Party. Casualties are highest in demolished buildings and the immediate release of buried persons is the first essential service. If sufficient volunteers join, Night Duty should not occur more often than one night a week and only when public warning is given. Unless called out for action the Party is at ease in the Cookery School. Beds &c are provided.

First Aid Party. Men are urgently wanted to train in FA. 3 ambulance drivers are wanted immediately (no FA training necessary). The Party is also in need of cars with drivers (petrol provided). Night Duty occurs about twice a week. Unless called out for action the Party is at ease in the Depôt. Beds &c are provided.

AFS. Men are required to train in Fire Fighting. Duty is required on alternate weeks when public warning is given. Unless called out for action, the Fire Party is at ease in the Cookery School. Beds &c are provided.

Day Watching and Report Centre Duty. A limited number of men and women are required for day or evening duties.

ARTHUR WALTON, Head ARW (Girton)
16 Girton Rd. *23rd January, 1941*

The Wellbrook Laundry was chosen as the GHQ for the Invasion Committee. The Laundry, established largely for the use of the College, was taken over by Modeluxe in the 1970s, and demolished in 1988

VOLUNTEERS
Please fill in the following form

Name and address of Householder:

Members of Household willing to volunteer

    Name   *Services offered*

Men between the ages of 18 and 60 who have not filled in the above form and who are not already members of the *local* Service are asked to give their names and state the reason why they are unable to volunteer.

PARTICULARS OF FIRE-FIGHTING EQUIPMENT
Please strike out the sentences and words which do not apply

Stirrup Pump
I own a stirrup pump.

I am the joint owner of a pump which is kept at ....

I wish to buy a pump at a cost of £1.

I wish to become joint owner of a pump.

Long-handled scoop and rake
I own a scoop and rake.

I wish to buy a scoop and rake at a cost of 4/6 per pair.

Other Fire Fighting Appliances
I keep pails of water, sand, half-filled sand-bags, fire extinguishers, in readiness in case of fire.

Ladders
I own a ladder and am willing to lend it in case of emergency.

Length of ladder or number of rungs ....

MOTOR CARS FOR EVACUATION
It might be necessary to remove families from damaged or threatened houses to the emergency rest centres at LHS and Girton College at short notice. If willing to lend a car and driver for this purpose please give the following particulars.

    Name   *Address*   *Telephone No*   *No of seats in car*

Third ARP Services Bulletin

PARISH OF GIRTON

No 3   ARP SERVICES BULLETIN   **June 1941**

Since the publication of BULLETIN No 2 many changes have taken place in the local ARP services, and it is felt that householders would care to know the present position. The response to the appeal issued last January for volunteers for the ARP services was satisfactory, and the thanks of the Parish are due to those who then came forward. Vacancies, however, continue to arise in all the services, and further volunteers are badly needed, and would be warmly welcomed. Offers to serve should be made to the Head ARW Dr Arthur Walton, 16 Girton Rd (Tel 76137).

Some thought has been given to the problems which may arise in the Parish in the event of invasion or other enemy action, cutting off the normal communications and services; a special Committee has been set up in the village to study the local problems to which such an event would give rise, *eg* the distribution of food, water, fuel, and medical supplies. In the event of such an emergency, an Administrative HQ and Information Office would be set up at the Wellbrook Laundry (Tel 76161).

Telephone numbers are given throughout this BULLETIN , but the public is requested to refrain from using the telephone system during an alert, except in cases of urgency.

This BULLETIN has been prepared by the Head ARW in consultation with the Heads of the various Services, and is issued to the public by the Parish Council. A note has been added on the salvage of waste in this village.

MICHAEL PEASE

June 25th, 1941   (Chairman of the Parish Council)

AIR-RAID WARNINGS

On Feb 12th of this year the system of sounding warnings by whistles and hand-bells was discontinued by order of the Ministry of Home Security. Whistles are to be used only in the case of incendiary bombs. Hand-bells are only to be sounded to give the All Clear after a gas alarm has been given by rattles. There is, therefore, no local warning at night. During business hours the Wellbrook Laundry will sound the Alert and All Clear as before, and messages by telephone will be sent to the Headmaster during school hours.

GAS MASKS

The public are asked to pay particular attention to their gas masks, and to wear them periodically for at least 15 minutes, in order to become accustomed to their use. Tests and adjustments will be made by the nearest Warden. Defects should be reported at once. Replacements will be made by the Head Warden for a small charge. No charge will be made in the case of children, if reasonable care has been taken. Babies' Helmets, however, must be maintained at the parents' expense.

Babies' Helmets can be obtained on application to Mrs Searle, 90 High St, or the Head Warden. Special masks for invalids with respiratory troubles &c are available. Application for a certificate to be signed by a doctor should be made to the Head Warden.

PROCEDURE IN THE EVENT OF AIR-RAID DAMAGE

Responsibility for the conduct of the ARP services rests with the ARP Controller (Mr Tabrum, Clerk of the CC), and all reports by the services are made to the Control Room (Shire Hall), where the officer in charge is responsible for supplying assistance if required. In the event of Air-Raid Damage the Wardens will be responsible for reporting the incident, for summoning the local services, and guiding them to the site, and also for making subsequent reports to the Control Room. The Wardens may establish an Incident Post at the nearest telephone, with the permission of the owner. Each Service called by the Wardens will be responsible to its own leader or deputy. In order to co-ordinate the work of rescue, reports will be made through the Incident Post. The Police are responsible for the control of traffic or access of persons to the neighbourhood of the incident and for the maintenance of law and order.

In the event of a major incident an Incident Officer will be sent from Police HQ, who will assume control of the Incident Post. The Incident Officer can order the evacuation of houses which he considers dangerous.

REST CENTRES

In case persons are rendered homeless by reason of Air-Raid Damage, or a delayed action bomb, temporary accommodation will be provided at Girton College (Tel 76219) and LHS (Tel 76129). A list of persons who have offered to put cars at the disposal of the Wardens for evacuation purposes has been drawn up: further offers would be gladly received by the Head ARW.

If persons rendered homeless by enemy action are without means, application should be made to the Assistance Board (Salisbury Villas, Station Rd, Cambridge), who will provide for immediate needs, including furniture and clothing. If the undermentioned things are lost, apply as follows:

Identity Card	Chesterton RDC (Tel 3422)
Food Ration Book	Chesterton RDC (Tel 3422)
Old Age Pension Book	Ministry of Health, Pensions Branch, Blackpool, giving full name, former and new address, and nearest Post Office.
NH Insurance Card	Post Office
Unemployment Book	Employment Exchange, Newnham
gas mask	Head Air-Raid Warden

DAMAGED HOUSES

A 'First Aid' service to make damaged houses again habitable is provided by the Chesterton RDC Application for this service should be made direct to the Council's Surveyor at the Old County Hall, Hobson St, Cambridge (Tel 3422), or to one of the local Councillors – Mr Pease, 1 High St (Tel 76134), or Mr Frank Skinner, 30 Pepys Way.

WARDENS' ORGANISATION

Head Air-Raid Warden	Dr Walton, 16 Girton Rd	Tel 76137
Business Hours	Tuesdays and Fridays	6–9pm
Deputy Head Warden	Mr Kelsall, 2 St Margaret's Rd	Tel 76222

Head Report Centre, 16 Girton Rd   Tel 76137

Wardens &	Dr Walton		
Messengers	Mr Kelsall	2 St Margaret's Rd	Tel 76222
	Mr Nisbet	21 St Margaret's Rd	
	Mr Hawke	6 Bandon Rd	
	Mr Hartnoll	26 St Margaret's Rd	Tel 76277
	Mr Tadman (Day)	Animal Research Station	Tel 76278

Night Watch,   116 Thornton Rd   Tel 76101

Warden	Mr Duckett
Watchers	Messrs Beaumont, Beaumont, Blott, Brading, Fairley, Franklin, Gibson, Havers, Huke, Lawrence, McFarlane, Monkman, Morris, Pinder, Rhoden, Secker, Sexton, Smith, Sumpter, Wolf.

Sub-Report Centre, The Wellbrook Laundry   **Tel 76161**
Warden   Mr HG Lilley   28 Pepys Way
Sub-Report Centre (Day)
                    St John's Farm, High St, Mr Hall   Tel 76263
                    92 High St, Mrs Martin   Tel 76163
                    (Alternate Weeks)
Wardens   Mr Porter   32 Cambridge Rd   Tel 76261
& Messengers   Mr C Nightingale   12 Church Lane
                    Mr Amps   Bridleway, Duck End
                    Mr Kidman   4 Dodford Lane
                    Mr Cornell   2 Dodford Lane
                    Mrs Searle   90 High St
                    Miss Fairey   90 High St
                    Mr Wilson   10 Duck End

Night Watch,   **ARP Post, The Cookery School**   **Tel 76334**
Wardens &   Messrs Porter, Nightingale, Kidman,
Messengers   Cornell, Amps, Wilson
Watchers   Messrs Barber, Barlow, Betson, Camps,
                    A Coe, G Coe, K Evans, WRG Evans,
                    Foster, Hawkes, Hort, Jeffery,
                    SV Nightingale, Rule, Shaddick,
                    Strachan, Teff, Watson

Sub-Report Centre, Madingley Turn,
                    Huntingdon Rd   Tel Madingley 210
Warden   Miss Walliker

Sub-Report Centre, Girton College   **Tel 76219**
Wardens   Miss Robertson
                    Miss Smith
                    Miss Jolliffe
Night Watchers Messrs Brett, Cockell, C Cole, W Cole,
                    Dean, Evans, Halls, Harpner, King,
                    Lofts, Muggleton, Pace, FS Sharp,
                    JF Sharp

Night Watches, which are not directly under the Wardens'
organisation, have also been established at the Wellbrook Laundry,
the University Farm (Animal Research Station), Catch Hall Farm,
St Margaret's Rd, Bandon Rd, & LHS.

THE SPECIAL CONSTABULARY

Head Special Constable Mr Newton, 'Ramsea', 135 High St
Section A

Sgt	Mr Rudd, Girton Garage, Huntingdon Rd	Tel 76128
	Mr Foskett, Llanberis, Girton Rd	Tel 76184
	Mr AE Garner, 26 Girton Rd	
	Mr G Lilley, 64 Thornton Rd	
	Mr Marchant, Sunnyside, Church Lane	
	Mr Purkis, 1 Pepys Way	
	Mr JF Rawlings, 84 Thornton Rd	
	Mr Wilderspin, 26 Girton Rd	
	Mr Frost, Pepys Way	

Section B

Sgt	Mr Fairey, 90 High St	
	Mr Chandler, Duck End	
	Mr Hunt, 79 Cambridge Rd	Tel 76108
	Mr Jones, 44 Woodlands Park	
	Mr Mitham, 101 High St	
	Mr Searle, 90 High St	
	Mr Holt, 159 Girton Rd	
	Mr Bailey, Homeleigh, Girton Rd	Tel 76122
	Mr Foster, 99 High St	

RESCUE AND DEMOLITION SERVICE

The official Rescue and Demolition Service is provided by the CC, and is centred on the Depôt at Histon. A local Rescue and Utility Squad has, however, been organised in the village under the Leadership of Mr Radford, 11 Pepys Way. Air-Raid damage to houses or public services should be reported to the nearest Warden or Special Constable. A member of the local party takes duty on Siren warning at the ARP Night Post in the Cookery School.

Leader	Mr T Radford	11 Pepys Way	
Deputy Leader	Mr P Skinner	59 Cambridge Rd	
Driver	Mr CW Fletcher	Hicks Lane	Tel 76177
Members	Mr V Chapman	35 Church Lane	
	Mr W Claydon	10 High St	
	Mr R Collinson	5 Cambridge Rd	
	Mr R Evans	3 Cambridge Rd	
	Mr JM Greenwood	37 Thornton Rd	
	Mr C Hancock	53 Hicks Lane	
	Mr S Hankin	15 Dodford Lane	
	Mr E Nightingale	64 Cambridge Rd	

Mr N Nightingale   5 Dodford Lane
Mr B Watson   40 Hicks Lane

FIRST AID PARTY

Leader	Mr Tingey	19 Pepys Way	
		(Messages to Mr Evans)	Tel 76250
		(During business hours)	Tel 3979
Deputy Leader	Mr Dark	17 St Margaret's Rd	
		(During business hours)	Tel 76119

Members

Mr Barrett, 6 Church Lane
Mr Bonsor, 52 Woodlands Park
Mr Chaplin, 15 Pepys Way
Mr Dymond, 31 Pepys Way
Mr Lamaison, 16 Girton Rd   Tel 76137
Mr Marshall, 1 Cambridge Rd
Mr Pease, 1 High St   Tel 76134
Mr Pinder, 47 Thornton Rd
Mr Smith, 10 St Margaret's Rd   Tel 76289

Ambulance & Car Drivers

Mr Hall, St John's Farm, High St   Tel 76263
Mr Ingle, The Stores, Cambridge Rd
Miss Potter, 60 Girton Rd

Dr LM Ingle, 19 St Margaret's Rd (Tel 76340), has kindly offered to go out with the FAP if they are called to an incident.

Members of the RC Detachment have volunteered for duty at the FA Depôt during Alerts which occur in business hours.

First Aid Party Depôt
Conservative Room, Cambridge Rd (Tel 76173)

Casualties should be reported to Wardens and Special Constables and to the Report Centres. Casualties may be reported to the FA Depôt, but this is not a FA Post, and severe casualties will be taken to Cambridge for treatment.

FIRE FIGHTING

Girton Parish is protected by the Cambridge Borough Fire Brigade and by the Borough Auxiliary Fire Service. An outbreak of fire should be reported direct to the Borough Fire Brigade from the nearest telephone (Dial '0'). The local Report Centre should also be notified at once. A Manual Fire Engine has been stationed at 12 Cambridge Rd, in order to provide 'First Aid' in the parish before the arrival of the Borough Brigade. This engine is in charge of Mr Irvine

King, The Bungalow, The Rec. Tel during business hours 76134.
Other members of the local service are:

> Mr Cyril Matthews, 3 Dodford Lane
> Mr Whitehead, 124 Girton Rd
> Mr Victor Watson, 125 High St
> Mr Ray Watson, 16 Cambridge Rd
> Mr L King, 29 Church Lane
> Mr S Matthews, 48 Church Lane
> Mr E Hales, 52 Hicks Lane
> Mr M Lipscombe, 14 High St

STIRRUP PUMPS

Orders for about 30 pumps, at a cost of £1, were forwarded to the RDC. The Council has been informed that supplies are still being restricted to the more vulnerable areas. There is, however, a plentiful supply of pumps on sale in Cambridge shops, at a higher price. Mr AGG Marshall, 'Broxton', Huntingdon Rd, generously supplied 10 pumps for the use of the Parish. These have been placed in public buildings, or under the care of Wardens. The present allocation is as follows:

Site	Responsible Authority
The Men's Institute	The Trustees.
The School	The Headmaster
The FA Depôt	The FAP Leader.
92 High St, Report Centre	Mrs Martin
4 Dodford Lane	Mr H Kidman
The Hill	Mr Porter
Burrell's Nursery, Huntingdon Rd	Dr Walton
Bunker's Hill Cottages	Dr Walton
Ladysmith Cottages	Dr Walton
Duck End	Mr Amps

Stirrup pumps to be of any value must be kept in good order. The shaft of the plunger should be greased. A drop of oil should be applied to the ball valve at the base of the pump. Pieces from the inner surface of the hose pipe may become detached and block the nozzle, and must be removed. The junction of the hose with the pump may become loose and must be strengthened. The pump should be used for practice at least once a fortnight.

SAND BAGS

It is expected that householders will supply and maintain in good condition their own sand bags for dealing with incendiary bombs.

These should not be filled more than half full, and should be kept dry and not allowed to rot. Sieved ashes from the fireplace may be used instead of sand, and the bags are lighter to handle. 350 sand bags were issued for distribution in the Parish, and have been allocated. A small reserve is available for further distribution if required.

LADDERS

A census of ladders in the Parish has been made, and lists are in the charge of the AFS Officer and the Head Warden.

SALVAGE

The salvage of Paper, Metals and Bones has been organised by a number of local volunteers, working under the general direction of the PC. Mr Palmer, 32 Church Lane, is the official Salvage Officer for the Parish. Bones should be put into the receptacles provided at several places in the Parish, and metal scrap should be put out with the unburnable rubbish at the ordinary monthly collection. The old metal is sorted out by the collectors and put on the official dump at Mr Searle's yard. With regard to paper, about 60 sacks are sent monthly from Girton to London. The paper is sorted under 5 groups, namely, newspapers, books and magazines, cardboard, brown paper and waste (including letter scrap, thin cartons and every kind of clean refuse paper). The work of the sorters would be simplified if householders (1) would exclude everything except paper from their contributions (eg feathers, kitchen and bedroom refuse are not wanted), (2) would send newspapers clean and folded, not rolled into balls. Householders are asked to make far more use of the Depôts kindly provided by local residents for this purpose. It is impossible to make a house-to-house collection throughout the village; but it is possible to collect sacks in cars from sheds or garages lent for this purpose. The depôts in use at present are named below, but offers of others would be much appreciated.

List of Depôts

Girton Rd	Nos 6, 135, 137 & 99
St Margaret's Rd	Nos 10 & 24
Thornton Rd	Nos 93, 80, 77, 43B, 34, 33, 21 & 6
Pepys Way	No 15
Woodlands	Nos 12, 19 & 52
Church Lane	Nos 26 & 46
High St	Nos 102 & 79
Cambridge Rd	No 12

CAMBRIDGE EXPRESS

Minutes of the Girton Invasion Committee
Joint Civil Defence Services Committee

A meeting of the Heads of the Civil Defence Services and others was held in the VI on June 12th at 8.30pm.

Present:
	Dr A Walton	Head ARW, Convenor
	Mrs Green	Women's Voluntary Service
	Miss Robertson	Girton College
	Mr Rudd	} Special Constabulary
	Mr Fairey	
	Sgt Read	} CC Police
	WR Smith	
	Mr King	AFS
	Mr Skinner	Rescue Party
	Mr Garner	Girton Endowed School.
	Dr Gane	Home Guard
	Mr Tingey	FAP
	Mr Pease	Parish Council

The Convenor explained that he had been asked by the ARP Controller to convene a meeting to discuss plans which might have to be adopted in the event of an invasion. He read the communication which he had received from the Controller and proposed the election of Mr Pease as Chairman of the meeting. This was seconded by Mr Garner. Dr Gane proposed the election of Dr Walton, who declined the office on the grounds that in the event of invasion the Office of Head Warden would be a sufficient responsibility and the duties of the 2 offices might clash. There being no further nominations Mr Pease was declared elected and took the chair.

The Chairman proposed the election of Dr Walton as Secretary and this was seconded by Mr Rudd. The Chairman then asked for a statement on behalf of the various Services. The Head Warden proposed the establishment of a GHQ which would at the same time coordinate the work of the different services and serve as an Official Bureau of Information for the General Public. Sgt Read proposed that before discussing details the membership of the Committee should be decided and that detailed proposals should be considered by a small executive for submission to the Committee at a later date. This was agreed to, and the Committee decided that the following should constitute the General Committee.

Wardens	The Head Warden and Deputy
Special Constables & CC Police	} 2 Representatives
FAP	Mr Tingey and Deputy

AFS	2 Representatives
Home Guard	2 Representatives
Rescue Party	2 Representatives
Girton College	2 Representatives
Parish Council	2 Representatives
RC Detachment	One Representative
WVS	
Women's Institute	
Men's Institute	
Church Council	
Chapel Council	
The Food Organiser	
The Wellbrook Laundry	
Littleton School	
Rudd's Garage	
Dr Ingle	Medical Representative
Mrs Pease	Resident Magistrate

Sgt Read proposed and Dr Gane seconded the election of a provisional executive committee.

The following were proposed: Dr Gane, Mr Pease, Dr Walton.

The meeting decided to call the General Committee for 8pm on June 18th.

[signed] M Pease 18/6/41

Provisional Executive Committee Meeting
No 1 High St. Monday 16th June 1941

Present: Mr Pease in the chair. Dr Walton (Secretary), Dr Gane, Miss Robertson.

Miss Robertson reported that the Managers of the Wellbrook Laundry had agreed to the establishment of a GHQ and Information Bureau at the Laundry in the event of an Invasion. It was decided to recommend to the General Committee the election of 2 representatives from the following organisations: The Wardens, Special Constables, FAP, AFS, HG, Rescue Party, PC and Girton College; and 1 representative from the list of other organisations invited by decision of the Meeting on June 14th; and in addition the Rural District Councillor Mr Skinner, the deputy Billeting Officer Mr Yale and the representative of the Nursing Association. It was decided to recommend the election of an Executive Committee of 8 persons of which one representative should be chosen from the Wardens, the PC, Girton College and the HG; and that 3 representatives should be elected from the General Committee

irrespective of office. It was decided to recommend that the term of office of the Executive should be one year. It was decided also to recommend that the Executive Committee should report back to the General Committee in about one month's time.
[signed] M Pease 27/6/41

Joint Civil Defence Services General Committee.
Held in the Men's Institute on June 18th at 8pm
  Mr Pease in the chair.
Present:

	Mr Tingey	FAP
	Mr Dark	FAP
	Dr Ingle	Medical Representative
	Mrs Leakey	Food Controller
	Mrs Stewart	Women's Institute
	Miss Robertson	Girton College
	Miss Smith	Girton College
	Mrs Green	WVS
	Mr Chaplin	Church Council
	Mr Evans	GDNA
	Mr Burgess	The Boys Club
	Mr Munden	Littleton School
	Mr Skinner	RDC
	Mr Garner	Girton Endowed School
	Mr Fairey	Special Constable
	Mr King	AFS
	Mr Monkman	Home Guard 90 Thornton Rd
	Mr Smith	Constable
	Mrs G Nightingale	Billeting Officer
	Mr Rudd	Special Constable
	Mrs Pease JP	CC
	Mr Sharp	Nursing Association
	Miss Bonsor	RC Detachment
	Dr Gane	Home Guard
	Mr Foster	Baptist Church Council
	Mrs Vellacott	Infant Welfare Centre
	Mr Lilley	Parish Council
	Mr Pease	Parish Council
	Dr Walton	Air-Raid Warden
	Mrs Macalister	
	Dr Hertz	

The General Committee ratified the election of Mr Pease as chairman, who then called upon Dr Walton, Head ARW, to make an explanatory statement. Dr Walton outlined the contingencies which might arise in the village in the event of invasion: Isolation of the village from supplies; Breakdown of official communications from Govt Departments and Authorities; Influx of refugees; Need for protection of the civilian population against air-raids, gas, tanks &c; Possible evacuation of the civilian population including refugees. The problems which might have to be dealt with locally concerned: Food distribution and the organisation of Feeding centres; Health Services; ARP Services; Water Supply; Refugees and billeting; Transport; and the distribution of information to the public.

The meeting then approved the recommendation of the provisional executive that the General Committee should consist of representatives of the organisations present, and that the Executive Committee should consist of one representative of the following organisations.

The Police
The Wardens
The Parish Council
Girton College
The Home Guard

And 3 members to be elected from the General Committee. It was also agreed that the term of office should be for one year.

The following were proposed and seconded for election to the executive: Mr Rudd, Mrs Pease, Mr Sharp, Mr Garner, Mr Fairey, Mrs Leakey.

On a ballot vote Mrs Leakey and Mr Garner were declared elected, and Mr Rudd & Mrs Pease tied for the third place. On a show of hands Mrs Pease was declared elected.

The General Committee approved the recommendation of the provisional executive that a Services HQ and General Information Bureau should be set up at the Wellbrook Laundry in the event of invasion.

The Executive Committee were instructed to prepare a memorandum dealing with the various problems which might arise in the event of invasion and to report back to the General Committee in about one months time.

[signed] MS Pease 10/10/41

Joint Civil Defence Services Executive Committee.
Held at No 1 High St on June 27th at 8pm

Mr Pease in the Chair. Also present: Mrs Pease, Mrs Leakey, Miss Robertson, Mr Newton, Mr Garner, Dr Gane, Dr Walton.

The preparation of the memoranda dealing with various aspects of invasion, was entrusted to the following members of the executive.

Food	Mr Pease and Mrs Leakey
Health Services	Miss Robertson
Water Supply	Mr Newton & Mr Garner
Transport	} Dr Gane
Fuel	
Legal Aspects	Mrs Pease & Mr Newton
Civil Defence	Dr Gane & Dr Walton

Members of the executive were authorised to co-opt outside help in the preparation of the memoranda.
[signed] MS Pease 11/7/41

Minutes of Joint Civil Defence Services Executive Committee.
Held at No 1 High St on Friday 11th July 1941 at 8pm

Mr Pease in the chair. Also present: Mrs Pease, Mrs Leakey, Mr Newton, Mr Garner, Dr Gane, Dr Walton, Dr Hertz (Co-opted).

The secretary presented the memorandum on Health Services prepared by Miss Robertson who was unable to be present. He reported that Dr Hertz had consented to take charge of the emergency hospital and medical requirements and had been invited to attend the meeting. The memorandum was then discussed. LHS was thought to be unsuitable as a temporary hospital as it was already allocated to the HG as Battle HQ and because of its strategic position might be the centre of hostilities. The Committee decided that several alternative buildings might be suitable. Mrs Leakey offered the use of her house. Mr Pease undertook to approach Mr Tucker on the subject of the Rectory, and Mrs Pease undertook to make enquiries concerning the Isolation Hospital Oakington Rd, and also to find out what medical supplies were there available.

Dr Hertz raised the question of her possible evacuation from the district in the event of invasion. The Committee decided that when their report was presented to the Authorities application for Home Office Permission for Dr Hertz to remain should be made.

The following additional Drs resident in the neighbourhood were added to the list of personnel. Dr Brereton 6 Howes Place & Dr Macirone 14 Howes Place. The following trained nurses were also added to the list.

Mrs Goff	Binfield High St
Mrs Hallam	7 Pepys Way
Miss Bruce	St Margaret's Rd
Miss Billequez	92 High St

Dr Walton reported that much of the equipment given in Miss Robertson's list was available at the Animal Research Station and that Dr Hammond, the director, had given permission for reserve stocks of instruments, disinfectants &c, to be held in reserve in the case of emergency.

For hospital use it was suggested by Dr Hertz that acetylene lamps and a stock of carbide might be kept. Dr Walton undertook to enquire about the possibility of obtaining a cylinder of oxygen.

Mr Pease undertook to inquire of the Nursing Association whether obstetrical instruments would be obtainable in case of emergency.

Mr Newton & Mr Garner presented a memorandum on emergency water supply. With the possible exception of Thornton Rd the Parish is well supplied with wells and it was thought that Girton College would be able to supply this district. Mr Pease undertook to raise the question of repairing some derelict wells and pumps at the next meeting of the RDC.

Dr Gane & Dr Walton presented a memorandum on CD, which is appended to the minutes.

Dr Gane reported that he had applied through the HG for a report from the RAF on the advisability of camouflaging the Laundry or other prominent buildings.

[signed] MS Pease 25/7/41

Minutes of Joint Civil Defence Services Executive Committee.
Held at 1 High St on Friday 25 July 1941 at 8pm.

Mr Pease in the Chair. Also present: Mrs Pease, Mrs Leakey, Dr Hertz, Miss Robertson, Mr Newton, Mr Garner, Dr Gane, Dr Walton.

On business arising out of the minutes of previous meeting.

Mr Pease reported that the repair of pumps and wells in the Parish had been raised at the Chesterton RDC who had decided that it could not authorise expenditure on this account but had submitted an enquiry to the Home Office.

Dr Gane reported that the RAF did not consider the Laundry to be particularly conspicuous from the air.

Mr Pease reported that the Nursing Association had undertaken to provide obstetrical instruments in case of emergency.

Dr Hertz reported that she and Mr Tingey had inspected the Rectory and the Isolation Hospital with a view to their use in the case of invasion. The Rectory was unsuitable for several reasons. The Isolation Hospital was ideal except for its distance from the Parish. Several minor repairs would be required, and provision made for Fire Fighting. Miss Robertson, Dr Hertz and Dr Walton were requested to draw up an inventory of requirements and submit it to the Clerk of the CC. Since the Hospital had been used for Scarlet Fever it would be unwise to use it for immediate surgical or maternity cases.

It was proposed however that if beds were provided at the FA Depôt, this could be used as a clearing station for surgical cases. Maternity cases would certainly be attended in private houses.

Mr Garner reported that he had been asked to house 40 mattresses and 80 blankets on behalf of the Education Committee in connection with the Feeding Centre at the School and it was decided that these could be stored at the Depôt and used in emergency.

Dr Gane reported that the inventory of vehicles was not complete but would be available at the next meeting.

Dr Walton reported that he had received communications on the subjects of Crop protection from fire and Contamination of crops from poison gas, and that he would take necessary action to inform the farmers concerned.

[signed] MS Pease 8/8/41

Minutes of Joint Civil Defence Services Executive Committee
Held at 1 High St on Friday 8th Aug 1941 at 8pm

Mr Pease in the chair. Also present: Mrs Pease, Miss Robertson, Dr Hertz, Mr Garner, Mr Newton, Dr Walton.

Apologies for absence were received from Mrs Leakey & Dr Gane.

Correspondence from Mr Tingey was read concerning the proposed use of the FA Depôt as a clearing station for casualties. He thought the Depôt unsuitable except for the treatment of minor casualties, as the Depôt would be in constant use during hostilities by the personnel of the FAP. Dr Hertz was asked to arrange with Mr Tingey to visit together Mrs Green and to report on the possibility of using her house [Culdrein] as a temporary hospital & clearing station. Mr Tingey also wrote to the effect that he considered the FA Depôt unsuitable for the storage of blankets. Mr Garner undertook to store the blankets at the Men's Institute.

Mrs Pease undertook to see that the CC made the necessary repairs to the Isolation Hospital.

[signed] MS Pease 29/8/41

Minutes of Joint Civil Defence Services Executive Committee
held at 1 High St on Friday 29 Aug 1941

Mr Pease in the chair. Also present: Mrs Pease, Dr Hertz, Dr Gane, Mr Newton, Dr Walton.

Apologies for absence were received from Miss Robertson.

Arising out of the minutes of last meeting Dr Hertz reported that she had interviewed Mrs Green who had expressed her willingness to put her house [Culdrein] at the Committee's disposal for an emergency hospital. Dr Hertz thought 10–20 patients could be provided for.

The Committee decided to call the General Committee on Friday 26th Sep subject to the Men's Institute being available. Dr Walton undertook to book the Institute for this date.

Miss Robertson and Dr Hertz were asked to prepare the final report on the Medical Services.

Dr Walton undertook to prepare the report on Defence Services. Dr Gane undertook to complete the reports on Fuel and Transport.

Mr Pease presented a preliminary report on Food and undertook to complete it as soon as possible. Mrs Pease presented a preliminary report on the Legal aspects.

Dr Walton reported that he had received a communication from the ARP Controller on the subject of incendiary 'leaves' used against standing crops and had taken steps to inform the farmers of the neighbourhood and had also asked Mr Garner to warn children against the danger of picking up the 'leaves'.

[signed] MS Pease [no date]

Minutes of Joint Civil Defence Services Executive Committee held at 1 High St on Monday 15th Sep 1941

Mr Pease in the Chair. Also present: Mrs Pease, Dr Hertz, Dr Gane, Mr Newton, Mr Garner, Miss Robertson, Dr Walton.

The report on medical services presented by Miss Robertson was finally approved. The secretary was instructed to write to the ARP Controller on the subject of Dr Hertz's position with regard to taking up the duties of medical officer in the event of invasion.

The report on the emergency water supply was adopted.

Dr Gane was asked to make some alteration in the report on fuel and submit it as an appendix to the Food Report.

Mr Pease undertook to complete the Food Report and Mrs Pease undertook to complete the report on Legal aspects.

The secretary was asked to collect all the reports and to make arrangements for their duplication and distribution to the General Committee before the General Meeting.

[signed] MS Pease [no date]

Minutes of Joint Civil Defence Services Committee on Invasion, held at the Men's Institute 10 Oct 1941

Mr Pease in the chair

Present:		
	Mr ML Cornell	Wardens
	Miss FM Smith	Girton College
	Dr Hertz	Medical Representative
	Mrs Macalister	Matron
	Miss Bonsor	RC
	Mrs Nightingale	Billeting Officer
	Mr Foster	Baptist Church Council
	Mr King	AFS
	Mr Garner	Girton School
	Mr FG Evans	Girton Nursing Association
	Mrs Leakey	Food Officer
	Mrs Chaplin	Church Council
	Mr Dark	FAP
	Dr Gane	Home Guard
	Mrs Green	WVS
	Mrs Pease	Magistrate and CC
	Mrs Stewart	Women's Institute
	Dr Walton	Wardens & Sec

The following sent apologies for absence

Miss Robertson, Mrs Yule, Mr Monkman Mr Tingey Mrs Vellacott Mr Smith Mr Redford and Mr Fairey.

On the recommendation of the Executive Committee the Committee decided to co-opt Dr Hertz and Mrs Macalister.

The Report of Executive which had been circulated to members and which is appended to the minutes was considered. Minor amendments were made and the final preparation of the Report was left to the Chairman and the Secretary.

It was notified to the Committee by the secretary that he had received a list of hospital equipment from Miss Bonsor.

[signed] MS Pease 2/6/42

Minutes of IC Executive held at 1 High St Apr 9th at 8.15

Mr Pease in the chair. Also present: Mrs Pease, Dr Hertz, Mr Tingey, Mr Garner, Dr Walton.

The Committee discussed matters arising out of the ARP Controller's comments on the Memorandum, and matters arising out of the Parish Meeting held on Mar 30th and adjourned until Apr 13th.

The Committee asked Mr Tingey to fill the place on the Executive rendered vacant by Miss Robertson's resignation and to report on the Medical Services at the Parish Meeting. Mr Tingey accepted the invitation and asked if he might co-opt Mr Dark and Dr Smith. This was agreed.

The Secretary was asked to communicate with the Chief Constable on the subject of Dr Hertz's exemption from the Aliens Restriction Orders, and on the subject of the signing of official notices mentioned in Par 1 of the Memorandum.

On Mr Tingey's recommendation the Committee decided to provide the 6 hurricane lamps, 5gal of paraffin and a funnel for the Emergency Hospital. Mr Tingey was asked to procure these and the Secretary was asked to apply to the PC for the expense to be met from the salvage account.

Mrs Pease undertook to enquire about disinfectants at the Isolation Hospital.

The secretary undertook to enquire about the possibility of procuring an emergency supply of certain drugs and anti-tetanus vaccine.

[signed] MS Pease 25.6.42

Minutes of Invasion Committee held at the Village Institute on Friday 29th May 1942 at 8.15pm.

Mrs Pease in the Chair

Members of the IC and the Defence Services engaged in the Invasion Exercise 'CC' held on May 16th – 17th were present.

In the absence of the Chairman, who attended a meeting called by the Regional Commissioner to discuss the Exercise in Cambridge, the Senior Umpire Mrs Pease took the chair.

The Head Warden described the various incidents which occurred in the village.

Points raised for further investigation were: The duplication of messages, and responsibility for the direction of fire fighting when the Borough NFS have been called. The lack of static water supply to the Thornton Rd section.

In the Umpires' report the advisability of arranging adequate rest periods for men on duty was stressed.

The leader of the FAP Mr Tingey gave a report on the work of the Party. He raised the question of co-operation with the RC, and also asked that the Committee press for a permit for Dr Hertz to be released from the Curfew Restrictions of the Aliens Act. Further discussion on the Medical Services was postponed until the

Committee met on Tuesday 2nd May. The Secretary notified the meeting of the time and place of this meeting.

Prof Green criticised the system of sending messages from the Wardens to the HGHQ. The Senior Umpire suggested that exercises should be held so that the sending of messages could be practised. Mr Pease reported from the meeting held in Cambridge, that the sending of messages, and the number of irrelevant messages sent to the Control had been much criticised. He also reported that in many parishes the official notice boards had not been kept under strict observation.

[signed] MS Pease June 2nd 1942

Minutes of Invasion Committee held at the Village Institute on Tuesday June 2nd at 8.15pm.

Mr Pease in the chair. Also present: Mrs Pease, Mrs Macalister, Mrs Green, Mrs Leakey, Miss Bonsor, Mr Tingey, Mr Monkman, Mr Dark, Mr Barrett, Mr Cornell, Mr , Dr Hertz, Dr Walton (Sec).

Mr Tingey presented the report of the Medical Sub-Committee a copy of which is appended to the minutes. It was agreed that IC's previous decision to regard the Isolation Hospital as the first alternative should be rescinded, and that some site in the village would be more appropriate. A number of sites are mentioned in the report and it was decided that as soon as a state of emergency is declared the choice should be made by a small committee consisting of the Chairman of IC, the Head ARW & the Leader of FAP in consultation with the Senior Military Officer in the village at the time.

Mrs Pease reported that the Isolation Hospital was in order and would be kept in good condition. It was agreed that a list of Medical requirements should be prepared by Mrs Macalister and submitted to the PC on Wed 10 June, with a request that they should be purchased by the Council. The secretary announced that Dr Chang had agreed to be responsible for the collection of instruments from the Animal Research Station and had also volunteered to join the FAP.

Mr Pease proposed that Miss Ashton 64 Thornton Rd be asked to co-operate with Dr Chang in collecting instruments.

Mr Barrett raised the question of training in FA for members of the YMG. Mrs Green, Miss Bonsor and Mr Barrett were asked to undertake the organisation of courses.

Mr Cornell offered on behalf of the Entertainments Committee to organise a Garden Party Entertainment in aid of the Medical

Services. The Committee gratefully accepted Mr Cornell's offer and expressed their appreciation.

Mr Pease reported that the Emergency food supplies had been received in the village.

The Committee decided to call the Annual General Meeting in July. The date to be fixed by the Executive Committee.

The Committee agreed that it was desirable that a new edition of the Parish Bulletin, containing the latest information on Invasion arrangements should be drawn up and distributed to the Public.

It was agreed that a local Invasion Exercise should be arranged within a month's time.
[signed] MS Pease 20.7.42

Minutes of the Invasion Committee Executives, held at 1 High St on Tuesday 23rd June 1942 at 8pm

Mr Pease in the chair. Also present: Prof Green, Mrs Pease, Mr Garner, Dr Walton, Dr Smith, & Mr Chapman (FAP Representatives).

Prof Green gave an outline of the proposed Exercise 'Speed' to be held on Sat 4th July as drawn up by Mr Monkman, and Dr Walton described the arrangements which had been made to procure Umpires, and obtain the co-operation of the Police and Borough Fire Services.

On behalf of the FAP Mr Chaplin asked whether incidents could be arranged which would involve the collection of wounded members of the HG from fields or places away from the village. He also suggested that if possible an incident should be staged in Girton College as the FAP had not had an opportunity of entering the grounds of the College. Dr Walton undertook to convey these requests to Mr Monkman.

Dr Walton reported that the Divisional officer of the NFS was anxious to co-operate in the Exercise and would like an incident staged which would involve transport of water from the Borough. He asked Dr Walton to get in touch with the Victoria Rd Station to make the necessary arrangements.

The Committee decided that a meeting of the services taking part in the exercise should be held soon after the exercise at a time convenient to the Umpires, who would be asked to present reports.
[Signed] MS Pease 6/10/42

The Invasion Committee's Report
PARISH OF GIRTON
Joint Civil Defence Services Committee on Invasion
REPORT OCTOBER 1941

1. General Provisions in the Event of Invasion

The Govt has already issued to each householder a leaflet on 'Beating The Invader' which instructs the public what to do in the event of invasion, and ARW have also received a supplementary pamphlet on how to advise the public on the instructions given, These instructions should be taken as a basis but require amplification by special local arrangements.

2. General Headquarters

The Committee recommend that the Wellbrook Laundry be used as a GHQ for all CD and all Administrative Services. Sanction for this has been obtained from the Laundry Directors. The RAF report that the Laundry is not particularly conspicuous from the air. Besides coordinating the Services the GHQ will keep in touch as far as possible with the National Authorities and the Military and will act as an Official Information Bureau for the public. Official notices will be posted outside the building and on official notice boards only. These notice boards will be as follows: Parish Notice Board, Rec; the VI; Parish Notice Board, Girton Corner; The HG Hut, Thornton Rd, The Post Office, High St. All official notices will be signed either by the Chairman of the PC (Mr Pease), the Head Special Constable (Mr Fairey) or the Head ARW (Dr Walton). This is intended to reduce the risk of spreading false rumours and unofficial orders. Official documents and texts will be kept in triplicate; one set of copies at the Laundry, one with Mr Pease, 1 High St, and one with Dr Walton, 16 Girton Rd.

3. Protection of the Public against Enemy Action

Many householders have already made some provision against Air-Raids, such as the construction of shelters, refuge rooms &c. Should invasion become imminent these can be extended. The Wardens in consultation with members of the building trade are prepared to give advice and several Govt pamphlets on the subject are available. It is not proposed, at present, to advocate any special programme of trench or shelter construction.

Should fighting break out in or near the village the public are advised to keep indoors or in their shelters. If the houses are made the objective of an attack and evacuation is ordered by the military or police, the public should on no account take to flight along the roads or across open fields but should take cover away from the roads but as near the village as possible. While circumstances would determine which sites would be most suitable for this purpose, the following possibilities are suggested:

District 1   Huntingdon Rd, Girton Rd (S of Laundry) and Thornton Rd to cover at Burrell's Nursery. Chivers' Orchards and Mr Skeel's Orchard, via Thornton Rd.

District 2   Girton Rd (N of Laundry) and Pepys Way to cover at Mr Skeel's Orchard.

District 3   Hicks Lane, Duck End, Church Lane and Cambridge Rd to cover at Messrs Betson's and Burrows' Orchards.

District 4   High St, Woodlands Park, Dodford Lane. Mr Coe's Orchard on Histon footpath and/or the Isolation Hospital and surrounding orchards.

Wardens and Special Constable would be required to conduct the public to these centres and keep in touch with HQ and the FA and other services.

4. Transport in the Event of Evacuation

The following census has been made of transport facilities available in the village.

Population	nearly 3,000
Private cars	132
Seating capacity	527
Vans	8
Horses	16
Cycles	about 1,000

The population could not be evacuated without extra transport, even if one third of the people were prepared to cycle. The vans would be required for invalids. The authorities would have to provide transport for about 2,000 people.

For rapid removal of the population transport should be directed from the General Services HQ at the Wellbrook Laundry to 6 collecting Centres. These are

Huntingdon Rd

St Margaret's Rd, Bandon Rd and Girton Rd (S of Laundry)

Thornton Rd

Pepys Way and Girton Rd (N of Laundry)

Church Lane, Hicks Lane and Cambridge Rd

High St, Woodlands Park and Dodford Lane.

It may be necessary to collect the population from Orchards and trenches where they have had to seek refuge. These have been specified already in the report.

Special Constable and Wardens would be responsible for the

arrangements at each of the collecting points,

5. Medical Services

The Committee have considered the question of the Medical Services which would be necessary and available for Girton Village in the event of all communication being cut off between the Village and Cambridge. The matter has been dealt with under 6 heads: Hospital Accommodation, Medical Personnel, Trained Nurses, RC Detachment, FAP and Equipment.

The Committee recommend that the Isolation Hospital at Oakington put in order for use as the main hospital for treatment of casualties and in case of epidemics arising. The Isolation Hospital is equipped with beds and bedding and contains most other hospital necessities. Some minor repairs would be required to put the hospital in working order, and stores and paraffin would have to be supplied. As the Isolation Hospital is some distance from the village, it was felt that accommodation situated actually in the village should be available for use at the outset of the emergency as a Casualty Clearing Station, the patients being transferred later, if possible, to the Isolation Hospital. By consent of Mrs Green the ground floor rooms of Culdrein will be available should the state of emergency arise. 10–20 cases could be treated here, and the situation of the house is particularly convenient, as it is opposite the Wellbrook Laundry, which would be used as the Services HQ and General Information Bureau.

There is no registered practitioner in the village. Dr Hertz, 17 Pepys Way has consented to act as the MO in Charge and the following doctors, who live in the village and immediate neighbourhood might be available to help if they were unable to reach their own base in Cambridge:

Dr Brereton, 6 Howes Place, Cambridge.
Dr Ingle, 19 St Margaret's Rd
Dr Macirone, 14 Howes Place, Cambridge.
Dr Paterson, 30 St Margaret's Rd
Dr Taylor, 7 Bandon Rd.

Mrs Macalister, 143 Girton Rd, will act as Matron in Charge of the Hospital, and the following trained nurses live in the village:

Miss Billequez, 91 High St
Miss Goodenough, St Margaret's Rd
Mrs Hallam, 7 Pepys Way
Mrs Strathey, 2 Pepys Way.

Miss Bonsor, 52 Woodlands Park, Commandant of the Girton Village RC Detachment, will be in charge of the members of her detachment, all of whom have taken the FA and Home Nursing Examinations of the BRCS and hold the necessary certificates. At least 8 members would be available for day or night duty.

The FAP at present consisting of 10 trained men will also be available to deal with casualties &c.

A certain amount of medical and hospital equipment will be required. The majority of the most essential items of the medical equipment for Culdrein can be provided in case of emergency by the Animal Research Station, Huntingdon Rd.

Medical Equipment Available   *Med Equipment Required*

Primus Stove & Fuel	Bicarb of Soda	Lysol
Steriliser	Iodine	A small supply of
Scissors	Dettol	Morphine
Dressing Forceps	Pot Permang	Camphor
Artery Forceps	Thermometers	Caffeine
Scalpels	Hypodermic syringes	Aspirin
Tourniquets	Glucose	Sal volatile
Alcohol		

Hospital Equipment Required for Culdrein

Hot Water Bottles	Sheets
Bedpans	Pillows and Pillow Cases
Bowls	Mattresses
Mackintosh Sheets	Blankets
Soap	Towels
Pails	Old Newspapers
Bandages	Long Kitchen Table

The RC Detachment have undertaken to prepare a list of householders who would be willing to supply these articles in the event of emergency.

The Divisional Food Officer would deal with the question of food supplies for the casualty Clearing Station and the Isolation Hospital.

6.   *FOOD*

In the event of invasion, the local Food Organisers, (Mr Pease, 1 High St and Mrs Leakey, 15 Cambridge Rd) will be responsible for making all arrangements necessary for feeding the village and ensuring a fair distribution of the available food. The local Food Organisers would have full powers to requisition all existing stocks of food stuffs (including animals for slaughter) in the Parish.

The Food Organisers hope to have at their disposal a dump of food, sufficient to provide 2 or 3 days 'iron ration' for each person in the village.

2 contingencies should be considered (1) that the village would be entirely isolated, without gas, electricity, or piped water supply; and (2) that while Cambridge and Cambridge services would be out of reach, contact with Oakington and other villages on the W would remain. The position with regard to the principal food stuffs would be as follows:

BREAD. As long as Oakington could be reached, all the bread needed for Girton could be baked there. Some increased storage of flour and fuel should, however, be made at Oakington. In the event of isolation the position in Girton would be extremely critical. Bread could be baked at the Cookery Room, and in several private houses. But at present no flour is stored in the village and there is no reserve of soft coal suitable for oven firing. A supply of yeast has been laid in by the Food Organisers. But there is an urgent need to provide proper storage for flour and soft coal now.

MEAT. Oakington too can provide all the meat necessary for Girton. It would be necessary to requisition animals in Girton and send them to Oakington for slaughter In the event of isolation arrangements would have to be improved in Girton. Facilities for slaughter could be arranged at Mr Searle's farm; Mr Pickett, 13 Pepys Way is a skilled slaughterman and has undertaken to take charge of a team of helpers who would act under him.

MILK. Girton is not self-supporting in milk. So long as supplies could be got from Oakington and villages further to the W, there should be no shortage. In the event of isolation, the basic ration would be about $\frac{1}{4}$ of a pint per day. Steps would be taken at once to ensure priority for babies, nursing mothers, children, and invalids.

GROCERIES. There are about 3 days of supplies of groceries in the village shops for those who are registered locally. In the emergency, the shops in the village would be closed for a few hours, while existing stocks are checked up, so as to ensure an equal distribution of food to everyone in the village whether customers or not of the local shop. As in the case of flour, it is highly desirable to make provision now for a far larger storage of essential groceries in Girton: at least one week's supply of essential groceries for the whole parish ought to be normally stored in the village shops.

CREDIT. The Food Organisers would, in cases of need, issue food against credit. All food stuffs requisitioned by the Organisers would become the property of the Ministry of Food. After the emergency, the Ministry of Food would pay for the food requisitioned and would collect the debts due from those to whom food had been issued on credit.

The matter of fuel is so important in connection with Girton food that it is dealt with separately in a special report below:

7.   *FUEL*

In the event of a breakdown in the supply of gas and electricity to houses in the parish most of the inhabitants would have to rely on domestic fires for cooking arrangements. Householders are therefore urged to have in reserve a fortnight's supply of coal for this purpose, as it is improbable that there will be any reserve dump of fuel for private (as opposed to communal) use.

For baking there is a limited number of ovens heated by coal which owners could share with their neighbours if fuel were available and so reduce the demand on any communal ovens which may be in use. A certain amount of cooking could be done on paraffin burners, but since paraffin supplies are limited the users of it will not have large supplies in reserve, nor are there any stocks in either of the village shops nor the local garage, The normal weekly consumption of paraffin is estimated at   gallons. [The number is not entered.]

In the event of more of less complete isolation of the Village from both Cambridge and Oakington the parish would have to produce those foodstuffs normally brought in. Bread would be the most serious deficiency to be made good and would have to be produced by a communal effort. Of the few large kitchens available, Girton College and LHS both rely entirely on Cambridge for fuel and could not be operated for a long period on their present reserves.

The Committee would be prepared to set up and operate a number of field ovens. To do so would require a supply of soft coal immediately available. There is no such supply of coal in the parish. The stocks held by the largest consumers (Girton College and Wellbrook Laundry) are unsuitable for burning in grates not equipped with forced draught.

To make 1,000 loaves daily the output would be 42 loaves per hour by working 24 hours per day. If each loaf occupies $\frac{1}{2}$ sq ft of shelf space and with 2 shelves in the oven, the oven floor area would be about 10 sq ft. To maintain an oven of this size at the required temperature would need about 1cwt of coal to make the bed of fire and about 2–3cwt to keep going for 24 hours. Such an estimate as the above must be considered very approximate, since ovens vary greatly in fuel requirements, but a round figure of 5cwt per day should not be too wide of the mark. One ton of coal would suffice for bread making for 4 days.

Small field kitchens and ovens would be more wasteful with fuel than one large unit, but may be required for communal feeding, eg tea, soups, stews &c. If such were the case then the daily consumption of coal could be as high as 1 ton. A dump of 10 tons of coal would meet most contingencies for at least a week, The coal should be stored under cover at the site selected as most suitable for the erection of field ovens.

8.   *EMERGENCY WATER SUPPLY IN GIRTON*

The following sources of water in the village would be available in the case of emergency:

(1) Bored well, hand-pump, at Mr A Coe, Histon Fields, could supply Mr Camps, White House, Oakington Rd and Mr Hinkins.

(2) Bored well, hand-pump, at Manor Farm, (Mr G Coe) could supply all houses to Red House Farm (Mr TH Searle).

(3) 3 surface wells, one mechanical pump, 2 hand-pumps, all water drinkable at Red House Farm (Mr TH Searle). Could supply all Dodford Lane.

(4) Parish Pump opposite St John's Farm, could supply all houses to the Hill.

(5) Littleton House School. Bored well, pump electrically driven. Could supply all houses from Hill to entrance to Woodlands Park, plus all houses in Woodlands Park.

(6) Bored well at Reynolds Close (Mr Pease). Mechanically or hand driven. Could supply all houses up to entrance to Woodlands Park.

(7) Bored well at Mr S Chandler's. Could supply all Duck End and Church Lane to entrance to Hicks Lane.

(8) Surface well at   } Could supply houses in Church Lane
    Mr F Cole   } from Hicks Lane entrance to Green
    Surface well at   } Alternative supply at
    Mr C Nightingale   } The Close (Mrs Leakey)

(9) Hicks Lane. Surface well at Cherry Orchard (pump out of order). Surface well at Mr B Watson (pump out of order). Surface well at Mr Amps (pump in working order). Committee suggest steps be taken to put these pumps in order, then this district would be covered.

(10) Bored well at The Close (Mrs Leakey), Could supply from Hill to Church plus part of Church Lane if necessary (see 8).

(11) Bored well (pump needs slight attention), one surface well (pump electrically driven) at The Mount (Mr E Porter). Could supply houses from Church to Red Gate Cottages.

(12) Surface well (new pump recently installed) at White Gate (Mr S Barnes). Could supply from Red Gate Cottages to Hicks Lane.

(13) Bored well, hand-pump at 'Avondale' Girton Rd, (Mrs Skeel). Could supply all houses in Pepys Way.

(14) Bored well, hand-pump at 112 Girton Rd (Mr W Lingley, Senior). Could supply all houses on Girton Rd, from Mr Duke's, No 159 to No 112 Girton Rd.

(15) Water supply at Wellbrook Laundry. Could supply all houses from 112 Girton Rd, to entrance to Thornton Rd.

(16) Girton College, (with Girton Grange). Bored well, pump windmill driven at the Grange, underground tanks in Main Court of College, partly surface water, can be controlled by mechanically driven pump. Could supply all houses, Thornton Rd to Girton Corner, plus houses at Girton Rd end of Thornton Rd.

Arrangements might have to be made to cart water from Girton College to St Margaret's Rd and Bandon Rd.

(17) Bored well, pump requires attention, at Burrell's Nurseries. Could supply houses on Huntingdon Rd, from Travellers' Rest to College Corner, plus houses at Huntingdon Rd end of Thornton Rd. Steps are being taken by the Chesterton RDC to put this pump in order.

(18) Good supply of water at Howe Farm House (University Farm). Could supply all houses from Girton Corner to Animal Research Institute.

(19) Ladysmith Cottages, Grange Farm, Madingley Turn, and Catch Hall Cottages each have their own supply.

9.   *LEGAL ASPECTS*

After consulting the local Police, the Clerk of the Peace and the Chief Constable, it appears that there is at present no special provision for maintaining law and order, if the village is cut off from the Central Police Station. The local magistrate and policeman have normally power to issue summonses and warrants and to remand accused people in custody for a very limited time, but one magistrate alone has no power to try and sentence. In an ordinary court of summary jurisdiction at least 2 magistrates must be present, the trial must take place in the court house, and a police prosecution is not initiated or conducted by a policeman below the rank of inspector. If Girton were isolated there would be only one magistrate and one Constable available, therefore though criminals could be detained for a day or two they could not be adequately dealt with. Presumably the area would be under martial law, but the military are likely to be far too busy to deal with minor offences or to check such things as looting before it has become serious.

Much trouble, and ultimate shooting, might be prevented if the public knows someone in the district has power to deal at once with any trouble that may occur. We suggest that this can best be done by a declaration, which should be made as widely known as possible, that in the event of a village being cut off, *one* magistrate only and the local policeman, will have all the powers of a court of summary jurisdiction (and possibly of a coroner's court as well). A local lawyer could probably be found to act as clerk of the court. Any offender could then be at once arrested and brought to trial and where necessary imprisoned in the custody of the HG. There appears to be no place suitable for a police cell, so a guard would be necessary.

In any case it is clear that whatever arrangements the Govt does decide to make for preserving order in an isolated village should at once be made quite plain to the magistrates, the police and the public. The present uncertainty as to their powers would lead to weakness should an emergency arise.

RECOMMENDATIONS

1. That the arrangement to make a GHQ for all Civil Defence and Civil Administration at the Wellbrook Laundry be approved.

2. That all official notices should be signed by the Chairman of the Parish Council or the Head Special Constable or the Head Air-Raid Warden and posted only on official notice boards.

3. That should evacuation of the village be necessary it should be directed from the GHQ.

4. That the Isolation Hospital, Oakington Rd, be sanctioned for use as an emergency hospital and put into a state of repair, and that small stocks of disinfectant and paraffin for lighting should be purchased and kept on the premises. For emergency operations an acetylene lamp with stock of carbide should be purchased and placed in charge of the FAP.

5. That Dr Hertz, 17 Pepys Way, Girton, notwithstanding that she is an Alien, be authorised to carry out the duties of a voluntary MO in the event of invasion.

6. That Dr Hertz should be supplied with morphine, camphor, caffeine, sal volatile and aspirin for use in emergency.

7. That provision be made for increasing the stocks of groceries, flour and soft coal in the Parish of Girton.

8. That in the event of invasion one magistrate and the local policeman be authorised to exercise the powers of a court of summary jurisdiction and a coroner's court.

Correspondence

GIRTON PARISH COUNCIL

TD PALMER, Clerk   19th June 1942
Meadway
32 Church Lane
Girton
Cambridge
Dear

I have been asked to convey the thanks of the parish to all who took part in the Invasion Exercise on the night of May 16th–17th. It is realised that the exercise involved all concerned in a sleepless night and in many hours of boredom, but most valuable lessons have been learnt and warm thanks are due to all whose patience and good temper enabled the exercise to be carried out. I would be grateful if you would convey this message of thanks to all the members of your Service and to any volunteers whom you may have called in to help you on the occasion.
Yours very sincerely

Chairman of the Parish Council and
Chairman of the Invasion Committee

THE WAR OFFICE,   11th Sep, 1944
LONDON, SW 1

Sir

I am commanded by the Army Council to inform you, for the information of Mr Herbert Morrison, that the continuance of ICs is no longer considered necessary. The work of these Committees has been invaluable from the military standpoint, and I am to request, therefore, that you will convey the Army Council's appreciation to the civilian members of these Committees for their assistance. I am, Sir,
Your obedient Servant,
(Sgd) GW LAMBERT.
The Minister of Home Security.

3: Replies to Freddie Barrett

M Parnwell

In Mar 1943 Mr FC Barrett of Girton started to correspond with villagers on active service by a monthly newsletter (see *KiT*). Below are extracts from the replies he received in response to those newsletters.

From RM Depôt, Kent, Apr 1943

I am now in a village much smaller than Girton, but I can get some idea of what Girton looks like. But instead of going to Washpit or Woody Green for a stroll, we go along the cliff tops or the Beach.

From RAF, Northern Ireland, June 1943

You asked for a bit of news from me for your next letter. It is very difficult as our letters are rigidly censored, besides most of the things which do happen would lose their amusingness, unless one happened to be very conversant with the RAF 'slang'.

From Northern Ireland, June 1943

This is a very amusing part of the British Isles and I believe most people will agree that the inhabitants are very hospitable. I am looking forward to coming home again, which should be in July. It's one of the pleasures the folks who have never left home know nothing about. The most hardened of fellows act in the way one used to as a child when going on a SS treat. 'Fags' are handed around generously, presents appear from hidden places for their loved ones at home, chocolate (which is rarely eaten by those who have children waiting to welcome them) is carefully counted over bar by bar. No! you don't realise what you've missed. The topic is always turned to 'Leave', that's the one thing we look forward to. You don't hear so much as you would expect to about the War ending, but it's always 'Leave' and 'Home'. If one asked me what struck me most in the Forces, I would immediately reply, the lads' thoughts of those at Home; even the worst of fellows talk about 'Home' with a wistfulness.

From Caterham Barracks, June 1943

I certainly agree that there ought to be some Scheme for further Education of young people up to the age of 18 to 19. It is a surprise to know that the old school where we spent our happiest time of our lives is nearly 100 years old. I am very sorry to hear that the FAP has been broken up, they are doing a fine job of work which could be put side by side with the forces in the front line.

The Entertainments Committee is doing a good job of work for us in the forces and it's very nice to know that we all have so many friends in the village backing us up and working so very hard indeed, because it certainly is hard work preparing and running the Dances, Concerts and Socials &c, and we all appreciate what is being done for us.

From MEF, July 1943

I guess you are all busy Digging, and Fruit Picking &c, for Victory. It's good to hear there are signs of a good harvest, what cause for gratitude to God. 'There shall be seed-time and harvest'.

It is now over $2\frac{1}{2}$ years since I left good old Girton for Egypt. Much could be written on what has happened between then and now, much more will happen, but it's encouraging to reflect on the famous victory of the gallant Eighth Army, among which our village was represented, now they are off again after 'Jerry' in Sicily. We wish them God-speed.

Many of you know from past experience in the 'Great War' of the 'Glamour' (and sweat lost) of the ME, but the tourists have the Pyramids and Sphinx. They are very wonderful, but one can have enough of them, believe me. It will be just grand to breath the fresh air of good old England and gaze on the green fields again. May that day be near.

May I record my appreciation to the Entertainments Committee? Yes! Those half-crowns have been received and I trust acknowledgments safely delivered. It's a grand effort, the Savings Certificate for those of the boys who are unfortunate in being prisoners of war.

The new Education Bill, may it bear much fruit for our children, much is going to fall on their shoulders eventually in the rebuilding of the chaos which will remain after this struggle is over and to work for a Peace which will bring 'Freedom to All'; and one of the weapons which they will need is a good education. If this is achieved, it will be no small consolation to us, who in one form or another are doing our bit and as we remember those who have been called upon to pay the supreme sacrifice, let it be said 'Their works do follow them'.

From HMS *Ganges*, Ipswich, July 1943

Do you know I think this is a life for any man, it is a good life, believe me. I hope to be going on the same work as Ron Lipscombe when I have finished my training. I shall be home on leave in 2 weeks from today for 7 days, then I get posted and wait for a ship.

From 13 Field Dressing Station, Sittingbourne, July 1943

I am one of the lucky ones to be still at home, though I did have a rough trip in Apr 1940 trying to get into Norway. We got within

30 miles of the coast and then our ship was turned back and the evacuation of Norway was started.

I played quite a lot of sport in the army until last Nov when I twisted my knee badly and so finished my football for last season. I was in hospital for a month expecting to have my cartilage removed but the specialist I saw decided it was not necessary and I hope to be fit to start this season off. I am within easy distance of my club at Fulham and do hope to play for them often providing my knee does not let me down again. I have been able to play cricket in spite of my knee and have had a few enjoyable games, 58 being my best knock, and still keeping wicket.

From RAF India Command, Aug 1943

I note with interest that the local CD Services are getting well into their stride, especially the NFS who have 'been in action' which proves that if and when the time comes for them to do their stuff they will be able to have everything under control. I also hope the FAP did very well in the County Competition, according to your letter they should at least pass with honours.

I'll now give you a brief account of my experiences since leaving home. The trip over was uneventful all the way. We stayed in S Africa 4 weeks. I had a very good time there, just imagine, spending a few weeks on a troopship and then being 'let loose' amongst every type of fruit one can think of. Well you can guess what happened. I just 'scoffed and scoffed' bananas, mangoes, &c, &c, &c, but I suffered after. Anyway, the time came to leave, so we proceeded on to this country. We arrived, anxious to hear from home, also to write home now we had completed our sea voyage. It was very hot at first; one who drank very little tea &c, at home soon starts out here, a terrific thirst develops, the chief thirst quencher being tea (or 'char') consumed without exaggeration by the gallon. I'll bet I can now drink any woman (noted tea drinkers!) under the table, whereas at home I drank well below the average. Work came hard at first owing to the heat, but I'm gradually getting used to it now. I'm keeping fit, getting a game of football now and again. I hope to play regularly this winter. I am at present enjoying a rest in the hills, away from the heat and scorched plains. It's really beautiful up here, about 5,000' up, it's quite a change to see the green grass and vegetation, more or less equal to spring at home. It's also nice to sleep in a bed instead of on top.

From Chatham, Aug 1943

It was good to hear in the last letters that news had been received of some of our men from Singapore.

From MEF, Aug 1943

Since I received your last NL I have moved about quite a bit and I am now somewhere in Syria, which I think is much better than Egypt, it's more like good Old England.

From RASC, India Command, Sep 1943

It is now 1 year, 9 months since I left England to do my duty in this part of the globe, during this time I have spent some of it in Africa and Egypt, finally arriving in India. It seems to me like a lifetime but having travelled so many thousands of miles, seen so many places and had so much excitement, it hardly seems possible that so much could be packed into so short a space of time, although during the time I have spent out here I have been in Hospital on several occasions owing to illness and accidents. However, I'm now managing to keep fit and hope to remain so. The more I see of this country the more I realise that there is most definitely no place like the old country. There are a few advantages such as fruit, eggs and cheaper cigarettes but these are nothing compared with what is offered at home.

Regarding the 'tough spots' you would like to hear of, I'm sorry to say our friend the Censor would have something to say in the matter. Security is very strict and one has to be very careful when writing. Without breaking security rules I think I am able to say a little as to what happens in my Unit. As you will know by my address, the work consists of transporting tanks on vehicles, which when loaded weigh about 60 tons. The Unit is half British and half Indian. I am in charge of a section which consists of 5 British soldiers and 5 Indian, and 4 transport vehicles. The work is very hard, especially the maintenance of the vehicles.

From RAOC, BNAF, Sep 1943

Everyone seems to have enjoyed themselves at the Sports on Whit [see *KiT* 13], even though the Army won the challenge match, but then if they had the NZ champion to help them along, it is not very surprising. I was more than glad when I learned that the wives and mothers of the lads in Singapore had at long last had news. It must have been a great day after the long suspense of waiting.

I had to laugh over the episode of the fire at Jack Gunn's [see *Kit* 14], all those fire engines there and then someone puts it out with a stirrup pump, it struck me as being very funny, and I bet the firemen felt rather small as well.

Mr Pease has added a very fine postscript to this NL [*KiT* 15–16], his description of the functions of a PC are very lucid and I realise how much the village owes to him and his untiring efforts, and the village can consider itself very lucky in having a man like him with its interests at heart and able to further those interests by his being on various Public Bodies.

There is quite a variety of fruit grown here, grapes are in season at the moment and we have had some very nice bunches at different times, the vines are actually bushes and they cover the whole countryside for miles around. It is very interesting to watch the Arabs pick them and cart them off to where they are pulped and turned into an amazing variety of wines (and believe me, they are very potent, I've had some). There are also oranges, tangerines, lemons, gorgeous peaches, pomegranates, dates and figs, in their respective seasons, so you can see we do very well for fresh fruit.

From HMS *Howe*, Sep 1943

I have had one or two kicks at the old football, but it's a lot different playing on these hard pitches and very hot as you can imagine, but none the less I enjoyed it although I'm longing for the day when we shall all be home and having another game on the village ground.

From HyAA Regt RA, Lincoln, Oct 1943

The German planes seem to have too much work on their hands to come here. Some nights we are called from bed for some planes, perhaps miles away and then after having us all standing around for some times an hour, shivering with cold, they let us go back to bed. Nearly all of us grumble for being pulled from bed for nothing. Nearly all of us here are learning to drive the transport which keeps arriving every day ready for us to go mobile. We have a course to do of 5 weeks at Leigh on Sea soon and needless to say leave will be stopped while we are there, which pleases no-one at all. We had a concert here on Friday afternoon given by some of the people who are at the Theatre Royal in Lincoln. Jane of the Daily Mirror was here too in the same outfit she wears in the Mirror, also with the little dog. The Gloria Sisters are here too with 6 musical instruments. Martha Green was singing some of the favourites both old and new. 2 of our lads are singing songs too. We had $2\frac{1}{2}$ hours' entertainment. It was very nice. Everyone enjoyed themselves.

The weather is very bad here and living in bell tents makes it a lot worse. I hope our next place will see us in huts again. I started to write this letter just before tea, but now I am trying to finish by candle light. The way we are living here would surprise most people, but we are happy. Our friend the rat comes every night at the same time from the farm buildings which are near at hand. They are not too bad under the tent boards but when they come inside the tent it's beyond a joke.

From HyAA Regt RA, Leigh on Sea, Nov 1943

As you can see from the address we have moved yet again and how I wish I was home again, although I am very lucky still being in England. We are here for just over a week, but still have yet another 4 weeks. We are being taught the right and wrong way a Bty should work as a mobile one. After we pass here we go to join the field Army. I think everyone knows what it will mean.

How many things have changed in the village since the days when Mr Palmer first came to Girton [see *KiT* 32]. Who would have thought that we who were still at school then would be trying to do our best in a war which is the most terrible in history. The war news has cheered everyone up this last few weeks. We are lucky, our billets are in London Road, we have a post office across the road and a paper shop next door. It's the first time for months we have been able to get a paper every morning, being on a gun site in out of the way places. It's good too to be in Billets. We have been pinching coal and coke from the cookhouse and it's real nice sitting in

The Rev PNH Palmer, former Rector of Girton

front of the fires which are going in nearly every room in the house. Some of the Sgts are very worried as we can dodge parades very well, the Billets being spread over a large part of the town. I went to the pictures yesterday afternoon when I should have been on a Drill Parade.

From HMS *Howe*, London, Nov 1943

There is one thing I can tell you and that is it's certainly lovely to feel cooler, it is real cold at times but I would rather have the cold than the heat. I suffered with the heat a lot and had what we call prickly heat, which was terrible. Every time one bends down one would think that somebody had stuck a load of needles in him.

From RAF Weeton, Nov 1943

As you may know I have just finished 8 weeks training at Skegness, where we had rifle drill, fieldcraft and general service training. I am now on a Technical Training Course for 3 months or so, as Instrument Repairer. Am finding the course very interesting so far, and am glad that I came in on this trade. Of course there is a lot of 'swotting' and I expect I shall be very busy during the coming weeks. I feel certain that big things will happen when the chaps all come back and strengthen the foundation already there.

From the short time that I have been in the Service I am convinced that the life is mainly what you make of it yourself. Also have the privilege of visiting places which would otherwise be beyond our reach, and although we don't always visit these places under ideal conditions, we at least gain a wider knowledge of the world in which we live.

From MEF, Nov 1943

When I was coming up by train through Palestine just over a week ago, we passed through a lot of the Palestinian orange groves and I said to myself I wonder what the children of Girton would do now if they are suddenly placed around the village. I don't think the oranges would be there very long.

Where I am now instead of having a rambling rose over your door you have a vine and what lovely grapes they have on them.

From Barry, Dec 1943

As you will have seen by the address I am in S Wales at the moment. I am billeted in a big hotel about $\frac{1}{2}$hr walk from the sea and I don't have to tell you it is very cold here at the moment.

I am working on the docks, driving vehicles from about a mile away, loading them on to ships. It is an extremely interesting job and I wouldn't change it for anything.

I don't expect to be home for Christmas, but according to all accounts I shall have a good time here. The officers are organising a party for us on Christmas Day and we get Boxing Day off as well. So far my Army life has been one big holiday and I don't for one minute regret my volunteering. Sometimes, of course, I get 'browned off', but that's natural. Everyone has a grouse now and then.

From India Command, Dec 1943

I am in the best of health and enjoying active service. It's much better than back at home, we feel that we are doing something to help win this war. I am in the jungle, which is a very interesting place. My pal and I often go for a walk and have a good time looking for snakes and catching butterflies.

We live in a small tent which we stretched out to its fullest to make more room. We have a gramophone which we can play to relieve the monotony of the place. My pal is just putting on his pyjamas so bedtime must be getting near as we go to bed most nights at 8.30pm when not on duty as there is nothing else to do.

From Beds & Herts 54 Div BSHF, Dec 1943

How is the YMG going this year, as I hope there are still many new faces and an enjoyable evening to be had. I'm stationed out in what seems the wilds of England and the house seems haunted to us as it's surrounded by trees and on top of a hill.

I will wish you a Merry Xmas and a Happy New Year and may this be our last war-time Xmas.

From Seighford, Dec 1943

My first thought is to wish you a very happy Xmas and a successful new year. I also wish all the members of Girton serving in HM Forces at home and overseas all the best for the season. No doubt those serving abroad will find it more difficult at Xmas. I know they will get as good a time as they are able. As for myself, all being well, I shall be home for Xmas this year. Last year was my first Xmas in the forces and I sincerely hope that next year a great many others may have the privilege and good luck to be with their families for Xmas.

It is with great interest that I read the NLs and postscripts and I know that it means a great deal of work on your part and I am sure it is appreciated very deeply by all who read them. For those abroad especially it brings, besides their own letters from home, a touch from the village as a whole.

From Cumberland, Dec 1943

As you can see I have moved again, this time into the wilds, in many ways this place reminds me of Iceland with its snow capped mountains, at least they were when we first arrived. Now we are having a spell of mild weather.

The address of our quarters sounds rather grand but I am afraid its grand days are over. Built in 1658 it looks it too. I should hate to think it was my property. Anyway I don't expect our days in it will be long, then, who knows where.

The men of this unit are a fine crowd, they are all out to help and cause very little trouble, something to be grateful for. We have only been here a short time and in that short time the boys have created such an impression that half of them are entertained to tea and supper and Sunday by the local people, who are also putting on a supper tomorrow night. You can gather from that we are not too badly off in the wide open spaces.

From HyAA Regt RA, Leicester, Dec 1943

We have been so unsettled with our address that I could not write. We will be going to firing camp again before the New Year. The NL is very nice and it seems more than nice just before Xmas when those of us who cannot be at home have a letter which brings home very much nearer to us. While we are here it's a rest as we are not operational. I wish you all a Happy New Year and may 1944 see peace once again.

From US Naval Air Station, Brunswick, Maine USA, Jan 1944
Right now I am having a great time, and for Xmas was entertained by an American family and had a really wonderful time, helping to polish off a 22lb Turkey with all the trimmings. Being RN, I can tell you nothing of my sea voyages, or very little else, except that I am hard at work at my present address, though tomorrow, who knows. Please excuse short note, but time is very short indeed, it is now 12.10am on New Year's Morning, and I will have to get some sleeping time in.

From YMCA, Canada, Jan 1944
I had my first leave at Vancouver, and I must say that my stay there seemed to go too quickly. It's a very nice place, but at present there's only one place I would like to see right now, and that the little place on the map called Girton.

From CRE Aerodrome, MEF, Jan 1944
Since I last wrote you I have travelled hundreds, yea thousands, of miles, up into the Western Desert as far as Benghazi and back again – don't think I'm a 'desert rat', no, I haven't had to endure what those boys did and would not dare to take any of the 'glory' due to them. What a grand job they did! Nevertheless, those of us who are rather more in the shade are, I hope, doing our bit.

Just a word on Benghazi, a place that before the war was perhaps hardly a name to many of us. Alas! Hardly a house stands complete, I doubt if there is one. I walked its streets for about 2 months and at the end of that time began to feel morbid as I looked at the desolation. One thing stands erect, though scarred here and there by bullet holes – the Cathedral with its 2 stately Domes, left as it were to remind us that whatever happens around us, one thing will stand – the Sovereignty of Almighty God. Is it not through Him and Him alone can come that 'Peace' for which we are all longing?

I was favoured Xmas Eve in that I was able to get to Bethlehem. I wanted to get to a Service but time forbade, nevertheless could hear the carol service from outside and also visited the spot, down in the crypt of the church, reputed to be where the 'Holy Child' Jesus was born. The birthplace is marked by a star in the floor, whilst near at hand is the 'manger' and a small cave in the rock, now all covered in tapestries, incense is burning, great is the pomp and show, but let us not lose sight of the fact that in those far off days it was just a cave in the rock, no comforts or homes as we know them, it is quite easy now that I have seen the like, to picture what it was in those days, the stable, very small, an ass or two perhaps up one corner and the manger being utilised as a crib for Jesus. It was rather striking too as my friend and I looked away down the valley. What did we see, Shepherds tending their flocks, perhaps sitting by a crude fire? No, but I think we realised a little of their 'fear and astonishment' as on that memorable night the stillness was broken by 'Peace on Earth, goodwill towards men'. Ah, the wonder of it all, it would take reams of paper to tell you of all one sees, perhaps ere long we may be able to sit by our fire-side and relate a few experiences and sights we have seen, which I'm sure would carry many of us back to childhood days.

Xmas has past, we had a grand time too, we were about 33 strong in my unit. Our cook being a 'civvy street' chef knew how to do things. How's this for a menu. Tomato soup, Fish, Turkey, Pork, Potatoes – baked and mashed, Cauliflower, Green Peas and Carrots, Xmas Pudding and Brandy Sauce, Cheese Biscuits, Beer of course finishing off with Turkish Coffee, though for the most part, by the time the Pudding course was over no-one had room left for the rest. It was a really grand 'do' and everyone thoroughly enjoyed it. Then came toasts, the toast to 'absent friends' brought you all into the picture, my mind scanned that little spot in Cambs and I thought of as many of you as could be squeezed into the mind during those few seconds the toast took. I certainly hope you all had as good a time as we did, marred only by being away from loved ones, yet we hope as we did last year and the years before, that it will be the last one away from Home. It's a good tonic to look forward to that reunion day, may it not be far away.

I am forcibly reminded of the English climate today, it is simply teeming with rain, a gale is blowing and it's very cold, though here one has to be more thankful, as it were, that it's raining as it all comes in about the first month of the year, the rest of the year is very hot, it's wonderful how the earth retains the moisture to bring forth the harvest in 6 months' time, how truly wonderful is God's creation.

Oranges! Ha, no doubt you all remember what an orange is like. I passed a remark the other day as I passed 4 or 5 great heaps (I mean heaps too, just as you in England see a heap of potatoes or mangolds, so at the moment we see heaps of lovely Jaffas). How lovely it would be if we could tip a lorry load just outside our schools at home, my, what a time the children, yes and grown-ups too, would have. This however, is only a pleasure in abeyance and we are all looking forward to the day when our ships, instead of carrying weapons of destruction, will again be transporting these good things to England, and other things from England in return.

One last word, as a souvenir of the war I think the NLs with postscripts should be bound and made purchasable in volume form – here's order No. 1.

From MEF, Jan 1944

At the moment we are having a bad thunder storm, also plenty of hail and rain. In England we look for the thunder storms in the summer to get the rain, but here it is in the winter that they look for rain, and they get it too, one minute the ground is dry, the next it is flooded.

From CRE, Persia & Iraq Force, Jan 1944

Roy Naylor

I have a special interest in learning from the NL of the whereabouts of various lads I know. Such familiar names as Stan Dixon, Carlos Griffiths, Roy Naylor &c, who were all members of the Girton Scout Group of which I had the honour of being a Leader with Mr J Rule. I would deem it a great favour if you would send them all my very best wishes and tell them that after the War, and our ultimate return, I am going to organise a magnificent Scouts' re-union in the Village, and am looking forward to seeing them all there.

I am in Iraq, at the moment feeling very cold, but we shall make up for that in the summer when the temperature will soar up to 130°F in the shade, or thereabouts. Then for plenty of iced drinks and plenty of fans to cool the bungalow.

Whereabouts unspecified, Feb 1944

Well, after being on 3 different ships, the one we are on at the present is more like a floating barracks. That is HMS *Nelson*, a grand ship, but we won't be on here for long, I don't suppose. Well, Mr Barrett, time is getting short, so I must leave you now, with best wishes to all at the YMG, and hoping all the boys overseas are fit and well, as this leaves me fit and in high spirits. By the way, not so much spirits, as I am not old enough for RUM.

From Beckenham, Feb 1944

Dear YMG, Just a few lines to thank you all very much for the Xmas present which I was very pleased to receive.

How's the YMG going this year, as you seem to be losing members slowly, but I hope you are getting more members to take their place; let's hope this Blue Pencil war is soon over so we can spend some enjoyable nights at the YMG.

From Enderby Camp, Leicester, Feb 1944

I hope you are right when you talk of this year ending the war in Europe [see *KiT* 46]. It would be so nice to know that those who have been away so long will soon be home. I think that the well-known figure who everyone knows and is so used to seeing around the village, Miss Hibbert-Ware will be missed by many, both old and young. On letting my thoughts go back it does not seem so long ago since I was going with those at school and with Miss Hibbert-Ware to Hatfield and Epping Forests. When someone like her leaves us it brings home how much was done.

It will be no surprise to us all in this Bty to be in some way 'in' on this much talked of Second Front. We cannot complain, if we left for duties overseas tomorrow we have been lucky. It will be 3 years in Sep since I joined up. We have been lucky to stay here so long.

I would have liked to have seen the concert by the boys of LHS. Auntie wrote and told me it was very good.

From AA Bty, Manchester, Feb 1944

I have been to many parts of England, but have never met anyone that I know, nevertheless one is greatly cheered by the kind way in which those at home remember us who are away, how we all look forward to the day when we all return. I think too we shall all strive for those things in the future for which we are fighting, not only for ourselves, but for those of you at home, who have worked and given much for us.

May I in closing thank you and all the kind people in Girton who are giving up so much time and rest which I know you need, to give us pleasure, also for the very kind gifts of Postal Orders.

From RAF Officer's Mess, Mar 1944

My stay in Canada has been a wonderful experience and I have seen many of the wonders of the New World. The people here are looking eagerly forward to the peace to come and realise that they will play no small part in the rebuilding of our own New World. Who knows, there will be hundreds of our friends at home who with adventure in their hearts, with peace and goodwill in their pockets, will see a new, perhaps better way of living among the prairies of Canada.

From HMS *Howe*, Mar 1944

I look forward to receiving your most welcome NLs more than words can explain. The last one was just over a week ago, that being Jan copy in which you give a Report on the Homecoming Fund and very kindly ask us to give our views on the matter. Well, I'm sure it was very nice of you to ask us, Mr Barrett, but all I'm going to say is that I shall be more than satisfied with whatever you decide. Perhaps you will think well that's a good way to get out of it, but I can assure you that that was my point of view as soon as I read your report and what's more you at home are making the fund a success and should therefore have the satisfaction of sharing it out.

It is now over 12 months since I was home and since leaving the old country I have been to some very nice places which have taught me a lot about different things. One place opened my eyes on the housing situation very much.

We are now working with the American Fleet and the mail might now take longer. The mail hasn't been getting home too good, so I'm hoping it won't be much worse.

From RASC, MEF, Mar 1944

Many thanks for the NL which I received a few days ago. The letter came one evening when it was rather wet, so after I had looked through it I passed it round the tent for the other lads to read, also some of the other NLs, they all said what a good thing it was, 2 or 3 of them said they wished that they would start the same sort of thing in their village. Later that evening I had to pack my kit for a move to a much colder part of the world, a place I hadn't been to before. I came to the place where I am now by train. It was so fast in some places that you could get out and walk and keep up with it. At one place I put my hand out of the compartment window and picked some fern that was growing on the rocks. At some parts, if you stepped out of the compartment door you would fall anything from 10 to 500'. We were passing through mountains all the time. It took the train 12 hours to cover about 70 miles.

It's good to hear once again how and where some of the lads are. If there are any of the lads in any of the fighting just now I wish them all the best of luck. I am glad to say I am still OK.

From HyAA Regt RA, Hampshire, Apr 1944

We went to the pictures and saw 'This is the Army', as if we don't see quite enough of it. Still I am in hopes of going again at the weekend.

From Rockingham Camp, Northants, Apr 1944

As you will see we are still this side. would like to know. It's not bad here but small town as it is, not as large a place as Girton, but it has a Picture House, where all the lads when we are out spend most of our time. One would think one were in Scotland here, with all the people being here and working at the Scotch firm's Steel works. We are nearly cut off on this site with pits all round us. The noise of the diggers awakens us each morning, as they grub up the ore. It's quite a network of railways here too with the trucks being pulled and pushed everywhere by little 'Coffee Pot' engines. They are very small, but they make some noise. Still I think we are lucky to have a camp with huts, tents is what we mostly get. Those we carry around with us need burning they are just rotten from the looks of them. One would think they have been left over from the last War.

From HyAA Regt RA, Chorlton-cum-Hardy, Apr 1944

I received last week yet another of your very interesting NL. One's mind truly went with you [see *KiT* 40] to the familiar places you mention, many places are now built on, that as a child I can remember were either fields or allotments.

As you see we have again changed our abode, we are now more in the country, it reminds me of Thornton Road. It is a built-up area, and in spite of Manchester's rather grimy outlook, spring has shown itself and the weather too has looked that way.

No doubt you have read in the papers of the 'Salute the Soldier' week. Here, on Saturday, it was opened with a parade and a march past, in which our Bty took a leading part, also the ATS band. On Piccadilly there is a miniature gun site, in various shops there are exhibitions, in the Art Gallery there is an Allied Nations Exhibition, which I found very interesting, on the walls pictures of the distress caused by bombing, the work going on to build up the attacks, the attacks that are taking, or rather have taken place, and the areas covered by allies and enemy, in one room, on a table is a miniature war base of Germany, lit here and there, the lights go out and one sees flashes representing fires, and the noise just as it was during the raid by our bombers. Another room, called 'Sanctuary' is a tribute to the soldiers, sailors, airmen and civilians who have given and will give their lives in the cause to which we are fighting. Another part is given to Germany, the promises Hitler and his staff have made to their people, and what they have ended up in. Finally, the exhibition ends in a tribute to the gallant men of the Navy.

Last week we had a lecture on the Dominions. One question was 'Should Africa be self-governed?' Some were for, some against, some thought that without Religion they could not make a success of it, others said that if they had their own Govt would we be turned from that country. The decision was, I think, against it, although they should be given a fair chance.

From GHQ India Command, New Delhi, May 1944

It was with great anticipation that I opened Father's letter today knowing quite well that inside would be the NL giving us that feeling of being once again in the village circle. It is truly amazing how close letters can turn our minds back over all the miles until it seems that all the life here is blotted out. To you, all the folks at home and all the lads and lasses who, like me, are so far away I send all the very best of wishes and hope that before long we may once again all meet.

From Grenadier Guards, CMF, May 1944

I look forward to the NLs arriving very much and I still have every one that my Father has forwarded on to me and I often get them out and read them. I am the only one from our village in my Battn, but I'm sure you will be pleased to know that quite a number of my men read the NL and some have even wrote home asking for the same thing to be done in their own district.

I'm afraid I can't give you much news from this part of the world but I don't think the censor will mind me telling you that I have just spent a glorious week's holiday at a seaside resort 30 miles S of Naples. Most of the time was spent on the beach, swimming, boating and sunbathing. Oranges and nuts were very plentiful and most of the gardens consisted of lemon trees and grape vines. Last year during the grape season I was in N Africa, this year it is Italy, and I'm hoping next year it won't be grapes but home and a drink, or maybe two, at The George.

I received an air-letter from my young brother Walter, who you may know is now a Corporal in the RAF stationed at Nassau, Bahamas. He had been in hospital for a month but at the time of writing was fully recovered and said he was having a good time, but like us all is looking forward to returning home.

From Indian Command, May 1944

I am hoping that one of these days when we are pushing our way through the jungle I have the luck to bump into Carlos Griffiths, as they say he is in here somewhere'.

From CMF, May 1944

As you already know, I am now doing my bit in Italy, which in my mind is a much better country than N Africa, the people are much more hard working, also it's not so hot. The good old Rec, as you know my heart and soul was there. It will be grand to get kicking that ball, and getting the willow out. I have played quite a lot of football for our Unit, but not in goal, at centre half.

From Air Command, SE Asia, June 1944

Whilst on leave, which I spent in the hills in the N, I saw some snow. Wouldn't I like to be there now, it's like an oven here.

You will be pleased to hear that I met Tom Impey here on the same camp. I was really amazed. I could hardly believe it at first. It seems very like home being able to have a chat with someone I know.

From Persia & Iraq Force, June 1944

It is getting very hot. The other day the shade temperature reached 113°F. However, it will get much hotter than that very soon. I have known 128°F to be reached. The worst of it is, there isn't much relief after sunset, as the tent seldom falls lower than 90°F all night. You can imagine it is rather 'sticky'.

I was surprised to learn from the NL that Basil Wallis is in Cairo. As I think Miss Wallis types your NL, would you be good enough to ask her if she would send him my best wishes? I have known him since I was very young.

We out here are very encouraged at the Allied invasion of Normandy, and wish all those taking part the very best of good health.

I can imagine that Girton is looking lovely at this time of the year? I would give a lot to be able to see it, if only for a few minutes. One gets very bored having nothing but a desert to look at, with one or two palm trees scattered around.

From RN, Malta, June 1944

I'm back in Malta, now that war in Italy is over. We all expected a rest when we got here after 12 months ops with our MTBs, to find the Navy have gone back to peacetime routine, which gives us plenty of work.

From Flotilla RM, London, Sep 1944

Only yesterday I was going through some stuff and I picked up the latest one [NL] I have received, that's the July edition, and while reading through it (for the tenth time at least since I received it) I thought then how all the other boys feel when they get them, they certainly raise our morale 100%. I am sorry that I am unable to say anything about the place where I am at present, all I can say it is too hot for my liking and the sooner I get back to Girton the better. By the news we are getting from different sources I am hoping that very soon we shall all be back there, and getting down to a normal routine, not forgetting, of course, those who will not be back.

From RAF, MEF, Sep 1944

I am writing to thank you for the most welcome NL which I enjoy reading so much. I look forward to receiving it every month as it brings news of the village and the boys which are serving, although I don't know the lads personally I do by name and I am hoping I shall come across some of them sometime.

From Searchlight Bty, RA Kent, Sep 1944

I am now looking forward to my release from the army. I have now served 7 years, 2 as a territorial and I do feel now that I have done my bit for my country. Although I have not been abroad I have seen a great deal of action on the SE Coast and during the last few months we have taken part in successful actions against Doodlebugs. Some at times were shot down very close to our positions. I have served 2 years now as a detachment commander, in rank of a Lance Sgt and 2 months ago I was promoted to full Sgt, my ambition was to reach this rank, so now I can sit back satisfied with myself making the grade. We are under canvas here and miles from the nearest town. For months now we have been without a wireless set, we have appealed to the local welfare and also to our officers without success, we have no recreation of any sort on site. Could you help us? Hoping you will give this your kindest consideration.

From Field Regt, SEAC, Sep 1944

Owing to security reasons I am unable to tell you a great deal about myself, but I will try to tell a few things which may be of interest. I am at present out of action taking a well earned rest. We have managed to make ourselves fairly comfortable with the aid of tarpaulins and bamboo poles, and of course, the inevitable pieces of string and wire. I have 4 men in my 'basha', as these home-made huts are called. We have made ourselves a bed each out of bamboo, and believe me to a battle weary soldier a bamboo bed is the next best thing to the 'Ritz'. This bamboo is exceedingly versatile stuff, you can make huts, beds, fires, cooking pots for rice out of it, yes and if you are really hungry you can even eat it. Young green bamboo shoots are very tasty when boiled. My job at present is in the signal section of the Bty. This consists chiefly of keeping communications open between the Observation Officer and the guns, it is done sometimes with wireless and at others by telephone, either way it is very interesting, as we sometimes get mixed in with the infantry and have a little hand-to-hand skirmish with our 'little brown brothers', the Japs. The Japanese snipers have a nasty habit of cutting your telephone line and then waiting for you to go out and repair it, but we can shoot as straight as them. Whilst out on patrol recently I was caught by a Japanese booby-trap, but luckily got away with only a slight wound in the head. In spite of an awful haircut given to me by an Indian medical officer, my hair is growing again, and I should be soon quite presentable.

From RA Suffolk, Oct 1944

Duties have been altered so there is very little chance to write except when off duty, which is every 4th day if we are lucky. We have to sit up at night now and rest during the day, and believe me, we don't like it one bit, seems very strange having a hot meal in the middle of the night, still I suppose we will get used to it. Perhaps the Doodlebugs will stop very soon. At least we hope so. One good thing is there are not so many here as were along the S coast, and it's a very good thing too. I managed to get home for a 24 hrs on Sunday. I hitch-hiked home. I did not leave here until 2pm and was in Girton at 5pm, not bad I thought. When everyone gets home again perhaps the School and Village Hall will then be built. Girton has increased quite a lot during the last few years before the war and it should get larger soon as this war is ended and we enjoy peace once more. Everyone is longing for that day and I believe people everywhere will take more interest in the way their country is being run so to prevent the horror of war again.

From SEAC, Oct 1944

Well, things are about the same and I am feeling very fit. I might say this that I was very proud to be with the 1 Army in the recent fighting which took place on the Indo-Burma border. I must say we gave old Japs a sound pounding which I don't think he will forget.

From BLA, Nov 1944

My life up to the last 2 weeks or so has been very hectic and has taken me many miles, but unfortunately, I have been unable to do much sight-seeing, the very few odd hours I have had have been spent sleeping. Anyway, I don't grumble because the job I am on is so worthwhile. I wouldn't have missed it for anything. Perhaps one day I may be able to tell you about it. I did say I hadn't done any sight seeing but I was lucky enough to get a 48 hr rest leave in Brussels which was naturally interesting but at that time I was too weary to go dashing about, but I was able to see a little of the town and came to the conclusion I could manage 10 days quite easily (what a hope).

From SEAC, Nov 1944

I suppose you have heard that I am in hospital, well I am going on fine now and hope to be back soon at my batt. I haven't received any NLs lately, but I hope to soon as I miss them very much. I wish all the boys serving abroad and at home a very happy Christmas and New Year. I had a letter from my brother not long back and he said that the YMG had started again. I wish I was there as I used to enjoy it very much, especially making the toys.

From General Hospital, Halifax, Dec 1944

Will you please convey my very sincere thanks to the members of the YMG for the very pleasing gift which I received today, it is very gratifying for all of us away from home to know that we are not forgotten by the people of 'dear old Girton'. As you probably know, I have been in hospital for the last 5 weeks. I haven't been feeling so good until a few days ago but I feel much better now and I hope to be going to a convalescent home in about 10 days, after a month there I should get 10 days leave, but as you know the Army changes its mind so much that it doesn't pay to look forward too much. I hope to be home some time in Jan anyway. I will close by wishing all the members of the YMG a very happy Xmas and a New Year which I hope will see victory for us all.

From Royal Signals, ATS MEF, Dec 1944

I am afraid this is a bit late in the day but I would like to thank you very much for the NL which I have received regularly since I've been abroad. I've been in Palestine some time now after a year in Egypt, and am very happy up here among all the orange groves &c, but I am looking forward to seeing Girton again, whenever that may be. I hope you will all have a very happy Xmas and New Year in the village, and that I will be able to be with you again before next Xmastime.

From Flotilla RM, London, Dec 1944

A Christmas card sent to FC Barrett, Dec 1944

I sincerely hope that this letter finds everything going along OK in the village and with the YMG. As for myself I am still keeping fit and well, and doing my best to keep cheerful, which is not very difficult when you have a grand crowd of fellows with you as we have here. Since you last saw me, I have travelled quite a bit, over half way round the world in fact. Our first port of call was New York, then on to Bilbao, Panama, Society Islands, New Hebrides and New Guinea, a round the world trip before seeing Blighty again. I had quite a surprise 2 nights ago, when I picked up the 'Ditty Box', that by the way is a monthly magazine, published by the Navy. One of the first things I saw was a photo of IVC. It's a real treat to see and read about all these places to bring back happy memories. No doubt other naval men from the village have seen the same photo. Much to my regret I have not yet had the luck to get any monthly NLs through yet, but I am hoping every time we get a batch of mail in. I realise now how much they are to be looked forward to, they came as a break whilst serving in UK, but when abroad they are more valuable still. I sincerely hope that news is good from all the other lads from the village, and I send my best wishes to them all for the New Year and may 1945 bring us much nearer to the time when we shall all be together again.

Whereabouts unspecified, Dec 1944

Just a few lines to thank you and the YMG for my Christmas Gift. I am hoping to be home for the party on 23rd.

From 'A' Troop, 542 Bty RA Woman Private, Dec 1944

We are at present packing kit bags once more, though not for a very long journey. I have received this afternoon Dec's NL and was very interested to read of all the men in the various parts of the world. I was very impressed by the greetings from the children and members of the many organisations in the village and thank them very much for them. Our Christmas here was very jolly. On Christmas Eve there was a concert in the NAAFI by some of our men and girls; I say girls, as we always call each other by that expression, it was good, songs, dancing, sketches and music. On Christmas Day we had our much looked forward to cup of tea in bed at 7.30am and a biscuit. At breakfast we had some of the men in, one was Drum Major, another played the Bagpipes, another the Drums, then came some men dressed up in PT kit. They went all round the camp. During the morning we just pleased ourselves, then we had our dinner all together, after that everyone was in high spirits, we had our beds all turned over by the men, so of course we dashed round to do the same to them, after that we had a comic football match by the men. It was meant to be football, but it was football and Rugby combined. After tea, which we found a job to eat, we had a rest. In the evening there was an ENSA 'B' show, that is a good one, it was all music, very good indeed, ending with a dance until small hours of the morning. On Boxing Day we spent most of the time as I have said before packing up. In the evening was another dance until small hours. The weather was seasonable too, very cold and frosty, it has I think been the worst for many years. I would like to wish you and Committee a Happy New Year, and with it the hope and wish of us all in the Forces, the longed for Peace. My New Year wishes to all our men serving in all parts of the World.

From RAOC, CMF, Dec 1944
Let us hope that the time is not far distant when we can all get together again and this long separation is but a memory, but we must do our utmost this time to ensure that the peace is really a peace, and not just another interim period between wars, and to ensure that our children never know the horror and cruelties of civilisation's greatest crime.

Things are going along very much as usual out here at the moment, plenty of work &c, we have said goodbye to summer and KD again and the winter is very much with us now. We miss the freedom of shorts and open neck shirts and the delights of sunbathing, and begrudge the intervening months between now and the spring, when we shall see blue skies and hot again. I'm afraid that is one of the things we shall miss most of all when we get back to Blighty, but will nevertheless jump at the chance when it is our turn to go back.

I see by your letter that the various organisations are still going strong in the village and was particularly interested in the proposed memorial for Miss Hibbert-Ware, a very practical and sound scheme, and one I am sure she would heartily approve of, besides being an attractive centre of the village.

From BLA, Jan 1945
Dear Youth Clubbers, Thanks very much for the Xmas present which you all so kindly sent to all us members now in the forces.

As you know, I'm in Holland, we were some of the first in. I, like many more, thought of Holland as a land of canals, clogs, windmills, boys with trousers of many patches and girls with pretty dresses and those funny looking bonnets. Well, there's certainly canals, clogs and windmills, but the rest either doesn't exist or so far we haven't had the chance to see them.

The Dutch, like the Belgians, are grand people to know and the Dutch language is very much like ours and it's surprising to find a great many speak English. The children learn the phrases quickly such as 'cigarette for poppa' or 'souvenir for big sister'.

From RAOC CMF, Jan 1945
Just a line to thank you very much for the Nov NL received recently, as welcome as ever, as you can guess, full of news of the village, and I was especially interested in Mr Pease's letter to Mr H Morris [see *KiT* 95] on the proposed Community Centre for Girton. I see that you ask us to consider this and make suggestions or comments; but all I can say is that if the proposals can be carried out as they are contained in the letter, no suggestions are necessary, everything

seems to be catered for and to my mind cannot be improved. If the PRC can only get the plans approved and passed, and the project becomes a reality, Girton will be a village in which anyone could be proud to domicile. There is no doubt that the most essential question is a new school. That is wanted very badly and should be pushed through before anything else is attempted, and the proposed site seems as suitable as anywhere could be, and I sincerely hope that the difficulties can be overcome and the necessary permission obtained.

From Exeter, Devon, Jan 1945

The day the NL reached me we had spent all afternoon on booby-traps and mines, and on reading that part in the NL [see *KiT* 111] just made me think of what the Sgt instructor had been saying. That there is always something new happening with booby-traps. We are in one of Butlin's Camps, quite nice. The Major who is top boss of training thinks it's fine for training, but the boys have their own ideas about this place. There are too many hills. The town is in a valley and there is a 5 mile climb every way out of it. We had a 15 mile march today but was nearer 20 before they finished. A fall of snow on Monday night and Tuesday morning made it hard going. We spent that morning on the range. It's 20 miles from here on top of the hills. There was a good depth of snow there. Still it was a good day. We had our greatcoats on with equipment over the top, but it was a job to keep warm. I hope my letter is not too much shop for you, but it's all the news. When they bring rations in here they ask what the outside world is like so you can quite understand what the place is like.

From RAF India, Jan 1945

First of all regarding the NL – I can only express my appreciation by saying thank-you to you and all those concerned. I really enjoy reading it – and quite often go through it several times. It takes on an average 3 months to reach me, but as you say – time is of no consequence, especially to us in distant parts. It is really a great asset to us overseas. Usually letters from home have to be very brief – it's a question of writing little and getting here in good time, consequently they are more or less confined to family affairs so the NL certainly lives up to its name. I have in front of me your Nov copy, received yesterday – and your description of the village is indeed a delightful memory, being so different here – no green fields surrounded by hedges, trees that shed leaves in autumn and green again in spring. Instead of having 4 distinct seasons there are several and it's really a job to tell the difference – apart from winter and monsoon when it's slightly cooler.

Regarding the Post-War PRC, they certainly have a stiff task in front of them, and I do hope they get full support. The suggested Community Centre is in my opinion a good idea – and the 8 items on the agenda are all very much needed – especially the Assembly Hall.

Yes, the local football team must have lots of new faces. I've only been away 2 years (seems like 10) and I think the majority of the younger lads of my time are now in the Forces. Still, I'm sure – as always – there is plenty of enthusiasm.

From Topsham Barracks, Jan 1945

Knowing that I was going on infantry training I thought it best to wait until I got settled. We have 10 weeks of this training here before moving again. We have just completed the first week. I hope we get a leave when finished here but it remains to be seen just what is happening as to how badly they need us across in Germany. Have you still snow? We have had a little here but not to stay but it is still very cold here. I wrote to Mr Bradfield early last week, so if you have seen him you know of this transfer.

From Essex, Feb 1945

I think the 'Welcome Home Fund' is a very good idea. Those of us who have not met for so long, we will be able to have a good old chat of the years gone by, and many of us our childhood days. You ask for our point of view. I think those who need it most should have the biggest share, such as those who have several children, those with no definite job to go to, and those of us who have no home ties share equally after those who I have mentioned have been helped along; the wounded too should be thought of. May the reunion day come soon – sooner than all of us expect. I must close now, as the time is getting late, it will soon be lights out.

From 558 Flotilla, RM, Feb 1945

Thank you very much for the Dec NL which I received along with a most welcome present. I appreciate them very much. I was very glad to get the NL, as it is the first I have received since leaving England and it has news of nearly all the boys in it. I often think of these NLs as milestones in the war, because for at least 18 months now, as we get our letter, we have been able to look back on a month which has held a big success, or steady progress to the end of this lot. Our one big hope now is that month is not far off when you write your Grand Final NL which will be at end of the war and everyone back home. I think if circumstances permit we shall have to have that a decorated affair which can be kept as a souvenir.

From SEAC, Feb 1945
You may have heard by now that I am in the jungle in Burma, another one of the Girton lads to join the 1 Army.   Life here is naturally far different from the life we were having in India but considering all things I personally think we fare quite well. Rations, of course, tend to be monotonous, being generally tinned or dehydrated but combined with an occasional piece of fresh fish we manage okay. Some of us are getting quite expert at catching fish, usually about 1lb in weight, which are quite abundant in these rivers. I guess the hook and bit of dough is a novelty to them and we are naturally reaping a harvest while we can. I won't bother to describe to you the various type of bird and animal life met with out here or bore you with details of our tasks as I am sure you must now be quite familiar with the general way of living. I read with great interest your news of the 'Welcome Home Fund'. I think it a great idea and eagerly look forward to the time when all the lads and lasses can congregate again. As to my suggestions regarding the distribution of the Homecoming Fund you mention, I have little to say, except that, in my opinion, there should be no difference between those who serve at home or overseas. I personally am many thousands of miles from home but good luck to those who are lucky enough to serve at home. None of us can decide for ourselves where we serve. Anyway of one thing I am certain and that is we are all looking for the day when we can join in the life of the village once again.

I see from the NL that some of the lads have met one another again. So far I have only met Claude Kidman, but am continually on the look out for a familiar face as I know we are quite well represented up here. To be on the safe side however I must take this chance of sending my best wishes to everyone both in the village and in the Forces.   To my brother in Italy, I will just repeat his greeting to me, namely may we soon have that long awaited pint together again. Little more remains for me to say today except to add my name to that long list you must have sending

Claude Kidman

my thanks and appreciation for all the work you put in to each NL

Believe me if you could just see the expression on our faces (I'm sure they must be the same) you would be duly rewarded.

From Shillong, SEAC, Apr 1945

I am in the best of health and enjoying a spot of night duty at the hospital. Every day I look out to see if I can see any of the village lads who might come in, but no such luck as yet, still perhaps it's just as well as we don't want any of the village lads to get wounded or sick do we? I am in contact with my old school pal A Evans, the last letter I had he had been in hospital with a split head through being kicked by a mule which must have been very unpleasant for him. I was pleased to know he got over it OK. I must admit I have travelled a lot since I arrived in India but once you have seen a few towns out here they are all alike. Last year this time I was up at the forward area and was proud to be in with the troops that captured Kohima. things have moved fast out this way against the Jap. Let's hope it will soon be all over.

As I read the NL through I must say the village will look a bit bare on the corner of the park with those elms cut down. I can remember when I was at school Dick Evans fell down one of those and broke his arm. I expect by the time I get home the memorial and garden in remembrance of Miss Hibbert-Ware will be looking fine. I also think that it will become a beauty spot of Cambs and many people who knew Miss Hibbert-Ware will come to it. I must say that we are going to appreciate the home-coming fund which I know the work and spare time you kind friends of the village are doing so well. Maybe in some way or another when we all get back we can do something good for the village in return.

From Nassau, Apr 1945

During my tour of duty here in the Bahamas which is now coming to a close, I have always looked forward and thoroughly enjoyed receiving and reading the NL which is a most wonderful and interesting letter and must prove a great heart uplift to our fellow Girton friends much nearer to the fighting lines than I am. A great lot of history is found here in the Bahamas and when they all get back and we all meet, I am sure I shall have some interesting stories to tell. I would like you to forward my very best wishes to all our Girton friends in the Service. I shall be looking forward to meeting you in the very near future. The very best of luck to all concerned with the distributing of the NL.

From SEAC, Apr 1945

It is very pleasing to hear that the war in Europe is nearing its conclusion, and I am sure this one out here cannot last much longer.

The 1 Army have had some big successes and I'm definite that they have the Japs on the run now. To which I am proud to say that our Battn have played no small part, and have done some very good work. I myself am in very good health, but am looking forward to the time when we can all meet again in peace.

From Flotilla RM, London, Apr 1945

It [the NL] seems to form a link with the people at home, what goes on, and all our friends who may be serving in different parts of the world. I always look on the NL as 3 things all in one, 1) a personal letter from yourself representing the folks of the village 2) an annual report 3) a gossip column, perhaps 'gossip' is not quite the right word to use, but I think you will get what I mean when I say that you give us a lot of little bits of news that we might not get otherwise, you bring back old memories of the lads of the 'sight' on the Rec, with Sgt Gill Digger and at the time those lads seemed to be part of the village, and I think I can safely say were very popular amongst the children especially. Now in about $4\frac{1}{2}$

Cyril 'Son' Wilson, killed 23 April 1944

years everything has changed so. We saw fresh faces on the Rec and then none at all. There was the football and cricket teams disbanded and now its members and players all over the world, which includes many who attended your first YMG meeting, and small alterations in village scenery, such as trees missing here and there. You don't really notice such things so much if you are on the spot, but when you come home after being away for some time you notice these sort of things. Where our football team took touch line advice from such men as Sid Gawthrop, Tom Impey, Son Wilson and others, we look like being the chaps who are going to give it to Charlie Matthews, Vic Hancock and those who are the present team, which by reports are doing pretty well.

I haven't yet met up with any of our lads, but I hear that Dick Watson went somewhere to tea where I had been only a week before, and I got nearer to seeing Jack Collings than he will ever realise, but let's hope that the day is not too far ahead when we shall all meet again, not India, Burma, Europe or such places, but the one place that is in all our thoughts, Girton.

From Beckenham, Kent, May 1945

I am looking forward to the reunion of all us members scattered all over the world and that meeting isn't so far off now. Now I must thank you for your gift and also the NLs which I receive regular and look forward to reading the news. I don't know what you Youth Clubbers think about keeping the NLs going after the war but I have been thinking it a good idea to do so and I'm sure the people in the village would enjoy reading it as much as we all do in the forces and I agree with the idea of binding the NLs, so I'm placing my order now.

From CMF, May 1945

Here's a few lines to tell you that I'm doing well now. I saw in the NL of Apr how you had heard that I was in a Convalescent Depôt in Southern Italy. I've been here now nearly 5 weeks after spending some time in hospital with a broken arm. I'm very glad to say that I now feel very fit and well, in fact I feel well enough now to get back to my unit, but the powers that be think I should stay here a bit longer. We all waited eagerly for Mr Churchill's speech telling the world that peace had been signed. What a thrill it was for all. We held celebration on VE day at the camp, sports in the afternoon and an outdoor tea, had some beer and cigarettes afterwards which we all enjoyed very much. Of course the real day will be when we all get home and have our own celebration, which I'm hoping won't be very long now. How did you celebrate VE day at home, I suppose you held something on the Rec didn't you, also a dance at the Hall. I hear you have had some very bad weather at home this month, much damage has been done to the fruit &c. I'm so sorry to her that. The weather is getting hotter here every day now, have been issued with our shorts and are making full use of them, getting PT 3 times a day, the remainder of the day resting and sunbathing, much different to what we had up in the N last winter and the beginning of this year. I don't think I ever felt so cold in my life. Conditions were terrible, still all that is over now and all that's in our minds now is when we are coming home.

From RASC, CMF, May 1945

As you may probably guess I am in Italy just outside of Florence, it's lovely country up here with miles and miles of vineyards. It's much nicer than Southern Italy, although Naples is a lovely slight looking at it from the sea, but you get a different impression as you go through it. I have also visited Rome and the Vatican City and there are some really lovely churches and public buildings there. The football matches here between rival Italian villages are much the same as the Derby Day match with Girton and Histon. There is usually plenty of 'nice' language being exchanged.

From Air Formation Signals, c/o RAF Ceylon, May 1945

Although my home is in Pepys Way, I have only had the privilege of spending 2 leaves before I came overseas, but being a lover of country life I found profound pleasure in Girton and its surrounding district. I often picture my rides to Oakington and walks across the fields toward Histon. Speaking then as a stranger to Girton I must admit I like it immensely, and like other lads am looking forward to seeing it, may be sooner than any of us expect. I was deeply touched by the words of your letter that there would be little or no enthusiasm for V Day [see *KiT* 130]. I think that we away from home should celebrate, because we are no longer in fear that some flying bomb might destroy our homes. Now we know you at home are safe and will be able to carry on till victory is ours.

From BLA, May 1945

It must have been good to hear that it was all over in Europe and to hear that it is going well in Burma. I do not think it will last long when our bombers get there. I hope it ends this year so we can all come home for good. It will be good to see them all again for it is a long time since we have been together. The boys are doing a good job out there. I guess I will soon be going there for I am a young man and they want all young men out there. I won't worry for if I go I will be doing my job to make this a peaceful loving world to live in. Well, now the censor is finished I can tell you whereabouts I am in Germany and some of the places I have been: Ghent, Eekloo, Walkeren Island, Weert, Gennep, Goch then to the Rhine crossing. We were at Xanten, Bocholt, Öding, Bocken, and then we came out of action and went back to Öding for a rest.

From RAOC, CMF, June 1945

Strange as it may sound, we have been busier than ever since VE Day. We are now in the process of clearing up the ammo dumps and there are quite a number of them in Italy. God only knows where it is all going to, but we are bringing it out as fast as labour and transport can handle it. Well, the great news is now nearly a month old, but the relief of knowing that it is all over, in Europe anyway, is still quite overwhelming at times. My wife wrote and told me of some of the scenes which occurred on VE night, and I can well imagine the joy and relief which everyone at home must have felt when the news was announced. All that we need now is the news of Japan's capitulation to complete the good news. We are at the moment just outside Florence, and on a couple of visits to the city I have been quite surprised at the apparent normality of everything. All the shops are open, there is everything on sale that one can think of, and it is not until the question of prices is raised that the shock comes, everything is terribly dear and the Black Market is flourishing, but the city is a beautiful place, wide, clean, tree-lined streets and a beautiful cathedral. As soon as I can find time I intend seeing the Ponte Vecchio, which I have heard so much about. I have seen the famous Leaning Tower of Pisa, and it is a truly amazing sight.

From India Command, June 1945

I have just about got settled here now. It's not at all too bad. Things have improved since we arrived here. We now have quite a nice writing room, much nicer than some in the camps in Blighty, carpets, easy chairs, and a wireless that goes very well until it's time for news, when a huge crowd appears from nowhere and that part of the room becomes one mass of boys. There is quite a lot of fresh fruit here but of course we have to take care what fruit we eat and so on. Bananas we get quite a lot. I had half a dozen this morning. I guess the children at home would like to have them as plentiful as we find them. The Fruit Walla, like the Char Walla, keep walking around the huts which they have so many to supply. One thing we always know when it's time to get up because the Char Walla is always around on time and hear his voice at the window. No turn over, for a while longer, as was favourite at Blighty. The tea to most of us is too big a temptation. I guess it won't be so long now before some of the boys will be coming home for good. Those who have been away for so long will see quite a lot of difference, but I hope with all the excitement of those coming home, those lads who have gone are not forgotten and their people at home. It will seem more hard to them in a way when the lads they went with come home. I guess you will, perhaps, wonder what I was thinking about, and I think perhaps you have guessed. I was thinking before I started to write of those wives of the lads who have gone, also the parents, it will be hard for them. I hope our new Govt will do more for those than has been done in the past. I have met quite a lot of lads who were in my first Unit here. Some I have not seen for 3 years. I came all this way and they seem the first I see when I arrived. How is the progress on the Miss Hibbert-Ware Memorial getting along? I guess it's completed by now.

From MEF, June 1945

I was pleased to read in Apr NL that all the boys are doing well, and that leaves me the same. It looks as if Girton is all over the World, some here, some there, some everywhere. You can't keep old Girton down.

I suppose Dad has told you that I have been travelling about quite a lot in these last 3 months, first going to Greece, then back to Italy and then on to the MEF. I am at the moment near Cairo, which as you know is a very nice place.

Now for a bit of cricket news, am doing well with the ball. Yesterday I took 5 for 16, but with the bat as you know, I could always hold my own, but I'm just a flop now, all the wickets are matting, which makes them very fast, so please tell the boys to look out for themselves when I do get home.

I believe the people of Girton are doing well with the home-coming fund, which will be very helpful to us all. How nice it has been that all the time those abroad have not been forgotten.

As you know, the demobbing has started and with a bit of luck I hope to be out early in the New Year, then we can have a good long chat together.

From India Command, July 1945

The news of VE Day are very interesting and I would rather have been enjoying them there than where I did. A free glass of tea at a YMCA and standing in a queue for an hour to get it, so you can guess some numbers were around at the time. Bananas, oranges and custard was on the menu too so had quite a grand do of it as far as was possible. The 1pt of beer, promised for V Day arrived just 8 days after it and cost about 1/- for a small bottle labelled Lions Beer, was worse than any I have ever seen or tasted before but has saved quite a bit of money for me. Still it's one thing that is seen from time to time now. But I have gone to Char, it's always the same, one thing which is not short.

From RE Works Section, MEF, July 1945

It seems a very long time ago since I wrote you, and since then I have had one or two changes of air and scenery. Now, at the above address I think I shall remain until I return home on demob in Aug. Somehow, I do not yet realise that very soon I shall be back in Girton again. You can imagine how impatient I am to be getting back.

The main reason for this letter is to thank you so very much for the regular supply of your NL. For the past 2 years it has been a very welcome periodical from home, and has been a means of keeping in touch with the village activities, and the whereabouts of the Girton lads on active service. Your efforts as Editor of the NL surely ranks very high in the form of War Service, and I, for one, will always remember the pleasure I have derived from it since I have been overseas.

Girton, I imagine, is practically unchanged? Except for a few iron railings that have been removed for ammo. The great day will be when the War in the Far East is over and *all* lads and lasses of Girton are back home again. Surely, that will be Girton's 'D Day'.

From India Command, Aug 1945

I guess very soon that a good many lads will soon be home again and we hope to jobs. I guess the fields around the village are showing signs of harvest. One thing I miss seeing around here, a harvest. When one sees the harvest nearly finished it reminds one very much of the winter quickly coming on.

VJ days were spent very well. Sports were in full swing for $2\frac{1}{2}$ days, mostly football and races, both were very good. We managed a concert party from amongst ourselves which was very good since it has given one show every night.

From RAOC, BAD, CMF, Aug 1945

I have moved right down S since last writing to you, and am now in the Bari district, up to my eyes in work. What a contrast from Northern Italy. All one can see on the roads here is an endless vista of olive groves. The dialect they speak is practically unintelligible, very difficult to pick up, no more like Italian than is Chinese.

I had quite a nice trip down here by road from Florence, passing through some of the well-known places, Leghorn, Rome, Naples, Cassino and Freggia.

I was quite surprised at the very large majority secured by Labour in the Election and we must now wait and see what sort of a job they make of things. They have the full opportunity and should be able to make a decent job of things. I think the Cambridge Borough result has made history hasn't it, if I remember rightly, a Labour member has never been returned before.

From Darjeeling, India Command, Aug 1945

I've been in hospital for 10 weeks with skin trouble, but am glad to say I'm being discharged tomorrow and having 14 days at the Convalescent camp near here. After that I shall be going back to Calcutta. You see I was evacuated from Burma by Hospital Ship to Calcutta and it was like going into Fairyland to get on that boat and enjoy a lovely bed without mosquito nets &c. It was a grand experience although I was a bad patient having penicillin injections by the score.

I was sent up here in the hills because of the cooler climate and I've certainly had a most comfortable stay for the past 5 weeks. I've even done a spot of pony riding and played bridge during the rainy periods which just now are considerable, it being about the height of the Monsoons.

It was an exceptional piece of luck to meet Tom Impey right in the heart of Burma. He happened to be dumped where we were stationed, and was waiting for an air lift.

He knew I was somewhere about and very quickly found me. You can imagine my complete surprise at hearing his voice once again. We spent the rest of that day together, the latter part with me on duty in the Guard Tent and Tom laying in our apology for a deck chair. We fixed him up with a meal and also a bed in our tent and he left very early the next morning.

Tom Impey

In the meantime I am making the most of my time here and seeing plenty of really wonderful sights of which I have read but never imagined I would see.

Kanchenjunga is really marvellous and on a clear day we can see it quite easily, towering up in the sky like a fairy castle. Darjeeling, as you probably know, is built on terraces on the side of a very steep slope. Even the hospital blocks are built in the same way and all the flat spaces are artificial. We overlook a big tea plantation and one gets a feeling of tremendous space and height (we are about 7,000 ft up and often shrouded in cloud).

Burma was better than I expected but everything is very primitive and most of the buildings badly knocked about. All kinds of flying pests and crawling reptiles, apart from the usual heat and mosquitoes.

From Blenheim Camp, Bury St Edmunds, Dec 1945
I have been informed by mother that the YMG supper is on Friday evening of this week. I am very sorry I cannot be present, the last I remember very well, the food was very good but I could not eat much, the reason being that I had to introduce the Guests after the supper, and I was a bit jumpy all through the meal. I hope that this supper goes off as well as that last one.

4: Service Records

R Lipscombe

WJ Claydon

I was a member of the Rescue Squad, spending many nights in the old tin hut at the entrance to the Rec. When the squad was disbanded I joined the FAP where I met Freddie Barrett. My last attendance was on Mar 8th 1943 on an exercise to Oakington to deal with casualties from a bombed house. I was given the task of helping a charming young lady restore the circulation in her legs.

A few days later I joined the army and was posted to the Royal Signals. After a few months in Yorkshire, working on overhead telephone lines I went to Spurn Point for 6 months. On the evening before D-Day, I was posted to British Second Army Mobile HQ and embarked at Gosport on D+3 for Juno Beach. We went to Creully and Army HQ with General Sir Miles Dempsey, sometimes working in his caravan. I was later made a member of a crew of 3 on a mobile telephone exchange and test room. There were 2 of these vehicles at Main Army HQ and 2 at Rear Army, the HQ of Lord Glenarthur, the Army Quartermaster. They leap-frogged from one location to the next, as we made our way across France, Belgium, Holland and into Germany. On the third or fourth move we were in convoy when we came to a stop, due to a broken fan-belt. The rest of the convoy left us. We were saved by a German armoured car, driven by British soldiers who had captured it. They found a spare fan-belt in the tool-kit which fitted. There was a terrible row going on when we reached our location. The loss of such a vehicle would have been disastrous. I was told that 12 months had been spent installing the equipment, including 14 miles of wiring, in each vehicle. After that, each time we moved we had an escort of 4 Sergeant Majors in a Jeep.

For 3 nights I lay in my tent and watched Falaise burning. I was among the first to pass through the ruins and across the Falaise pocket. There were bodies everywhere, along the road and across the fields as far as the eye could see, thousands of them. They were the enemy but they were also human beings, cut down in their prime. It was the most disturbing journey imaginable.

The Rhine crossing in early Apr 1945 enabled us to enter Germany. We took over part of a furniture factory. The owners lived in a large house next to it. At least 3 generations were living under one roof. In the morning we made use of their wash-room and were supplied with plenty of hot water. In the evening we were invited into the house to join the family with the radio tuned in to the BBC for our benefit. We were forbidden to fraternise with the Germans but found that the vast majority of ordinary citizens were very friendly and anxious to please. At the end of hostilities in Europe my Section (51 T/E) was awarded a Mention in Dispatches and granted an extra home leave.

Some time later we went to Potsdam Conference, using the late Frau Goebbels' house as the communications centre. This was followed by a year in Berlin, most of the time on duty in various telephone exchanges. I was then sent to Glandorf near Osnabrück where we laid 2 telephone cables about 28 miles long to exchanges in outlying villages. My first job was to survey the underground telephone ducts from Osnabrück exchange to the edge of the built-up area. From there the cables were laid in the grass verges and across open country.

On the day in Sep 1946 when I left with one of my comrades to be demobbed, a crowd of the local inhabitants assembled to wave us goodbye. Not because they were glad to see the back of us, but they were genuinely pleased that we were about to be united with our loved ones. I made many friends during my sojourn in Germany.

R Coe

I was called up 12 Dec 1939. I enlisted at Ipswich and became 1545113 Gunner Coe R. I joined the territorial regiment of the Loyal Suffolk Hussars (RA) 220 Bty, serving in various parts of Britain.

During 1941–43 when there was fear of invasion the 220 Bty was taken from the Regt to form an independent unit in the potential defence of London. When this danger receded, the 220 Bty disbanded. Some were posted back to the Regt, others, like me, received overseas posting. I found myself boarding a troopship in Liverpool, which after 4 weeks at sea and passing through the Suez Canal arrived at Mombasa, from there by rail to Nairobi, then on to the EAA Depôt at Athi River, firstly learning basic Swahili then training African tribesmen to become soldiers and to integrate with us to form regiments for service in Burma.

J Collings (see photograph p283)

'Gummy' Naylor wrote to Fred Barrett saying I would be surprised to know how near to each other we once were. This, I think, was at Ulithi in the Pacific, when an ammunition barge came alongside *Illustrious*, to stock up on ammunition. Unknown to us both, he was sending it up to our flight deck, and I was running it to the hoist. I was in Colombo twice, before I read in one of Fred Barrett's letters that Ron Lipscombe was there. Sadly, on a further visit, we docked at Trincomalee, so I missed the chance of seeing him. Around that time an invasion of Ceylon was a good possibility, we were then part of fighter defence. We were inundated with new stores – machine-guns, rifles, hand grenades &c in case of invasion. However, my Pilot, Lt Morgan (Canadian) said 'not to worry jumper, we need you air mechanics to service our planes. We will chuck out the radio, and a bod will curl up in there, another will sit in the pilot's seat, the pilot will sit on him, and one other tied under each wing to fly you to India'. I was sure glad they did not invade!

L Collings

My Boys' Brigade pal and friend Fred Chalkly and I decided to join the Cambs Regiment when a big drive for recruits was on. I was told that Cambs 2nd Battn was full, but men were needed for the 250th RE. We enlisted on 22nd May 1939 in No 3 Section 250th Field Co RE reporting to 2nd Lt RE Strong, JE Oxenham (Capt) TA 4 yrs service.

I was working in a field helping to put a new gate up with Bert Sandell, head carpenter at Fulbourn Mental Hospital when someone told me the army reserve had been called out and I had better report to my unit. To best wishes from the staff, I cycled home to Grange Lodge. There awaiting me was the blue Mobilisation Form telling me to report to HQ. We all guessed things were dodgy by now.

With a day's ration and gas mask, wearing my battle-dress uniform, I reported at 9am that Sep morning. We duly fell in with the Cambs Regt on Parker's Piece. Rumours swept through the ranks of TAs as we waited for orders. Section after section marched down to the Drill Hall, to be given billets for the night. A Mr & Mrs Brown found themselves having to put up myself and one other. One or two of the lads were actually billeted next door to their own home. Of course, they soon swapped.

Some of the initial duties were digging trenches at County High School; Practice for night whistle for supposed star shell burst; Route marches round the Gogs. Once the Coy stopped outside the Mental Hospital for a practice. We went into an imaginary train, entraining and detraining from an imaginary carriage. The thought that passed through my mind was we ought to have been the ones locked up, it seemed so far fetched! As I had worked at the Hospital, I was only hoping no-one who knew me could see me!

We drilled at the Drill Hall and in St Matthew's School playground. My marching training in the Boys' Brigade came in very handy. I went to first TA Camp 14 days at Canterbury where we did explosives, bridge building over dry ravines and rivers. I enjoyed it under canvas. One afternoon a load of us after duty went to Herne Bay, missed the last bus, so marched back passing the Buffs' barracks. The sentry called out the guard, thinking we were a troop on duty going past. The result was they took us in their barracks, we had a mug of tea and one of them pointed out a short cut through their barracks so we arrived back at our camp just in time for parade Reveille, 6am.

We did stints of guard duty manning a Lewis Gun on top of Parkside House. Also outside our HQ, a favourite 'meet-up'. The policeman who patrolled the area would pop in and have a break.

The 250th were off to France while I and others only 18 at that time were not to go overseas till 19. They came back via Dunkirk. We were transferred to 288 Field Coy, sent to Cranwich Heath Camp and were billeted at Weeting Hall, a big country house where I encountered my first Nazi prisoners, very arrogant, they gave the Nazi salute and *Heil Hitler* when we were at our ablutions. I remember one incident when coming off guard unloading our rounds one lad pulled his trigger and shot through the ceiling. Luckily no-one was hurt.

While at Cranwich Heath Camp we all lined up outside the camp and we had our first feeling of what it would be like to be buzzed by 2 RAF twin engine planes flying very low. At Woodbastwick our building was turned into a mini-hospital which contained wounded soldiers from Dunkirk, one of whom was being treated for a leg wound with leeches – first time I had heard of that happening.

My job was as runner between the telephone situated in the hospital and our camp 300–400 yards away. I had a chair bed to rest on beside the phone. I was kept very busy mostly at night. Our Capt Harper, a Cambridge man, also spent a lot of time over there. That phone was our only connection with the outside world, except of course the comings and goings of Duty Officers and DRs with orders. While there one of our lads ran amok. Our guards had to knock him out with a rifle butt and tie him up and for a time he was in our main guard tent till the MP took him away.

We had just come home from laying mines on the coast on a very hot day. A pal of mine was put on guard by a gate entrance to our camp. He laid his rifle against the gate, himself also. I expect he just closed his eyes for a second, when Sergeant Major crept up, snatched the rifle and held him up. 'You would have been dead and also your mates if this was in France.' Very serious offence. We were on a war footing. My mate was charged and into the glass house he went. We never saw him again. His being put on a charge was more to frighten the rest of us to keep awake and alert at all times. We were not playing games.

At Caister-on-Sea we sat having our break in the Lifeboat Station when 3 'crumps' nearby told us Jerry was about. Red Alert had been sounded, when we heard the oncoming roar of a plane coming fast and low as it flew by I looked at it and could see the head of the pilot looking quickly left, right and up as he roared out across the sea and home to Germany.

We mined Gorleston-on-Sea, Winterton, California, Hemsby, Horsey and all bridges inland. I worked on Yarmouth, Acle, Potter Heigham where we lived a life of holiday makers on a cruiser *The Gleaming Light*. We stayed to guard Ludham Bridge, prepared for demolition in case of invasion. With us there was a Section of Pioneers led by a Lieutenant who was a famous film star pre-war days. We lived in a Summer House beside the river. While at Ludham we fancied some fish to supplement our diet. One of our lads devised a way with a depth charge in a Golden Syrup tin. A lot of stunned fish rose to the surface. A rather bigger explosion which shook the bank and slopped water over the banks made us stop! Back to Cambridge. Billeted with Mr & Mrs Twinn and their 2 sons and daughter. Wonderful people. Mr Twinn drove a Dale's Brewery van delivering beer to the pubs in surrounding villages. On leave I went round with him. It was just heaven.

Our section of men had been chosen to carry out experiments to Prof Inglis' bridge [the Inglis Military Bridge], putting it up and seeing how long it took to completely build. This was done in a field behind the University Rugby grounds. I believe the bridge parts were made in the University Engineering Labs. On one occasion the paint was not completely dry when we handled them, consequently while working I was not quick enough to get my hand out before the lads let go the weight. My thumb was squashed flat. Our FA man was a Sapper, a bricky by trade. Sapper Ladlow quickly bandaged the thumb and I was excused that day's training work.

After Dunkirk we ended up at Langley Park. Our tents were positioned under the trees. We dug latrines in the woods then dug trenches in defensive positions round the camp and we manned it every day. 1 hour before dawn and 1 hour before dusk dressed in full battle order. I think the Top Generals were expecting a glider attack on our mainland to follow their victory over us in France, Belgium and Holland. Very tense times. A big pit was dug and loads of ammo and explosive deposited. Rumour had it, it was one of the biggest reserves of explosives in East Anglia. We had to be very careful not to cut across the field as a short cut because enemy photos taken by Recce planes would let Jerry know troops were hereabouts. A bomb nearby was followed by rumour that a Jerry was in the woods flashing a light signal to Jerry planes. We had a search of the woods, found signalling apparatus but no-one found.

We went out each day on defence work. Some of us laying mines, making sand-bag defence, I remember doing a stint building a sand-bag defence round coastal guns on a high position overlooking the cricket ground at Sparrows Nest. There were 2 guns firing out to sea and covering the harbour entrance. RMs tough, bronzed, just back from Malta positioned the guns, the first big guns I had seen. It was a lovely day, stripped to the waist in the sun. Those RM had finished their task before we were three-quarters done, It was a friendly against time with plenty of banter about us part-time soldiers. We had to go round all the buildings and houses to tell the inhabitants to open their windows before the guns were fired, the ones that didn't were broken by the blast.

Another of our jobs at that time was mining road and rail bridges which were hastily done in case of the invasion. At Beccles Bridge Road I was building a box to contain gun cotton to blow iron bridge girders and jarred the thumb I'd squashed in Cambridge. Our MO was attending to our lads coming back from Dunkirk. He arrived back in our camp in the evening, saw my thumb which by now was causing blood poison. He took my nail off, did 2 crosses under where nail had been, squeezed the pus out, said I wish you had fainted.

I agreed with him. Took 3 weeks to clear up and about 6 months before I could bend my thumb.

From Jack Collings: My brother Leslie was discharged from the Army with valvular disease of the heart. However, as a dedicated conjuror, he still did his bit entertaining troops and workers with his bag of tricks, some with the Girton Follies.

CB Cundell

Although I wanted to be in the navy I signed for the infantry in June 1939 to do my 6 months; or so I thought. I was called up on 15 Nov 1939 to the Suffolk Regiment. After training I was sent to Rouen. On May 10 1940 when the Germans broke through Belgian lines we were told to go to the canteen store and help ourselves to anything we might need. A lot of men were taking cigarettes but an old soldier called Tom Gordon advised us to take food so we did. That night we slept in a field and it rained all night. The next few days we marched about 30 miles, I can still hear the Stukas and see those poor people dragging their prams and carts across France. We arrived at Dunkirk around 22 May 1940 (what a way to spend my 21st birthday). After days of bombing I managed to get on to a paddle steamer. I slept all the way and did not know what day it was.

We were then sent to Cumberland to join 2/5 Battn Queen's Royal Regiment 56 London Division, then on to Ashford to guard 25,000gal of aviation fuel, where I stayed all through the Battle of Britain and trained to be a cook.

My next move was to Dimchurch and then to Suffolk. In 1941 I had 3 days' leave, I returned home and married Lily.

The next move was to Sudbury in 1942, I had 2 stripes now and my own section and Corporal Leach from Cambridge. My pride and joy was a sub machine gun from the USA.

We were waiting to go to Iraq. We arrived in Basra and travelled by train in a cattle truck to Kirkuk to guard an oil field This was now 1943, the division was then moved 4,500 miles packed 15 to a lorry to near Tripoli to join the 8th army. We carried on fighting until the 12th May then we rested at Tripoli. The King, Monty and Churchill came to see us march past.

The next move was to Salerno. I was sick with hepatitis. I was sent to England on a ship and into hospital on Mill Road. When I was fit again I was promoted to Sergeant. I had to train 18 year old 'call-ups' for $2\frac{1}{2}$ years until I was demobbed in 1946. A bit longer than the 6 months I expected. I also lost some good mates; Stan Cornell of Cottenham in N Africa, Tommy Thompson in Italy, Len Harvey of Mill Road in N Africa, Harry Mansfield at Singapore so of the 5 of us I was the only one to return.

K Dean

I was employed at Marshall's, then Short's Factory on Madingley Road before being called up. Then sent to Ireland for Anti-Tank training, near to Mountains of Mourne. Stationed at Newcastle for a time, then down to London. Went to France 1944, attached to SHAEF HQ until the end of the war.

SR Dixon (see photograph p17)

Joined RAF Volunteer Reserve 1938 as Observer (navigator) flying weekends with ground lectures at Marshall's airfield – all for 1/- an hour! Called up 3 Sep 1939.

After scraping through navigation, bombing and gunnery courses on Anson, Heyford and Fairey Battle aircraft, posted Mar 1940 to 254 Sqn, long-nosed Blenheim fighters at Bircham Newton, operating over the Low Countries trying to help stem the German invasion. One memorable sortie was against about 50 Heinkels and Ju 88s bombing Rotterdam without, I have to say, much success losing our number 2 unfortunately shot down in flames.

Following the German invasion of Norway in Apr 1940 our sqn was hastily sent to Lossiemouth, our role being offensive patrols against enemy airfields and shipping. On one sortie my hare-brained pilot, with his petrified navigator, shot up the airfield at Stavanger destroying several Heinkels and Ju 88s and then on to a nearby harbour also destroying a few Bloem & Voss seaplanes where, by some miracle we avoided some very unfriendly AA fire. It was a glorious spring day with just a few clouds when we spotted and attacked a Ju 88 off Peterhead which we left with smoking engines – claimed as a probable. We collected quite a few hits and despite being injured my pilot got us back to base with his luckily unscathed navigator – despite the 40-odd bullet holes in the aircraft!

The Sqn then moved to Sumburgh in May where we continued ops over Norway including escort to dive bombers from the *Ark Royal* operating against the *Scharnhorst*. Then we moved to Aldergrove, where our role switched to more gentlemanly convoy escorts and anti-sub patrols over the Atlantic. After being commissioned in

Nov 1941 posted to 608 Sqn, Hudson bombers on shipping strikes in the North Sea. Then 'rested' from ops and became a Navigator instructor on Sunderland and Catalina flying boats at Invergordon. I was there when the Duke of Kent was killed in a Sunderland *en route* to Iceland.

In Apr 1943 the Air Ministry decided that I was to go on a pilot's course in Canada. On gaining my Wings there in Apr 1944 I returned to UK and flew Wellington and Lancaster aircraft ready to join the 'Tiger' force against the Japanese. However, the war suddenly ended with the atomic bombs. After a short spell flying Dakota aircraft on the European routes I was demobbed in June 1946 and returned to my old job in the Pathology Lab, but not for long. I succumbed to itchy feet and rejoined the RAF Jan 1947, retiring in 1975 – but that's another story!

R Ellis

Arthur Evans and I joined up together. We trained at Norwich and Lincoln and were sent to Bury St Edmunds to await posting. I went to the Beds & Herts and Arthur was posted to the Northamptonshires, who went out to the Far East. Come the invasion my Battn was broken up and I was transferred to Queen's Regt (Bermondsey Battn) Infantry Brigade 7th Armoured Division (Desert Rats) which I served with from Normandy to Holland. In Dec 1944 the Battn 1st 6th was broken up and I was transferred to the Herefordshire Regt 11th Armoured Division Infantry Brigade. We were in Schleswig at the time of the German surrender, and German soldiers came in all sorts of conveyances to give themselves up [see p127]. At the end of the war we had reached the Baltic, so I consider I was lucky to have survived from Normandy to the Baltic. I was transferred to the Provost Coy No 1 Internment Camp (war criminals) until it closed, and I saw the last few months with the Yorkshire Light Infantry until I was demobbed.

T Evans

I spent 3 years 8 months down the pit as a Bevin Boy, years I shall never forget. The thought of the pit cage, you would hear the bell to say the cage was ready to go down. The first 40' was like a free fall, your stomach would come up to your mouth. When you came up from the pit, sometimes the winder would bring you up too quickly, then you would apply the brakes, causing the cage to go up and down like a yo-yo.

Tom recalls the times he witnessed '6 tubs of coal running away out of control, with only a little hole to jump into, while the tubs went shooting by at 60 mph, then they would crash, bringing in the roof, into which you could get 3 double-decker buses'

You went down the pit at 1.30pm knowing that was that day over as you never saw daylight again for that day ... also that there was no toilet. If you worked at the pit bottom it would be freezing cold, but on the other side the temperature would be above 90°F. – The others working in the pits, where always one for all and all for one.

The one thing I regret the most was that the only thing I got was a return ticket home when I had served my country for 3 years and 8 months. We did not get a medal, or any recognition for the service we gave.

MW Fordham

Horace Bradfield (bless him) formed the grand-sounding 'Young Men's Discussion Group'. We used to meet in either the school or the VI. We came out to a most glorious Sep day, not one of us knew what to expect. Would we be bombed before nightfall? Nothing happened, except a very bad thunderstorm. I had started work with Jack Moore in Aug 1934 at the village garage he ran. By the early 1940s new cars were no longer available and

trucks and vans were becoming hard to come by, so worn out ones had to be rebuilt and reconditioned, and Moore's had come into their own.

One event comes to mind, cycling to work one morning. Sitting on Freeman's tennis court was the sad sight of a crashed Wellington bomber, the crew had bailed out earlier on, set the controls to clear the town – very difficult to do at night. Luckily no-one was hurt or killed, but a few yards further on and it would have landed on

Moore's building and Freeman's house next door [Map site D].

I had not joined the HG but it was then announced that all had to join one of the defence units. I thought a volunteer better than a pressed man, so to 90 Thornton Road and Lt Monkman. Was instructed to attend the next Wed at the WI at 7.30pm. Wilf Monkman was the man of the hour as far as Girton's No 8 platoon, 1st Cambs Battn went. A blunt, bluff, Yorkshireman, with a touch of the bully in him, plus a bit of 'Captain Mainwaring' too. He wanted to make No 8 platoon into a first rate one, and he achieved his aims, with dear old Jim Thompson in the background as second-in-command, and liked by everyone; and a real live soldier we must not forget, Jesse Kidman who knew what the real thing was like in the 1914–18 conflict.

One memory I have was a weekend scheme at Madingley Hall. We arrived one Saturday evening, slept on straw palliases, up on Sunday morning looking forward to breakfast. It must have been good because when the cooks announced those who wished could have a second helping, greedy me and others did just that. But greed does not always pay, because the orders came, Prepare to move off, so it was gobble down what you could and all kit on ready for the off. about 6 of us in this small group. We moved off slowly, which was just as well as it was then the pain came on, and for the next half hour I was in agony.

We came to the Madingley–Dry Drayton road, which we had to cross. Some rolled over, some just scuttled over. We hung around while the inquest was held, and when the finding came out, it was of no consolation to be told every man was killed by enemy machine gun fire from the ditch up the road. Even to this day whenever I go past I think back and if I have anyone with me say to them 'this is where Fordham died many years ago'.

Histon Despatch Riders

I had a visit one Sunday afternoon from Sgt Fred Garner, the Sergeant in charge of the motorcycle DR section, stationed in Histon. Would I like to join the DRs? Would I! I knew them all well. Wilf Monkman agreed. I'm sure he knew I was a hopeless soldier and would be much happier at Histon.

Histon was in one sense a doddle. 3 hours Sunday mornings

cleaning and adjusting the bikes, a total waste of time as we only went out about twice a month and not then if it were wet or too cold. We never got to know the area as we should, a most unsatisfactory state of affairs for the DRs and those depending on them.

With hindsight I am sure that from the time Germany invaded the USSR the powers that be were certain that this country had very little fear of invasion and the HG was allowed to carry on as a morale booster.

S Gawthrop

Called up in 1940, sent to Norfolk training with Tank Regiment. Went to N Africa, going right through that campaign, then on to Italy with the 25th Tank Brigade supporting the 1st Canadian Division with great success. So much so that the Canadians invited them to wear the Maple Leaf on their berets and the emblem on their tanks. Eventually demobbed after spells in Greece and Cairo.

L Hales

My call-up arrived stating I had to report to Felixstowe on Jan 2 1940. Ken Matthews had been notified of the same arrangements, but after arriving there I lost contact with Ken. On arrival at Felixstowe Station we were marched down to the sea front, then put into empty houses with no heating. Next day, our civilian clothing was replaced by army uniform. This was the RASC, a transport Coy. From then on it was Drill, PT, Driving Instruction and Lectures. Naturally, Guard Duties had to be done and at that time we were armed with pick axe handles. After 6 weeks I was transferred to a Troop Carrying Coy and moved to Wiltshire, eventually moving down to Southampton to load our vehicles &c on board for France. We docked at Cherbourg, Dunkirk at this time was being evacuated. Our job was then in the cover of darkness to pick up troops cut off by the German advance. My last journey on this mission was making for St Malo. We were evacuated. Our vehicles were left by the roadside with no petrol and smashed engines. I was on a coal barge, standing only, but glad to leave France. As we left St Malo the docks were blown up. Reaching Southampton, we boarded a train and finished up in Chesterfield. After a few nights sleeping on the floor of Baythorpe Drill Hall we were allocated to private billets which turned out to form a life-long friendship.

In 1941 I left Chesterfield for Greenock. Once again out to sea, not knowing where to, but rumoured Singapore. At this time U-boats were tracking our convoys so this became a little scary at times. Singapore was overrun by Japan, so awaiting further orders we docked at Durban. After a short stay once again out to sea, and landed in Egypt, doing short spell of duty there. Once again on board ship bound for India, landing at Bombay. We were then trained for Tank Transporting. I was in charge of 4 transporters. The Indian Army joined our Coy and I was training them to drive and maintain transporters, so back to school to learn Urdu and also unarmed combat. At the time I didn't think it would be $4\frac{1}{2}$ years before I left for England, so learning Urdu was a help. Our duties here were carrying tanks, carriers &c to Dinjpur *en route* for Kohima and Imphal for the 14th Army. Later on I visited the cemetery at Kohima and found the grave of Cyril Wilson. I took a photograph and brought it home, giving it to his mother and father.

TC Impey (see photograph p205)

I enlisted in the RE in Cambridge on 18th Feb 1940 and later on in that year I was sent to 5th Training Battn Land Forces at Black Camp, Clacton. Having completed my initial training I was posted to a coy of RE in Devon but on arrival I was informed by the OC that I was too qualified to be wasted on the work the unit was engaged on. I was posted to a depôt at Ripon. On arrival I met 2 other sappers in similar circumstances and we were all posted to a new Corps to be formed at Leeds. When we arrived nobody had any news of us and we were sent to Gibraltar Barracks where once again we were not wanted. They put us in some old chicken huts, wet and cold, and after 2 days all 3 of us were very ill, one in hospital with pneumonia. We were then sent to a nearby Catholic Seminary for sleeping accommodation. Eventually all 3 of us were sent to 9 Corps (new) at Catterick. They immediately sent us to a camouflage school at Darlington where a group of 'civvy' plasterers were engaged on building a dummy village to teach camouflage. We spent a year or so travelling around the North carrying out camouflage work.

I was posted on my own to GHQ Southern Command at Oxford. Here I was allowed civilian digs for 18 months or so. I spent my time measuring up buildings for storage and assisting the Americans setting up a hospital unit. This was a good life, but it had to end and I was posted to Halifax which I knew meant an overseas posting. Surely enough, I embarked at Glasgow not knowing where we were going, but I had recently heard from a friend posted to India that if an appeal was made for a librarian on board to apply for it as it made life very good. I applied and was appointed. Instead of being jammed in the hold I lived on B deck in comfort for the whole trip which as I guessed was India.

I was posted to GHQ New Delhi doing design work for camps. After a couple of months I was sent to Jalandhar where there was a RE depôt. All good things come to an end and I was again posted, this time to report to the Railway Transport Office at Calcutta. This meant a journey through the whole length of India in a train crowded with Indians – nobody to talk to for days on end. Eventually I arrived in Calcutta and after a night's rest was told to go by train to Lanipur. After a couple of days I finally arrived only to be told that my journey was not over and that I had to go to Kohima to find my new unit who were with the 14th Army. The only way to get there was to thumb a lift. By the time I arrived the war had moved on towards Imphet where the fighting was extremely heavy. In fact the whole area was trapped in a pen surrounded by Japs. It was a case of all hands to the pumps. This turned out to be the turning point of the whole war. Eventually Jap was broken and started to retreat. The monsoons had started and we all expected a rest but it became plain we had to push on through the jungle, the one thing everybody thought impossible. We built a road 100 miles long through the jungle against all odds and eventually reached the Chindwin river, 1400' wide. The only way to get our vehicles across was a floating pontoon, which we built under Jap fire and in spite of appalling conditions our vehicles crossed and we continued to chase the enemy. towards Mandalay. Here conditions were far better and we made good progress. The night before we attacked Vera Lynn arrived to give a sing-song. It was grand. The attack was successful and Mandalay was ours. Before moving on I was asked to help in the repairs to the Ava bridge where the 2 central spars had been blown by our troops on the retreat in 1942. The only possible answer was a suspended bailey bridge – after a struggle we finished this and all our vehicles entered Mandalay.

I then moved with the Army towards Rangoon, but at Pune I was called back to 14th Army HQ. Here I was promoted and told was urgently required in Rangoon. The only way to get there was by plane.

Some months later, the war in Europe being over, I was told my work was not over and I was again sent back to Calcutta. Here I was re-kitted and told to go with a force being prepared for the re-capture of Singapore. I was flown to Colombo to go by landing barge to Singapore. Fortunately, before we sailed the 2 atom bombs were dropped. We therefore had an uneventful trip to Singapore where we landed amongst great excitement. For a further 6 months I was engaged on repair work such as getting the brewery going again and many other important and interesting jobs.

On 23rd Apr 1946 I embarked for Blighty which we reached on 16th May 1946. I was demobbed on 17th and at long last returned to my family.

RD Lipscombe (from his diary)

Nov 1942. Received call-up papers and instructions to report to RN Training Establishment HMS *Glendower*, Butlin's Holiday Camp at Pwllheli. Not a Redcoat in sight, only CPOs shouting orders. After being kitted out went straight into Seamanship training. One very clear memory was of Life Jacket testing in a huge tank of icy water, a Petty Officer with a long pole made sure you went deep enough. Issued with Pay Book with rate of pay of 14/- per week.

Jan 1943. Given 72 hours leave after passing Seamanship exams. Then on to Gunnery drill, drafted to training establishment at Liverpool HMS *Wellesley*, practising firing 4" and 12 pounders at dummy targets at sea. During this time was selected in a squad of 100 ratings to march through Manchester to mark Salute to Red Army Day. I had not felt well for 2–3 days and next day went to the Sick Bay, diagnosed as having yellow jaundice, kept in for 12 days on low fat diet. Resumed Gunnery course until end of Mar, passed exam to be awarded rank of Acting Able Seaman Gunner, with a pay rise, so much that I don't remember how much it was. We were called 'the 10 week Sailors'.

Drafted to HMS *Chrysanthemum*, a training ship moored on the Embankment, then 7 days' leave during which time old pal Roy Naylor was also on leave from his RM training base at Deal. It was 2 years before we met again.

Back to London to board night train, destination unknown. Next morning we were back in Liverpool embarking on the P&O *Athlone Castle* as a troopship. Sailed that night, manning AA Guns with Maritime RA Gunners, joining convoy in poor visibility and rough seas, repeated action stations warning as unidentified aircraft approached so that convoy broke up. Weather was getting quite warm. Ordered to change into Tropical Kit.

Apr 28 arrived at Freetown, lots of diving boys asking for 'Glasgow Tanners' (silver 3d pieces) to be thrown into water. Sailed from Freetown in heavy rain, able to have a good wash on deck.

May 18 arrived Capetown in thick fog, nearly hit breakwater, able to go ashore where the locals treated us like Royalty (Cape Brandy quite lethal!) On leaving we joined a convoy for a few days, then we were unescorted until reaching Bombay on June 10th.

June 13 sailed from Bombay after transferring to troopship *Strathmore*, slept in hammocks on deck.

June 16 arrived Colombo in monsoon, taken to St Joseph's Barracks. Next day DEMS Gunnery School and football crazy CPO Bailey who signed me on for the DEMS team playing in the Interservices League. After a refresher course I was drafted to the Gunnery Officers' Launch taking over as Cox with a crew of 3, a RN Stoker below decks and 2 Singhalese on deck. This became my duty for most of the next 2 years, apart from a couple of short spells as relief Gunner on 2 vessels plying between Ceylon and India. During this time, feeling I needed a change of scenery I requested a transfer to sea which the CO turned down, saying they needed me in Colombo. At one point, a letter from home said my calling-up papers for the HG had arrived. CPO Bailey said 'bad luck Son, you don't get home as easy as that'.

Aug 1944 not feeling too good, sent to Sick Bay, diagnosed as having Dengue fever. 10 days in Sick Bay, then 14 days sick leave. Went by train to rest camp in the hills at Dujatalawa, much cooler there but 12 hour journey on wooden seats – not to be recommended. Back again in Colombo to resume Harbour duty. One of the hazards of walking down to the Jetty in the morning was dodging the red juice that the betel-chewing ladies seemed to take great delight in spitting over our freshly Blanco'd white shoes.

Mar 22 1945 received unexpected good news. Told to prepare to leave for home. Next day joined RFA *Gurna*. We were assured that we were going home, but not too sure how to take that when we discovered that the holds were packed with mines.

Mar 25 sailed from Colombo calling at Aden, Suez, Port Said, and Alexandria, where we had some shore leave.

Apr 25 left Gibraltar in convoy and arrived at Portsmouth on May 2. Granted 21 days leave. A lasting memory was walking home from Girton Corner and how wonderfully green were the trees and hedges, great to be home after 2 years away.

May 6 VE Day, great celebrations. Downed a few pints in the

Crown. That 21 days just flew by, then it was back to RN Barracks, Portsmouth for another 12 months or so before eventual demob after $3\frac{3}{4}$ years.

K Matthews

I joined up in Jan 1940 in RASC, sent to Felixstowe to do my basic training and to France in June 1944, D-Day + 4. My number was T/139036. My rank started as driver but became private because I was a tradesman in Workshop Platoon of 224 Coy RASC attached to the Guards Armoured Division. I went through France, Belgium, Holland and finally into Germany – finishing at Cuxhaven when peace was declared. I came back to England for demob in Jan 1946.

K Mayes

In order to pursue my interest in athletics and firearms I replied to an advertisement for training as an armourer in the RAF July 1939. Having passed a medical and general knowledge exam I duly signed for 6 years' service. What I didn't allow for was a war, which created all manner of disruptions.

To await my armourer's course I was posted to S Cerney, and enjoyed my first 'flip' in a Hawker Hart. My posting came through for my course in Manby, for 6 weeks where I lapped up weaponry and bombs. Qualifying, I was then an AC2 armourer who was posted to No 19 Spitfire Sqn, Duxford. I was given 2 machines to maintain (16 Browning machine guns).

The airfield became crowded with the arrival of 2 more sqns (No 66 and 222). Our sqn was moved to a farm on the outskirts of the perimeter. Then to another farm at Fowlmere where I, plus 3 others, lived in stables. Later we had the luxury of Bell tents.

On alternate fortnights A or B flight would go to an airfield at Horsham St Faith's. Here I witnessed Douglas Bader up-end his aeroplane taking off, bending his legs in the process! Further excursions in Norfolk were Matlaske and Ludham. A move to Sheppey lasted 3 days due to the attention of the Luftwaffe who flattened hangars, aircraft and huts.

The Battle of Britain was hotting up and as reinforcements we were sent to Hornchurch. We had no billets and spent most of the night in the shelters making up belts of ammunition, cleaning guns, and re-arming the returning aircraft. I was posted to Bolt Head in Devon, in charge of the armoury and one airman (I was then a Corporal). A brief encounter with an explosive ensured my sick leave for best man at my pal's wedding in Girton Church.

Next step Acklington on a ground-to-air firing range (Sgt then), Cardington on a senior NCO course. Back to Acklington. Passed a Selection Board in Edinburgh for pilot training. No more pilots required and I didn't fancy being an air gunner! To Grantham in charge of RAF Regiment equipment. An officer, one Warrant Officer and me in the office. Demobbed Dec 13th 1945.

D Mills

Douglas Mills, at 16, was the youngest to take part in the Battle of the River Plate aboard HMS *Ajax* in 1939. At Dunkirk his bleeding hands were evidence of his working non-stop for 26 hours. He also saw service in Tobruk, the siege of Malta, the Battle of the Atlantic and Java. He was sunk on HMS *Encounter* suffering shots in both arms, and was a Japanese PoW for $3\frac{1}{2}$ years. He was tortured and could have been executed, but was saved by 2 Gurkhas. On his release from captivity he weighed $5\frac{1}{2}$ stone. He received a letter from the King and a cigarette case in recognition of his service.

R Nightingale

Volunteered mid-1942 for RAF. Taken to Cambridge Station by friend Mitchell Fordham on the back of his trusty motor-bike. Took train to Cardington RAF base. After being kitted out sent to Redcar. Billeted in civilian houses. The training consisted mainly of 'square bashing'.

Went to Melksham RAF Training Camp. After 6 weeks passed out as Instrument Repairer. On to Stradishall which had Wellington bombers and sustained heavy losses in the notorious '1000 bomber raid'. From Stradishall to Chedburgh working on

Stirling bombers. Able to bike home from there when there was a

chance. Back to Melksham for more training courses which resulted in promotion to Leading Aircraftman. Posted next to the Flying Fortress (B17) base at Sculthorpe.

In spring of 1945 detailed to join Transport Command destined for India on board *Nea Hellas* which left from Greenock. On the journey taken ill and transferred to hospital in Aden. By this time the Atom Bombs had been dropped and the war was virtually over. Came home in a hospital ship carrying men who had been rescued from the hell of Japanese PoW camps. Landed at Liverpool and was back in 'dear old Blighty' once more. After more treatment was discharged and demobbed in late 1946.

D Watson

I was a member of Girton AFS which had as its HQ the Pump House at the top end of Woodlands Park.

I was called up for the Army (Oxford & Bucks Light Infantry) in 1944, after being deferred for a time because of my work at the Pye Granta instrument works in Cambridge, and sent to Fort George in Scotland for training and kitting out. In 1945 embarked on Troopship *Empire Ken*, *en route* for India. Based at Alikan near to Calcutta during race riots in which reportedly 100,000 people were killed. Returned home on the troopship *Île de France* and demobbed in 1947.

R Wilson

If your registration number ended with a 0 or 9 you had to go down the mines ['Bevin Boys']. I was unlucky enough to end with a 9 so having just turned 18 I was sent to Stoke on Trent. There were about 30 of us from all parts of the country. We were billeted in private houses and given one month's training and sent to different mines. I was sent to Mossfield Colliery where I remained until demob.

The colliery employed about 800 men. Every day you arrived at the pithead baths where you had a clean side of lockers and a dirty side with shower baths in the middle. You changed out of your clean clothes and put on old clothes for going down the pit. You filled your water bottle, then to the Lamphouse to get your lamp. You were searched to make sure you had nothing that could cause an explosion, then you went to the pithead to get in the cage that would take 20 men at a time 500yd down the shaft to the pit bottom. You then walked about 200yd and got into a miniature train and travelled about $\frac{3}{4}$ mile to the coal face, about 3' 6" high.

I was mainly employed on haulage, getting the coal from the coal face to the pit bottom. We produced about 4,000 tons a week.

Josef Kominek (see photograph p49)

Although not a local man, Sgt Josef Kominek had a Girton girl friend. He was based at RAF Duxford with Czech 310 Sqn, and shot down three enemy aircraft in the Battle of Britain. On 8 June 1941 he was preparing for night action in his Hurricane and changed his route to fly to Girton where his girl friend lived in the Thornton Road area. While doing prohibited low flying at 9.45pm he crashed at Manor Farm and was killed [Map site B]. The crash was seen by Mr Ron Foster of St Vincent's Close, who was working in a field nearby and was first on the scene. The Searchlight Bty then attended and secured the area. He was originally buried at Royston but is now in the Military Cemetery at Brookwood.

Those Who Died

The War Memorial commemorates the names of 11 men who gave their lives in the conflict. The *Roll of Honour* website records brief details of their Service careers (at the time of writing this is at http://www.roll-of-honour.com/Cambridgeshire/Girton.html) and includes the name of WHH Johnson (see p36). Three other men mentioned in these pages however also gave their lives in the conflict but are not commemorated. Mr Dennis High was married in St Andrew's Church in May 1942, and the Church Magazine records his subsequent death in active service. Mr Alex Ulyatt was reported missing in April 1942, though no confirmation of his death was posted in the Church Magazine. Mr AH Wagstaff was killed in action in Sep 1942. Mr Johnson and Mr High are not even recorded in the Village Roll of Service (nor is Ken Dean, who appears to have moved to the Village during the War), though Mr Johnson is in the Girton section of the Ely Cathedral Second World War Book of Remembrance. Beyond what is recorded in these pages it appears nothing else is remembered of them.

ROLL OF SERVICE
Names of those from the Parish of Girton who served in the World War

1939~1945

Alexander, A.	Cornell, H.	Hart, G.H.	Martlew, T.	Rooke, H.W.
Alton, J.M.	Cox, T.H.	Hawkes, D.F.	Mathews, K.	Roper, S.A.
Andrews, E.M.	Crabbe, B.	Hills, L.F.	Mayes, K.S.	Rose, O.E.
Anthony, H.	Cranfield, A.P.	Hind, J.	Milne, G.S.	Rosenthall, M.
Archer, T.M.	Cundell, R.	Hodson-Smith, A.	Moore, C.	Rudd, J.E. w
Arthur, T.G.	Cundell, C.B.	Holt, A.R.	Mortimer, E.G.	Rudd, R.G. w
Ashton, N.C.	Cundell, L.R.	Hoppitt, E.	Moyce, D.A.	Ruffer, C.M. w
Austin, R.G.		Huddlestone, G.		Rule, F.J.
Ayres, R.J.	Dean, H.	Hulger, B.F.	Naylor, G.	Roote, L.
Brading, R.	Dean, L.	Hunt, J.O. w	Naylor, R.	Saffin, H.E.
Balsom, J.	Dimond, W.H.	Hurdy, G.B.	Nelson, D.	Saunt, T.
Barber, R.H.	Dixon, S.R.		Nightingale, E.	Scott, E.T.
Barnes, G.V.	Dixon, W.P.	Ibbett, W.	Nightingale, R.	Secker, J.F.
Berry, S.G.	Dupont, F.	Impey, T.C.	Nightingale, V.	Siddall, D.
Betson, G.W.	Durham, W.H.	Impey, L.G.	Nisbet, W.	Smith, C.A.
Betterman, M.L.		Imrie, A.		Smith, J.G.
Betts, B.C.	Edmunds, G.C.	Ingle, S.	Oliver, H.D.	Songer, M.
Bird, D.	Edwards, A.W.	Ison, J.H.	Oliver, M.C.	Spalding, J.R.
Blunt, K.R.	Ellis, R.B.	Ison, W.H.	Oliver, P.R.	Stearn, E.J.
Broad, F.H.	Ellwood, S.A.			Stearn, E.
Brown, S.C.	Engledow, C.M.	Jackson, A.	Palmer, T.D.	Suttle, P.C.
Buck, G.A.	Evans, D.	Jaggard, R.J.	Parfitt, K.M. w	Swift, H.M.
Burgess, L.	Evans, F.G.	Jardine, R.S.	Pauley, C.V.	
Burrows, J.C.	Evans, R.H.	Johns, L.M.	Pauley, C.	Thurlbourne, P.
Burrows, R.S.	Evans, T. m	Johnson, A.	Pauley, T.A.	Trethowan, H.N.
Bright, R.S.	Evans, W.	Johnson, A.G.	Pearce, S.	
Campbell, J.M.		Johnson, F.	Penney, L.	Ulyatt, A.
Chapel, B.	Gawthrop, S.A.	Johnson, P.	Pettit, G.R.	
Chaplin, B.M.	Gerrard, T.C.	Kidman, C.	Pigden, E.S.	Wagstaff, A.H.
Chapman, H.J.	Goodman, L.M.	Lamb, R.H.	Piggott, D.C.	Wakelin, J.
Chapman, A.J.	Green, D. w	Lane, J.L.	Pinder, D.A.	Wallis, B.R
Chivers, P.C.	Green, F.C.	Leuchars, G.	Plane, D.L.	Wallman, H.W.
Chivers, W.N.	Griffiths, C.	Lewis, E.R.	Potter, J.W.	Watson, D.
Clare, R.C.		Lewis, N.	Povey, W.T.	Watson, P.
Clark, S.	Hales, L.M.	Lilley, H.G.	Pritchard, H.	Watson, R.
Claydon, W.J.	Hall, A.J.	Lilley, S.C.	Purkis, R.J.	Whitehead, D.
Coe, R.	Hancock, K.R.	Lipscombe, R.	Purkis, W.J.	Wilderspin, G.P.
Cole, D.	Hankin, C.R.			Williams, R.
Cole, R.H.	Hankin, S.C.	MacAlister, E. w	Rawlings, J.F.	Wilson, C.S.
Collings, J.K.	Hankin, V.W.	MacDougal, J.	Rayner, E.M.	Wilson, E.C.
Collings, L.H.	Harrison, R.M.	Mack, C.H.	Reading, J.	Wilson, R. m
Chandler, W.R. m	Hart, B.R.	MacAlister, J. w	Risebro, R.F.	Kitteridge, K.E.

w Indicates Womens' Services.   m Miners.

The Roll of Service

5: Adult Reminiscences

R Scrine

These reminiscences come from people resident in the village in the War years. Some, sadly, have died before publication. With an operational aerodrome at Oakington and a Flying Training School in Cambridge, which used Girton as part of its training circuits, the RAF was very much in mind, particularly when aircraft went missing or crashed in the vicinity. The sites of all crashes in Girton are marked on the map (*Frontispiece*). In the interests of clarity we have edited the notes or transcripts of tapes they made, and this chapter should not be taken as a verbatim account. Nor should it be assumed that these memories are always accurate.

Mr John Brooks: The University Farm

The war caused an urgent need to maximise food production to reduce dependence on imports. County WAECs directed the campaign and farmers were required to follow orders. The University Farm was well placed for the ploughing-up campaign. In 1939, 116 acres of grass were ploughed to grow wheat and a further 60 acres in 1940. Throughout the war the emphasis was on the maximum acreage of wheat possible. The farm was also required to grow not less than 60 acres of potatoes and sugar beet annually and this meant growing 20 acres on the clay, with all the problems of harvest in a damp autumn.

Livestock policy had to be severely changed as a result. The beef breeding herd was immediately disposed of, and the ewe flock drastically reduced. The dairy herd was increased to 40 cows and all calves reared. The pig breeding herd was halved to 15 sows, and poultry reduced from 1000 laying hens to under 100. Practically no experimental work was possible with the emphasis on food production and the shortage of staff.

In 1939 most of the work was done by horses and there were 43 Percherons of various ages, 17 in regular work. Some 7 or 8 foals were bred each year, and young horses sold. Two mares, full sisters, over 20 years bred and reared 39 foals between them, probably a world record. The horses were gradually replaced by increasing mechanisation, the last horse leaving the farm in 1968.

Mrs CE Parr

We had Land Girls lodging with us who worked on the University Farm. On one occasion we had a mother and two daughters. One day there was a knock at the door and the mother stood there absolutely exhausted. The work that particular morning had proved too much for her. The Land Girls stayed about a month then after they were trained they were moved on. One girl we had was very lively, she always had RAF chaps calling to take her out.

After the Land Girls we had evacuees. One boy returned to see us not very long ago. I knew who he was because of his red hair, although I hadn't seen him since he was a boy.

Mr R Parr

I worked at Marshall's, so I was in the HG there as well as in the Girton platoon. At any one time only one had a rifle, my neighbour and I had sticks. However, the Girton platoon was very efficient and won trophies. When the Eighth Army visited we all paraded together and to their surprise, our drill was as good as theirs, and we all saluted as one.

Girton HG Platoon. Mr Monkman holds the shield awarded to them in 1943 for the best fieldcraft in the country.

We used to patrol the hedgerows and fields looking for paratroops. One evening we gathered a lot of mushrooms and asked the cook to fry them up for our breakfast. However, we had some officers visiting, and they were given to them instead. We used to patrol the bridge on Oakington Road some nights as well – with sticks as our only armament.

Mrs E Matthews

My husband was an ARW. Sid used to do fire-watching around Girton. There was an old water tank in Washpit Lane which they used for water as there was no other available in Girton. They used to push it on a trolley. We had a shelter in our garden for the family and the evacuees whom I used to carry down there. We had two evacuees during the war, a boy and a girl whom they wouldn't split up and we were paid 5/- a week. When they came to us they had head lice. The older one didn't want to go home but wanted to stay with my Charlie. As we were outside the 3 mile limit there was no school bus and the County Council supplied bicycles.

We had everything in the garden, vegetables, rabbits and chickens, so we didn't have to buy very much.

I remember seeing a plane crash on the golf course [Map site A]. My son said it was German. A Mosquito crashed near Ladysmith Cottages on the Huntingdon Road after hitting the treetops in the coppice [Map site F]. One of the crew died in the crash and the other on the way to hospital. All my ceilings came down when it crashed.

Prisoners of war were billeted in Washpit and they used to help at harvest. Dad got on very well with them. When he walked to Huntingdon with the horse and the siren went, the horse would bolt.

The HG blocked off Huntingdon Road with carts to keep tanks away.

Mrs Miriam Doggett

My father and Stan were in the HG. When there was a raid Mr Porter used to come round and ring a bell. I remember watching them drill on concrete behind our house, marching up and down with pitchforks because they hadn't any guns. My husband used to go fire-watching and he was there when 19 bombs fell down by the Animal Research Station.

Mr Tom Evans

Before being called up as a Bevin Boy, Tom and his twin brother Dick joined the HG. Sgt Jack Coe, an ex-regular soldier, was very strict. Ted (Tubby) Nightingale was always late on parade, but was found without fail either in The Crown or The George.

Tom remembers Spigot Mortar exercises in the field next to The Crown. Someone put the wrong

Tom Evans with his brothers Will (L) and Dick (R)

shells in the Mortar so the shells were going well over targets and the heads of watching members.

On an exercise in Madingley Woods they had to crawl through a wood to capture enemy on the other side. They turned out to be in the wrong wood.

Once they were ordered to the Conservative Hut to march a captured German prisoner to HG HQ. The prisoner, in full uniform, was in fact an impostor from the University.

Mrs Vera Goddard

My husband was a volunteer fireman in Cambridge. We did not have a phone, and the only indication of a siren was a man cycling round the village blowing a whistle, which did not wake us up. Mrs Bonny next door had a phone, so when the sirens went off in Cambridge the Fire Officer rang her. They fixed up a wonderful contraption. Mrs Bonny had a thick rope dangling from her window into our bedroom window, on the end of which was a 14lb weight that thumped on our bedroom floor when she pulled her end. Three times in one night George dressed and went off on his bike to Cambridge only to get to Girton Corner in time for the All Clear. Poor Mrs Bonny!

There was an 'ack-ack' post behind the Church and one night they brought a German plane down and we heard them cheering. We picked up shrapnel in our front garden next day.

Mrs Betty Impey

I was married in Dec 1939, my husband went in the army in May and I lived with my mother-in-law and worked in the office at Eaden Lilley. My husband was away for three years in N Africa and in Italy. There was a lot of air activity, I was really and truly frightened.

The only bombs were up on the Huntingdon Road and they killed a cow or two, I think. It was still a bit frightening when the sirens went off but I think I was more afraid of the Doodlebugs than anything. When we heard them we used to sit and hold our breath until they had gone.

Jim Ison and Leonard Cornell used to get up concert parties in the VI in aid of the Homecoming Fund.

I can't remember whether they were given money, but my husband was given a little radio. And of course, we loved the concerts as well. There was singing and the children used to do dancing.

There was a Pig Club based at The George and we all used to keep our swill. My father-in-law was in the HG and they used to take it in turns to take the swill and then have part of a pig, maybe 4 times a year because there were quite a few members of the Club.

Mrs HW Leakey

Alice Hibbert-Ware had a great friend in Switzerland, also a very well known naturalist and they decided to write to each other about the birdlife in their respective countries as the seasons went on. After the war, on holiday Miss Hibbert-Ware was paged for the telephone and the two people next to them said 'You are not Alice

Hibbert-Ware? We could never crack your code'. How much time they must have spent trying to crack ornithological notes!

There were academics living in the Huntingdon Road, and I got into awful trouble when as Billeting Officer I wasn't allowed to billet in any of those houses. These were the code-breakers and their work was terribly important; they couldn't have anyone billeted in those houses. But it was terribly difficult to persuade people that it wasn't gross favouritism.

In 1941 we had a simply abundant fruit crop. We had no sugar. The government decided that they would allocate sugar for jam making if we turned ourselves into a Produce Guild and had proper instruction. It was a time when the village became conscious of itself. Our Treasurer was Dr Margaret Martin, the archaeologist. She realised this was something she could do with the village. I was so glad. We were supervised by government people. We had days when we made jam and days when we did canning. Children were allowed to come in and crack the nuts with a hammer. We did 4 tons of fruit in the village.

The Pease Family
[Extracts from letters to their evacuated children, Richenda ('Chen'), Dora and Fabian ('Fabs') in Canada.]
Some time in 1941
It's a long time now ... Are you getting real Yankee now, have you started to talk their way yet? Reynolds Close is rather lonely without you ... although we have got a little 'Ref' [evacuee] boy staying with his mother here.

Yesterday I brought back the little cow from over the farm, making a total of three, getting quite a herd of cattle now but we cannot get more than $1\frac{1}{2}$ pints daily from them, although we will get more in a week or two when a new calf arrives. But there won't be you around this year to make a fuss of it.
16 Feb 1941
Yesterday we had quite a fine show in the air over the garden – three of the vast new bombers (we think they are the American ones) sailing through the sky like ships rolling from side to side and round and above them groups of fighters dancing about like gnats. It was an impressive and cheering sight – pleasant, contrasting with an awful Sunday in June when we could see and hear no planes round here and we wondered if our last fighters and even trainers, had been thrown into the battle in France! Last Sunday an unfortunate bomber (not one of these giants) went sailing round and round above the village for 6 hours. The landing wheel was jammed and they

kept up as long as their petrol lasted, trying to get it down. Finally they had to make a 'pancake' landing which the pilot managed with extraordinary skill, to the admiring applause of 3 villages. We did not applaud when a damaged bomber returning from Germany crashed into houses in Histon Rd, the pilot and crew having baled out 10 miles away. It is true only 3 old women were killed, but what with the road deaths, many of which are said to be due to furious driving by the army and now the RAF chucking aeroplanes about like this it is a hard world for civilians! (NB This crash, with details of place and time, was given out on the wireless, so I hope the censor will not say I am giving away information to the enemy).

13 Mar 1941

We have a small evacuee boy with us temporarily – a very nice little fellow, and pathetically appreciative of any attention. Joanna has been reading to him in bed which he likes very much. She was reading him some stories (out of *Puck of Pook's Hill*) about attacking castles with bows and arrows; he exclaimed 'What a silly owl to try bows and arrows, I would take a stick of dynamite!'

The other night I was chasing the calf in our field with a bicycle light. It was pitch dark and I had just got it where I wanted it when a man's voice spoke from behind the haystack 'Is it all clear?' and out stepped a uniformed figure. He was HG and apparently thought I was signalling to him! He was much too proud to help chase the calf, but anxiously enquired if there were any bulls in the field. I said no bulls, but about 3' of mud. However he didn't mind that and splashed off to the other side. They were evidently having their night practice attacking or defending the tank trap.

There is another alert on tonight and poor old King will be up again. He is the only one in the Fire Squad who can drive, so he has to be on duty every time.

13 Oct, probably 1941

I am very sorry I was a long time answering your letter but I have been very busy lately with the two children I have got living with me now. Girton is getting very full now with all these evacuees.

We have the siren going every night. Dodford Lane had 4" bombs dropped which caused great excitement but no damage done. It's really maddening the way Jerry goes around dropping bombs anywhere ... 8 o'clock, siren has just gone.

20 Oct 1941

The bombers are going out over us now every few minutes as I write. Margaret Engledow is in the WLA at St Neots, but doing cows, not tractors.

The other night, when Daddy was at his post, he was wakened by a succession of heavy bangs which seemed to shake the hut to pieces. 'Ah' they all thought as they jumped up, 'it has come at last! A stick of 6 bombs in the middle of Girton!' So they ran out. And what do you think it was? The sand-bags bursting and falling against the tin wall of the hut! So we still remain unbombed. The nearest we have had were some small ones a little while ago that managed to get the sewer, water main, electric and telephone cables in the main road opposite what used to be Cousin Ida Darwin's house.

4 Nov 1941

Enclosed is a ring from Mrs Matthews, meant for your birthday present, but it will be about right for Xmas. It is made from aeroplane glass (of which, as you can imagine, there are a good few bits lying about England!). Mr Cornell (you will find him in your ARP list) made it for her to give you.

10 Dec 1941

Locally we had some light relief a little while ago (I trust the censor will let me reveal it now) in the form of manoeuvres combined with ARP exercises. I was 'Chief Umpire Search' for Girton (don't ask me why that title!) Of course it was all rather absurd really, but it did reveal weaknesses and provide a useful rehearsal. I and my two co-umpires had to stage certain 'incidents' and report how the services worked. A land mine was supposed to flatten the whole of our road, and the Laundry was hit, &c. I had to stage a direct hit on Girton College tower: and while I was trying to get my fire cracker to work, a too zealous HG arrested me and it took 20 minutes to convince them that as I was a white-badged umpire they had no business to interfere with me. So in retaliation I labelled them all casualties. We also had a fire down Dodford Lane which nobody noticed so I had to report it myself! And King's Fire Squad turned up in fine style and proved conclusively what we wanted proved, that the hose was too short from either end. We used the LHS boys as casualties and they did enjoy themselves, only they all wanted to be stretcher cases and they kept on showing their labels and asking what sort of gory wound they had got. The principal anxiety of the proceedings was to see that they all got home safely in the blackout! All night and all next morning tanks and armoured cars (real ones) came down Washpit and were 'diverted' round Duck End (on account of the alleged land-mine in our road). Jockey Jones was very indignant because one convoy refused to recognise his authority to block the road and pushed past him 'absolutely brushing my coat'. I must say they looked an awesome sight and we thought of the villages the

German tanks have really torn through.'
Jan 1942
Thank you very much for the parcel received safely from you for
Xmas. Yes, as you put it, the box should have contained whisky as
it's just a little scarce nowadays. I wear the gloves daily and they
are very nice, but the tea we have not used, we are saving it for a
rainy day.

Mr Michael Pease with his cattle

Reynolds Close is about the usual in appearance, the cow has a
little calf 3 weeks old, which we generally get this time of year, but
with the shortage of poultry foods there's no Muscovy chicks and
only three of Khaki Campbell, 12 fowls, which is different from the
crowds you used to remember.

Now this afternoon we have been over to IVC to see a film sent
from Canada of Dora and Fabs. It was very nice to see them running
and rolling on a new lawn. I took Mirelle, Mrs King, and Mrs
Matthews over in the car, the others cycled.
From Mrs Matthews; probably Jan 1942
The old village is about the same. We have a searchlight on the Rec.
It lights the village up at night.

Oh, the ring is made out of a Jerry plane shot down nearby. We
have had quite a peaceful time just lately, not a Siren in two months,
perhaps more. I expect you have your worries out there now with
Japs. The news looks bad out there, especially in Singapore. Every
time I put my blackout up I think about you out there ... What do
you think to Russia. They are marvellous, the news has just said
they have taken Možajsk. I went with your people to see the film of
Dora and Fabian, it was lovely. They have grown, it was taken in a

lovely garden. They both look very well and happy. Can you send me a snap of yourself for a keepsake, as I expect you are getting quite a young lady now ... I do remember the girl Turner, it must be very nice to have someone from Girton so near to you.

Mrs Amy Williams

There was a great movement of people – Girton residents going to join the Forces or to work in special war industries and other families coming in to work at Marshall's or other Factories. Pre-war there had been the arrival of many Jewish refugees to the Cambridge area.

Another group who arrived were a Non-Combatant Corps of the Army. They were mainly conscientious objectors and expecting to go overseas on certain duties. They were well received and we met them at dances in the WI Hall. Some had been university students. The young wife of one of them stayed with us for several weekends. She had been trained as a Court Dress-Maker and worked in London. I also remember the Sergeant Major – very much a Regular Soldier – he and the men put on Concert Parties at the VI which were much enjoyed.

Blackout and Rationing were outstanding in our minds. Cycle and car lights were well dimmed by order and it was often difficult to get batteries. Roads and kerbs were not very well maintained with little street lighting. My father made light wooden frames covered in heavy black paper to fit in each window. Sometimes searchlights scanned the sky at night and on occasion you could see an aircraft caught in the beam.

My father dug a trench alongside Mr Skeel's orchard to shelter us in the event of an air-raid but it was no use as it soon filled up with water. We then shared a metal shelter with Mr & Mrs Read who kept the shop next door, Mr & Mrs W Lingley our very good friends, and my godmother, Mrs Amy Graham. It was set up in our orchard and camouflaged with extra branches. I can well remember sitting inside it and listening to German bombers passing overhead and being told the next day that Coventry had had a devastating raid. There were clear summer nights and bombers' moons and a nightingale sang in an old pear tree at the bottom of the Reads' garden – such a strange mixture of the bad and the beautiful. We were in that shelter the night bombs were dropped on the University Farm – there were no human casualties as I recall but we picked up shrapnel from the garden path the next day. As the months went by we abandoned the shelter and stayed the nights in our houses. The Air-Raid Siren caused fear and the All Clear relief. I can also remember one sunny afternoon at the bottom of our garden in 1940 prior to the evacuation at Dunkirk we could hear the distant gunfire and explosions.

People living in the country and growing their own fruit and vegetables had a distinct advantage and my mother had always made jam, preserved fruit in kilner jars and eggs in large earthenware pots of isinglass. We were allowed sugar to feed the 5 hives of bees in winter time and our rations were managed very well.

My father did Fire-Watch duties at the College on some nights. Mother helped with the accounts for a canteen for the village school children which was run in the VI. Mother also had a small group of people she called on each week to sell them National Savings Stamps to help the War Effort. Neighbours were all very supportive of one another. On fine summer evenings we would congregate by the drive of Mr Secker's bungalow. He had been a RSM in the Boer War and had many ideas to offer about the conduct of this one! All were welcome and war news and progress were discussed at length.

At the beginning of the war it was mainly the RAF cadets one would see marching in town along St John's Street back to the Colleges where they were billeted. Convoys of army vehicles would travel along the Huntingdon Road but information about troop movement was heavily restricted and the posters warning us about 'Careless Talk' very prevalent. Mail overseas was censored and we could buy Aerogram forms at the Post Office to write a short letter. These were filmed and printed out in the country of destination and this photograph was then delivered – all to reduce the weight of overseas mail.

I had a friend who was a Flying Instructor at Marshall's and he used to fly low over the tennis court at the bottom of our garden and wave – I guess it was against regulations!

I had Scottish cousins in the RAF who would come over from Waterbeach or Stradishall at weekends. Our greatest shock was when one went missing: an Observer in a Wellington. The aircraft was shot up and ditched in the Channel. I can still remember that very stormy Sunday night sitting in the house and saying how terrible it would be for men at sea. Little did we realise that Jock and the crew were tossing around in their dinghy for 57 hours and were eventually washed up on rocks at Ventnor. We had a letter from his sister on the Monday morning telling us that he was 'reported missing', and then a greetings telegram about three days later to say that they were all safe and in hospital. Their survival was headline news with details as to how they had tried to put out flames in the aircraft with anything available.

Not long after I started work at Addenbrooke's there was the bombing of Vicarage Terrace in Cambridge and I remember the casualties being wheeled along the corridor for admission. Towards the end of the war German Casualties were brought over to a sand-bagged ground floor ward kept empty for any special emergency which might have struck the town.

There were many political rallies in the Guildhall. We went to hear Bernard Russell speaking and Ernest Bevin's speech was relayed to crowds standing in the Market Square. We also went to dances – cycling home was difficult but comparatively safe.

Janet Cracknell

On 29 Nov 1986 we were out with our metal detector in the wood opposite Washpit, near the Pillbox, when I got a bleep. I started removing the soil and found a batch of bottles with metal tops. There were about a dozen.

At this time Frank found a notice saying 'PRECAUTIONS AW Bombs fire instantly on breaking in air. If fire is

Girton's Pillbox still stands by the Huntingdon Road

started accidentally, use water freely. Store bombs (preferably in cases) in cool place, underwater if possible. Do not store near inflammable material, avoid storing many bombs close together if possible. Stringent precautions must be taken to avoid cracking bombs during handling. The caps must never be removed'. I stopped digging immediately and informed the Police, who informed the bomb disposal squad. The next day the A14 was closed and the bombs were detonated. These were obviously set up as a Tank Trap, near the Pillbox.

On raid nights we could read a newspaper by the flares dropped to illuminate the air fields. Also, on other nights we would listen to that droning misfire noise made by the Buzz Bombs, one hoped they would continue to buzz, for if not they were on their way down.

6: Children's Recollections

P Graves & H Naylor

Alison Baker (née Bonny)

I was born at 3 Woodlands Park on 18th Nov 1939. I went to the village school when I was 4. There was a stove to warm it. The lavatories were outside, a row with unpolished plain wood seats, and newspaper on a string on a nail.

We had a garden full of fruit, so my mother bottled plums and made jam. We used to have eggs from Miss Amps and probably let her have fruit.

Sometime our books or presents were pre-war stock, due to shortages of paper in the war. We 3 sisters were given silver spoons, and my younger sister's was for Hunstanton Bowling Club, the only one my parents could find.

The three Bonny children

We were the only ones with a telephone in our area and we took messages for the neighbouring houses. I think we were the ones who took the call that Cedric Smith (2 doors down) was safe and well and not dead (he was in a Japanese PoW camp). When the Americans came on the scene, we used to get calls from them for Barbara Scott opposite, and I ran across to ask her to come to the phone. Various of the older girls went out with the Americans. My father brought one home for tea one day and he arrived in a jeep, khaki with a white star, which stood outside our house. He took us for a drive round the village. He brought sweets and chewing gum. I have an abiding memory of King's College Chapel with a khaki American truck, white star in front of it driving past, with a smiling black face looking out.

When a group of soldiers marched through the village with a band, we would march along behind. We all sang 'Maisy Doates' and 'You are my Sunshine' and 'She'll be coming round the mountain'.

There was great excitement when a plane crashed in the field at the end of Dodford Lane [Map site A]. We all went to see it.

My father took me outside the back door one night when it was dark, to see the glow in the sky, which he said was London burning.

On VE day on the Rec a huge bonfire was built which we danced round. There was also a slow bicycle race, a wheelbarrow race, a

3-legged race, an egg & spoon race, and a sack race.

Isabel Wilson (née Bonny)

Looking back to war-time Girton through childhood eyes is not so easy, for I was born in 1942.

One visitor was a German PoW from Oakington. He made us all rope sandals Many years later when holidaying in Bavaria, we happened on a village garage. The owner was delighted to learn we came from Girton – he too had been a PoW at Oakington and had loved every moment. By sign language and a few words we gathered many Germans had tried to be captured – a better life for them than their own.

I remember seeing a gas mask in the landing cupboard, my sisters' had animal faces I'm told, but they were never needed.

Hazel Baggaley (née King)

My brother and I cycled in to Guest Road, Cambridge to School. Cycling was certainly the easiest and best way as the bus No 102 from Girton Corner was a mile to walk and the fare I think was 2d. My brother and I did this for most of the war years and taking our gas masks with us at all times.

My father, Irvine King, was the Fire Officer for the village and he used our car to tow a small Fire Engine about the village. The Fire Station was the Pumping Station building at the top triangle green of Woodlands Park. There were about 12 firemen from the village, Mr Ray Watson, Mr Fagg, Mr Vic Watson (an ex West Ham footballer), Mr Whitehead, Mr Hales, Mr Nightingale, Mr Matthews, my Uncle Mr Les King; and my brother Neville was the Messenger Boy. 3 of the Firemen slept each night at the Fire Station and the weekly drill period was Sunday morning from 10am to noon.

During this time my father and any other villagers who had land had to grow more potatoes and wheat and at harvest time a threshing machine from Cottenham used to come and thrash the corn. Horses and carts were used to carry the wheat-sheaves to the threshing machine.

Hay making was another thing. Mr Luke Cole used to cut the hay with his old hay cutter, then the hay was put into heaps by hand and left to dry.

The ladies used to take cans of tea and jam sandwiches to the men in the afternoons and then the men would work on until 8 or 9pm. Some of the ladies used to collect the wheat ears left on the ground, my Gran did this. Potato picking was mainly done by the ladies.

June Beavington (née Mayes)

My brother was in the RAF. On 3 Sep 1939 we listened to the

wireless; Mr Chamberlain declaring war on Germany. I believe the Air-Raid siren sounded soon after – so we put on our gas masks (which were kept in a small cardboard box with string attached to hang round our neck) expecting we knew not what.

My father was in the ROC at HQ in Cambridge and cycled on duty day and night. My brother told me I had to be brave like a soldier to look after my mother.

IVC opened at that time, a number of us set off for our new school, on bicycles our parents had bought from the Education Authority, complete with oil lamps! the gas mask always in our bicycle basket, and we were told to get into a ditch if the siren sounded.

One afternoon playing on the Rec (ignoring the siren), I saw a plane in the Histon direction drop a string of bombs.

We spent numerous nights sitting in the hall of our house. The German planes came in with our bombers after raids to bomb the airfield – we knew the drone of the enemy planes. I remember the bombers taking off to join in the 1,000 bomber raid on Germany – like a swarm of flies.

One Doodlebug went over one evening spouting fire and making a screeching sound.

A summer Sunday afternoon a fighter plane flew over the village very low. We watched in horror as the plane flew lower and lower, and heard the sound as it crashed into a field [Map site B].

Then, of course, there was the 'Blackout'. My mother answered the front door one evening – Mr Herbert Jones told Mother a chink of light was showing. Mother stepped out onto the lawn and onto Herbie's foot – the sky lit up! My poor mother nearly died of fright.

Soldiers stationed in the WI Hall had a very good choir and gave concerts.

Phyllis Bickel (née Skinner)

We were allowed 2 weeks off school for potato picking during late Sep–Oct. This was cold, hard work.

The old FA ambulance had no doors at the back, only canvas flaps. We children spent a lot of time playing in it (I don't think it was ever used). We used to emerge through the canvas flap, pretending we were on stage.

I attended the village school and remember being happy there. The Field Club, started by Miss Hibbert-Ware, was a particular favourite lesson.

Frank Cracknell

On the Rec there was a searchlight unit, but I still remember clearly, with other lads, our eyes popping as we watched the arrival of the

NAAFI girls who were warmly greeted by the soldiers and had to beat a hasty retreat each day.

Chivers' Farms were billets for Italian PoW, which we used to supply with Ally [aluminium] and Perspex, in return the prisoners made us rings, crosses &c.

On one occasion Benny and I found 6 incendiaries joined by wire, which we took home and our parents called the Police. We also found, with the assistance of Geoff Norton from Grange Farm Cottages, an unexploded cannon shell. Being inquisitive we pushed it into the ground so only its firing cap was visible. We took position behind a haystack and with catapults fired stones at it. As nothing happened and we got braver, we approached the shell until we were standing directly above it. There was an almighty bang and a shower of dirt blew into us. Luckily, no-one was hurt and we stood looking into a large hole.

A plane crashed a few fields away from us, it was trying to make its way back to Oakington after a raid [Map site F]. This was night time but we went to see what had happened. A member of the crew was still alive, but trapped under part of the aircraft. When the rescue team got him out, he died.

Janet Harradine (née Pluck)

I remember seeing flares drop overhead one evening in Feb 1941.

On the afternoon of 21 May 1941 a plane crashed in the second field over the stream at the end of our farm (University Farm) [Map site E].

About 10 bombs fell in our field about 11.20pm on 8 Sep 1942. Some didn't explode, and there were lots of flares around.

Roy Ellis

In 1940 on a misty afternoon, my mother pointed out fires in the field. Incendiary bombs had been dropped in the field beside the Old Crown. Claude Kidman and I went out to look for shrapnel and found fins from the bombs lying in a line, about 100' apart. I have still got 2 of the fins.

I joined the HG as soon as I was old enough. On one exercise a man left off and was asked where he was going and he said 'the bloody cows need milking'.

Shrapnel picked up by Roy Ellis in 1940

Peter Graves

When the evacuees arrived in the village there was no room in the school, so the VI was turned into a classroom. Old desks and chairs were brought in and a row of toilets with buckets was built at the back. With the arrival of evacuees we had an outbreak of head lice and fleas. The District Nurse inspected all our heads once a month (I was OK). Some days there was no-one to teach us. Some children were sent to work in the school garden next to the VI. All children considered under-nourished had a spoonful of cod-liver oil and malt every morning at school, owing to food rationing.

As the war came to an end the first bananas came to Girton. My father had the job of selling them 1lb per ration book. I had the job of marking everybody's ration book.

I helped Miss Hibbert-Ware and her brother to collect waste paper in her old car which was stored in Mrs Green's garage. After school I worked on the farms at harvest time, setting the sheaves of corn up and leading horses. Everybody worked till dark.

Most people kept a few chickens. Household scraps we boiled and pollard was mixed. We were allowed 14lb a month from French's Mill. Surplus eggs were stored in a big stone jar and covered in waterglass. All surplus vegetables and fruit, chickens and rabbits, were collected twice a week by Luke Cole and his horse and cart, and taken to the Mart in King's Street Auction. Bone bins were put around the village for our bones.

The WI, leader Mrs Thomson, knitted socks, scarves, mittens, which her son and I delivered round the village to folks with men away fighting the war.

As D-Day approached, convoys of military vehicles passed along Huntingdon Road. We stood at Girton Corner watching all the tanks, lorries, guns &c go by.

Keith Lawrence

I remember seeing a number of searchlights scanning the skies for enemy aircraft. I was kept awake at night by the soldiers shouting orders.

My father used to spend long cold nights fire-watching from the roof of the Shire Hall in Cambridge where he worked. He would go off to work in the morning with his gas mask and tin helmet. I have no idea when he slept!

Sometime during the war, we had billeted with us an airman, who I believe was a rear gunner in the bombers stationed at Oakington. My memory is limited to a single brief encounter when Mr Young was in the bathroom when I wanted to be there.

Walking home with my mother one afternoon, soon after Hitler's death, I remember seeing the effigy of a man hanging from a lamp post or a telegraph pole and being told that it was Hitler.

One evening a Doodlebug passed over not far from our house. I could clearly hear the noise and see the sparks from its ramjet engine.

Maureen Littlewood (née Cranfield)

Maureen remembers staying home from Church for Chamberlain's announcement. Life suddenly became grim. She was 11 years old and joined the first intake of children at IVC. Bicycles were provided for children to ride to school, only those who weren't able to cycle could ride on the bus.

As a Girl Guide Maureen (in uniform) helped to take evacuees to their host families and introduce them. She remembers queueing for gas masks and the nuisance of carrying them everywhere.

In 1942 Maureen left school to join NIAB and was annoyed not to be allowed to fire-watch as she wasn't 18 years old.

She remembers the drone of bombers *en route* for Coventry, later the glow in the sky from the fires in London.

Harry Naylor

When I was about 11 or 12 we used to deliver laundry to Longstowe Hall. During the war there was an army field bakery there. My father used to hammer along down the hill at Caxton, with his foot on the floorboards and doing at least 60! We thought that was a tremendous speed.

During the war the cream of the teachers were called up. Jimmy Garner who was headmaster was a very old man. His method of teaching was a lot different to what it should have been. When I was 11 I went to IVC. Before I started there others kept on about the periods. I asked what they were and they said it meant you move from one room to another for different subjects. They rattled the subjects off and said 'English' and I said 'What's English?' My elementary education was so backward I didn't even know what 'English' was at age 11.

Fabian Pease

The first night we got home from N America a stick of bombs fell well within waking-and-shaking-us-up distance (we assumed it was Oakington) followed by the air-raid sirens. For our first letters back to the Bells I wrote enthusiastically all about it only to be told that we couldn't include that kind of information.

I recall watching the Lancasters taking off each evening while we had dinner on the verandah, a B26 crashing at the foot of Dodford Lane [Map site A] and looking at a wrecked Mosquito over on the Farm on Huntingdon Road [Map site F]. I also remember several stray V1s disturbing the peace.

The George Inn, one of Girton's two pubs

Also walking up to The George to listen to the King's speeches on VE and VJ days. They had set up a loudspeaker on a pole outside, so we listened to the King's speech standing at the side of the road, and then the celebratory bonfires at the Rec. My brother got his picture in Picture Post as one of the crowd outside Buckingham Palace.

Dora Pease

My younger brother and I were sent to Devon in the summer of 1940, but I had forgotten this until I saw some years ago the national register for ration books and identity cards, listing everyone in Girton High Street in lovely black copperplate writing with a later note against our names as having moved first to Bishop's Teignton and then being evacuated to Nova Scotia in Canada.

Many of my pre-1940 memories are due to the care of our Canadian foster-parents who were meticulous in seeing that we wrote home weekly with drawings, to which they added their covering letters. Chenda had been sent to the USA. Alas, she got into trouble for writing a letter to the parents about all the exciting ships she had seen in Halifax harbour – Royal Navy destroyers MTBs &c, and the 2 *Queens*, frightfully sensitive material. Luckily the foster parents were very kindly censors, so the letter never went off.

The parents wrote regularly and sent us books and there were often messages from Gladys Matthews, Irvine King and Gerda Senser. But of course they couldn't say anything much about the war. We were thrilled to hear that Gladys had a baby daughter, Veronica.

Chen came back in autumn 1943 and Fabian and I in Apr 1944.

We used to listen to the planes from Oakington, Lancasters and Liberators, flying out at night on bombing raids and back in the early morning. Fabian and I were avid readers of the Govt pamphlets. A few lost Doodlebugs came overhead and one or two stray rockets. During the day, planes would be practising in the sky, Chipmunks, Dragon Rapides, Tiger Moths, Spitfires, Hurricanes, and, later, Mosquitoes and others I can't now remember. All quite different from the great seaplanes we knew in Canada, the Catalinas and the Short Sunderlands.

We didn't see much of Jo or Bas. Jo was away training to be a doctor. Bas was in Bomber Command working on radar and used to come home with mysterious black briefcases.

VE day: Bas and Chen went up to the celebrations in London, and came back with 2 enormous flags which we used for bedspreads. I can't remember the atom bomb being dropped, or VJ Day,

Sally Robey

It was 1938 and the Munich crisis was casting a long shadow over the country. But this meant nothing to me as I peered through the banisters, fascinated but also more than a little scared. The lighted hallway below was full of men wearing khaki capes down which water was streaming. As I watched, Father ushered everyone towards the kitchen and out of my sight.

The next morning our large farmhouse kitchen was full of soldiers eating bacon and eggs, Mother having banged on Mrs Parsley's shop door long before opening hours in order to get supplies for the Searchlight Bty that had landed up in the field behind our house the night before. They were Derbyshire territorials, coal miners who had been mobilised straight from their shift and had set out for a map reference that happened to be Home Pasture on Howe Farm in the parish of Girton. When they arrived it was already dark and there were neither provisions or tents waiting for them. Luckily my father noticed something amiss and went out to see what was going on. Hence those weird figures dripping water all over the hall.

It was several days before an officer turned up relieved to find the men in good hands, for after breakfast was served on that first day Mother had knocked on more doors and obtained enough camp beds and bedding for each soldier. Darts, bagatelle, cards and a radio were also provided in this makeshift barracks as well as regular hearty meals. Indeed, the officer was so well satisfied that, whilst guaranteeing that the men would in future receive proper rations as well as tents, he asked Father if he'd been in the war (1914–1918) and, on learning that he had, asked him to take charge.

Many of these men kept in touch and, eventually, my parents received letters from numerous war zones. Unfortunately, these have long since been lost.

We had ack-ack gun batteries on the pasture behind our house on several occasions during the War and, although these soldiers were properly cared for, they always used our kitchen as a mess, consuming countless drinks of tea and cocoa, and the cards and games were in action again.

Sometimes the gun crews would give my brother and myself roundabout rides on the gun. However, there was one gun that was shrouded in mystery. It used to arrive at dusk and leave each day before dawn. The idea was that, if hidden away in the woods during the daylight hours, German reconnaissance planes would not be able to spot it, and thus it could be effective at night. This was at the time of the so-called Baedeker raids when Hitler threatened to bomb a number of historical towns, one of which was to be Cambridge. These nocturnal soldiers, too, got a nightly hot drink, and once Mother remarked, jokingly, that they had not yet shot down a German aircraft. 'We'll get you one tonight' they said. And they did!

Then there were the PoW. First came the Italians. Cheerful, thankful that they no longer had to fight, they sang their way through the days. Indeed, we children had a wonderful time with our neighbours living on the other side of the fence, and on many a sultry summer evening my small brother was swung up onto broad shoulders and carried home as we all trudged up from the harvest field.

Haymaking, here by the Pease family

Mother's belief was that everybody is somebody's son, and she always sent for the PoW to help themselves to some of our garden harvest. The same belief meant she somehow provided them each year with a Christmas hamper. She applied the same rule later, when some German prisoners came to live in the cramped hut.

A Mosquito crashed tragically killing its crew of 2 [Map site F], and 19 bombs fell in one field, harming no-one.

Josephine Pringle (née Wilderspin)

On Sep 3 1939 we did not go to Church but stayed at home to listen to Chamberlain's announcement.

We all went to the WI Hall to get our gas masks, which had to be carried everywhere. This was a nuisance when combined with a school satchel. The cardboard boxes containing the gas masks soon became battered and were fitted into mackintosh cases.

At school the cloakrooms were reinforced and surrounded by sand-bags. If the sirens sounded everyone took their books to the cloakrooms and continued working, sitting on the shoe lockers, until the All Clear went.

The sound of planes was constant. Tiger Moths for pilots in training by day and bombers going out at night. We used to count the planes leaving Oakington and hope to count the same number returning. One morning a Lancaster went over minus its tail fins. Searchlights – 3 making a beacon, but more on less clear nights. Occasionally the sound of a German plane, a distinctive engine sound. We called the Tiger Moths 'Marshall-smits'. They used Girton College and the distinct pattern of our garden paths at Syxtene for a turning point.

There was always a houseful of people, airmen and civil service personnel were billeted on us. Unfortunately father was on permanent night duty so needed quiet days.

On Saturdays it was time to deliver wool to the knitting circle ladies. They met on Monday afternoons to make 'comforts' for the troops: dark blue for the navy, khaki for the army and grey-blue for the air force.

Telegrams always seemed to bring bad news. So many Cambs troops lost in Singapore, and school children lost crossing the Atlantic for the safety of Canada or America. Airmen just disappeared.

During the school holidays we helped to make camouflage netting, and went to the Leys School, which had been converted into a military hospital, to help with cleaning.

Margaret Sharpe (née Wilderspin)

On Sunday 3 Sep 1939 we were called in to hear Chamberlain's speech declaring that England was at war. The next week there was a special visit to Town to buy what looked like miles of thick black cloth, to make blackout curtains.

Everyone had to go to the WI Hall to be fitted with a gas mask. These fitted into cardboard boxes which soon became rather battered. People bought mackintosh covers to protect them, and some used them as a safe nesting place for identity cards. As children we had to learn our card numbers. Later they became NHS numbers.

Evacuees arrived and empty houses were furnished for them. Everybody helped, providing furniture, and toys for the children. However, village life proved too dull and soon the evacuees departed taking their 'spoils'.

Airmen in training were billeted on us. They were very ingenious in their methods of cheating to pass their exams so that they could join the fight. Sadly only one of the many who stayed with us survived the war.

The nearest air-raid shelter was at the Wellbrook Laundry. My parents decided that it would be safer to stay at home!

My sister and I went to the Convent School in Cambridge where the cloakrooms were fortified with sand-bags and we practised 'Siren Drill' – how to get there safely, quietly, and, of course, with one's work, whatever the lesson.

Gradually the blackout, shortages of food, lack of fuel and no buses on Sundays became the norm. Street lights were installed in 1939 in Girton but not used until after the war. The one at the corner of St Margaret's Road became a tit-box. Bicycles were the best form of transport but with the shortage of tyres and inner tubes a lot of time was spent on repairs. Cycle lamps had to have white, not chrome reflectors and in order to keep the light down were fitted with little 'jockey' caps.

The drone of planes setting off on raids over Germany made going to sleep difficult. On the first circuit from Oakington 'drome they just cleared the Girton College trees – and the roof of our house. The return was sporadic, not the steady notes of the journey out. Seeing a late plane returning, minus most of its tail, one knew that the rear gunner was not making it home. Occasionally there was a ground-shaking explosion when a plane didn't get off.

Great care was taken not to waste food. Food coupons were precious. All scraps were kept for pig swill. Mr Ward (Shepherd on the University Farm) would walk down from the Bunker's Hill cottages with some eggs – a thank-you for the swill which he collected. Clothes were a problem when you were growing and children gained a lot of 'pass-ons' to be cut down for them. Miss Pauley in Hicks Lane was a tower of strength in the clothes making and altering business.

On Monday afternoons there was a knitting circle, making 'comforts' for the troops. There were concerts and whist drives to raise money for the 'Home-coming Fund' which was to give money to every returning serviceman, or his family if he didn't come back.

Dr & Mrs Stewart at Girton Gate, Huntingdon Road let the Girton Tennis Club use the court in their garden.

At the beginning of the war my father, a Scientific Instrument maker, was in a reserved occupation. My brother Geoffrey had been turned down by the RAF owing to poor sight, so became an aeronautical engineer at Marshall's. My Grandfather Wilderspin lived with us, but many more when relations from London and Manchester came for respite from bombs, plus the pairs of Airmen. It was a big change for my mother, no more maids and with so many people. The shortage of sugar meant less jam making. I remember her saying 'How shall we manage, I've only made 100lb of jam this year'. The surplus fruit had to be preserved in Kilner jars. Surplus eggs went into big crocks of isinglass.

Ann Tole (née White)

The sound of planes flying heavy and low over the house and trying to count them, then waiting for them to return. The returning ones had a different sound.

Standing outside the house in the dark looking for lights in the sky, watching them go out. Being awakened and taken down stairs with my sister and later my brother to sleep in the hallway until after the All Clear.

The only thing I remember about the production of *Michael* [see *KiT* 54] was sitting on the edge of the stage with my sister Janet in the Girton Follies (I did not remember the name). I did a tap dance and was in a skit. I remember Mr Ison very well. I know we visited American Bases and Hospitals and I always enjoyed this as we were given sweets and presents. Once we entertained some Polish and many British soldiers. We would be picked up at the top of Woodlands Park and a lorry would transport us.

My father was an aeroplane mechanic and was away from home, so we would go and stay with him for a few weeks at a time; sometimes he would come home unexpectedly and stay for a few hours.

Girton Follies in 1944

7: Evacuees
R Scrine

As part of war preparations in the late 1930s, a programme was drawn up to evacuate children from areas deemed to be at risk from enemy action. Most came from the Greater London area. Evacuation was not compulsory, and during the 'phony war' many returned home.

To some children it was an adventure, to others the thought of leaving home was unbearable. For some it was the only way to continue education as whole schools were uprooted. Teachers and Welfare Officers were supposed to accompany the children. For all it had a considerable impact, particularly on children entering puberty with no one to talk to at time of greatest need. The clash of cultures often led to the unfortunate children being relocated, perhaps more than once. Yet many survived the experience, some remaining in their adopted countryside.

In designated areas Billeting Officers were appointed to find suitable homes. This must have been a thankless task.

Mrs HW Leakey: Chronicle of a Billeting Officer

It is mere nonsense to think that you can be well-prepared for 'Evacuation'. On paper the thing looks fairly simple ...

At 2pm two bus-loads of London children are due to arrive in our village. Some 50 householders have in these early days been persuaded that they are ready and willing to offer homes, on Govt terms agreed ...

- 2 girls to Mrs B
- one small, very quiet boy to Mrs W
- one, possibly two, girls, aged 8–10, to No. 44
- Mrs L must have girls who speak well, because of her own children
- Mrs S will take little girl if she can be guaranteed well-behaved

Then comes the Bus, and out of it surge hordes of bright-eyed, sturdy boys, all looking about 8 or 9, with a small sprinkling of very small children, and only a couple of the popular-sized little girl. Each child is labelled, and with their bundles or string-tied suitcases they stand – quite undaunted, for is this not the country, and are they not Evacuees?

The Nice Little Girl of Twelve: 1940

The long day ended, and I had billeted 30 of the London children in what I hoped were permanent homes in our safe area. There only remained for the following day the 6 who had been fitted in for the night, but for whom proper homes must be found on the morrow.

Night came, with splendid peace, but all too soon the morning.

I made my list, consulted notes and records. There were the twins aged 6, two jolly little boys of about 11 or 12, a mere wisp of a girl-baby alleged to be 5, and the tall, lanky Johnnie whose thin wrists stuck out far beyond the frayed cuffs. Hollow of eye was Johnnie – all bones – but possessed of a grin that lit the face, till shyness cloaked him again ... But first I must milk my goats, and deal with family breakfast.

Then off we went. There was kind Mrs D, and this early in the morning I found her at home, sleeves rolled up, welcoming. 'Poor little lambs!' Of course she would help, she had come up yesterday, but found me out. Heartened, I took a twin in each hand and said 'Jennie and Veronica, Mrs D, could fit into one bed as they are only 6'. She smiled, and patted Jennie on the head. 'I'd love to, Ma'am, but I'm out at work most mornings; by evening my legs are so tired I can't be running up and down stairs. Could you find me a nice little girl of 12 who could do for herself at bedtime?' I offered each of my flock as substitute, but adamant she remained – 'A nice little girl of about 12 ...'

3 doors on, my hopes leapt up, as Mrs J opened the door, smiling. 'Well I never,' she said. 'And I'd just told Dad I'd really like to take in a nice little girl of 12 who'd like taking the baby out in her pram of an evening'. How hard I worked ... but oh so reluctantly did she take in Freddie, and I left an unwise promise to exchange him later.

But at least our party of 6 was now reduced to 5 ... Across the road, down the lane, brought us to one of our small farms, whence I had earlier extracted a promise of a billet. I took out my notebooks. There it was: 'Mrs T – girl, 10–12'. Gone was the sunshine of the day. Should I offer the twins or the hungry-looking Johnnie? But the door opened and we were all swept into the spotless parlour. How the twins managed it I don't know, but we emerged without them, and I blessed the motherly hearts of the country women whose kindness has no limits.

'Now Johnnie', I muttered to myself, 'and Tom, who is undoubtedly a boy, and this mere baby ...'

Off we went to find Mrs H and her already big family. 'You're welcome, Ma'am,' she said. 'Of course I will, though Dad do say I shouldn't. But some one can sleep in with my Barbara, for though she's 12, she's very small. Now a nice little ...' I pushed Tom forward and grabbed Elsie the baby firmly by the hand. 'Mrs H', I said, 'you're an angel. Keep these two till tomorrow ...' And I fled with Johnnie, in search of the villager who yearned for a long, lean lad with an endearing grin and a doubtless enormous appetite ...

But does anyone know any Nice Little Girls of Twelve?

The Naughty Boy from London

'It isn't that he means to be naughty, Ma'am, but he just isn't used to our ways, and he's not been brought up the way we do. Meals! I'd be ashamed to send out a child of mine no more accustomed to good food than this one. Always hungry, he is, and asking for "a piece". And that's what they feed them on – a piece here, and a piece there – and often as not no butter nor jam to it either. It isn't that he means to steal. He just takes things when I'm not looking being as he is hungry. I've no patience with these London mothers and their ways.

And Mr Hall's cow – Now, did you ever hear the like? A bow and arrow which he had made himself. But to shoot at the cow! Well, well! Young Mr Hall, he pulled the arrow out quick, and the old cow is still milking well, never or more. But when our Constable did come along, I felt real ashamed, for we'd always lived respectable and I've always kept myself to myself. As for him stealing apples – well, Dad did get fair angry, for the fruit was still quite green, and fine keepers too, right into April, planted by Grandad over by the pump.

But do you think that the WVS ladies could help with a piece of stuff so I can mend Jackie's trousers? The Ladies did send along a nice pair of shorts for him – but stand in them as he can, poor lad, there's no sitting down. I reckon his old ones will give a lot of wear yet. O yes, he has another pair, but those are his Sunday ones. I wouldn't like him not to look neat-like when he comes out with Dad and me of a Sunday evening'.

The Seven Sisters of Islington meet the Blitz of the Countryside

'Well, how are things getting on?' I asked, as I saw the harassed face of the official who had travelled down on the bus that fateful Sunday.

'Not too bad', he replied, 'but I wish you'd keep your eyes on that lot'. He pointed to 5 names starred on his list. And so I was introduced to the Seven Sisters.

The eldest was 26, the youngest 18, each had left a husband at home, most of them had a baby or two with them, too young to walk, and whose meal times were public and incessant. They were sitting all together, expostulating against the idea of being billeted separately. Never, it seemed, had they lived or slept apart. Fresh air, space and separate beds were horrors they had never before envisaged. Some sobbed, some continued to expostulate and a sort of chorus came:– 'I want to go home'.

At length the sisters, in pairs, were promised that they should be billeted in houses as near each other as could be. I took them along with relief just as the next bus-load full of children arrived, and hoping for the best I slipped home for 10 minutes' peace while medical inspection of heads went on among the children. Brief and blessed peace.

But at the Hut I found some of the Sisters – for, though billeted in different houses, they expected at least to be able to sleep together in decent warmth and comfort. Stemming the tide of talk, I saw them back to their 'homes'.

Seen as a group, they were not unlovely – dirt, babies, distress and all. Gypsy-type, I thought, as I tried to help them – and discovered that in London it seemed that they all slept in one gigantic bed, any interstices being filled with husband or baby. At long last I persuaded them to suffer the barbarities of country life and go back for the night to their billets. 3 of them had made return a delicate matter and we bedded them down with their sacks of luggage in the sitting room of the kind villager whose goodness of heart was beyond belief and praise.

Before I was fully awake next morning, the telephone rang. Could I come along at once to the house where '2 of the Sisters had slept'? With praiseworthy calm, the villager explained that one of her Sisters had woken up with a rash and temperature that looked like Scarlet Fever suspected and later confirmed by the doctor. The history of that day shall not be written about in all its awful length ... Sanitary Officials, Doctors, forms – the unfruitful endeavours to extract details from the Sisters – and the constant chase to keep them all in a garden allotted for the days of quarantine.

Later that afternoon the Ambulance arrived and all the Sisters were packed off to the local Isolation Hospital for the next 48 hours of danger.

The following morning I went forth to see how they had fared in the kindly hands of the hospital's small staff. A sort of unrealistic peace reigned over the place. I knocked at the front door and went in.

'Funny lot you sent us,' said a woman cleaning.

'Funny lot they sent us,' I said. 'But where are they?'

'They've gone – all gone!'

And so they had. The space and intolerable quiet of the bare neat rooms held fears which could not be borne. Authorities or not – and very early that morning – out-witting the enemy by sheer numbers

– babies, baggage, germs and all – the sisters had escaped and made
off up the road. They had 4 hours' start and the wide welcome of the
fields – making for London.

Has any one met them? We reported the facts to the authorities –
and heard no more.

M'Ankle Straps

'But Doris,' I said, driven at last into argument with the small but
determined girl, 'of course, they won't give you another pair; these
are perfectly good shoes to wear indoors at school'.

'Them's not shoes,' said Doris, 'them's m'ankle straps. And Mum
said m'ankle straps are for Sundays'.

I looked helplessly at the low-heeled patent leather shoes which
were causing such trouble and time. Authority took the not
unreasonable view that only children without house shoes could be
considered. But then shoes that looked quite ordinary was part of
London's Sunday Ritual, together with a preposterous white silk
dress ...

'Doris,' I said, 'I'm sure your Mum would want you to fit in with
our ways and to do as we ask you'.

'I'm a good girl, I am,' said Doris, 'but m'ankle straps are for
Sundays'.

Routed, I returned home, and searched among my own daughter's
shoes for a pair which should fit Doris, and leave her undisgraced as
a true child of London.

Footnote

Girton placed 188 children from Stoke Newington and Bethnal
Green during the war years. We never saw a Welfare Officer, or
teacher. Our school was packed, but happy – as were the children in
their adopted homes.

Sundays used to be 'Visiting Day' for some parents. When they
came to The Close, I used to move them gradually from the warm
fire-side to the Oh-so-chilly window-seat of the lounge. Although
they were nice and grateful, time was scarce, and my goats had to
be milked, Sunday or no.

Evacuees who live in Girton

Few evacuees still live in Girton, and no survivors of the evacuation mentioned by Mrs Leakey. Several who were evacuated from London to Cambridge came to Girton at a later date. Robin Scrine was evacuated to Beccles in 1939 and arrived in Girton in 1957. Chenda Huxley and Jennifer Turner were among the more fortunate ones who went to N America, though they were lucky to have arrived there and returned home safely.

Mrs Babs Hancock

My time in Cambridge started as a London evacuee. To be a London evacuee one had to have, believe it or not, a haversack. It cost 1/- and was just a sack, horrible brown sacking. There had to be a label on the bag, and also a label on myself and a list of clothing. I said goodbye to my mother and had no idea that I would literally be leaving for ever. My brother and I just walked to the corner and waved goodbye. We went to the school, and were put in a crocodile and walked to the tube station. We ended up at Liverpool Street station, boarded a train and still didn't know where we were going.

When we arrived at a big station we were taken off the train and bundled into buses. I realised afterwards that this was Cambridge. The buses took us to Newnham Croft and fussy ladies in white coats pushed us along to the classrooms and into the halls. We were called by name and sat in a chair, a lady started combing my hair, and looking in my ears, checking to see if I was clean. We were then walked round the streets and the Billeting Officer knocked on the door of each person and asked who they would take. Gradually the crocodile became shorter. Nobody would take us as brother and sister so my brother had to go with one landlady and I had to go with another, an elderly couple, who were very kind.

People could have been forced to have a serviceman, war worker or evacuee. and often they thought it would be easier to have an evacuee. This rather put an onus on us because the Billeting Officer would say, yes she can clean, yes she can sew, yes she will help to do the housework, yes she will do this and she will do that, but as an 11 or 12 year old I am afraid I wasn't able to.

Anyway I found myself with this elderly couple. It was rather traumatic because I was made to strip and take a bath in a tin bath in the kitchen. I felt very humiliated. Then I found I had to sleep with her! Just imagine, the first night you are evacuated you have to sleep with this old dear. I felt sorry for her and I certainly felt sorry for myself. The next day we found ourselves at St Mark's Church, where our teachers were trying to control us and understand our problems. My first weekend in Cambridge was spent having a lovely time. The war hadn't been declared and my brother and I and our other friends walked right through from Newnham to Grantchester meadows. It was absolutely wonderful, because there was an orchard, and we could scrump apples on the way. On the Sunday we were told to put on our school uniform and we had to walk all the way from St Mark's to Great St Mary's. During the service they announced that war had been declared. Oh good, we whispered, we will get our 3 weeks holiday. We won't be sent home just yet.

As time went on we realised it was going to be longer than we thought, the nights began to get dark and the landlady felt that perhaps I was rather difficult and a bit of a handful. I suddenly found myself in one of the grand houses in Grange Road with the staff of the family. I spent all day in the kitchen in the servant's quarters and my bedroom was upstairs in a garret room, so when the maid went home at night and all the staff had gone, yours truly had to take herself off to bed with a candle all by myself. There was nobody to say goodnight to, nobody to kiss me goodnight, there was just the stars, God and myself.

I remember longing to get a letter. One morning the postman came and I ran through to the hall and picked up the letters. Hilda the maid said sharply 'What have you got there?' 'The letters', I said. 'You can't have them'. I thought how awful to live in a grand house like this and you can't have the pleasure of picking up your own letters.

I was used to coming home from school starving and going into the cupboard to see what there was to chew. I remember seeing this dish which I thought was apple and custard left over from lunchtime. So I took a bite and it was awful, white sauce over cold marrow! So I left it and thought nothing more about it. Once again Hilda said I had to go in to see Mrs So-and-so, and I went into the study. 'I'm going to report you to the Billeting Officer'. 'Why', I said, 'I haven't done anything wrong'. 'You've been stealing food. Don't you realise you have taken the Master's supper?' Well, I just couldn't understand it. What I had taken a bite from wasn't big enough for anybody's supper, leftovers like that at home would have been thrown in the dustbin.

On another occasion I had to go into the study, was taken up into my bedroom and given such a telling off because I hadn't looked after my bedroom properly. I didn't realise I should strip my bed every day, shake the mattress and shake the blankets out of the window.

I was told off for not dusting properly. When I got to bed that night I sobbed my heart out and found myself hating my mother because she had not taught me to strip my bed and shake it out every single day, and had never taught me to dust on top of the doors. I vowed that if I had children they would be made to manage for themselves because I found that was one of the worst things in my memory – one was expected to be self reliant and be able to do things otherwise one suffered.

I got billeted with another lady who had a daughter in Girton. She was very nice and she would bring me over to Girton and I got to know the local people. This lady became too old to keep me, but I wasn't allowed to come to Girton because I was a city evacuee. But I kept in touch with her and the Girton people.

The Billeting Officer said to me one day 'You're C of E aren't you? The people I am going to billet you with are Salvationists'. I didn't know what she meant. The only Salvationist I could think of was the chant we had 'Salvation Army – all gone barmy'. But that was the best billet I ever had, because on that first afternoon 'Uncle Tom' who came to mean so much to me over the coming years, sat me in the armchair by the fire, and asked me if I would like fish and chips for supper. He actually asked me if I liked fish and chips.

It was while I was at Church that I met the Girton people again. This man had friends who used to attend the chapel at Girton and they wanted somebody to help with the SS. They asked me if I would go and we started the Girton Bright Hour on a Thursday night and that's how I met the young man I later married.

I found a billet in Girton, as I was then 17 and was no longer counted as an evacuee. The war was still on, but I had left school and gradually met more Girton people.

I noted the differences between living in a city that had been bombed like London and a country city like Cambridge. I could hear my billeting landladies worrying about their spring cleaning, whether there would be enough material for curtains, or would they get enough soap to do the cleaning. In London there was no worry about spring cleaning because the bombing was so bad you wondered if the windows would still be there the next morning I did go home occasionally in the summer to see my mother and baby sister. My mother could only get the food from the shops where she used her ration books. For example, one was allowed $\frac{1}{2}$lb jam, or $\frac{1}{2}$lb of sugar. My mother had the jam. the country housewife would take the sugar and if there was fruit in their garden they would make their own jam, so by magic their $\frac{1}{2}$lb of sugar became 1lb of jam. We only had one egg on the ration book but in Girton nearly every other person had their own chickens. People even had their own pigs. You couldn't do this in town, and I realised that country people were certainly that much better off where food was concerned.

I recollect one Easter, my brother and I feeling so desperately homesick, buying carrots and walking to Byron's Pool, cleaning the carrots in the Pool and sitting chewing them instead of Easter eggs.

I remember a sailor coming home on leave while I was in Girton. There was great excitement as he had brought home a lemon, it was such a prize that they had a special raffle for it. Just imagine, the whole village having a raffle for one lemon!

Mrs Alice Pritchard

When my husband received his call-up papers I had a live-in job in Huntingdon Road with my daughter aged 2. I was very unhappy there, the family were not at all kind, like many I was looked down upon because I came from London. My working hours were long though I was well fed. When my husband came home on leave I became pregnant, had my baby in Addenbrooke's and subsequently went to Great Wilbraham for 3 months to live with the Vicar.

Following this I came to Girton in 1943 to 68 Cambridge Road where I was very happy as people were very kind. After the war my husband worked at the Animal Research station, and we went to St Vincent's Close in 1948.

Mr Robin Scrine

In the summer and autumn of 1939, we had prepared ourselves for leaving our home town of Gravesend, Kent, finally embarking on the *Royal Daffodil* on Sep 3, this ship being somewhat irreverently referred to as a 'Fish and Chip' boat.

Gravesend Grammar School for Boys had approximately 500 pupils a large number of whom went on board at about 8am together with a number of girls from the Girls Grammar School – probably about 250–300.

We all thought this was a jolly adventure, but we were strictly segregated from the Girls School! By the time we were in the vicinity of the Sunk Light Vessel the calm water had become choppy. Needless to say, sea sickness began to take its toll and most of us who had eaten were wishing we had not!

At Lowestoft there was a queue for the only berth and we had to wait for what seemed like hours, rolling badly. Those who weren't already ill soon succumbed, those already ill thought they were leaving this mortal earth! However, once we had disembarked complete with suitcase and gas mask we were taken to the Odeon

Cinema where we stayed in rather insanitary conditions for the next 2 days.

It was a short journey to Beccles which was to become our home for the next 10 months. My younger brother John and I together with another boy from my form were billeted with a retired coastguard and his wife, who although about 65 years of age made us most welcome and looked after us through the winter with all attendant problems of illness and no antibiotics to treat them.

School consisted of lessons in various buildings – the local Grammar School, and any other available space, but it must have been an awful problem for the Staff, not only suffering from a shortage of fellow teachers, but in the early days, lack of books and equipment meant that lessons were rather rudimentary and the school day was mercifully short! This state of affairs lasted for around 2 months when the School acquired the use of a disused Workhouse in a village called Shipmeadow about 3 miles W of Beccles. The rooms were all heated with coal fires with the blackboard on the mantlepiece which made the teacher rather warm especially when early arrivals had piled all the coal from the scuttle on the fire!

Nevertheless, it was very cold, we had to cycle or walk 3 miles to the school and the return journey was often in the teeth of an E wind well laced with sleet or snow. When the snow was deep it was easier to walk, the school day being shortened to allow us to return home before dark. On the whole it was quite safe with few vehicles (apart from the army) on the road.

After about 10 months we were forced to move as the town was placed in a danger zone. We ended up by moving a mere 6 miles to Bungay. Although smaller it coped well with school numbers, as by this time many pupils had returned home to Gravesend, just in time for the Battle of Britain! We did see some of the air war, the odd German plane being pursued by fighters with the accompanying rattle of machine gun and cannon fire. One memorable afternoon, a Dornier 215 bomber flew round and round Bungay eventually dropping its bombs on the marshes which hurt nobody.

There were many bombing raids on the larger towns of East Anglia, Norwich burned fiercely when the Boulton and Paul aircraft factory was heavily bombed – we could see the glare from 20 miles.

Being small boys we were interested in collecting empty cartridge cases and fragments of bombs which fell in the fields leaving a large crater. Apart from these excursions, I found the countryside very enjoyable and spent many an hour cycling and walking around the lanes in the vicinity of Beccles and Bungay. We went blackberrying in the autumn to earn pocket money, and gathered acorns in the winter (these were fed to pigs and we had to pick up an awful lot to earn a few pennies). Tame rabbits were also a source of income when sold at the local markets to augment the weekly meat ration of $\frac{1}{4}$lb.

We stayed with 2 families in Bungay, the first for quite a short time and the second for the remainder of our stay there. Both looked after us very well, but were an anti-climax after the love and care we received at Beccles. Coincidentally, both husbands worked at Richard Clay, a well known printing firm which is still operating.

As time went on, those remaining at Shipmeadow used to go back to Gravesend for the school holidays – usually we spent most of the nights in the air-raid shelter. However, by 1942 the Luftwaffe had turned its attentions elsewhere, the danger of invasion had virtually disappeared and our time at Shipmeadow came to an end in July.

Apart from occasional air-raids at night, the war front was fairly quiet for a while and school continued without too much disruption. We were shaken out of our complacency in 1943 and 1944 when we were bombarded by the V1 and V2 Rockets which arrived without warning. At least with the V1 you had a few seconds to take cover when the engine cut out! During our holidays when working on local farms to earn pocket money, we used to see these Flying Bombs being chased by fighter planes and were always glad when they came down somewhere else.

My mother, brother and I were very fortunate to avoid being killed when a V2 landed 2 doors away at about 4.45pm in 1944 killing some of our neighbours and severely damaging our home. Thanks to the kindness of friends we were given accommodation in their house for about a year until our bungalow was rebuilt.

Mrs Jennifer Trusted (née Turner)
We were in N Cornwall when War was declared. I was 14. I remember Chamberlain on the radio saying that there was a 'state of war'. I remember feeling glad that we had at last 'stood up' to Hitler. The year before I had been appalled that we had capitulated over Czechoslovakia.

The first few months were 'the phony war'. We were back in Cambridge and I think I heard that it was the first place to experience an air-raid. We came downstairs when the siren went but I don't recall any bombs. I didn't really worry about defeat but my father did and we 6 children along with my mother went to America in July 1940. We were part of a group of 50 children of Oxbridge academics who were invited over by some E Coast American universities. I was very seasick and did not worry about U-boats. We came up the St Laurence and were met by Mrs Calvin Coolidge. I did not know that her husband had been President.

We travelled to Northampton, MA and stayed with Mrs Lyman, whose husband was a cousin of the Roosevelts. It was a lovely big house, and most unusually for the States they had 3 resident servants – nearly as many as we had had in Cambridge! They were ardent anglophiles. I went to a private school there. I loved it; it was warm, the food was very good and the teaching was excellent. But unlike England! The next year, when I was 16, I won a scholarship to Radcliffe College, attached to Harvard.

Jennifer Turner at her 17th birthday party

The War hardly impinged until Pearl Harbour; I came back to Northampton MA for the holidays, great excitement because Mrs Roosevelt was coming to stay. But she had to go to the W Coast after the attack and so I did not meet her.

In July 1942 we came back to England. On the crossing we were with a lot of Merchant Navy officers who had been torpedoed and were getting back to England for another ship.

Queen Mary College was evacuated to Cambridge and I did some lab work under their auspices and took the Girton entrance to read Natural Sciences in 1943. I had my first room in the new wing – it was a little bed-sitting room. We had coal fires – and not a great deal of that. The building was cold and I imported a small electric fire – which fused a number of lights. The transgression was detected and I was rebuked.

Of course we bicycled everywhere but there was a bus service from Girton Corner and at that time we could go back to the College through the wood – no fears of attacks. We had lunch at the Girton waiting rooms just off King's Parade. We did not have to fire-watch, the only real war effect was the blackout.

After VE day my father opened some champagne but it was old and had gone quite flat.

8: The Women's Institute

M & S Hornsey

Introduction

The Minute Books for both the Committee and the Monthly Meetings record the discussions, preoccupations and the actions of the WI each month. Items selected from these books reveal the impact of war on villagers during the years from 1939 to 1945. The entries follow a chronological order, month by month, and inevitably there is repetition as matters of concern recur season by season or annually. On many occasions the Secretary has clearly recorded events as they happened at the meetings and, since those involved were perfectly familiar with the situation under discussion, notes can be tantalisingly brief. Over the succeeding months details about a subject might emerge from subsequent discussion or report; then it is possible to re-create the event more fully. In the following account of the war years the Minutes have been extracted and reassembled to provide rather more coherent descriptions within the framework of topics. Episodes in each topic are treated chronologically to preserve the sense of developing events and to allow some cross-referencing with other happenings within the village. In doing this, we lose some sense of the immediacy of the times and miss the intense divergence of interest and preoccupation that went on simultaneously each month. It can only be hoped that we gain in clarity from the chosen approach.

The WI Hall

With the advent of war all WIs received a letter from the National WIHQ, in September 1939, urging them to continue as normally as possible during this period. In her letter Lady Denman (Chairman of the National Federation of WIs) said 'It is not easy always to maintain courage and cheerfulness in war time. Our Institute meetings should be centres not only of the many forms of war-work which we shall be asked to undertake, but of neighbourliness among ourselves and among the visitors who war has sent to live among us.' One change was that monthly meetings would be held from 2.30 to 4.30pm in order to meet blackout regulations; however, this restriction only lasted until the end of the year. The HQ request particularly affected institutes with their own halls since the needs of both the WI members and the larger community had to be satisfied. Girton Hall was already used by the village Brownies and the Infant Welfare Clinic and a further complication was introduced by the possible requirements of the Military. Added to all of this was a proposal that County Council classes and the VAD might use the WI Hall for their meetings. With evacuation of the civilian population already in place the Girton institute decided that evacuated women and children would be welcome on Monday afternoons and that a group which was concerned with the making of bandages could resume work when the need arose. Within the village there was talk of establishing a First Aid post in the Hall but the required sand-bagging of the small room would have shut out too much light; the decision was to move the post to the Conservative Hall. The WI Hall was seen as being especially suitable for the Dances and Whist Drives which were organised to raise money for good causes, such as the Red Cross or 'comforts' for the troops. With so many diverse claims to be met, it was decided to appoint a working-party to coordinate all these activities. Already the increased costs of heating and lighting were posing problems and the WI had to ask the Infant Welfare Clinic to raise their payment from £2/2/- to £2/12/6 per annum.

In January of 1940 Dr Walton sent a request to the WI that he be allowed to store 80 gas masks for babies in the WI Hall. This was allowed and the committee volunteered to help with fitting these on the children if the occasion arose. By June the Hall had been requisitioned by the Military and the WI moved all their chairs down to the home of Mr Pease (Chairman of the PC), at 1 High St, as he had agreed to allow the monthly meetings to be held, on a temporary basis, in his hut. Now it was necessary to seek the permission of the Military for the use of the Hall for events such as Whist Drives. Eight months later (early 1941) the WI moved its venue for the monthly meetings again, to the Village Institute in Cambridge Rd; this was rented for at least 6 months at 2/6 per meeting.

The Military made no use whatsoever of the Hall they had requisitioned and the building remained quite empty for several months. During that interval children broke in and Mrs Leakey (the President) complained to the Military; as a result the authorities made it clear that they had the power to commandeer and alter premises without the consent of the owner. The WI would have to take the alterations at value or have any additional buildings removed at their own expense. On a rather more accommodating note, in October the Military did agree to Mrs Leakey's request that Brownies and the Infant Welfare Clinic be allowed to use the Hall free of charge – on the understanding that they would evacuate at 24 hours notice for military or other war emergency. With this permission the WI arranged to have the Hall repaired and cleaned, so that it was fit for use by the Infant Welfare Clinic; at the same time the gas system was repaired by the Drill Hall authorities. The woes did not end there and in December the water pipes froze. Mrs Leakey wrote to the Military once again – and where were the WI cups? Either there was no reply to this or, perhaps, the response was not fit to minute!

Perhaps there was no connection with these complaints but in January 1942 the Military handed over the Hall to the Home Guard. The Brownies and the Infant Welfare Clinic were allowed to continue as usual although, later that year, the Home Guard applied for permission to make permanent the new outhouses, which had been attached to the Hall by the Military. The skeletal walls were converted into a store room, a rest-room and an office. Mr Thomson, who had built this conversion, showed the committee what had been done (Jim Thomson was the second-in-command of the Home Guard unit in the village) and the WI thanked Mr Monkman (the Captain in charge of the Home Guard: he lived in Thornton Rd and had a builders business with its yard at Oakington: the site is now occupied by Dean & Sons) for permission to view the premises.

In the summer of 1943 there was a suggestion that the Infant Welfare Clinic should see to the provision of helmets for babies. Volunteers would be asked to help the mothers with their children in the event of a raid. This new aspect of war precaution produced the information that 28 mothers had no gas masks for their babies.

Happily, this crisis seemed to recede and by July of 1944 the outlook appeared to become more optimistic and there were discussions on what would need to be done if the Hall was to have a greater use by the village. Members of the WI were quite clear that there would have to be better sanitation, a canteen and a cloakroom. The Infant Welfare Clinic would continue, with a welcome still extended to evacuated mothers, but there was expressed a hope that the Hall could be let for parties and wedding receptions. It was realised that considerable sums of money would be required to improve the sanitation and to provide a piano for entertainments. Exciting news was received, indicating that the Home Guard would need the Hall for only a short time more and that de-requisitioning would soon take place – but there was the warning that the Military might continue to keep the Hall for the Territorials.

This did not happen and the Hall was de-requisitioned in January 1945, when the Military offered to hand over fixtures at valuation, viz: buildings at £140, the shutters at £10 – and barbed-wire at

£2. Perhaps that final inclusion was too much for the WI and Mrs Leakey wrote to refuse this offer and provided a list of dilapidations which had occurred during the tenancy of the Military. With the initial moves accomplished, there was a meeting of the WI with a Captain Floyd, who proved to be both friendly and generous. The WI was offered £102/14/4 for restoration and they could have the outbuildings.

Money in hand, the committee had Mr Mitham (the local carpenter and undertaker: he lived in the N end of High St) to work on the closet, putting in an Elsan toilet, making a partition and adding a door. He was also willing to make a door into the hall in order to save members having to go outside in order to reach the dressing-room. Mr Monkman's estimate, of £88, for internal repairs and decoration was accepted, part of the repairs being to render the building water tight. The ceiling and upper walls of the main room were to be painted a cream colour, above a green wainscot and the boundary between the 2 was to be a cherry coloured stripe. All the paint was to be sprayed on and Mr Monkman was able to do this as a priority because there had been some kind of delay in work at the aerodrome (Oakington). He would start at once if the permit from the Office of Works could be signed by the following day. A limit of £100 for repairs and decoration was allowed on the permit, so the outside painting of the Hall had to be left until a later date. In the process of regaining their Hall the WI had to dispose of an organ and a piano and, for the work of renovation, clear all the furniture into a storeroom.

On April 11th of 1945 the re-opening of the Hall was celebrated by holding a tea-party for all the members, followed by a Public Dance – for which an entrance charge of 1/- each was made. Mrs Cole was appointed as the caretaker of the Hall at the rate of £5 per annum but by August she had resigned, the Minutes giving no information about the reasons. By May the WI activities were back in business, with the suggestion that the Hall might be used for the village VE celebrations. Although the Parish Council enquired about the use that the WI might make of a proposed new village hall, there was no record of the response; perhaps the question was inopportune at a time when the WI members had just recovered their own premises.

Food

Produce Guilds & Fruit Preservation Centres

In 1939, as war became a reality, there was the general sense that the whole topic of the Nation's food would have to be taken very seriously by everyone. The first essential was to grow the

maximum amount of food, in order to reduce the amount imported
in ships, and the national Dig for Victory campaign was aimed at
ordinary householders with gardens and allotments. As a part of
this effort the members of the WI pooled their orders for a bulk
purchase of seed potatoes in November 1940 and for fruit trees in
the September of 1940 and July of 1941. The Government had
given a grant of £500 to the newly formed Produce Guild (see below)
and, apart from providing courses for members, it made available
fertilisers, seeds, fruit bushes &c at slightly lower prices. There
were several other moves to create national organisations to meet an
increasingly urgent country-wide need for the coordinated handling
of such produce.   Preservation of surplus in the form of jam or
by bottling required the use of sugar; the Government recognised
the need and official forms were sent to WIs, seeking orders for
the necessary quantities. By early 1940 our WI was seeking its
allocation in this way. In May of that year the committee received
a letter from WIHQ regarding a scheme for establishing Produce
Guilds, whereby 'all produce from our gardens should be used to
advantage'. These Guilds were the outcome of a scheme which had
been proposed as early as 1927, in the agricultural depression. The
WVS had been put in charge of organisation by the Government in
1938, and this body had asked the WI to participate in the schemes.
The surplus produce, if not required by the local community, was
to be sent to a depôt. From there the food would be distributed
to areas where the produce was not grown or the amounts were
insufficiently abundant. In exchange the grower would receive a fair
market price for the food. Miss Warrington (who was Hon Secretary
of the County Agriculture Sub-committee and a Voluntary County
Organiser of the WI) had the task of explaining about the scheme
to WIs, enrolling interested members and organising the County's
contribution to the national effort. Girton WI heard a talk from
Mrs Leakey, in July, on the topic of jam making within the Produce
Guild; during this talk she discussed the details of distribution
and the prices. It was decided that a suitable venue for the sale
of jam would be the Group Meeting, which involved the institutes
of Girton, Oakington, Histon and Long Stanton (this last WI had
to leave the group during the war because the road to Oakington
was closed when the airfield was built). Even at this early stage
(1940) small scale canning equipment was widely distributed and
some members of Girton WI were involved in the canning of fruit.
Locally this was not specifically part of the WI activity and the
process was organised within the village community – Mrs Leakey

was prominent within this group besides being President of the WI. A different aspect of this whole scheme concerned the storage of produce, since the supply of preserves and the demand for their purchase were unpredictable. One proposed solution involved WIs buying the preserves, thus distributing the storage problem to a larger number of smaller locations; in the event this need did not materialise and Girton was not requested to buy any. Mrs Yuell (a member of the committee) was responsible for ordering a large number of preserving jars and Miss Hibbert-Ware (a member of the committee) wrote to the BBC about obtaining tops which would fit 2lb jam jars; these lids allowed the jars to be used for preserving fruit &c and so relieved the shortage of the Kilner-type preserving jars. The Balance Sheet for the Produce Guild in 1941 shows that they made £51/17/2, of which £12/19/4 was sent to the Federation of the WI, £10 was donated to the Nursing Association and £28 was paid into the Post-Office Savings Bank. At the same time it was noted that if the Guild were to function again they would require some new equipment and some improvement to the organisation. With the success of the Guilds, the scope of food production was widened to include the growing and preserving of vegetables and the keeping of small livestock. It was proposed that Produce Centres should be established in 22 Cambs villages and, once again Miss Warrington promoted the scheme. Quarterly conferences for the members of the centres would be held, so that speakers and demonstrators (supplied by the CC) could inform and encourage producers. Participating WIs were asked to suggest topics which they would welcome as subjects at one of these conferences. Girton indicated that 'fruit pulping' and 'the preservation of tomatoes' would be useful; both of these figure in the first conference in May 1942. The programme for the meeting was advertised:

CAMBRIDGESHIRE

This is an invitation from the County Home Produce Committee to all women in Girton who are interested. A conference will be held in the Village Hall, Girton at 7pm on Wednesday May 27th 1942 to consider whether a Produce Club should be formed in Girton.

PROGRAMME

1. The idea of the Produce Club – Miss DM Warrington.
2. Hints & Recipes for packed meals – Miss P Kelly.
3. Are rabbits worth keeping? – Mr WS Turner.
4. Methods of preserving fruit & tomatoes in present day difficulties – Miss P Kelly.

This meeting has been made possible through the kind assistance of the Girton Women's Institute.

Miss Kelly was a County Council Instructor for Rural Domestic Economy.   Mr WS Turner was a circuit-judge who lived on the Huntingdon Rd; he kept goats and other livestock. in his large garden. Later meetings dealt with 'Drying fruit & vegetables', a 'Brains Trust' on gardening difficulties and 'Pruning fruit trees'.

Girton Produce Guild was a success and in 1945, at the close of the war, the profits amounted to £29. Instead of spending this money on some local concern they allocated £10 to the WI Federation and the remaining £19 to the Netherlands Red Cross Relief Fund.

Tomatoes & Onions

Part of the effort to grow more food involved the national drive to produce more onions. In February 1941 Miss Hibbert-Ware attended a 'Communal Feeding' meeting and on her return to the WI she proposed that the institute form an Onion Club. Each volunteer in this club would undertake to grow at least one extra row of this vegetable. The general aim was for the WI in Cambridgeshire to contribute 7 tons of food to the national surplus. To encourage the start of these activities in the Girton club, Mrs Leakey offered to supply seed of the Bedfordshire Champion variety. All of these plans came to pass and, in October, the crop was collected and then stored by Mrs Dupont (a member of committee). What should be done with this surplus harvest? There came the suggestion that the onions be sent to Middlesbrough, where the regional supply failed to meet the demand; more specifically, the onions would go to a local WI which was prepared to distribute them. The institute selected was that of Marton-in-Cleveland (it would appear that all the relevant records of this institute over the period have been lost) and the members there welcomed the offer, indicating a willingness to pay the cost of carriage. Consequently a sack, weighing 109lb, was dispatched to Marton by goods train, at a cost of 3/1. The residue of Girton's crop was sent to men who were serving on the minesweepers.

During the following year (1942) some of the initial enthusiasm had dwindled but the members still grew what they could; another load (60lb) was sent to Marton.   It arrived in time for their 21st birthday celebration and their letter of thanks described the occasion.   In the December Girton WI received a gift from the WIs of Ontario (Canada); this consisted of three packets of onion seeds and one packet of tomato seeds (unfortunately the Federation in Ontario failed to respond to requests for further information).

Once again Miss Hibbert-Ware's enthusiasm led her, assisted by Mrs Betson (a member of the committee), to sow the tomato seed under glass during February; in the following month she distributed the onion seed to volunteer growers. A letter of thanks for the Canadian gift was sent to the Superintendent (Miss Mary Clarke) of the Federation of the WIs of Ontario, in Toronto. By summer both tomatoes and onions were growing apace and in August the onion crop was stored by Mrs Leakey before being sent to Marton. This time there was some delay in the delivery of the load because of 'congestion on the railways' but in January a letter of thanks was received from Miss Jenny Donaldson of Marton.

Onions seemed to be a serious preoccupation across these years, presumably because some pretty dull, and much used, wartime recipes needed enlivening. The Home & Country magazine of 1942 had mentioned 'the onionless waste of last winter' and had commented upon the absence of onion-milk to relieve the miseries of common colds. Even as late as 1944 the Red Cross organised a national onion growing/distribution scheme and invited Girton WI to take part. Preferring to continue their gifts to Marton, the institute elected to operate their own project but leave the Allotment Association to support the Red Cross. With possible victory offering sweet respite to a war-weary community, there was no enthusiasm to grow more tomatoes although the Canadian seed continued to arrive in the March of 1945. For some reason the gift of onion seed did not arrive until June, too late for the Spring sowing; consequently the committee resolved to distribute the seed to volunteer growers during the Autumn meetings of the WI.

Milk & Meals

There was much anxiety about the health of growing children as so many foods were becoming increasingly difficult to obtain. Apart from the uncertainty over the quantity of food, the main concern focused on the supply of proteins and vitamins. By 1940, these fears influenced the WI resolution calling upon the Government not to increase the cost of milk for school-children. While at school each pupil received (and was actively encouraged to drink) a daily issue of milk; this was in a bottle, containing one third of a pint, which was closed with a cardboard lid (a hole could be pushed out of the middle so that a straw could be inserted through the lid). Now it seemed essential for this milk to be distributed throughout the long summer holidays. Mr Garner and the WI organised the distribution of the milk over the period in which the children were not at school; during this stage of the war 740 bottles of milk had passed through this system. Wider fears about general malnutrition increased somewhat in the mid-winter and Mrs Green proposed to the WI that there should be a 'Communal feeding of Girton children'. Volunteers were to be responsible for the serving of mid-day meals. The fears were reinforced by reports during early 1941 that cases of scurvy (caused by lack of Vitamin C) had been detected in Cambridgeshire. The WI sought for a conference to be held on the theme of 'Health in children'.

Harvesters' Meals & Meat Pies

The Government used the WVS as an 'organising' service for many national systems which directly involved civilian women. In the dark days of 1941 there was developed a project for supplying hot meals (chiefly in the form of pies) to farm workers who laboured long hours away from home during the vital period of harvest time. Girton WI quickly established that the local need for such meals was very small; furthermore, they argued, the cooking facilities here were totally inadequate. In addition, it was noted that these agricultural workers already received extra rations in acknowledgment of their strenuous physical activity.

Other workers, however, did not benefit in this way and some had no canteen supplied by their employer. The agricultural scheme was therefore widened, in 1942, to include these extra categories of employees. Meat pies were to be distributed and the WVS again sought the help of the WIs. Girton responded by forming a committee to deal with the problem and arranged with the Co-op to deliver the pies to the Village Institute, for distribution by WI volunteers on Tuesday and Friday afternoons between six o'clock and quarter to seven. With the agreement of the County Council and the Education Authorities, the pies were cooked and distributed at the Village Institute (which was being used as additional classrooms during the war and possessed the means of cooking school meals). Initially 82 people applied for these pies but by the following month (July) demand had fallen so much that distribution was reduced to one session each week. The scheme continued into the winter, the number of applicants being increased by advertising in Ingle's village shop (which was the Post Office). At this time there were problems relating to the variable quality of the batches and the irregularity of the delivery, despite complaints from the WI. Many recipients were disappointed, disillusion set in, the demand sank to twelve customers – from a high point earlier in the winter when 90 had been registered – and by March 1943 the WI had withdrawn from the enterprise.

Helping the British Services

The Local Men

Much of the help provided for troops was summarised by the word 'comforts' and generally these resulted either by the spending of collected money or by the personal efforts of individuals, although sometimes the 2 systems were combined. Such was the case in February 1940, for example, when a Whist Drive raised £4/7/6 and some of that money was used to purchase 10lb of wool, with which volunteers of the WI knitted socks. The rest of the money bought cigarettes and chocolates for men who didn't need socks. Such attentions brought letters of appreciation from the men, so more such events were organised within the village. As the year rolled on increasingly firm control was exercised over materials and permission had to be obtained to secure a voucher which could be exchanged for coupon-free wool (which was, like so many items, severely rationed to individuals). In order to secure this concession, the recipients of the knitted garments, such as socks, had to be named and khaki was the only colour allowed. Mrs Thomson (a member of committee) took charge of the arrangements and WI members volunteered as knitters, each indicating the quantities of wool that would be needed. By 1942 the regulations concerning wool were tightened yet further and the WI learned that 'No-one could have wool without coupons now but a serviceman could apply to his Medical Officer for any garment he felt he needed. If the MO agreed, a permit was issued for coupon-free wool'.

Of course, the WI was not the only village group concerned with the welfare of local men and in 1941 the village formed a committee to organise the production of comforts; representatives from all of the interested bodies were asked to join this coordinating committee. In addition, the Parish Council organised activities for servicemen that were based in the area around Girton. Many of the money raising events involved Whist Drives but there were also dances (one, for example, was organised by Mr Morris and took place in the WI Hall during early 1940) and Sales of Work (that of December 1943 allowed the WI to donate £5 towards the troops' Christmas Fund; another in 1944 produced another £5, to be divided between the 'Boys out there' and the 'Home Coming' Funds). Some of the peculiar conditions operating during the war can be gleaned from the arrangements for the ARP Whist Drive of May 1941. The entrance charge for each person was two 6d War Savings stamps; prizes were taken from this entrance income and the First Prize was 10 of these stamps stuck to a card , the Second had 5 stamps and the Consolation was of 3 stamps. With due regard to food rationing, there were no refreshments provided.

Alongside these fund raising events which aimed to support specific, and often local, projects, there were organised entertainments making contributions to national organisations with wider commitments. With so many men in the services families often had quite limited budgets, perhaps made more difficult by the presence of evacuees. Nevertheless, surprisingly large sums were repeatedly raised within the village. Mrs Hall (a member of the committee) provided a whole series of Whist Drives and other entertainments at her home (St John's College farm) throughout much of the war, contributing impressive amounts of money to the Red Cross. During 1943, for example, she sent £162 to that organisation; in July alone she also enriched the fund for POWs by £20 from a Whist Drive in her garden. As an organisation, the WI had given £15 to the POWs but had also dispatched materials with pattern books, to provide some occupation in toy-making and other crafts to relieve the boredom of captivity. At their monthly meetings WI members donated scraps of material and a large box full of this was taken, by Mrs Hall, to WI House in Cambridge. All of this activity had been stimulated by an exhibition of photographs of the men in the POW camps, which had been circulated through the WIs of the county.

General military personnel

Books, too, were greatly in demand to enable all the service men, including those on active service, to while away the tedious hours of boredom when nothing else was required. The Red Cross asked the WI to help with the bookbinding needed to repair books and these women, coordinated by Mrs Moule (in December of 1942) collected yet more volumes for the Royal Navy and the men on the minesweepers. Clearly members of that section had an especial appeal because every fortnight hampers for them were organised by Mrs Burrows (of Whitegate on Cambridge Rd; she was the wife of Sterndale Burrows, solicitor) as part of the WI war work. Plums, beans, onions &c, each in their season, went into these parcels. In addition WI volunteers knitted garments for these men; by 1942 the scheme for allocating vouchers for the necessary wool had been discontinued and the WI had to seek supplies from the WVS (who had been burdened with the task by the Government).

As part of the general economy drive to sustain the war effort in 1941, there was concern about the maintenance of military uniforms in the face of normal wear and tear. Again, the WI was seen as the obvious choice of organisation to help. Each Welfare Officer sent a plea for help to its local WI asking for volunteers to do mending, especially of battle-dresses. This additional request came at a time when women battled to cope with their families, 'make do & mend', needs for clothes, making of rugs &c. Where did villagers find all the time and energy to grow extra food, knit for themselves and others, mend clothes endlessly, go to dances, attend Whist Drives, look after evacuees &c?

Help for Civilians
British

The assistance afforded to our civilians ranked as a fairly minor part of the WI's official activity. In the summer of 1941 there were grave concerns about the effect on Girton people should Cambridge be bombed. It was feared that such action might sever the village supplies of water, gas, electricity, telephones, transport &c. In response, the village established an Emergency Committee to report upon measures which might be adopted to re-establish vital links with the town.

Children, again, were in the forefront of the villagers' worries and the WI sought ways of supplying toys, toy-making becoming one part of their monthly activities. In the winter of 1940 money was collected to allow three toys (of unspecified nature) to be sent to the Infants' School at Shudy Camps. Girton youngsters at Impington Village College had to walk to school and in the winter this involved them being in rubber boots throughout the day. To remedy this undesirable situation the WI provided patterns (in 1942), so that the pupils could make slippers that could be worn in school.

In Cambridge itself, the war brought problems for some young women who had either arrived to do war work or had been stranded overnight, as they passed through the town, by the frequent disruptions to the transport system. In either case they needed accommodation and this was hard to obtain in a town that was bulging with additional civilians and military. During 1942 the YWCA had appealed for £1500 to start up a hostel for young women; the County Federation of the WI had promised to furnish and provide for one bedroom (holding 6 beds), costing £60. Girton WI contributed £1/1/- towards this fund. In 1944 an emergency hostel was established to help these women and the WI was one of the organisations asked to help with donations of money. Girton duly raised £3 and the institutes generated a total of £52; Mrs Pemberton expressed thanks on behalf of the hostel and said that the money would be used to buy a piano. During May the hostel had an Open Day and the WI members were invited to attend.

The greatest demand on the resources of the village was undoubtedly made by evacuees. Preparations had been required in 1939 and children, some with their mothers, had arrived in Girton homes. This went on throughout the war as vulnerable young people were moved away from the terror-bombing by the Germans on so many towns and cities. Even in March of 1944, 26 lads of the North Polytechnic arrived in the Cambridge area and needed accommodation. Only 13/- a week was offered to support each boy and the WI committee was adamant that such a sum scarcely paid for the extra food. It might be thought that, by mid-1944, the threat of the Blitz had receded and that the evacuation programme could be reduced; however, the arrival of the new 'terror weapons' (the so-called V1 & V2) posed a threat of even more massive, indiscriminate destruction of life and property. At the June monthly meeting of the WI, Mrs Leakey (the President) was called away on urgent business related to her work with evacuees. She announced that '48,000 from Wandsworth, 25,000 from Eltham and 11,000 from Woolwich were being evacuated and that all possible accommodation would be required'. The WIHQ was asked to provide help in every possible way but, at the August meeting, Mrs Leakey told the Girton members that 'Girton had shown good will and good work under four years of persistent billeting and had reached saturation point. Evacuated mothers were welcomed at the Welfare Centre, Country dancing and at WI monthly meetings'. As one of the Billeting Officers, Mrs Leakey was in an excellent position to make informed judgment about Girton's contribution to this aspect of war.

Foreign

Despite the many demands upon the compassion, time, work and money of WI members, they still managed to turn their attention outwards to consider the plight and needs of foreigners (albeit allies) in addition to those of our own people. During the autumn and winter of 1941 there was much interest in Russia, especially in the women; at the Group Meeting there was a talk about 'Russian women in the war'. This was followed by the sending of a WI delegate to the meeting, held in Emmanuel Church Hall. to consider the topic of 'Aid to Russia'. As a consequence of this, Girton WI resolved to carry on knitting, if there was any wool; but there wasn't! Instead, they collected money to send soap and other comforts, the items being gathered at a couple of homes in the village; eventually 17lb of soap were dispatched (at a time when it was difficult for households to find enough bars of soap for their own needs; ingenious gadgets were bought or made to ensure use of the

very last fragments of used bars) and 14 rabbit pelts were donated
– presumably by the Rabbit Club. These skins were sold and the
money used to add further gifts. In a separate venture the Red
Cross had asked WIs to help in the collection of money; apart from
the national Flag Day, each member paid 1d per week and the total
collection went to the Red Cross at the end of the year. From the
proceeds of this initiative the Red Cross was able to send a mobile
X-ray Unit to the Russian Red Cross in April 1942. Rather more
unconventionally, WIHQ asked each institute to donate three rabbit
skins, which would be used to line the coats that were destined for
Russia. Girton WI asked the Rabbit Club to supply the required
pelts and HQ sent the instructions for the correct method of drying
the skins; by September the items had been dispatched. Perhaps
this incident sparked a train of thought because, in February, there
was to be a conference upon 'The use of rabbit skins' – to which the
Rabbit Club would also be invited.

January of 1944 saw another shift of concern, to the subject of
'European Relief', when the WVS asked members of the WI to
knit babies' vests; the white wool and the necessary patterns were
supplied and each vest was to be 14" long – 48,000 were required
from this area! Shawls were also needed and the WVS aimed to
distribute all of this relief after the cease of hostilities. The WI
responded nobly and by September four shawls had been produced
(and displayed at the WI's monthly meeting) but, meanwhile, the list
of requirements continued to lengthen and now included coats, made
of material rather than wool, cap-scarves and pilches (for babies).
In the September the wool had been supplied for the cap-scarves
and material came for the cut-out boys' knickers. By the November
Girton WI had established itself as the most productive institute
of the area and had finished 72 garments. Sixteen blue coats had
been made and yet the volunteers kept on with the work, taking
boys' trousers to sew up at home. The knitted garments were to
be transported by air, probably to Greece. Sadly, this activity in the
WIs had stimulated the spread of some unpleasant rumours and Mrs
Shufflebotham was asked to dispel, emphatically, the story that this
aid was being sent to Germany.

The New Year (1945) brought a jolly monthly meeting and a
collection for the relief of Norwegian refugees; by the February
£6/10/- had been donated in Girton and this money was spent on
haberdashery. Advice on the best selection to make was given by
the buyer at Messrs Lilley and the purchases were sent on their
way to Norway. Still the knitters worked on behalf of European

Relief and the Produce Guild donated £19 to the Netherlands Red Cross Relief Fund. May saw the introduction of one more strand to this international aid when there was an appeal for volunteers to make aprons for French children – the material to come from blackout blinds. What joy it must have been to dispense with this unpleasant element of wartime precaution, with its attendant fears, restrictions and inconveniences. In addition, what pleasure it must have been to make items for children, knowing the uplifting news that France was beginning to emerge from the horrors of occupation. By August of 1945 Girton and Whittlesford still topped all other local villages, by a comfortable margin, in the production of knitting for the European Relief.

Collection for the War Effort

In order to reduce the country's dependence upon imported materials, carried in valuable and increasingly scarce shipping, there were highly organised national campaigns to conserve strategic raw-material by the process of salvage and collection of wild or garden products.

Salvage operations for paper, scrap-iron and bones were well under way by early 1940; the boys of Littleton House School (housed in the Old Rectory – now the Cambridge Academy of English) did much of the collecting around the village but WI volunteers helped to sort out the paper. The needs grew ever more pressing as 1942 dawned, tin and rubber being added to the list of salvage materials; the need for rubber became increasingly urgent as time passed. Naturally there were some initial problems in the organisation and the Girton Parish Council was asked about the procedure for collecting what the WI was gathering together. At the same time, the Clerk to the Parish Council (Mr Palmer) was encouraging a special effort to salvage paper; Mr Barrett organised a group of young men to go around the village, on January 31st, to collect paper which people had salvaged. This party used a cart, borrowed from Mr Coe (George Coe was a tenant farmer at Manor Farm in the High St), and the whole enterprise amassed three and a quarter tons of paper. Books had been freely donated and, ever aware of the need to supply recreational reading, Miss Hibbert-Ware volunteered to sort out useful volumes and forward them to the Red Cross.

Although the Dig for Victory campaign, and others directed at the increased production and preservation of food were well established, there were additional requirements. In June of 1942 WIHQ asked each institute to collect two pounds of herbs. The WI Country Herb Committee was established at the request of the Ministry of Supply to collect medicinal herbs *eg* nettles, foxgloves, raspberry leaves and rose-hips. Children were to be paid to collect these and the products were to go to local packing stations, from which they were to be dispatched to chemical factories. In addition there was to be a collection of culinary herbs. Apparently requests for these had come from Culpeppers (on a commercial basis), local military camps (for use in their kitchens) and PoW camps. The main problem lay in the proper drying of the collected herbs and Girton decided to seek the help of Chivers (at Histon). All the contributions from Girton were accumulated at the home of Mrs Stewart ('Girton Gate' on Huntingdon Rd; she was secretary of the Girton WI and a former President – until 1941). In September three bags of the dried herbs had been sent to Culpeppers in London.

A major preoccupation for those concerned with the welfare of children centred upon an adequate amount of vitamins in the diet. It had long been known that rose-hips were rich in Vitamin C and the abundant harvest of these fruits in the hedgerows was there for the gathering. From the October of 1941 to the July of 1945 this harvesting was a feature of WI activity. Only occasionally do the Minutes record the quantity gathered; Mrs Leakey (who recommended the making of a purée based upon a Danish recipe – which was not recorded) dispatched thirty pounds of hips in November 1941 but in October 1942 the amazing total of 19 stones were sent. Such quantities represented many hours of tedious and prickly picking. Girl Guides were well in the forefront of the collectors and in the autumn of 1943 members of the Girton WI were urged to emulate the girls' fine achievements.

Rather less well known were the manifold virtues of the common conker (just the seed of the horse-chestnut, not the prickly case) but these, too, were seen by the authorities as a potential source of useful materials. Apart from the high protein content (which offered a source of animal food), these seeds held large amounts of saponins (forms of fatty substances) which could be used to make soap or in this case, the foaming agents of fire- extinguishers. The conkers could also be used to produce tannic acid which could be incorporated in creams or lotions and used to treat burns of the skin. During the autumn of 1942 no less than three hundredweights of the 'shelled' conkers had been gathered in the grounds of Girton College and an equal amount had come from the village. By the January of the following year Miss Warrington had received £1/2/6 for the village share of the harvest. However, the extraction of useful products from conkers rapidly proved to be practicable but too expensive on a large scale; no more were to be collected towards the war effort and conkers resumed their traditional place in autumn games. Throughout 1942 Mrs Green was in charge of the dispatch of the hips and conkers to the regional collection centres; she continued to make arrangements for the hips right on to the end of the war.

Activities other than those of the war-effort

Throughout the six war years the members of the WI met regularly every month, when they had talks, debates, discussions &c and entertained themselves with games, dancing (eg the Lancers) and/or singing. A Folk Dance group was successfully maintained over the period and, from 1940, the choir proved its merits in the local WI Choral Singing Competitions. A Certificate of Merit was awarded to them in 1941 and in the following year they earned praise for 'their polished performance'. Meanwhile the Drama group produced short plays, excerpts and sketches, also winning judge's commendation at the WI Drama Festival of 1942. All three associations of these lively people contributed to the varied activities of the monthly meetings. Other members turned to craftwork, made soft toys as gifts (eg for the War Nurseries) or for the WI Fairs or Sales of Work; they also exhibited at WI Craft shows (eg Oxford in 1942).

At many meetings members articulated their views in debates, the subjects of which ranged widely and were sometimes light-hearted but more often touched upon serious concerns. Thoughts were aired upon the nature of education, its suitability and its future developments. Equally important in the members' minds were ideas about housing and the design of post-war homes; there was great eagerness to see the new Government dwellings in the local villages (Oakington, Bourne and Caxton), much effort put into the completion of a questionnaire about their requirements in the design of houses and Mrs Sadler represented the institute at a Housing Conference in the Guildhall (1944). It was not only the individual homes that were considered to be important and debates ranged over comparisons between the village as it then existed and as it had been in the past, while pondering on the changes that might come to the community after the war. Connecting all of these themes together was the nature and working of Local Government and members had their suggestions about that, too.

Girton WI members had their ideas shaped and informed by an impressively diverse programme of talks. Those which were broadly Social in emphasis included topics such as Housing & Sanitation, Town Planning, Parents & Children, Ourselves in the Community, Citizens of the Future, Special Schools and the Coal Industry. Some talks and demonstrations naturally focused upon immediate, more pressing problems – Uses of Fats, Food in Wartime, Appropriate Recipes & Methods of Cooking, Bottling, Dietary Needs of Children, Household Jobbery and Make do & Mend. Beyond these essentially practical areas there were talks on music, the production of plays, craft, literature (*eg* Shakespeare & the Elizabethan Theatre: Martin Chuzzlewit: The Village in Literature), many on Natural History, on Witchcraft, Joan of Arc, the Girl Guides, the Red Cross, Life in a Leper Colony &c. As their war work clearly showed, the WI looked outwards, beyond the narrow confines of our village or, even, our country. Over the years speakers brought the world to Girton; personal experience and knowledge, usually illustrated with lantern slides, described Canada, Australia, New Zealand, the USA, France, Italy, Russia, China, W Africa and Czechoslovakia. Fortunately, the electricity supply had been installed in the Hall during October 1936 (when the Cambridge Electric Supply Company charged £4/10/-), with three lighting points and a plug for the lantern.

It must be remembered that this WI activity took place along with all the war work. These women simultaneously coped with, and were actively involved in, this great diversity of demands and interests which covered the present and the future, at home and abroad. While keeping themselves entertained in a social atmosphere, they acquired new knowledge, ideas and skills. They dealt with present practicalities, gave thought to the shaping of the future and demonstrated apparently endless compassion for their compatriots and foreigners. Girton WI members were certain that the future involved change in the village because they themselves had experienced rapid changes during those momentous years between 1939 and 1945. However, nowhere was there any doubt expressed about the continuing value of the WI within the community and within the country.

9: Girton College

DR de Lacey

The College journal, the *Girton Review*, gives glimpses of life in the College during the war years and, where not otherwise acknowledged, quotations in this section are from its Editorials or News. Towards the end of the 1938–39 academic year, the editorial (Easter Term, Apr – June 1939) reflected on the shadow of impending war: 'A term normally overcast by nothing more serious than anxiety about the Tripos [the University examinations] is this year overshadowed by fear of war. The fact is brought home to us by FA Classes, by notices in the Post announcing the Govt's interest in our careers, by the echoes of Hitler's voice in the corridors, by the phenomenon of political conversion at meals in Hall'.

A 21-year-old contributed a poem whose dark thought must have echoed the fears of many:

> I came from the womb
> To the sound of a bomb
>
> ...
>
> I go to my tomb
> To the sound of a bomb ...

By the Michaelmas Term (Oct – Dec) 1939 Girton was hosting the displaced Queen Mary College, London, whose 56 students more than made up for Girton's own decrease. '2 of our Research Fellows have left College to take up war work. 10 students decided not to return to College this year and most of them are engaged in war work of various kinds'.

Another major change was in the College gardens, already a significant source of food but now dedicated to the war effort, as Miss Procter the Garden Steward reported: 'During Aug, 3 Land Girls received an intensive training in market-gardening at Girton. Some "Dutch Brown" beans were procured from Holland to "grow on" for seed'. 'An extra temporary garden boy (financed out of Gift Funds) and a beautifully wet summer have helped to produce record harvests of food crops in great variety'.

In the Lent Term (Jan – Mar) 1940 'Rationing, Arctic weather and measles have provided much extra work for the household and rich topics of conversation for all'.

Over the Long Vacation of 1940 students offered themselves for war work, and wrote up their experiences. The Michaelmas edition has an extended essay by Anne Cohen, recording her experience of assembling telephone cables. She spent much time in the Air-Raid Shelter to which some workers even brought the family. '9d an hour, $8\frac{1}{2}$ hours a day, $5\frac{1}{2}$ days a week, works out at 35/3d less 1/6d for National Health and Unemployment Insurances. Barely a living wage. But the work was not too hard when one got used to it, the girls were good-hearted and friendly; and I was very sorry indeed to leave'.

LE Trench also had factory experience. 'Everyone in London is always wanting more helpers', she wrote, 'but in June they seemed to have little use for you unless you could speak Polish, or type, or decipher mysterious codes'. So she ended up in a cheese factory 'under the kindly despotic rule of George, the head cheesemaker, who found that "the girls," as we (an ex-housemaid, a dairy maid, a mathematician, an arts student and a geographer) were collectively called, could not only scrub floors, learn the technique of cheese making, and clean vats, but enjoy the funny side of the factory too'.

More soberly, Edith Burbeck was torpedoed while escorting 320 evacuee children to Canada. After over an hour in the lifeboats, and 26 hours before they reached shore again (back in Britain to the children's disappointment), she could still make light of her ordeal: 'In comparison with the terrible disaster of *The City of Benares*, our experience was practically a holiday and it had its lighter moments. One lifeboat rowed up to a tanker, asked to come aboard and with the courtesy and calm worthy of a Stanley, an officer offered profuse apologies but added that he was sinking too!'

Also over that Long Vac an appeal was made to old students for an Ambulance Fund, and by July 2 ambulances had been bought (at £550 each) and presented to the Lord Mayor of London, together with nearly £310 for running costs.

During Michaelmas 1940 a RC detachment was formed. The Lent Term *Review* reports that it is 'representative of the whole college, and includes many members of the household staff' – and students in Term. A former student, GD Rattenbury, of the London WVS and organiser of the Invalid Children's Aid Association, was awarded the George Medal for bravery during air-raids.

After the 1941 Long Vac the *Review* reports 2 Fellows absent on National Service and a Research Student become a Petty Officer

in the WRNS; but an exceptionally large student body remained
in residence.   4 were refugees, supported by a Fund set up in
1939. A Czechoslovak was reading Natural Sciences, 2 Germans
were reading History and Modern Languages, and an older German
scholar was a Visiting Fellow.

Helen Thomas writes of evacuation from Greece and of the poor
but loyal allies she left behind. AP Pearce in lighter vein records
her factory experience: an $11\frac{1}{2}$ hour day in which as a concession
to the weaker sex she was permitted two 10 minute tea-breaks as
well as the lunch-break. Pay was fair 'but no amount of money
could make up for the cutting down of actual living time. I seemed
to spend most of my free time getting home, getting clean, and
getting comfortably full of food'. In a 4 day town holiday 'the whole
population moved *en bloc* to Blackpool. People liked going because
they were sure of meeting other people there whom they knew. It
seemed to them that, at the end of my month, I should be going back
to a perpetual but much duller Blackpool. They were wonder-struck
at the phenomenon'.

The Dutch Brown beans re-appear in the Garden Report: the
Steward's foresight had come to the attention of HMI, and the seeds
were requisitioned and had to be sold on. However, 'The seed fetched
a fabulous price and the College did not seem broken-hearted to
be without it. Dried beans are as dull as they are nourishing!'
Bedding plants now consisted of carrots, beetroot and tomatoes. The
tomato was an unnamed but prolific variety, and the College named
it 'Girton Glory'.

HMI also provided 'enough Forms to paper a house! The 5
pages of interpretation which precede the 22 pages of rules relating
to potatoes begin in a deceitfully simple way. But, after this,
it gets much much more difficult and goes on until (n), and (k)
is subdivided (i) to (xiv) – you are not sure whether you are a
licensed auctioneer, grower-salesman, buyer, potato merchant or a
seed potato merchant? Cautious persons get licences for everything.
But even then one is not safe. A Cambs market-gardener has been
fined £5 for Growing Pears Without Permission – an awful thing to
do in cold blood, one does realise! – but still...'.

In Michaelmas 1941 the *Review* records an MBE for MG Reid, who
left the College the previous term, for gallantry in the evacuation
from Norway. 2 OBEs were reported in Lent 1942.

The Easter 1942 copy records a great flurry of excitement in 'The

Issuing of Biscuits' on which 2 members wrote a spoof Archæological Report dated 'July 2642'.   Each student was offered $\frac{1}{2}$lb, an unprecedented treat.

In Michaelmas 1942 the College started full.   But resident housemaids had dwindled from 20 to 8, and students had to help by looking after their own rooms, waiting at meals and acting as messengers. Those staying up for the Long Vac as fire-watchers also had to help in house and garden work.

They assisted in a record harvest. The Garden Steward records her gratitude: 'they did not fail me as the emergency schoolboy labour did.   The boys went sick with acute colic after only 2 days of serious work on the greengages. We have also had a phenomenal caterpillar crop, and, but for the students' timely attentions, winter greens would by now be merely ribbons of white lace-work; it was a neck-to-neck race. We have now too huge a programme of food-production for the professional Garden Staff to manage without amateur help – especially at "peak" periods.   It is truly war work of the very highest importance'.   She also mentions silage making – a relative

Jack Collings, Deputy College Groundsman, joined the Fleet Air Arm in 1942

innovation in England – and the gathering of rose-hips, dandelion crowns and conkers for various purposes. Her report ends 'David Whitehead – the College groundsman – is now a Leading AC in the RAF. His deputy – Jack Collings – has just joined the FAA. Our present groundsman is a gallant boy of 15 years old. He is holding down a man's job very well – even to driving the big motor mowers and motor roller.   But he is somewhat young for such work and becomes a little disheartened when his grass gets full of shrapnel. Shrapnel and bomb splinters, I'm told, are so bad for the blades of motor mowing-machines'.

Lent 1943 saw a bumper issue. It records an abortive attempt by the Mistress to foster international relationships by inviting eligible US servicemen to a party – a success in itself, but swiftly followed by the posting of the guests to 'an unknown destination'. Food, that major topic of conversation in a rationed nation, was the subject of a Brains Trust followed by an 'animated discussion in which it became obvious that most of us must make an effort to overcome our personal fads and prejudices and eat what Lord Woolton tells us'.

But the bulk of the issue is given over to a 'Newsreel' including reports from students of the previous 5 years on their work experiences. Many had to maintain secrecy: 'I can't tell you anything about the work and even my letters can't be sent to me direct. Really you shouldn't notice the name of the station where I get out. There are a lot of Cambridge people there but no one is supposed to know where it is'. Almost certainly she, with many other Girtonians, was at Bletchley Park.

Others were able to be rather more communicative. A Billeting Investigating Officer's patch covered evacuees in the whole of Central and Western Scotland. An administrative assistant in the BBC found her attempts to research information for broadcasting made her a pariah among other public service organisations. A mathematician found herself analysing aircraft engine failures in the design office of 'a well-known Aircraft firm', located incongruously in a chocolate factory. She confesses 'I know very little statistics but as most of the others know even less it doesn't seem to matter'. Another was immediately commissioned (because of her maths degree) as a specialist Instructor Fire Control; the training convinced her that her degree was far less relevant than her trainers supposed.

One had spent the whole of the war as secretary to the Czechoslovak Military and Air Attaché, re-writing his speeches in grammatical English. Another writes: 'This factory is being used as an experimental and training centre for labour officers; for labour management is new in Royal Ordnance Factories and rather distrusted by the old Woolwich men'. An economist applied for the Economics Branch of the Ministry of Agriculture and was disconcerted to be asked at her interview 'Well, Miss Elworthy, if you are so interested in farming, why don't you join the WLA?' But she was accepted and began 'to devote myself exclusively to problems of farmers' taxation, more interesting than I would have expected'. One in housing management for Abingdon discovered the interest in explaining almost everything 'from the return fare to Scotland to how much it costs to have a tooth out' while rent-collecting in a new estate.

Another reports 'There are 8 Girtonians working in the special war-time branch of the Royal Institute of International Affairs, evacuated at the beginning of the war to Balliol College, Oxford. We are all engaged in scrutinising the foreign press of allied, neutral and enemy countries and in collecting and collating information and writing press reviews'.

There is a long letter from the Republic of Ireland, harshly rationed despite its neutrality and suffering a crippling fuel shortage: 'nobody here has had any house coal at all for over a year ... People really have been going back to the rush lights that old women remember in use in their childhood'. She notes 'the absence of most of the young people of both sexes, who have joined the British forces. They come home on leave occasionally, wearing peculiarly assorted garments, for they have neither Irish nor English clothes coupons and must not appear in uniform. Anyone in uniform would be interned.' She finds this paradoxical neutrality depressing.

The 1943 Easter issue begins: 'The present Easter Term has been distinguished by several remarkable phenomena. To begin with, it really included Easter, which, for the first time in living memory, fell on the first Sunday of Full Term. No lectures were given on Good Friday but Easter Monday was a working day for the University, though not for the bus services, and the full effect of having no lecture bus of our own (another of this term's phenomena) was brought home unpleasantly to the non-cyclists'.

Students at the Fruiting Campaign in Wisbech

There is also a report of the Long Vac Fruiting Campaign to help the families of itinerant fruit pickers. The *Review*'s intrepid reporter describes arraying herself 'in pleasing Florence Nightingale fashion in apron and headsquare' before plunging into the joys of a crècheful of Cockney children ('Certain new-comers one soon learns to occupy immediately they arrive, to prevent outbursts that would rouse the dead; at first I wondered why murder has never yet been committed') and ministering to their parents' ailments with a 'confident but inexperienced medical student'. 'Most sufferers complain of gooseberry thorns "gone sceptical, nurse" or strawberry walk (variation of the vulgar backache), sunburn, and sundry bites'. 'At one farm, much to our dismay, a girl was prostrated by what was evidently acute internal discomfort, being surrounded by a group of sympathisers to whom she was apparently dictating her will and specifications of the funeral. It is revealed eventually that she has eaten large numbers of green gooseberries, and we give doses of Aspro all round and everyone is happy'. Saturday is a 'tay donsong' with Conga and the Hokey Cokey; 'a special technique is required for Cockney dancing which reminds one, faint but pursuing, of mediæval paintings of the the dance of death'. Sunday means SS 'greatly hampered by small persistent saints who clamber all over us'. Finally the week closes as 'all and sundry sing "Erbide with me" with touching abandon'.

In Michaelmas 1943 the College recorded its largest first-year intake ever (108 students), though the third year had dwindled to a mere 41 and there were only 65 in the second. Anne Womersley (née Cohen) contributes an extensive article on the making of official films. Again the Garden is a major topic. Pest, disease and soil impoverishment have sounded the death-knell of both College orchards, and with typical energy and foresight Miss Procter reports preparations for a new one to be well under way. Besides providing all the College's needs the garden has filled numerous extra mouths. 'More people are up now in the vacations, and we had a large Summer School to feed on top of ourselves. We also supply the Cambridge Waiting Rooms and sell a surplus'. 'The great adventure this year has been mushroom growing – for the benefit of the gardening student here who was about to take a horticultural examination. The manure cost us nothing: we get it from the University Farm in exchange for vegetable refuse. The beds were made in a dark tin hut at midwinter so there was nothing extravagant about the venture. We spawned one on St Paul's Day and one on St Valentine's Day and raced them. Rather surprisingly St Valentine won hands down! – giving a beautiful crop of perfect mushrooms throughout the May Term. And our gardening student (trained here, and now on the garden staff), Miss Ruth Finder, passed the Royal Horticultural Society General Examination in March. She did not get a question on mushrooms but she might have'. Miss Procter also stars in the RC report, for both lecturing and passing courses.

The Lent 1944 issue reports not merely the digging up of the tennis courts for cultivation, but associated archæological studies, which result in an extensive article by Dr Cam on the Hamlet of Howes. There is also a report that Mrs F Woodhead (C Layland) has been appointed to be one of the 2 Deputy Directors of WAAF. She had taken her pilot's licence in 1937.

By Michaelmas 1944 the scent of victory was palpable. 'Hopeful signs are in the air. A summer during which the College flag waved in celebration of the liberation of Paris and Brussels has been followed by a Michaelmas Term when fire-watching has ceased and the

College Tennis ended in Lent 1941

lights have gone up in Girton corridors. The present Second Year has been granted a third year at the University: the Grange has been de-requisitioned (and it is hoped it may be re-opened next term); and the Garden Steward has planted wallflowers as well as cabbages'. The Garden Steward is also congratulated on her election to the Council of the Women's Farm and Garden Association.

The College's 75th birthday is noted, though with muted celebrations because of the war. As at the start of the war, it took under its ægis other students: this time 27 Student Nurses from Great Ormond Street Children's Hospital to allow them to train safe from flying-bombs. 'The pleasing pink uniforms and tall white caps struck a cheerful note in Chapel and in Hall, and their zest for housework (part of their training) set an excellent example to one and all. They were the best possible type of evacuees, and we enjoyed their visit as much as they did'.

'We were sorry to lose our friend and neighbour, Rev G Hibbert-Ware during the course of the year. Mr Hibbert-Ware has taken services in chapel and been an occasional preacher for many years. Now, on the death of his sister, he has left the village and moved into Cambridge. The many Girtonians who have been hospitably entertained at *Hilary* and who admired Miss Hibbert-Ware's work as an ornithologist may like to know that an Alice Hibbert-Ware Memorial garden is being established in Girton village. Miss Procter is honorary adviser and has planned an attractive scheme which will add considerably to the amenities of the village'.

The extensive Garden Report extols the virtues of grazing sheep on a lacrosse pitch, looks forward to post-war gardening, and reports that 'A wren called Maria has made natural history at Girton this summer by nesting in a sack flung over a low beam in the garden toolshed – so that she and her children could be closely observed at every stage in their family life. When the shed was locked she had to enter and leave it by a small hole in the wall so that it was possible for a naturalist to photograph her at close range from a "hide", and also to try some friendly experiments on her. One day a stuffed wren was perched on a stump just outside her hole so that her reactions to it could be noted. Another time a wren-song was played on a hidden gramophone record just as she flew out. Valuable information was thus obtained by the distinguished naturalist and author – Rev EA Armstrong, Vicar of St Mark's, Newnham – who is working on wren-behaviour at present. Her 5 children all left the nest on Trinity Sunday and were one by one first coaxed to the hole and then out through it with pale green caterpillars carried by Maria – an enthralling sight!' The only drawback of the experiment was that it coincided with rumours that German paratroops were to be dropped in Madingley Woods dressed as Clergymen with Notebooks. Miss Procter comments 'I was relieved when the experiments were safely over'.

This issue also reported what appears to be the College's only fatality on active service: 4 Aug 1944 'from injuries sustained while flying HM aircraft in England, the Hon Mrs Margaret Fairweather, Flight Captain, ATA'.

In Easter 1945, 'Our local VE celebrations lacked perhaps the fine careless rapture of the Armistice rejoicings of 1918 (no bonfire in the court in 1945) but they were marked no less by a genuine feeling of relief and thanksgiving. As a College we have been extraordinarily fortunate. Our buildings have escaped damage from enemy action. Our numbers have never been depleted. Our garden has kept us supplied at all seasons. And now, if we do not face a future of unclouded skies, we intend at least to have unclouded windows. The blue paint is our immediate problem'.

The issue includes a comparison of English and American education by one who experienced both, being evacuated to America in 1940. She sees strength and weaknesses in both, though younger generations may be surprised at some of the things she finds remarkable in the American system: co-education, a national curriculum, a movement away from early specialisation.

War was over, but the Michaelmas 1945 *Review* reports an attack potentially as deadly as the Luftwaffe: *Salmonella Thompson* hit all indiscriminately and closed the College kitchens. Happily, Newnham College stepped in and fed the survivors; the College could even fulfil its plan to host a Summer School. 'ERH' reports 60 'fugitives from "The pestilence that walketh in the noon-day", right in the heart of it [Newnham], keeping its rules, eating its meals, enjoying its privileges. It must have been an event without precedent; it certainly was an unequalled feat of adaptation and catering, an unrivalled instance of hospitality and generosity, a new and unusual experience of our underlying affinity. Would that all exile were as comfortable'.

With the lifting of censorship the *Review* again presents records of student experiences, with 2 extensive reports from Europe. The first chronicles life in occupied France: the initial relief at German discipline, quickly changing to fear and hatred in the light of repression, torture, and arbitrary requisition; the immense value of the wireless, the words '*Ici Londres*'; the propaganda; the deportations; the *Maquis*; finally the dawning of hope and freedom.

The second, from the first student to benefit from the Refugee Students Fund, describes her eventful return to Prague. A 4-week wait for transport in Egypt allowed her to play the tourist; then through Palestine to Baghdad, Tehran, Pahlevi and by Soviet boat to Baku. Thence by trains (including goods trains) for 3 weeks through Rostov and Kiev and scenes of almost total devastation to Prague, to join in the rebuilding of the shattered nation. She was grateful to discover there was no reproach against those who had managed to escape and 'that meant a lot to me, because I did not find any of my family. My father had died my mother was sent to a concentration camp and has not returned and my brother who was in a forced labour camp has not returned either. Unfortunately this was the fate of many'. But Prague looked to the future and she was working in the University Physiology Laboratory. 'With the help we are receiving, I think that these difficulties will soon be overcome and though we are far from Cambridge standards, the prospects are good'.

How do students now feel, looking back on those experiences after 60 years? We are grateful to the College Alumnæ Office for encouraging war-time students to share their memories with us. Over a dozen did so, and what follows is an attempt to place their varied remembrances into some sort of framework.

Student Memories, Sixty Years On

Despite privation, all its students seem to have happy war-time memories. As in the men's Colleges, the rules were strict and evading them was seen as something of a sport. Visitors had to be signed in and out and were severely restricted in number.

'I have no memories at all of real discomfort or inconvenience; the atmosphere at College was very friendly and calm although there were strict rules about the hours and number of times we were allowed to go out in the evening. There were, however, one or two windows where one could "climb in"' [Margaret Weale].

'Rules enjoined us to dine in Hall and be on the premises by 10pm unless granted an official Exeat. As for the curfew, this was widely ignored because although the ground floor rooms were fitted with bars, there were a few exceptions for no particular reason. I was the occupant of one such set and my sittingroom window provided ingress for assorted Cinderellas without disturbing my sleep in the adjoining bedroom. The possibility of burglars did not enter into consideration: either they were busy elsewhere or the reputation of Girtonians was enough to deter even hardened criminals' [Eira Sallis].

'Everyone must have memories of signing visitors in and out of the college – visits were for afternoon tea or after-dinner coffee. We heard with amazement that the Mistress signed her visitors in and out too. We also signed on at dinner in hall.

There was talk of some students arriving back late in the evening and climbing over the gates. One reputed offender later became Mistress. The rule about visitors was eventually changed to cover afternoon and evening. The one problem then was the eventual hunger of the visitor' [Mavis von Proschwitz].

Heat

The winter of 1939–1940 was cruelly harsh. 'I don't suppose today's students can imagine the "War Years"! I remember my first year – that bitter winter of 1939–40 – in the bed-sit in the Tower. 3 outside walls and a fireplace across the corner by the door. No old blankets would stop the draught up the spiral staircase. The bed with a very thin mattress shut up to the wall under a shelf. I slept in bedsocks, cardigan, mitts, earplugs and sometimes a woolly hat. We all washed in our hot-water-bottle water and cracked the ice on the water jug. Fortunately the threat of air-raids made a compulsory move to F Chapel wing and I was also able to "inherit" the Blackheath High School sofa – a luxury indeed. Of course we just took it as it came at the time, but the memories are rich and the grandchildren think they are hilarious!' [Joy Hollings].

'My principal memory is of the organisation needed to keep warm. I shared a warmed room with 2 friends. If anyone had a single (male) visitor, however, she had exclusive fire-side rights. We were careful to save last night's cinders. Public rooms, libraries &c, were heated, corridors barely, and these were permanently bathed in a chilly blue light as the windows were painted navy-blue. One of our tasks on the cessation of hostilities was to help scraping paint' [Margaret Weale].

'Food was much more difficult (bread rationing) and the gas in the gasfire was very low – it was one of the famous winters when everything was frozen for ages and I remember the piles of snow in Sidney Street being carted away on lorries' [Phyllis Smart].

'Fuel was so short that we were inclined to pool resources – share a fire with a neighbour – in my case Mary Stead who later went to NZ' [Helen Scholfield].

'Also unknown to us was central heating and we survived the East Anglian winters by crouching over small fires emitting more smoke than heat. I seem to remember that the coal ration was one bucket per 2 days and we therefore teamed together alternately in each other's rooms to eke out the meagre portion. As we had nearly all experienced a fairly spartan upbringing in war-time we were well equipped to withstand some hardship: moreover any hint of complaint was invariably squashed by "Don't you know there's a war on?" Also we were very conscious of our privilege in being at college at all while our brothers and friends were dicing with death on land, at sea and in the air' [Eira Sallis].

'There was a black line painted on the bath to show the level of water allowed. We had, I think, 3 scuttles of coal a week, so much time was therefore spent reading in the beautiful library' [Mavis Genge].

Food

Despite the valiant efforts of the Garden Steward, feeding the College was not easy. While her famous Dutch Brown beans were plentiful, bread, butter, jams and fruit were not. Remarkably, Fitzbillies' cake shop managed to continue to maintain its reputation; and for many remembering friends meant remembering shared coffees and cakes, there or in their College rooms.

'The feeding of the flock at College was also well organised although I mainly recall one large potato in a bowl of soup for lunch. Yes, we all queued up for our ration of NAMCO, and once we had a an issue of 2 oranges each. For quite a while I positioned mine in a different place each day, just to look at them' [Margaret Weale].

Eira Eadie and Jean Atkinson, the 'infants' of Girton College

'One singular benefit bestowed upon me and at least one other, Jean Atkinson, was a minuscule ration of milk – one gill per day – because of our age. As we had been admitted at age 17, we were officially classed by the Govt as Infants until we reached our 18th birthdays and, lest deprivation might stunt our growth, we had to be "topped up". As this was the only milk available for brewing up in our rooms, we became very popular at teatime. As bread and crumpets were not rationed at this time, and we had usually brought from home some butter or jam, we were thus able to supplement our diet. As for our meals, they were uniformly dire. Any identifiable item, such as a weekly egg or scrap of bacon was ruined in the cooking and the rest was mercifully mysterious. I do remember a regular dish of meatless beans, to which I looked forward because it was actually edible. Nevertheless, we thrived on the fare and nobody suffered from obesity or malnutrition. Smoking was fairly universal as no-one had told us that it was not healthy. Drink and drugs were not a problem. There was no pub culture, instead we drank coffee and we thought drugs meant aspirins for a headache' [Eira Sallis].

'I had a jar of a new product, just come on to the market, called *Nescafé*, given to me by Mrs Armstrong next door, who said it would make it easy for me to make myself a cup of coffee. Food rationing was in force and caused complications, for we each had to have our own little ration of butter on its dish, kept in a cupboard in Hall, and likewise sugar, I think. Jam was in scarce supply, though sometimes there was honey as a great treat for Sunday tea. Meat was short, too, and now and again we had swan for Sunday lunch. It was dark, fishy and not at all nice. But Fitzbillies' sticky buns and dough-cake were somehow still on sale, so between lectures at the building in

Mill Lane we would repair to Fitzbillies' and buy buns to eat then and cake to take back for tea, which we mostly had in our rooms' [Pamela Gregory].

'The food I thought was wonderful, but must have been extremely stodgy to give us the necessary calories for cycling into town, sometimes 2 or 3 times a day, standing in the queue at Fitzbillies' for buns if you had guests for tea' [Jocelyn Finch].

Clothes

'In 1943 I advanced upon Girton in some trepidation, complete with blackout curtains and a cobbled-together "trousseau". After 4 years of war and school uniform the rationing of clothing by the points system meant that a basic adult wardrobe could be assembled only by appealing to sympathetic mothers and aunts. We could be said to have been at the chrysalis stage of development and very anxious to metamorphose into butterflies, especially as at least one full length evening dress was advised – sophistication indeed. Fortunate and much envied were those few girls such as Jenny Turner and Philomena Guillebaud who had been evacuated to America and returned with such exotica as non-utility garments with unrestricted pleats and yards of material. At the other extreme the young things who had been incarcerated in Cheltenham for the duration were mostly obliged to continue wearing school coats and skirts. At this time nylons were unknown to us and our stockings required constant darning so we mostly went barelegged or in trousers, then known as "slacks". At dinner we were expected to be suitably dressed, although not in full evening attire. This however was worn by the Mistress who appeared in black and cabbage roses, floor length, during her whole term of office' [Eira Sallis].

'Around College most of us wore trousers, although not for Hall nor for lectures. We did cycle into Cambridge in socks and slacks, but once outside the lecture theatre we rolled up our trouser-legs and donned a skirt on top' [Margaret Weale].

'I hung up my new clothes in the wardrobe; I had been taken to Jane Hardy, where we bought all our things, and she had found suitable attire for me. I remember a navy dress, which Jane said was a nice little dress "that you could go to lectures in", but I always kept it for best' [Pamela Gregory].

The Blackout

To comply with blackout regulations, the windows of the College were painted blue. Mavis Genge remembers 'The windows in the corridors were blackened and lights low'.

Students were instructed to bring their own blackout curtains with them: 'The Michaelmas Term start was postponed until mid-Oct so that the College could adjust to blackout regulations, and we were sent the measurements of our room windows to bring suitable curtains, thick or lined' [Joy Hollings].

'Most people's memories of 1940–43 were like mine, battling against the cold with our 2 buckets of coal per week. The windows were all painted blue, very depressing, and we all had to supply our own curtains, lined with black heavy material' [Jocelyn Finch].

'In term time we went in pairs after dark to check that all blackout curtains weren't letting out any light. My partner had poor night-vision and I spent a lot of the time preventing her from getting tangled up in the rose bushes' [Veronica Tillyard].

War Work

While the fear of incendiary bombs remained, students were expected to volunteer for fire-watching duties, both for the College and for Cambridge generally. There was an ARP look-out point on the UL tower, and students who volunteered during the Long Vac were given free board in the College.

'We were expected to do some war work each week – I can't remember how much – between 6 and 10 hours, I think, which might (in turn) include College fire-watching, sleeping in a room with an alarm for amber alerts when you then went outside. With luck you got a reasonable night's sleep. I remember another night on top of the Cavendish Laboratory watching a pulsating glow in the southern sky and realising that London was on fire – and my Father would be on duty in Westminster. He was a scientific adviser to the Ministry of Defence. As I had some FA and home nursing training I joined the VAD and did a shift at a convalescent home and a FA centre in town' [Joy Hollings].

'We did some "fire-watching" in one of the Reception Rooms, and in the company of Hermione Grammatike. Did we have any training? Any fire-drill? Nothing I think to compare with that famous Fire Brigade photo. We certainly decided that we should save Hermione first' [Margaret Wcalc].

'I did it [fire-watching] over Christmas, which was easy for me to do, as I lived in Cambridge. The fire-watchers shared a room with Hermione Grammatike, the Girton mummy' [Veronica Tillyard].

'There was also fire-watching at the UL for which I think we were paid something like £2 odd per time: I saved it up to buy a book' [Phyllis Smart].

'We were enrolled for ARP fire service on the roof of the UL and thought Cambridge looked mediæval in the moonlight' [Mavis Genge].

'My sister was working at NIAB on Huntingdon Road, for her war work. She was allowed to have some sprouts from there, so I picked some on my way home from firewatching. It was a frosty morning, and as I turned my bicycle into Storey's Way I skidded on the ice and sprouts were spilt all over the road. It was no problem to gather them up, as there was no traffic (not possible these days!)' [Veronica Tillyard].

'I went back to Cambridge during the Long Vac. It had always been possible to do this, for those who wanted to put in some more study, but it cost money. However, in war-time, if one volunteered

Hermione Grammatike, a first-century Egyptian mummy, was presented to the College by Flinders Petrie. Her name (painted just above her right shoulder) means either 'Hermione, woman of letters' or 'Hermione the Teacher'.

for fire-watching, one could live free. So Nan and I fixed up to fire-watch at the UL. We used to cycle down there at about 11 o'clock at night; it was still light then, because during, the war we had Double Summer Time, 2 hours ahead of God's time, something to do with saving fuel, I believe. I still envisage the 2 of us cycling over Garrett Hostel Bridge, and settling down on camp-beds in the foyer of the vast UL, with its imposing tower. These were, I think, the only times I actually entered it, because I found all I needed in other libraries. Had any fire-bombs dropped, I have no idea whether we should have been the slightest good at putting the fire out. There were buckets of sand, and mysterious things called stirrup-pumps, but we had had no training in using them. I'm sure Nan, who was eminently practical, would have risen to the occasion, just as I'm sure that I should have fumbled about uselessly. Luckily, this was never put to the test' [Pamela Gregory].

Gardening

'I don't know anything about the agriculture except that there were pigs and I would have evaded even seeing them (London born)' [Phyllis Smart].

'Our war work consisted of spending a few weeks in the summer vac either on domestic or agricultural tasks. I tried both and found neither to my liking, although perhaps being taken away on the back of a lorry to plant vegetables in a Cambs field which disappeared over the horizon was the more dispiriting. In term time we did fire-watching and kitchen duties' [Eira Sallis].

'All I remember about agriculture was helping with hoeing rows of vegetables for a few afternoons' [Veronica Tillyard].

Joy and a friend begin the morning's activities.

'I've been trying to find someone who remembers the French Farmer refugee who set up an early silage silo. A French refugee was working on the college land and he had introduced this new way of making cattle cake. An appeal came for students to go and tread down this silage, which was layers of green stuff (chiefly pea and bean haulm from the fields) and molasses. So we put on bathing costumes and old cotton dresses and tied up our hair in scarves and cycled down to the farmyard about 6am. The photo shows how the large wire cages were lined with roofing felt, or something like it and ladders were tied together for access (no H&S regs then!). I am the elegant girl on the top! 6 or 7 of us climbed in and stamped around on this sticky mess, dancing "Gathering Peascods" or "Strip the Willow" for an hour or so, and then dashed back to college where hopefully a friend had saved a bathroom for a quick swill down in the 5" allowance of hot water – all brown and smelly when we dried off and met the challenge to be in Chapel by 8.15.

That silage silo! I'm sure it ought to be "recorded" somewhere but I can't remember who else responded to the cry for help from the French refugee farmer. Who would want to know about it now?

Dutch Brown beans. No one seems to remember these. The Garden Steward grew masses of vegetables especially anything which would keep through the winter (no freezers then). A good crop of these beans, which were particularly rich in protein and could be dried, gave us bean soup and cutlets. Then a WAEC Inspector declared the Girton beans to be the only ones in England and commandeered the crop for seed. Anyone with a Veg Garden could have 6 seed beans. I took mine home and my Mother grew them for years. No one seems to have heard of them now. I have never seen them in a seed catalogue' [Joy Hollings].

First Aid

Phyllis Smart remembers Miss Cartwright, the Mistress, in her RC uniform. However, despite her brilliance as a mathematician, she was not cut out for medicine. 'The fire-watchers shared a room with Hermione Grammatike, the Girton mummy. One evening I went along to the room I occupied in term time, as I wanted to change into my old pair of slippers. On my return, I met Miss Cartwright. She invited me to have some refreshment and talk, though she was generally a shy woman, and I realised that there was some fellow-feeling here, because she and I had failed our FA exam, which we were all urged to take' [Veronica Tillyard].

'Fairly early in the war there were some FA courses at Addenbrooke's Hospital which you could take and I went to one of those when I was at the stage of wondering what to do next because I knew I couldn't go on as a research student' [Alison Duke].

'We all did something, and my own effort was fire-watching on a rota at the Observatory, and running the RC detachment. We did the usual things like take FA exams and be ready for casualties. I think I must have qualified for this because I used to go every year to the Cambridge Fruiting Campaign based at Wisbech and the Hopping Mission when we ministered to the fruit and hop-pickers and had a wonderful time!' [Jocelyn Finch].

Teaching

Lectures were arranged by the University, and in a period when all eligible males were called up many lecturers returned from retirement, and seemed old indeed to Girton's students. Meanwhile the men were coming up early and seemed very young.

'Mostly the lecturers seemed very very old gentlemen. For French Prose an ancient had emerged from retirement from terrorising small boys, to hone his skills afresh on first-year Girtonians. Even the Scholar admitted to knowing less French with every session. An error was adorned with ×. If the mistake was repeated – as it was, because explanations lacked clarity, shall I say – then ×× or ××× and so on was scored. One day a less perturbed Girtonian held up her cross-stitched paper and said "Look, I have invented the Victorian sampler!" After that we no longer cared much about the comments of the sarcastic old monster as we – bemusedly – translated our way through *Puck of Pook's Hill*. The one thing I *did* learn was how *not* to teach!' [Margaret Weale].

'As for the French tutor, my teacher at school warned me about him. She had him at Girton in the twenties and said he used to throw books at his pupils' [Mavis Genge].

Margaret Weale 'was frightened of one particular instructor and I of another: I do remember that we were forbidden by one who shall be nameless to speak French at all as our accents caused her offence. As we were in no position to go abroad to improve same, this rather negated the point of our attending Girton at all. We did emerge passably well informed about classical literature while not competent to order a meal without being sneered at by a French waiter' [Eira Sallis].

Some of the 'few male students' did occasionally venture out to Girton

'There were very few male students in Cambridge, none of course in Girton. They were younger than us and waiting for their call-up. I went to English lectures as well as French and German and attended one given by Prof Quiller Couch. There were about twenty girls there and not more than 2 or 3 young boys present. The aged professor began his lecture with "Gentlemen ..."' [Mavis Genge]. Joy Hollings recalls that he would not lecture at all if only women were in the lecture hall.

'In our second year we went to an elderly man for Greek and Latin proses. One had to write prose in the style of one or other of the classical writers, and after our efforts had been marked we were given fair copies shewing how we ought to have done them. He was a funny old man, whose name I have forgotten, who always had tomatoes ripening on the sill of the room where we had our supervisions. Another elderly man used to come to Girton each week and instruct us into the mysteries of the pronunciation of Greek. He also had a great facility for translating modern expressions: (*hapte to fōs*; = 'touch the light') meant 'switch on the electric light', and tomatoes were '*sphærula rubra*' (= little red spheres). I suppose we had these ancients because the younger dons had been called up. Several of the younger Girton dons had gone into the intelligence service or such things. I suppose that the men must have come up a year younger than normal, to get in one year before they were called up. So the male undergraduate population of Cambridge consisted of these very young boys, often still a bit spotty, and older men, invalided out of the forces, between which 2 groups the gulf must have been colossal' [Pamela Gregory].

Extra-Mural Activities

'One friend and I did some war work entertaining the children at a convalescent home somewhere up on the Gogs. As we absolutely had to be back for Hall at 7pm, once too hastily I tried to dash in front of an army convoy coming up the hill. To this day I can see the expression on the face of the driver of the van into whose path I was riding fast. My bicycle was a write-off. I was concussed, with bruises and grazes, and I was – so I maintain – taken back to Girton on a gun-carriage. I did not think at that time, but it must have been a thorough bother for all concerned' [Margaret Weale].

'At that time there was a school in Girton Village for mentally handicapped boys, and a few of us from the College went every week to help run a Cub Pack for them. The moving spirit was Mary Callister (2 years senior to me) who was Akela. Pam Gregory (née Gregory, 1 year senior to me) and later Barbara Pepper (née Siddons, 1 year junior to me) helped Mary. In July 1943 we took the pack camping in a field near the school, and I was asked to do the cooking on a field oven, which was completely new to me! One night, a German bomber, presumably on his way home, opened fire with his machine gun and some bushes caught fire. There was no panic and the fire was quickly extinguished, but not before one of the boys said, "It's like Moses and the burning bush, Miss!" That summer, we took them in punts on the Backs, which seemed to be quite an exciting adventure for them, and for us!' [Monica Pritchard].

'2 extra-collegiate activities in which I was involved were the Fruiting Campaign and a Cub Pack. The former was a kind of mission to the East-Enders who came up to Norfolk in the summer to pick fruit. Medical students especially volunteered for this, and girls also took part. We used to go round the pickers' "bunks" as their huts were called, with medical boxes, to minister to cut fingers, sore throats &c, being known as "doctors" and "nurses". The girls also minded the children during the day, cooking lunch and running a kind of weekday SS. The Campaign was run by the Franciscans, who had a house in Cambridge.

In the evenings we got on our bicycles and did the rounds of the pickers' bunks, armed with medical boxes, to treat headaches, thorns in fingers, sprained wrists or ankles and such minor ills. Quite a few medical students used to be with us, and they were always called "doctor" and we "nurse"; one felt very grand. I had a feeling that some of these burly Cockney men, holding out a large and dirty hand to have a splinter taken out of a finger, "Please, nurse", just enjoyed having their hands held by young girls. One memory that has stayed with me is of cycling along, those fen roads in the light warm evenings, with that flat country spread out for miles around, with sometimes the odd very important-looking tree, because of its rarity, and quite often a superb sunset. When we got back to our camp, we would make cocoa and sometimes we did eightsome reels.

The Wisbech Fruiting Campaign

Mary Callister, a year senior to me, was in charge of a Cub Pack for some little boys from a mentally handicapped establishment in Girton village. When Mary went down she bequeathed the Cubs to me, me who had never been so much as a Brownie. How I had the temerity to do it I don't know, but once a week I collected 8 or 10 little boys and taught them knots – reef, clove-hitch, round turn and 2 half-hitches, none of which I can do today except the first. We also learned how the Union Jack was formed, I having had to mug up all these things from a useful manual. Fortunately, being mentally deficient, they had forgotten each week what they had learned the week before, so it was not very taxing. I then discovered *tracking*. This was an huge success, and so whenever it was fine I laid a trail of twigs in the form of arrows and the Cubs followed it with enormous joy and excitement. I really quite enjoyed it, and they were nice little boys and no trouble' [Pamela Gregory].

The Forces

'During the war we were not, I think, much aware of the Servicemen near us in Cambs. Yes, there were the Americans at "Bull College" –

the then Bull Hotel (now incorporated into St Catharine's and King's Colleges). They did invite Girtonians to dances, but I did not accept (why not?). We were aware however of the constant dull roaring of aircraft overhead at night' [Margaret Weale].

'Some RAF Officers invited a friend of mine to a dance at the Camp. She would not have been allowed to go alone, so begged me to go with her. We duly applied for late Exeats. We gave the names of our escorts who would pick us up in a staff car and promised to bring us back on time. We joined up with some other Officers, but our escorts disappeared. 11 passed and I was very worried about college rules. Finally Barbara and I told our Cinderella story to one of the other Officers who rooted our 2 out of the bar. It was well after midnight when we reported in, and next day we were on the Senior Tutor's mat in deep trouble. In vain we protested that it was not our fault. We could not get back – they did not keep their promise – she paced the room – no more late Exeats that term! We were in disgrace and I wrote quickly to my parents in case the college did. That was my fantasy – I don't think the escapade was taken that seriously. 2 years later as an ATS Officer on a gun site I was expert at rooting drivers out of the bar – especially American ones – to get my girls back to the site for duty' [Joy Hollings].

'Perhaps cycling in and out of Cambridge helped to keep us fit. On account of the influx of American servicemen in the area who could not be expected to understand the civilised rules of courtship, we were advised to cycle in the blackout only when equipped with (a) a whistle, (b) a hat-pin and (c) pepper. In what order and by what balancing trick we were to administer such rebuffs was not recorded but I do not recall any such incident as mugging was not then invented as a popular pastime' [Eira Sallis].

Social & Culture

'Entertainment. How different it was then. We made our own entertainment, talking, toasting crumpets; and there was music. Crammed into a practice room we listened to Beate playing. There was a madrigal society, directed by Mrs Bertha Jeffries. Of course we held parties (beer and squash) and we *danced*. I got into trouble for spreading French chalk onto the floor of the reception room where my 21st was to be held. Inquisitive passers-by had looked in to see what was afoot, and trailed the chalk up the corridor. I spent the last 5 minutes before my guests arrived washing the corridor floor – up to the spiral stairs' [Margaret Weale].

'I did join the Classical Society, and in my first year we gave a dramatic reading of the *Alcestis* of Euripides, in translation. I was

chosen as Alcestis and a girl called Daphne Pickard was Hercules.
I think she also directed the performance. Certainly it was her
idea that we should do it in modern dress and place it in Scotland,
because it took place in Thrace, which was northern Greece. Daphne
herself was Scottish, and provided plaids for us to wear across our
evening dresses, while the "men" wore kilts. To take the place of the
Satyr play which would have provided light relief for the Greeks,
Daphne taught us to do a Scottish Eightsome Reel, which we danced
with great enjoyment' [Pamela Gregory].

*Girton Students relax in the
College wood*

'But I must emphasise that it was *not
my* idea at all, but Miss Jolliffe's, our
much admired Classics don, that we
should place it in Scotland and do it in
Highland dress – I was somewhat taken
aback when Miss Jolliffe suggested
this, and thought she could not be
serious. I had several Scottish friends
and together we attended a Scottish
dancing group at St Columba's Hall,
and I suppose Miss Jolliffe must have
heard of my involvement in this, which
must have prompted the idea. I was, of
course, then, very enthusiastic about the production, and was able
to borrow kilts &c from the male members of the group. I have
sometimes had mixed feelings about this production in the past, or
at any rate my own part in it, but Pamela's contribution makes me
feel better about it!' [Daphne Pickard].

'On Saturdays the great thing was to go to the Dorothy Café in
the morning, where there was dancing and a sing-song; I remember
particularly "My Bonnie lies over the ocean" – which, now I think
of it, has a poignant echo, though I never thought in that way at
the time. It was all very naive and innocent, I suppose' [Pamela
Gregory].

Cycling

Buses were 'rare and unreliable' [Helen Scholfield], and a cycle
was all-but essential, especially for those wanting to take part
in any University student societies, which were located in central
Cambridge. Cycling in the blackout was not without its interest.

'There were no street lights and no lights might show from houses,
and only a circle about the size of a half-crown ($1\frac{1}{4}$"), was allowed in
one's headlights. There were American troops stationed somewhere
N of Cambridge, and as we cycled back to Girton huge army lorries

used to swish past us, sometimes much too close for comfort. There were occasion when there was only one bike between 2 people. This entailed one of you cycling on some way, leaving the bike by the side of the road and walking on. The second one would arrive at the bike and repeat the procedure. It was better than walking the whole 3 miles, anyway!' [Pamela Gregory].

'After Dunkirk we were instructed to leave College immediately after our exams. My friend Stella and I were among the last to leave. The Dunkirk evacuation had begun. We planned to cycle N and left at about 7am after dragging our mattresses down into the Hall. As we rode down the drive lorries were arriving. Exhausted and, dishevelled soldiers were just rolling out onto the ground. My cousin, who was at Bedford College evacuated to Cambridge, met us at the gate with some bread she had bought in the town. We had the remains of our butter ration and a bag of tomatoes and some water (we must have found a place for more food on the way!). Stella lived in Holm Pierrepont, near Nottingham and knew the way. We cut off the A1 on roads now under Rutland Water – no signposts and pathetic 'road blocks' of farm implements on the side roads. Invasion was expected any time. We stayed the night with Stella and my cousin and I rode on to York, found a B&B for the night and rode on over the moors. I lived in Goathland and my cousin in Whitby. My grandchildren think that is hilarious too!' [Joy Hollings].

'I do remember one occasion riding back in the dark being joined by a male unknown figure who escorted me back, along the Huntingdon Road. Before peeling off to Girton village he said "excuse me, Miss, but your skirt is riding rather high". This must have been the nearest I got to having a pass made at me, certainly I was never afraid, as today's young maidens might be in a similar incident' [Jocelyn Finch].

Helping

'We were allotted various domestic tasks: *eg* we did a week's spring cleaning. "Go and fetch the donkey" I was told when about to polish the corridor linoleum. It transpired that a rag-wrapped weight on the end of a broomstick was – "a donkey"! We waited at Hall and we "polished" plates. The antiquated washing-up machine did its best, but we had to flick away any scraps of food still adhering. I have a photograph of 3 of us happily performing this exercise. I believe that some of the photographs taken at the time (to recruit domestic staff?) appeared in the *Tatler*' [Margaret Weale].

'We took it in turns to serve at table, lined up against the wall until our Head Housekeeper (?Ethel) dropped her arm and we advanced in formation.   To my everlasting shame on one such occasion I distinguished myself by depositing the contents of a dish of stewed plums in the lap of a senior student' [Eira Sallis].

VE Day

'VE Day was declared a holiday. In the evening we all dressed for Hall, and we drank CIDER. In the day a group of friends cycled out to Madingley to picnic. I remember lying in a field of buttercups looking at the blue blue sky and thinking, No more droning roaring groanings. So glad, so glad. It was not until much later when first I visited the American Cemetery at Madingley that I thought of the cost, the sacrifice of so many young lives in that time of war – what really was happening in our world throughout, for me, such happy years' [Margaret Weale].

Postscript

In 1945 the College was visited by photographers and editors from *The Sketch*, and a double spread of pictures appeared in the issue of July 11 (pages 12–13). 'At Girton College, Cambridge' it was titled, and the accompanying text stated 'The students come from every type of school in Britain, Eire, Europe and India. At present a great number are temporarily in the Women's Services and the Civil Service'. Eira Sallis, now Eira Eadie, still recalls dressing up and posing for the pictures, and was particularly incensed that the paper managed to mangle both of her names, transforming 'Eira Sallis' into 'Lena Sivell'. Eira comments wryly 'We were conscripted to polish plates which had already been dried, and I remember that other students were required to don dressing-gowns and draw curtains in daylight to simulate a cocoa party. As a result I have always since taken a jaundiced view of what the papers say'.

Pretending to work in the College kitchens

Index
DR de Lacey

This Index consists of all references to people connected with the Village and selected references to other topics. Initials have been added, where possible, from the 1945 Electoral Register. Illustrations are indicated in **bold type**. It should not be assumed that all references under any name are necessarily to the same person (there are at least two S Gawthrops), nor that a person named without initials (*eg* Mr Coe) is different from all the other Coes.

Adams, AFG 2, 6, 56, 88, 96, 104, 112, 114, 116, 120, 124, 126

agriculture 11, 227, 239–240, 246, 248, 266, 280, 282–283, 286, 296

aircraft crash 48, 215, 225, 229, 232, 236, 238, 240–241, 243, 246, 248

air-raid precautions 2, 8, 18, 20, 22, 24, 32, 34, 38, 40, 44, 46, 48, 54, 56, 58, 60, 64, 66, 68, 70, 74, 76, 78, 80, 82, 86, 90, 92, 94, 98, 102, 104, 106, 108, 126, 128, 130, 132, 136, 140–152, 155, 159–160, 233, 271, 294–295

air-raid siren 24, 40, 148, 230

air-raid wardens 140, 142, 144–145, 152, 154, 162, 164, 228

air-raids 36, 38, 40, 42, 44, 46, 48, 52, 54, 70, 72, 74, 82, 96, 98, 100, 102, 229–230, 232, 234–235, 240, 243, 246, 260

Aldridge, MA 84

Alton, P **15**, 90

Amps, AJ 12, 147, 150, 170

Amps, E 62, 90

Amps, MA 60

Amps, Miss 238

Amps, Mr 147

Anderson, JR 120

Andrews, C 62, 66, 84

Andrews, HM 8

Andrews, ME 66

Armitage, Mrs 110

ARP Post 74, 76, 84, 90, 94, 98, 147

Ashton, Miss 162

Asplen, ML 46

Asplen, YP 66

Atkinson, J 292, **292**

Auger, FG 124

Auger, MB 114

Austin, RGC 92, 94, 138

Austin, WA 8

Averne, HW **77**

Aworth, KA 42

Bacon, WE 132

Baggaley, HDB (née King) 239

Baguly, Mr 100

Bailey, E 98

Bailey, I 124

Bailey, JW 128, 130

Bailey, K 28

Bailey, Miss 8

Bailey, Mr 148

Baker, AM (née Bonny) 238
Baker, LA 22
Baker, M 58
Balaam, J **15**
Baptist Church 2, 6, 10, 16, 18, 24, 26, 28, 30, 46, 114, 126
Barber, EH 38
Barber, Mr 147
Barlow, Mr 147
Barnes, GV 32
Barnes, S 170
Barrett, FC 50, 52, 64, 84, **85**, 130, 149, 162, 174, 184, 186, 206, 208, 276
Bartrip, R 58
Bartrip, TR 46
Bass, AE 72
Bawden, C 54
Baxter, H (née Scholfield) 291, 302
Baynes, RN 70
Beaumont, Mr 146
Beavington, J (née Mayes) 239
Bennett, FE 8
Bennett, Mr 102
Benstead, FE 64
Benwell, R 62
Betson, Q 4, 18, 48, 269
Betson, S 82, 84, 147, 165
Betts, B 90
Bevin Boys 214, 224, 229
Bickel, P (née Skinner) 240
Biggs, R 124
Billequez, DOA 156, 166
Billeting Officer 153–154, 160, 231, 250, 255–257, 274, 284
Bletchley Park 19, 284
Blott, BVR 128
Blott, FR 146
Blunt, K **133**
Boardman, AJ 42
bombing (of the Cambridge area)

38, 54, 72, 74, 76, 96, 141, 144, 150, 201, 211, 229–230, 232–233, 235, 237, 240–241, 243, 246, 259–260, 294
Bonny, AM 10, 238, **238**
Bonny, D 230
Bonny, IM 76, **238**, 239
Bonny, M **238**
Bonsor, FR 8, 149
Bonsor, JM **9**, 48, 78, 154, 160, 162, 166
Boot, PF 54
Booth, RA 118
Booth, W 104, 126
Born, RG 54
Bowyer, WE 6, 16, 18
Bowyer, YR 18
Boys' Brigade 208–209
Braddock, M (née Weale) 290–294, 298–299, 301, 303–304
Bradfield, H 20, 84, 88, 196, 215
Brading, R 146
Brading, TJ 128
Brereton, Dr 156, 166
Brett, Mr 147
Brind, KF 86
Broad, RK 42
Brooke, A 5
Brooks, J 227
Brown, LE 102
Brownies 262–264
Bruce, MCD 156
Burbeck, E 281
Burgess, L 126, 132, 154
Burgess, LA 138
Burgess, ML 138
Burgess, Mr 14
Burgh, Mrs **9**
Burkett, Mr 124
Burrows, MA 42, 118, 272
Burrows, S 134, 165, 272

Butler, F 108
Butler, KT 72
Cadets 116, 122, 124, 134, 136
Callister, M 299–300
Cam, HM 287
Camps, AJ 147, 170
Carr, AF 78
Cartwright, AR 76, 297
Chalkly, F 208
Chandler, AE 16
Chandler, F 56
Chandler, M 92
Chandler, S 22, 24, 28, 44, 148, 170
Chang, Dr 162
Chaplin, AF 102
Chaplin, CA 98
Chaplin, LR 130, 160
Chaplin, MF 138
Chaplin, Mrs 8
Chaplin, SII 126, 149, 154, 163
Chapman, T 4, 16
Chapman, V 148, 163
Chenery, AT 12
Chenery, Mrs 114
Chestnut Farm 68, 98, 102, 122, **123**
Childerley, D 8
Childs, KW 86
Church Lane 165, 170
Clark, CSC 116
Clark, M 116
Clark, NM 118
Clarke, CG 54
Clarke, FA 108
Clarke, JA 76
Clarke, M 269
Claydon, WJ 148, 206, **206**
Coates, DI 132
Cobb, AE 10
Cobb, Mr AE 6
Cockell, Mr 147

Coe, A 147, 170
Coe, CG 38
Coe, EI 128
Coe, G 147, 170, 276
Coe, GA 50
Coe, J 10, 229
Coe, LB 58
Coe, MJ 92
Coe, Mr 165
Coe, R 32, 207, **207**
Cohen, A 281, 286
Cole, B 100
Cole, C 147
Cole, F 170
Cole, K 58, 62
Cole, L 32, 42, 76, 82, 98, 100, 118, 130, 239, 242
Cole, M 88
Cole, Mrs 265
Cole, W 147
Collings, J 199, 208, 212, 283, **283**
Collings, L 208, **208**
Collinson, R 148
Collison, ME 94
Collison, VD 30
conscription 3, 11, 22, 35, 59, 61, 63, 76, 82, 101, 123, 281
Cooke, MA 10
Cookery Room 30, 32, 42, **43**, 48, 90, 141–142, 147–148, 168
Cornell, & Mrs 120
Cornell, L 62, 66, 230
Cornell, ML 147, 160, 162–163, 233
Cornell, Mr 147
Cornell, P 58, 62
Cornell, S 213
Cox, DCI 78
Coxall, DA 34
Crabbe, BE 134
Crabbe, H 84

Cracknell, F 240
Cracknell, J 237
Crane, JJ 12
Crane, MA 120
Cranfield, M 90, 243
Cranfield, W 118
Crawford, ASB 98
Crawford, PIJB 98
Culdrein 158–159, 166–167
Cundall, M (née Pritchard) 299
Cundell, CB 212, **212**
Cundell, EM 98
Cunningham, M 104
Daniel, EW 136
Dark, SOS 136, 149, 154,
    160–162
Darwin, I 233
Davis, AJ 112
Davis, JH 124
Davis, SJ 70
Day, LC 46
Dean, J 62
Dean, JA 138
Dean, K 213
Dean, MJ 92
Dean, Mr 147
Dean, RE 100
Dean, RL 40
Dig for Victory 3, 16, 65, 175,
    266, 276
Digger G 199
Ding, FK 34
Ding, MA 34
Dixon, LJ 74
Dixon, SR 4, 16, **17**, 78, 184, 213
Dixon, V 16
Dixon, WG 60
Dixon, WPA 90, 92, 136, **137**
Dodford Lane 6, 165, 170,
    232–233, 238, 243
Doggett, JR 136
Doggett, M 229

Donaldson, J 269
Duckett, Mr 100, 146
Duke, A 297
Duke, RV 171
Dupont, EFV 268
Dupont, EW 46
Dupont, FM 4, 6, 12, 18, 26
Dymond, FJ 149
Eadie, E (née Sallis) 290–292,
    292, 293, 296, 298, 301, 304
Easter, PC 10
Edmunds, BJ 98
Edmunds, GC 10
education 2, 86, 101, 107, 110,
    112, 130, 134, 174–175, 179,
    185, 195, 229, 236, 238, 240,
    242–243, 246–247, 254–255,
    259–261, 299, 304
Edwards, JO 124
Edwards, JV 38
Ellis, M **83**
Ellis, R 214, **214**, 241
Elwood, SA 2, 14, 22, 24, 26, 28,
    32, 36, 50, 52, 54
Elworthy, Miss 284
Entertainments Committee 28,
    42, 56, 58, 60, 62, 68, 108, 122,
    128, 162, 175
evacuees 3, 228–229, 231–232,
    241–243, 247, 250–261,
    272–274, 281, 284, 287
Evans, A 198, 214
Evans, F **121**
Evans, FG 4, 10, 30, 154, 160
Evans, K 147
Evans, LJ 38, **39**
Evans, MS 30
Evans, MW 30
Evans, R **9**, 148, 198, **229**
Evans, SE 40
Evans, T 214, **215**, 229, **229**
Evans, W 10, 60

Evans, WRG 147, **229**
Fagg, CC 126, 239
Fairey, F 24, 148, 152, 154–155, 160, 164
Fairey, Miss 147
Fairley, MG 78
Fairley, Mr 146
Fairley, SC 130
Fairweather, M 288
Farr, TL 66
Farrow, EJ 26
Farrow, Mrs 26
Fegan, Miss 24
Fensom, KS 40
Finch, J 293–294, 297, 303
Finder, R 286
fire services 2, 4, 6, 8, 10, 24, 26, 28, 38, 44, 56, 66, 78, 80, 84, 86, 90, 126, 141–143, 149, 151–154, 157, 160–161, 163, 176, 224, 230, 232–233, 239
fire-fighting 56, 58
fire-watching 37–38, 40, 42, 44, 46, 50, 52, 54, 56, 58, 60, 62, 64, 66, 68, 70, 72, 74, 76, 78, 82, 84, 86, 88, 90, 92, 94, 96, 98, 100, 102, 104, 108, 110, 112, 141, 228–229, 236, 242, 261, 283, 287, 294–297
first aid 2, 4, 8, 18, 20, 46, 48, 70, 74, 86, 90, 92, 94, 98, 106, 114, 118, 120, 122, 126, 142, 149–150, 152–154, 158, 160–163, 165–167, 172, 174, 176, 206, 211, 240, 263, 280, 294, 297
Fletcher, CL 18, 20, 50, 52
Fletcher, CW 148
Ford, JM 136
Fordham, MW 215, **215**
Foskett, A 148
Foster, ES 120
Foster, H 148
Foster, J 62
Foster, Mr 6, 147, 154, 160
Foster, R **87**, 122, 225
Foster, RL 122
Foster, SC 130
Franklin, Mr 146
Freeborn, TW 40
Frost, MA 8, 12, 24, 28, 42, 60, 62, 66
Frost, WHJ 148
Gane, J 38
Gane, JR 124
Gane, R 52, 62, 64, 126, 152–160
Garmant, AJ 38
Garner, AE 148
Garner, F 216
Garner, JH 2, 54, 60, 62, 64, 68, 82, 84, 102, 126, 152, 154–160, 163, 243, 269
Garner, Miss 8
gas masks 2, 20, 90, 145–146, 208, 239–240, 242–243, 246–247, 258, 263–264
Gathercole, M 70
Gauge, AR 120
Gawthrop, B 6
Gawthrop, R 36, 120, 124
Gawthrop, RM 118
Gawthrop, S 2, **15**, 66, 80, 82, 199, 217
Gawthrop, V 22
Gayton, Mr 26
Genge, M 290–291, 293, 295, 298
George Public House 188, 229–230, 244, **244**
Gerrard, TC 74
Gibson, EH 146
Girton College 5, 28, 30, 34, 38, 58, 68, 72, 74, 76, 82, 98, 147,

Girton College ...
152–154, 157, 160, 163, 169, 171, 233, 236, 247, 277, 280–304
Girton Corner 1, 56, 112, 128, 130, 138, 164, 171, 221, 230, 242
Goddard, V 230
Goff, Mrs 156
Goldbourne, B 62
Golding, AM 134
Goodchild, Mrs 18
Goodenough, Miss 166
Gordon, W 2, 66, 68, 70
Gow, C 8
Graham, A 235
Grant, GG 124
Graves, PP 124, 241
Green, AM 112
Green, FC 44, 46, 162–163
Green, MB 20, 22, 52, 62, 64, 118, 152, 154, 158–160, 162, 166, 242
Green, Mr 42
Green, Mrs 4, 270, 278
Greenwood, JM 148
Gregory, P 293, 295, 299–300, 302–303
Griffin, FT 8
Griffiths, C 184, 188
Guillebaud, P 293
Gunn, J 82, 100, 177
Gwillam, RA 86
Hales, E 26, 150, 239
Hales, L 217, **217**
Hales, PM 84
Hall, AM **9**, 272
Hall, GA 6, 60, 86, 128, 147, 149, 252
Hall, GW 8
Hall, PM 68
Hallam, Dr 80

Hallam, FE 8, 156, 166
Halls, S 147
Halls, WW 98
Hammond, Dr 157
Hancock, AE 108
Hancock, Babs 255
Hancock, C 148
Hancock, E 20
Hancock, I 108
Hancock, J 2, 34
Hancock, M **9**
Hancock, Mrs 8
Hancock, V 199
Hankin, ME 56
Hankin, S 148
Hankin, WC 12
Hankins, CH 62
Hardcastle, F 58
Hardwick, AH 68, 82
Hardwick, EP 98
Harper, GR 44
Harpley, W 46
Harpner, Mr 147
Harradine, J (née Pluck) 241
Harrison, CA 74
Hartnoll, Mr 146
Harvey, HA 24
Harvey, L 213
Havers, Mr 146
Hawke, KJ 146
Hawker, P (née Gregory) 293, 295, 299–300, 302–303
Hawkes, J 58
Hawkes, JM 54
Hawkes, Mr 147
Hayes, ML 72
Heinrich, A 96
Henderson, DA 22
Herrow, EJ 8
Hertz, Dr 52, 140, 154, 156–162, 166, 172
Hertz, E 58

Hibbert, Mr 116

Hibbert-Ware, A 2, 4, 6, 16, 22,
    24, 26, 28, 30, 32, 34, 36, 42,
    44, 54, 56, 68, 80, 84, 86, **100**,
    102, 104, 110, 185, 194, 198,
    230, 240, 242, 267–269, 276,
    287

Hibbert-Ware, G 12, 24, 28, 44,
    102, 110, **111**, 287

Hibbert-Ware Memorial 102,
    104, 110, 114, 120, 198, 202,
    288

Hicks Lane 165, 170

High, D 68, 88, 92, 225

High St 147, 150, 164–165

Hill, F 62

Hill, P 62

Hills, LD 110

Hills, LF 32

Hind, DC 104

Hinkins, Mr 170

Hirsch, RS 112

Hodder, JD 128

Hodder, KI 76

Hodder, ME 128

Hodder, OJ 128

Hollings, J 291, 294, **296**,
    297–298, 301, 303

Holt, Mr 148

Home Guard 19, 25, 27, 33, 44,
    59, 62, 64, 70, 72, 74, 76, 78,
    82, 84, 88–89, 113, 117, 119,
    128, 153, 156–157, 163–164,
    172, 216–217, 221, 228–230,
    232–233, 241, 264

Homecoming Fund 116, 120,
    122, 128, 186, 197, 230, 271

Hoppit, NB 120

Horrocks, MD 102

Hort, LF 147

Houblon, Mrs 60

Houghton, RA 74

Huddlestone, Heather **9**

Huddlestone, Honor **9**

Huddlestone, RC 92

Huddlestone, RJ 136

Hughes, D 30

Hughes, Mr 28

Huke, GA 146

Huke, PN 50

Hullyer, BF 32

Hullyer, E 12

Hunt, Miss 8

Hunt, WE 148

hygiene 10, 20, 100, 156–162,
    165–167, 172, 178, 238, 242,
    247, 253, 299

Ibbitt, Mr 1

Impey, E 230

Impey, LG 8

Impey, TC 2, **15**, 189, 199, 205,
    205, 218

Impey, TG 18, **19**, 36

Infants Welfare Centre 16, 18,
    94, 122, 262–264

Ingle, JS 116

Ingle, LM 149, 153–154, 166

Ingle, Mr 149, 270

Inglis, Prof 210

Invasion Committee 50, 52, 58,
    64, 72, 76, 118, 120, 152–173

Ison, J 58, 78, 230, 249

Jackson, GW 124

Jackson, Noel 84

James, SA 104

Jameson, Miss 62

Jane, Mr 44

Jarman, MA 32

Jeeps, MD 132

Jeffery, WT 147

Jeffries, B 301

Jobson, CW 120

Johns, LM 112

Johnson, B 132

Johnson, C 138
Johnson, EM **9**
Johnson, WHH 36, 225
Jolliffe, NC 147, 302
Jones, ADP 104
Jones, H 148, 233, 240
Jones, WD 92
Keith, EE 124
Kelly, P 267–268
Kelsall, AJ 146
Kidman, AM 86
Kidman, C 197, **197**, 241
Kidman, EJ 104
Kidman, H 124, 147, 150
Kidman, J 216
Kidman, Mr 147
Kidman, Mrs 6
Kidman, W 10, **15**
King, E 8
King, GG 86
King, HDB 12, 239
King, I 14, 24, 26, 60, **87**, 90, 92,
    94, **95**, 106, 126, 150, 152,
    154, 160, 232–233, 239, 244
King, L **87**, 150, 239
King, Mr 147
King, Mrs 60, 234
King, N **87**, 239
KiT 102, 174, 177, 179, 185,
    187, 194–195, 201, 249
Kominek, J 48, **49**, 225
Lamaison, Mr 149
Lamb, C 36
Lambert, GW 173
Lane, B 130
Lane, L 96
Larkin, AJ 112
Larrissy, D (née Pickard) 302
Lawrence, BJ 72
Lawrence, K 242
Lawrence, RM 116
Lawrence, SA 82, 84, 88, 96,

    104, 124, 126, 146
Layland, C 287
Leakey, C 8
Leakey, HW 4, 20, 46, 76, **77**,
    82, 84, 104, 106, 110, 124, 126,
    130, 136, 138, 154–158, 160,
    162, 167, 170, 230, 250, 255,
    263–266, 268–269, 274, 277
Leakey, P 8
Lee, AE **9**
Lennard-Jones, JE 18
Lewis, N **137**
Lilley, CM 126
Lilley, G 2, 14, 88, 148
Lilley, HG 147
Lilley, Mr 36, 40, 42, 44, 66, 72,
    80, 94, 96, 100, 104, 106, 110,
    114, 120, 124, 130, 154
Lingley, AV 235
Lingley, W (senior) 171
Lingley, WJ 235
Lintott, CE 74, 100
Lintott, DM 84, 116
Lipscombe, JM 12
Lipscombe, M 150
Lipscombe, RD 175, 208, 220,
    220
Littleton House School 12, 20,
    22, **23**, 28, 32, 38, 74, 114,
    153–154, 156, 169–170, 233
Littlewood, M (née Cranfield)
    243
Liveing, EH 60
Lofts, C 82
Lofts, Mr 147
Lofts, S 44
Lynn, J 54
Lyons, G **9**
Macalister, MG 154, 160, 162,
    166
Macirone, Dr 156, 166
Mack, AJ 118

Mann, H 110
Manor Farm 49, 170, 225, 276
Mansfield, AR 58, 124
Mansfield, H 213
Mansfield, IP 96
Marchant, AA 148
Marsdon, HG 68
Marshall, AGG 40, 150
Marshall, GW 149
Marshall, Mr 124
Marshall, Mrs **9**, 128
Marthen, R 62
Martin, C 54
Martin, CA 8
Martin, FA 147, 150
Martin, M 231
Mason, GCG 34
Matthews, C **15**, 150, 199
Matthews, E 228
Matthews, G 233–234, 244
Matthews, GM 16
Matthews, JE 104
Matthews, K 217, 222, **222**
Matthews, Mr 24, 26, 239
Matthews, RA 44
Matthews, S **87**, 150
Matthews, V 100
Maw, RH 92, 112
Mayes, I **45**
Mayes, J 239
Mayes, K 222, **222**
McFarlane, Mr 146
McGorian, Mr 98, 112
McMorran, HJ 110, 114
Medlock, DG 118
Melbert, E 16
Melbert, YG 66
Men's Institute 34, 36, 40, 42,
  56, 82, 84, 120, 126, 130, 164,
  242
Mills, D 223, **223**
mining 47, 59, 61, 71, 101, 103,

105, 107, 245
Mitham, B 90
Mitham, SF 54, 78, 112, 116,
  148, 265
Monkman, KM 124
Monkman, W 62, 128, 146, 154,
  160, 162–163, 216, **228**,
  264–265
Moore, CL 8
Moore, J 215
Morris, H 110, 146, 194, 271
Morris, M 66
Moule, Mrs 272
Muggleton, AJ 147
Munden, Mr 154
Murray, KME 68
Naylor, AC 50
Naylor, D **9**
Naylor, G **9**, 118
Naylor, H 243
Naylor, K **15**
Naylor, KG 12
Naylor, R 184, **184**, 208
Neep, MR 66
Newman, Mr 122
Newton, BA 22, 24, 28, 148,
  155–159
Nicholls, CW 66
Nicholls, RJ 94
Nightingale, A 124
Nightingale, B 62, 90
Nightingale, C 2, 12, 14, 40, 42,
  48, 50, 56, 66, 68, 88, 90, 92,
  94, 98, 104, 108, 110, 116, 124,
  147, 170, 239
Nightingale, DL 48
Nightingale, E 148
Nightingale, EM 138
Nightingale, F 100
Nightingale, G 62, 154, 160
Nightingale, I **9**
Nightingale, J 58

Nightingale, M 16
Nightingale, Mrs 36
Nightingale, N 149
Nightingale, R 8, **87**, 223, **223**
Nightingale, S **87**
Nightingale, SV 147
Nightingale, T **73**
Nisbet, W 146
North, Mr 14, 18
North, VM 32
Norton, G 241
Nursing Association 6, 16, 18,
    24, 48, 88, 94, 118, 120, 122
Old Crown Public House 222,
    229, 241
Orwin, Dr 134
Osborne, L 90
Osborne, RJ 128
Oxley, CD 40
Oxley, MJ 4
Pace, J 147
Palmer, HA 98
Palmer, J 70
Palmer, PNH 179, **179**
Palmer, T 28, 36, 64, 100, 151,
    276
Parish Church 4, 8, 14, 28, 40,
    46, 54, 58, 60, 68, 70, 72, 78,
    94, 96, 124, 128, 132
Park, TJ 48
Parr, CE 227
Parr, R 138, 228
Parsley, Mrs 245
Paterson, Dr 166
Pauley, DE 136
Pauley, EJ 64
Pauley, JT 68
Pauley, Miss 248
Pauley, PE 22
Pauley, TA 106, **107**
Pauley, V **93**
Peak, Mr 130

Peake, Mr 122
Pearce, AP 282
Pearce, DC 64
Pease, D 244
Pease, F 243
Pease, HB 6, 30, 58, 153–163,
    231
Pease, MS 2, 6, 14, 16, 18, 22,
    26, 32, 36, 40, 44, 46, 52, 56,
    58, 66, 72, 80, 88, 92, 96, 104,
    108, 110, 120, 124, 126, 130,
    131, 132, 134, 144, 146, 149,
    152–160, 162–164, 167, 170,
    177, 194, **234**, 263
Pemberton, Mrs 273
Pentlow, ME 12
Pepper, B (née Siddons) 299
Pepys Way 54, 171
Percival, ELM 112
Perry, J 110
Perry, M 110
Pickard, D 302
Pickett, PG 168
Pig Club 230, 296
Pigden, ES 122
Pigden, J **15**
Piggott, F 20, 32
Piggott, JM 48
Pike, A 118
Pinder, Mr 146
Pinder, Mrs 36
Pinder, RE 149
Pluck, CG 1, 37, **139**
Pluck, J 241
Plumb, E 34
Plumb, RM 92
police 2, 24–25, 63, 76, 78, 88,
    104, 106, 126, 145, 148, 152,
    154–155, 161, 163–165,
    171–172, 237, 241, 252
Porter, AJ 124
Porter, BS 104

Porter, E 76, 147, 150, 170, 229
Porter, JE 8, 132
Porter, MG 74
Potter, NA 149
Potter, NJ 136
Potticary, GBF 60
Pringle, J (née Wilderspin) 246
Pritchard, Alice 258
Pritchard, M 299
Procter, CPG 280, 282–283,
   286–288, 291, 296
Pullan, EM 42
Purkis, W 148
Rabbit Club 70, 82, 275
Radford, T 18, 20, 32, 34, 40,
   148
rationing 3, 13, 17, 25, 27, 35,
   39, 49, 57, 59, 61, 63, 65, 67,
   71, 167, 242, 248, 256–257
Rattenbury, GD 281
Rawlence, J (née Finch)
   293–294, 297, 303
Rawlings, JF 148
Rayner, AD 30
Read, AH 235
Read, HT 235
Read Mr 152–153
Reade, GB 32
Reader, S **41**
Reader, WMB 126
Recreation Ground 1, 10, 12, 22,
   44, 50, 60, 92, 114, 128, 130,
   134, 150, 164, 234, 238, 240
Red Cross 8, 18, 25, 28, 52, 72,
   81, 92, 116, 149, 153–154,
   160–161, 166–167, 263,
   268–269, 272, 275–276, 279,
   281, 287, 297
Red House Farm 151, 168, 170
Reddall, CJB 104
Reddall, SEJ 104
Redford, Mr 160

Reid, MG 282
Rhoden, Mr 146
Robertson, Miss 52, 147,
   152–161
Robey, S 245
Rogers, GW 134
Rose, E 104
Rowney, EWC 38, **39**
Rowney, JA 112
Rowney, JP 112
Rowney, ME 40
Rudd, FA 148, 152, 154–155
Rudd, O 32
Rule, CF 106
Rule, FJ 134
Rule, J 184
Rule, R 147
Ryder, J 20
Ryder, PA 78
Sadler, EA 6, 60, 112, 134, 278
Sadler, H 112
Sales, NE 76
Sallis, E 290–293, 296, 298,
   301, 304
salvage 1, 16, 18, 20, 22, 24, 26,
   28, 30, 32, 36, 38, 42, 44, 48,
   50, 52, 54, 56, 58, 60, 62, 64,
   68, 70, 72, 74, 76, 82, 88, 92,
   94, 98, 100, 102, 106, 108, 110,
   112, 114, 118, 120, 128, 130,
   132, 134, 138, 144, 151, 161,
   242, 276
Sandell, B 208
Sankaran, V (née Tillyard)
   294–297
Schick, FG 48
Scholfield, H 291, 302
school 1, **7**, 126, 128, **129**, 130,
   150, 152, 154, 160, 191
Schutz, GV 74
Scott, AB 130
Scott, B 238

Scott, BJ 92
Scott, K 122
Scott, WB 92
Scouts 8, 12, 16, 184
Scrine, R 258
searchlights 12, 14, 29, 32, 34,
    190, 225, 234–235, 240, 242,
    245, 247
Searle, TH 2, 4, 6, 10, 12, 14,
    16, 24, 28, 32, 34, 40, 44, 50,
    54, 56, 68, 70, 88, 94, 96, 104,
    108, 110, 112, 114, 116, 122,
    124, 126, 128, 130, 134, 136,
    145, 147–148, 151, 168, 170
Secker, EA 132
Secker, Mr 146, 236
Secker, RV 88
Sedgwick, NJ 124
Sellers, KC 112
Senser, G 244
Senser, V 244
Sexton, Mr 146
Seymour, DM 124
Seymour, L 62
Shaddick, FF 147
Sharp, FS 147
Sharp, GM 136
Sharp, JF 147
Sharp, Mr 18, 24, 154–155
Sharp, Mrs 106
Sharp, RJ 94
Sharpe, M (née Wilderspin) 247
Sharpe, Mr 48
Shaw, G 30
Shead, BR 32
Shead, EJ 10
Sheffler, F 100
Shooter, Mr 42
Shufflebotham, Mrs 275
Siddons, B 299
Skeel, AR 165, 235
Skeel, Mrs 171

Skeel, NF 100
Skinner, F 2, 6, 16, 18, 28, 36,
    48, 52, 70, 88, 104, 120, 122,
    124, 126, 146, 152–154
Skinner, P 148, 240
Slater, NR 98
Smart, P 291, 294, 296–297
Smelly, Miss 6
Smith, C 238
Smith, CJ 74
Smith, EJ 126, 136, 161, 163
Smith, FM 147, 154, 160
Smith, GLJ 134
Smith, JE 149
Smith, LM 136
Smith, ME 8
Smith, Mr 146, 154, 160
Smith, NAL 18, 36
Smith, SM 90
Smith, WR 152
smithy 42, 78, 86, 94, 102
Snell, JR 124
Snell, SW 68
Songer, M 16
St John's Farm 147, 170
Stead, BM 291
Stearn, F 72
Stearn, JE 48
Stewart, HF 84, 248
Stewart, JG 2, 24, 70, 80, 82,
    154, 160, 248, 277
Stock, PR 138
Stonebridge, AR 14
Stonebridge, R 58
Storrs Fox, J (née Hollings) 291,
    294, **296**, 297–298, 301, 303
Strachan, Mr 147
Strathey, A 166
Strugnell, HC 38
Sumpter, D 146
Suttle, ADJ 12
Suttle, P 10

Tadman, Mr 146
Taylor, Dr 166
Taylor, RD 116
Teff, M 8
Teff, MS 147
Teff, Z 62
Thomas, H 282
Thompson, J 216
Thompson, MM 66
Thompson, Mrs 8, 82
Thompson, T 213
Thomson, JR 124, 126, 264
Thomson, Mrs 242, 271
Thomson, PO'C 124
Thornton Road 14, 28, 94, 102,
    141, 157, 164, 171
Thurlow, AR 4
Tillgard, EM 10
Tillyard, V 294–297
Tingey, L 6, 32, 46, 70, 72, 88,
    104, 116, 124, 126, 149, 152,
    154, 157–158, 160–162
Tole, A (née White) 249
transport (bus) 22, 32, 56, 92,
    94, 128, 209, 229, 239, 243,
    248, 252, 255, 261, 285, 302
transport (cycling) 20, 80, 90,
    165, 223, 229–230, 240, 243,
    248, 259, 261, 293, 295, 299,
    301–303
Trench, LE 281
Trewren, PJ 18
Trillwood, AC 94
Trillwood, B 42
Trusted, J (née Turner) 260,
    261
Tucker, GE 58
Tucker, LG 156
Tucker, M 8, 58
Turner, BM **9**, 18, 82, 84, 88,
    104, 106, 112, 114, 116, 118,
    124, 130, 132, 134

Turner, Dr 74
Turner, J 235, **261**, 293
Turner, Mrs 16
Turner, WS 267–268
Twinn, F 10
Ulyatt, A 66, 225
Vellacott, Mrs 16, 18, 154, 160
Village Institute **35**, 150
Vinall, JP 10
von Proschwitz, M (née Genge)
    290–291, 293, 295, 298
Wagstaff, AH 74, 225
Wagstaff, S 62
Wallaker, AM 124
Walliker, Miss 147
Wallis, B 189
Wallis, Miss 189
Walton, A 2, 6, 18, 20, 22, 28,
    30, 32, 34, 36, 46, 52, 54, 64,
    70, 72, 74, 76, 78, 82, 84, 90,
    92, 100, 106, 114, 116, 118,
    120, 124, 128, 130, 132, 134,
    136, 138, 140, 142, 144, 146,
    150, 152–160, 162–164, 263
Ward, WE 248
Warner, GW 86
Warrington, DM 22, 24,
    266–267, 277
Washpit Brook 6, 8, 12, 68
Watson, A 64
Watson, B 149, 170
Watson, Bernard **87**
Watson, Bob **87**
Watson, Dick 199, 224, **224**
Watson, Mr 24, 147
Watson, Ray 26, 150, 239
Watson, SD 64
Watson, V 26, **87**, 150, 239
Watson, WF 10
Weale, M 290–294, 298–299,
    301, 303–304
Wellbrook Laundry 2, 68, **142**,

Wellbrook Laundry ...
    144, 147, 153, 155, 157,
    164–166, 169, 171–172, 233,
    248
West, G **15**
Weston, L 36
Wey, WP 42
White, A 249
White, RG 114
White, WSS 249
Whitehead, CE 32
Whitehead, D 283
Whitehead, H **87**
Whitehead, HA 26, 150, 239
Whitehead, Mr 24
Whybrow, V 62
WI Hall 8, 16, 38, 56, **57**, 120,
    216, 235, 240, 246–247,
    262–263, 271
Wilderspin, G 248
Wilderspin, HA 6, 48
Wilderspin, J 96, 124, 126, 128,
    130, 134, 148, 246, 248
Wilderspin, LJ 14
Wilderspin, M 247
Wilderspin, Mr (senior) 248
Williams, A 18, 235
Wilson, Cecil 10
Wilson, CG 147
Wilson, CS 66, 106, 199, **199**,
    218
Wilson, IM (née Bonny) 239

Wilson, R 224, **224**
Windmill, IM 98
Wiseman, CA 124
Wiseman, J 54
Wodehouse, HM 72
Wolf Cubs 299–300
Wolf, Mr 146
Women's Institute 4, 12, 18, 20,
    22, 24, 30, 36, 60, 70, 84, 86,
    132, 242, 262–279
Women's Land Army 9, 81,
    227–228, 232, 280, 284
Women's Voluntary Service 20,
    30, 62, 68, 84, 153–154, 160,
    252, 266, 270, 272, 275
Womersley, A 281, 286
Woodhead, F 287
Woodlands Park 6, 78, 90, 165,
    170, 224, 239
Wosencroft, WH 16
Wright, H 66
Yale, Mr 153
Young, EJ 108
Young, G 30
Young Men's Group 4, 8, 10, 12,
    16, 20, 22, 26, 28, 30, 46, 162,
    181, 184–185, 191–193,
    199–200, 205, 215
Young, SJ 108
Yuell, Mrs 267
Yule, Mrs 160